# DEVĪMĀHĀTMYAM

# DEVĪMĀHĀTMYAM

## *In Praise of the Goddess*

*Translator and Commentator*
DEVADATTA KĀLĪ

MOTILAL BANARSIDASS PUBLISHERS
PRIVATE LIMITED • DELHI

*First Indian Edition: Delhi,* ***2006***
*(First Published in 2003 by Nicolas-Hays, Berwick Maine, USA under the title* ***In Praise of the Goddess****)*



ISBN: 81-208-2931-X (Cloth)
ISBN: 81-208-2953-0 (Paper)

MOTILAL BANARSIDASS
41 U.A. Bungalow Road, Jawahar Nagar, Delhi 110 007
8 Mahalaxmi Chamber, 22 Bhulabhai Desai Road, Mumbai 400 026
203 Royapettah High Road, Mylapore, Chennai 600 004
236, 9th Main III Block, Jayanagar, Bangalore 560 011
Sanas Plaza, 1302 Baji Rao Road, Pune 411 002
8 Camac Street, Kolkata 700 017
Ashok Rajpath, Patna 800 004
Chowk, Varanasi 221 001



*Printed in India*
BY JAINENDRA PRAKASH JAIN AT SHRI JAINENDRA PRESS,
A-45 NARAINA, PHASE-I, NEW DELHI 110 028
AND PUBLISHED BY NARENDRA PRAKASH JAIN FOR
MOTILAL BANARSIDASS PUBLISHERS PRIVATE LIMITED,
BUNGALOW ROAD, DELHI 110 007

ॐ

*Lovingly dedicated*
*to the memory of my Guru,*
*Swami Prabhavananda,*
*and to my Guru Mā,*
*Ma Jaya Sati Bhagavati*

# CONTENTS

# ACKNOWLEDGMENTS

I gratefully acknowledge my indebtedness to Swāmī Jagadīśvarānanda's translation of the Devīmāhātmya, published in India in 1953. Its glowing devotional spirit was the initial spark that led me almost two decades later to devote eight years of my life to this work.

This book would not have been possible without the initial encouragement and continuing assistance of Pravrajika Anandaprana and Pravrajika Vrajaprana of the Sarada Convent in Santa Barbara. I owe them my inestimable gratitude for their editorial skills, sensitivity, constructive criticism, and selfless dedication, which guided and shaped the work from its inception. I would like to express my thanks also to Joseph Cooper, my partner, who read the manuscript repeatedly throughout its evolution and often contributed just the right word or phrase that eluded me. Thanks also to Swami Sarvadevananda of the Vedanta Society of Southern California, who provided his oversight and requested the inclusion of the associated texts that form the third part of this volume; to Swami Atmajnanananda of the Vedanta Society of Greater Washington, DC, who clarified several important points; to Swami Chetanananda of the Vedanta Society of St. Louis, who advised me to "meditate on every verse"; to my fellow Vedānta devotees—Shuddha Barnes, Radhika and Govinda Eschner, Amala Kenny, Connie Magwood, Nalini Tipple, and Deepti Zaremba—who read portions of the manuscript and were unfailingly generous with their encouragement and suggestions; to Kalishyam DeVito, whose enthusiastic questioning guided me in revising the manuscript; and to my revered Ma Jaya Sati Bhagavati for confirming the book's spiritual validity. Heartfelt thanks to my editor, Valerie Cooper, for the intelligence, sensitivity, and commitment she brought to the realization of this book. To Swami Tyagananda of the Ramakrishna Vedanta Society of Boston, I can only say that words fail to express my profound gratitude for the editorial expertise and spiritual authority he brought to bear on the work. By reading the entire manuscript from beginning to end with meticulous care, he invested the work with a legitimacy far beyond that which I could have envisioned. Finally, to the Divine Mother herself, my inexpressible gratitude for engaging me in what has been truly a labor of love.

# ABBREVIATION GUIDE TO WORKS CITED

*All quotations are the author's own translations.*

| | |
|---|---|
| BD | Bṛhaddevatā |
| BhG | Bhagavadgītā |
| BU | Bṛhadāraṇyakopaniṣad |
| ChU | Chāndogyopaniṣad |
| DG | Devīgītā |
| DM | Devīmāhātmya |
| HV | Harivaṁśa |
| KU | Kaṭhopaniṣad |
| MBh | Mahābhārata |
| MR | Mūrtirahasya |
| MS | Manusmṛti |
| MU | Muṇḍakopaniṣad |
| PR | Prādhānika Rahasya |
| ṚV | Ṛgveda |
| ŚU | Śvetāśvataropaniṣad |
| TA | Taittirīyāraṇyaka |
| VR | Vaikṛtika Rahasya |
| YS | Yogasūtra |

# PRONUNCIATION GUIDE

| | | | |
|---|---|---|---|
| **a** | *a* go | **kh** | sin*kh* ole |
| **ā** | f*a* ther | **l** | *l* et |
| **ai** | k*i* te | **m** | *m* an |
| **au** | r*ou* nd | **ṁ** | nasal, as in French bo*n* |
| **b** | *b* it | **n** | *n* eed |
| **bh** | clu*bh* ouse | **ṅ** | si*ng* |
| **c** | *ch* ip | **ñ** | i*n* ch |
| **ch** | ran*ch h* ouse | **ṇ** | u*n* der |
| **d** | *d* eed | **o** | h*o* pe |
| **dh** | re*d h* air | **p** | s*p* un |
| **ḍ** | a*d* roit | **ph** | u*ph* old |
| **ḍh** | mu*d h* ut | **r** | *r* un |
| **e** | m*a* te | **ṛ** | p*re* tty |
| **g** | *g* o | **ṝ** | like **ṛ** but longer |
| **gh** | fo*gh* orn | **s** | *s* it |
| **h** | *h* eart | **ś** | *sh* eep |
| **ḥ** | *h*, followed by a faint echo of the preceding vowel: e.g., a*ha*, ā*ha*, i*hi*, u*hu*, o*ho*, ai*hi*, au*hu* | **ṣ** | *sh* ut |
| | | **t** | s*t* ar |
| | | **th** | righ*t h* and |
| | | **ṭ** | *t* ry |
| **i** | b*i* t | **ṭh** | boa*th* ouse |
| **ī** | mach*i* ne | **u** | p*u* t |
| **j** | *j* ump | **ū** | b*oo* t |
| **jh** | he*dgeh* og | **v** | *v* ery |
| **jñ** | eg*g y* olk | **y** | *y* es |
| **k** | s*k* ate | | |

The cerebral consonants, **ṭ, ṭh, ḍ, ḍh, ṇ,** are pronounced with the tip of the tongue curled back against the hard palate, farther back than the English point of articulation. The dental consonants, **t, th, d, dh, n,** are pronounced with the tip of the tongue touching the edge of the front teeth, a position more forward than in English. Similarly, the cerebral sibilant, **ṣ**, is articulated farther back in the mouth than the palatal sibilant, **ś**. When following another consonant, **v** is pronounced like English **w**.

The accentuation of syllables in Sanskrit is weaker than in English. The stress falls on the penultimate (next to last) syllable when that syllable contains a long vowel, a diphthong (**e, ai, o, au**), or a short vowel followed by two or more consonants. Otherwise, the stress falls on the antepenultimate, or preceding, syllable. Thus: ahaṁ*kā*ra, a*dvai*ta, a*dhar*ma, a*la*kṣmī, *a*sura, apa*rā*jitā.

# INTRODUCTION

Fifteen or more centuries ago an unknown author or authors in northwest India wove together the diverse threads of already ancient memory and created a dazzling verbal tapestry that remains even today the central text on the Hindu Goddess. Called the Devīmāhātmya ("The Glory of the Goddess"), this poem of seven hundred verses is recited daily in temples and widely disseminated in the original Sanskrit and in vernacular translations. Part myth and part philosophy, part narrative and part hymn, it is a spiritual classic that addresses the perennial questions of our existence: What is the nature of the universe, of humankind, of divinity? How are they related? How do we live in a world torn between good and evil? And how do we find lasting satisfaction and inner peace?

Cast as the narrative of a dispossessed king, a merchant betrayed by the family he loves, and a sage whose instruction leads beyond existential suffering, the Devīmāhātmya teaches through a trilogy of myths. The sage's three tales are allegories of outer and inner experience, symbolized by the fierce battles the all-powerful Devī wages against throngs of demonic foes. Her adversaries represent the all too human impulses arising from the pursuit of power, possessions, and pleasure, and from illusions of self-importance. Like the battlefield of the Bhagavadgītā, the Devīmāhātmya's killing grounds represent the field of human consciousness on which the drama of individual lives plays out in joy and sorrow, in wisdom and folly. The Devī, personified as one supreme Goddess and many goddesses, confronts the demons of ego and dispels our mistaken idea of who we are, for—paradoxically—it is she who creates the misunderstanding in the first place and she alone who awakens us to our true being.

Our ancient ancestors, whose beliefs constitute this text, found enchantment in nature's bounty, faced terror in its destructive force, and revered both aspects of their experience as manifestations of the Great Mother. As relevant today as ever, the Devīmāhātmya has the power to reawaken us to a sense of wonder at the surrounding universe through a dazzling, integrating, and ultimately liberating vision of reality.

This translation is the fourth by a native English speaker but the first ever to combine Western scholarship with an insider's perspective, based on my 37 years of spiritual practice within the Hindu tradition. I attempt to convey, in modern English, a dignity and eloquence befitting a sacred text and to allow you easy access to its inspiration. I have included the Sanskrit original in Part IV in order to fulfill the needs of those who want to study the Devīmāhātmya in depth.

Translating an ancient, literary language poses challenges unlike those met in dealing with modern languages spoken today, especially when the languages differ so radically from each other as Sanskrit and English in terms of vocabulary, grammar, syntax, and modes of expression. The translator has to find simple, natural ways to convey the ideas of the original text when, paradoxically, fidelity to the letter often obscures the very meaning it seeks to communicate. Previous translations by Indian and Western scholars often provide context and historical precedent, but their guidelines are neither consistent nor infallible, and some decisions ultimately rest, by necessity, on the translator's personal judgment.

This edition is unique on several counts. A comprehensive historical and interpretative introduction prepares you for a meaningful experience of the Devīmāhātmya, whether you are approaching it for spiritual or scholarly reasons. The full commentary—the first ever in the English language—reveals the Devīmāhātmya as the spiritual classic it is, a universal allegory of human experience and a guide for the inner life. Additionally, this edition contains eight other texts closely associated with the Devīmāhātmya, for the first time presented with English commentary. Finally, I have included a glossary of Sanskrit terms and proper names for your convenience.

# Part I
# Origins and Context of the Devīmāhātmya

# A BRIEF HISTORY

The story of the Devīmāhātmya begins long before its actual composition. Throughout the Eurasian land-mass as far back as Paleolithic times, women and men observed the female's awesome capacity to create new life and identified that power with divinity. They left traces of their beliefs in figurines that display the universal physical attributes of female fertility and motherhood. These mute but eloquent reminders continued into the Neolithic period, reaching a high state of development in the ancient Near East. Fashioned from stone, clay, ivory, or bone, they convey a message across the millennia that our ancestors long ago understood feminine divinity as presiding over the natural functions of birth, growth, maturation, death, and regeneration.

In the winter of 1980, a team of Indian, American, and Australian archeologists and anthropologists uncovered what may be the oldest evidence of religious practice on the Indian subcontinent. Dating as far back as 9,000 BCE, the site is in the Son valley, below the nearby Vindhya mountains—a region that will play an important part in the story of the Devīmāhātmya. There, the researchers excavated what appears to be a circular shrine, measuring about three feet across and made of sandstone blocks. In the center lay another sandstone block, measuring about 12 by 6 by 4 inches. Its weathered surface reveals harder layers that stand out in relief to form a natural pattern of concentric triangles. Tribal villagers assisting in the excavation immediately recognized the stone as a sacred emblem of Śakti, the Goddess. Such stones, they confirmed, are still sought out today and installed in the local villages, in both individual and communal shrines.[1] According to the archeologists, this dramatic evidence of cultural continuity indicates that the veneration of Śakti in the mountains of north central India stretches back at least 10,000 years.[2]

## Reconstructing the Past

The early history of India remains a highly contentious field of study, where there are more questions than answers. Many pieces of the past are irretrievably lost, and attempts to form a comprehensive picture are complicated by nationalistic, ethnic, and religious feelings and the legacy of pioneering European scholars, who frequently injected the prejudices of a foreign worldview into an area where they clearly do not belong. At the heart of the conflict lies the problematic chronology, identity, and relationship of two peoples: those who created the great Indus Valley civilization in the third millennium BCE and the Indo-European-speaking Āryas, who composed the Vedas, India's oldest surviving sacred texts. Even in the light of emerging scientific data, wildly conflicting theories abound, and even the best are not without seemingly irreconcilable anomalies.

Out of this poorly understood cultural matrix the Devīmāhātmya emerged, encompassing the beliefs and practices of prehistoric agriculturalists, tribal shamans, ancient city dwellers, and nomadic pastoral clans whose early deification of natural forces eventually led to lofty philosophies on the nature of reality. Presently, there is no way to make historical sense out of all the pieces, but the legacy of this mosaic-like past lives on in the resounding verses of the Devīmāhātmya.

## Harappan Religion

Three thousand years before the Devimāhātmya's appearance, a civilization as advanced as those of Egypt and Mesopotamia arose on the vast flood plain of the Indus and Sarasvatī rivers and flourished in full glory between 2600 and 1900 BCE. Its cities of Harappa and Mohenjo-daro were among the largest in the world, and there is increasing archeological evidence that this India of the Bronze Age was as culturally and ethnically diverse as it is today. As in most of the ancient world, multiple religious cults probably coexisted there, more or less peacefully.

Long before the rise of the Harappan, or Indus-Sarasvatī, civilization, at highland settlements in Baluchistan, north and west of the Indus Valley, the pre-Harappan cultures regarded the Mother Goddess or goddesses in much the same way as other peoples throughout the Neolithic Near East. Predictable for an agricultural society, the pre-Harappan goddess images display themes relating to fertility and the cycles of nature. Made of baked clay, the figurines share common features, such as elaborately styled hair, ornate necklaces, birdlike faces, broad hips, and full breasts. Often they represent the female form from the waist up, as if to suggest an earth goddess emerging from the ground. Some, with hands on their breasts, suggest a benevolent, nurturing mother. Others, often hooded and displaying grim, sometimes skull-like faces, hint at an underworld goddess who is the guardian of the dead and perhaps of planted seed-grain.[3] Their gruesome faces and distorted mouths seem designed to evoke terror, and it is easy to envision the goddess they represent as an antecedent of Kālī.[4] Often the images of the terrible goddess have been found in connection with those of an angry and destructive wild bull. That association may express the idea of inauspicious or evil forces being subdued by a higher divinity,[5] and it is not beyond the realm of possibility that this goddess prefigures Durgā, who slays the buffalo demon in the Devīmāhātmya's central episode. Most significantly, the portrayal of goddesses in gracious and formidable aspects is a dual distinction that passed into the Indus Valley and continues to characterize Hindu religion to the present day.[6]

The pre-Harappan images lead directly to the later icons found in the cities of Harappa and Mohenjo-daro,[7] which appear to have been centers of goddess worship.[8] Thousands of terracotta female figurines, outnumbering male images by seven to one, display the same wide hips and full breasts to express the theme of female fertility and creative power. Although many represent ordinary women engaged in domestic tasks, those identified as goddesses share a set iconography. Naked but for a girdle and adorned with jewelry and an elaborate headdress, they match another figure frequently found carved on the exquisite Harappan stone seals.

The seals, thousands in number, bear brief, still-undeciphered inscriptions along with scenes of animals, mythical beasts, plants, trees, anthropoid figures, and deities. These images offer the richest source of information—and speculation—concerning Harappan religion. The pervasive motifs of pipal (*Ficus religiosa*) and banyan (*Ficus indica*) suggest that sacred trees or groves may have been the primary sites of religious observance. Indus Valley artifacts frequently display scenes of worshipers with water jars bowing before a tree, and both the pipal and the banyan endure in later Hindu mythology as symbols of fertility and protection.[9] The deity who is shown standing beneath an arch of pipal leaves on the seals from Harappa corresponds to the one portrayed in the terracotta figurines. On seals from Mohenjo-daro, a deity appears standing in the midst of a pipal tree.[10] Conceivably, the two are regional variations of the same goddess, or perhaps distinct goddesses. In either case, this early conceptualization appears to live on in an epithet of Tārā, an aspect of the Devī closely resembling Kālī; she is called Vṛkṣamadhyanivāsinī ("she who dwells within trees").

One seal from Mohenjo-daro illustrates a worshiper prostrate before the goddess in the tree, with seven identically-clad figures standing in the foreground. Some scholars regard these as seven sister goddesses, whose birdlike motifs link them to Neolithic fertility figurines.[11] They will return later in our story. A horned goddess fighting with a tiger appears on many seals, which seem to illustrate a particularly prevalent, but otherwise unknown, myth. Occasionally her hand is upraised in what appears to be a gesture of assurance, possibly foreshadowing the fear-dispelling *abhayamudrā* of later Hindu iconography.[12]

A few seals depict a bearded male deity on a low platform, seated in a yogic posture with knees widely spread and heels touching. Wearing a headdress of curving water-buffalo horns crowned with three pipal leaves, he combines human, animal, and vegetable motifs. Two surviving seals portray this horned god with three faces, looking left, right, and forward, similar to the *Trimūrti* of later Hinduism, which depicts Brahmā, Viṣṇu, and Śiva as the creative, sustaining, and destructive functions of the supreme God. On the so-called Paśupati seal from Mohenjo-daro, the triple-headed seated figure is shown with an erect phallus and surrounded by wild animals—a rhinoceros, a water buffalo, an elephant, a tiger, and two antelope. Paśupati, the lord of beasts, is an epithet of the later Hindu god Śiva, and after decades of debate scholars still disagree whether or not this ancient seal represents Śiva in a prototypical form.

Like Rorschach ink blots, the Harappan artifacts elicit widely varying interpretations that are, at this point, only conjectural. That said, it is evident that the Harappan goddess religion represents a continuum of the earlier and widely pervasive worship of female divinity that was connected to the earth and all forms of fertility. Certainly some features of it endure in later Hinduism.

## Goddesses in Vedic Religion

European scholars of the 19th and early 20th centuries hypothesized that Indo-European tribes from the north migrated to the Indian subcontinent and founded the Indian civilization around 1500 BCE. With the discovery early in the 20th century that a great urban civilization already existed in the Indus Valley a thousand years before the supposed arrival of the Indo-European Āryas, the theory was revised to present the Āryas as invaders who conquered the Harappan people. There is no archeological evidence to support such a conquest, and the idea itself arose from a misreading of Vedic texts.

On closer scrutiny, the textual evidence actually suggests a much earlier Āryan presence in the Indus Valley than 1500 BCE. The Saṁhitā of the Ṛgveda, consisting of more than a thousand hymns composed over hundreds of years, is India's oldest sacred text. It is thought by Western scholars to have reached its present form between 1500 and 1200 BCE, although Hindus have always claimed it is much older. There is compelling evidence for that claim in the Vedic hymns themselves: they describe a landscape that vanished hundreds of years before the hymns supposedly were composed. Those hymns describe the Indus-Sarasvatī region as the Land of Seven Rivers. Part of that region is known today as the Punjab (from Sanskrit *pañca ap,* "five waters").

Of the seven rivers, the deified Sarasvatī was celebrated as surpassing all others in majesty and might (ṚV 7.95.2). Since modern scientific data now confirm that the Sarasvatī began to dry up around 1900 BCE, the hymns extolling her glory have to date from before then, when the holy river still flowed abundantly and civilization flourished along her banks. If the Āryas arrived on the scene only around 1500 BCE, they would have had no knowledge of the Sarasvatī's former magnificence, nor would they have chosen to deify a dying or already vanished river.

A gigantic environmental catastrophe, not an invasion, brought the Harappan civilization to collapse. How the Āryan, or Vedic, people fit into this picture, if at all, is a problem archeologists and historians have yet to solve. The evidence of the Vedic texts, to which we will return, chronicles the gradual disappearance of the Sarasvatī beneath the desert sands and at least hints at interaction between the Vedic and non-Vedic peoples and their religions.

It used to be accepted that the patriarchal Vedic religion looked skyward to its gods and centered on a sacrificial cult directed to a pantheon of mostly male deities for the purpose of maintaining cosmic order. Indra, the chief god, wielded a mighty thunderbolt that rumbled throughout the heavens. He was the awesome lord who caused life-giving rain to fall upon the earth. Other, mostly male, deities had overlapping functions associated with the atmospheric phenomena of wind and storms and with the ordering of day and night. Sūrya, the sun god, was revered as the source of warmth and light, although he was heralded daily by the lovely Uṣas, goddess of the dawn. On earth, the celestial light existed as fire, deified as Agni, who delivered terrestrial offerings to the gods on high. The Sanskrit word for god, *deva*, derives from a verbal root meaning "to shine," and it implies the linkage of light to the concepts of sovereignty and transcendence.[13]

The earliest strata of Ṛgvedic hymns should reflect features common to the still older Indo-European cultural matrix from which the Āryas emerged. The supreme Indo-European deity was the sky god Dyaus, whose name derives from the same source as the word *deva*. In India, Dyaus had already lost his supremacy to Indra by early Vedic times, and his name signified little more than the shining physical sky.[14] Not so in other Indo-European cultures, where Dyaus Pitar, the sky father, survived until classical times as the supreme god Zeus Pater in Hellenic religion and as Jupiter in the Roman pantheon. In India, the sky father, Dyaus, and the earth mother, Pṛthivī, were originally understood as procreative partners, but from an initial relationship of parity Pṛthivī soon gained dominance over Dyaus. The Ṛgveda most often links them as Dyāvāpṛthivī, a grammatical compound which means "heaven-and-earth" conceived of as a single entity of feminine gender, and some hymns even present Dyaus without Pṛthivī as feminine.[15] This process, unique to India, suggests a dramatic reshaping of the fundamentally patriarchal Indo-European religion by a strong goddess tradition.

In reality, the presence of all kinds of goddesses in the Ṛgveda and the honor accorded some of them raises important questions about their origins and significance. The early Vedic period saw a multiplicity of deities with similar attributes and intersecting functions, and such richness already points to the confluence of diverse traditions.[16] It is important to remember that the Vedic hymns were composed over many centuries by members of loosely related, and not always mutually friendly, Āryan priestly clans. Although no consistent pattern of development emerges from the exuberant, overlapping, and sometimes contradictory profusion of gods and goddesses, the trend was toward the coalescence of deities that closely resembled one another.

The Ṛgvedic goddesses belong to four broad categories: the weak, poorly-defined consorts of gods, named after their male counterparts; the personifications of qualities expressed by abstract feminine nouns; the deities with a basis in the natural world; and the goddesses who were powerful in their own right.[17]

The goddesses who personified abstractions expressed by feminine nouns bore names such as Dhiṣaṇā ("intelligence"), Śraddhā ("faith") and Nirṛti ("decay") and represented both positive and negative qualities. Numerous Ṛgvedic hymns document the process whereby such deities arose from the observation of physical phenomena and then became philosophical abstractions and personified goddesses. For example, *śrī* ("light, lustre, radiance") appears first as the all-encompassing glory ascribed to Agni, Rudra, Uṣas, and other deities.[18] Only much later did Śrī emerge in her own right as a personified goddess who soon thereafter merged with Lakṣmī. Initially, Lakṣmī ("good fortune, prosperity") was probably a non-Āryan agricultural deity; and her negative counterpart, Alakṣmī ("misfortune"), suggests a further connection to the older, dual-natured Neolithic goddess. The Śrīsūkta, a hymn appended to the Ṛgveda in late Vedic times, documents the merging of Śrī and Lakṣmī into a single goddess, whose propitiation grants protection from Alakṣmī, her dark aspect.[19]

Some Vedic hymns celebrate feminine power in the beauty of night, the forest, the rivers, and the earth, personified as goddesses who, for the most part, played a smaller role in the pantheon. An exception is the frequently and ecstatically hymned Uṣas, goddess of the dawn, who in earlier Vedic times figured prominently among the sky deities. Likewise, the deified Sarasvatī River figured as a powerful goddess, extolled for annually bringing new life to the farmlands and sustaining the towns and villages along her banks. A singularly beautiful hymn (ṚV 10.146) glorifies Araṇyānī, whose name (from *araṇya,* "forest") identifies her as the guardian of the wilderness and the mother of beasts and all sylvan things. This elusive Lady of the Forest, gently rustling like the tinkling of bells, is sweet-scented, benevolent, and protective, giving forth an abundance of uncultivated foods. She slays only murderous enemies, understood by the 14th-century commentator Sāyaṇa to mean tigers.[20] Assuming a Harappan-Vedic interaction, could this unique hymn to Araṇyānī be addressing the tiger-vanquishing goddess of the Indus Valley seals? Whatever the historical reality, the distinguishing feature of the Ṛgveda's goddess hymns is their joyful wonder at nature's luminous visage. Thousands of years later, their words still evoke the same ineffable feelings that must have stirred the hearts of the seers who composed them.

Among the few female divinities who were powerful in their own right, the primary Vedic goddess was Aditi, whom the hymns extol repeatedly as the Great Mother.[21] In what is believed to be the earliest stratum of Ṛgvedic hymns, she appears fully formed and surpassing any specific natural phenomenon from which she might have arisen. Writing in the late 19th century, the great Indologist Max Müller described Aditi as one of the oldest Āryan deities,[22] although more recent scholarship sees her origins "largely shrouded in pre-Vedic religion."[23] The Vedic hymns repeatedly praise Aditi as a universal, abstract goddess who represents the boundless expanse of physical creation and everything it contains.[24] According to one hymn: "Aditi is the heaven; Aditi is the atmosphere; Aditi is the mother, the father, the son / All the gods are Aditi, and the five [Āryan] clans; Aditi is that which is born; Aditi is that which will be born" (ṚV 1.89.10).

Her Sanskrit name means "boundlessness" and speaks of unity and inconceivable vastness. By later Vedic times, Aditi had gathered an array of attributes relating to both transcendence and immanence. On the one hand, she was the impersonal, limitless, and imperishable One, encompassing existence and nonexistence alike. On the other hand, she was the universal mother and protector, nurturing and upholding the world, and guarding the cosmic order (*ṛta*). Absolutely free, she could grant liberation to those who took refuge in her.[25]

A comprehensive statement of the one supreme Goddess is formulated in a hymn of the Ṛgveda known as the Devīsūkta ("Hymn of the Goddess," ṚV 10.125). Its eight verses, ascribed to the daughter of the sage Ambhṛṇa, are the vehicle through which the goddess Vāk, who is identified with both Sarasvatī and Aditi, reveals herself. First-person utterances are rare in the Ṛgveda, but here the Devī, who is the shining consciousness, proclaims that she works through all the gods and reveals herself in manifold ways. In her, all live who see and breathe and hear what is said, not knowing that they abide in her, the mother of all, who rules and upholds the universe. So vast is her greatness that, pervading heaven and earth, she transcends their limits. The Devīsūkta is of incalculable importance, because it is widely regarded as the Devīmāhātmya's point of origin.[26]

## The Late Vedic Age

On the evidence of the Vedic texts, the division between the early and late Vedic periods coincides with the drying up of the Sarasvatī River. To the early period before 1900 BCE belong the hymn portions or Saṁhitās of the Ṛgveda and Sāmaveda; to the later period belong the Saṁhitās of the Yajurveda and Atharvaveda, along with the later Vedic texts known as the Brāhmaṇas, Āraṇyakas, and Upaniṣads. Sweeping religious change rarely takes place in a vacuum, and the altered circumstances after the collapse of the Indus-Sarasvatī cities initiated the gradual and complex transformation of the old Vedic religion into modern Hinduism. Historically, the rise of Brāhmaṇical religion seems to coincide with the Harappan economic collapse and the disappearance of the Indus Valley script around 1700 BCE.[27] The theological treatises known as Brāhmaṇas address the practical concerns of a priestly class and the proper performance of sacrificial rites in the post-urban setting.

Additionally, the Brāhmaṇas document the gradual drying up of the Sarasvatī River between 1900 and 1300 BCE.[28] Once mightier than the Indus and believed to originate in heaven, the Sarasvatī was known to flow on earth from the Himālayas to the Indian Ocean. Ṛgvedic hymns and the Brāhmaṇas alike allude to sacrifices performed along her banks,[29] and the discovery of typically Indo-European fire altars at the town of Kalibangan are persuasive evidence for a Vedic presence along the Sarasvatī River in the third millennium BCE.[30] Long before the Gaṅgā took preeminence as India's holiest river, the Sarasvatī, whose name means "the flowing one," claimed that honor. Understandably, fertility and purification must have been among her earliest attributes, but even the Ṛgveda extols her not only as the great flood but also as the bright goddess of intelligence, who illumines every righteous thought (ṚV 1.3.10–12). With the onset of desiccation, the Sarasvatī appears in the Brāhmaṇas less often as a holy river and increasingly as a personified goddess. By the fifth century BCE, Yāska noted in the *Nirukta,* the oldest surviving commentary on the Vedas, that the Sarasvatī's flow to the sea could be taken figuratively as the flow of thought into the great, shining sea of consciousness.[31]

Additionally, the Brāhmaṇas repeatedly identify Sarasvatī with Vāk,[32] the creative Word personified as the Ṛgvedic goddess who proclaims her own universal power and transcendence in the Devīsūkta. As such, Sarasvatī-Vāk represents the intelligent power of creation, and her vast network of subsequent associations, including her later and current role as Brahmā's consort or power (*śakti*), perpetuates her reputation today as the beneficent goddess of knowledge and the arts.

Reflecting the growing popularity of other female deities, the Brāhmaṇas introduce many new goddesses unknown to the Vedic Saṁhitās. The tendency for similar deities to coalesce at this time indicates the contact and mingling of diverse religions, likely to have taken place in the new village settlements that proliferated in the outlying areas between the 19th and 17th centuries BCE[33] as a direct result of the widespread abandonment of cities and towns, especially along the Sarasvatī River.

Following the Brāhmaṇas in the Vedic canon, the slightly later Āraṇyakas ("forest treatises") likewise reflect life in the new, post-urban environment, and the name of this class of texts in particular refers to the emergent ascetic tradition of seers who retired to the forest to practice spiritual disciplines.

The Vedas reached completion with the composition of the principal Upaniṣads, the earliest of them overlapping the late Brāhmaṇas and Āraṇyakas. The Upaniṣads are sometimes called the Vedānta, owing to their physical position at the end (*anta*) of the Vedas and to the culmination of spiritual knowledge they reveal. Concentrating on the mystical experience, the Upaniṣads follow the course of later Vedic hymns that had already ventured boldly toward the knowledge of a higher, nontheistic reality. The word *upaniṣad* means "sitting down near" and evokes images of disciples circled around an enlightened seer, who addresses the fundamental questions of existence and imparts the answers revealed in the state of deepest meditation. Reflection on the transience of life led the Upaniṣadic seers beyond time and space to the eternal, unchanging reality called Brahman, and in the silent depths of their being they discovered that the indwelling Self (*ātman*) and the supreme godhead (Brahman) are one.

Toward the end of that murky, unsettled period that saw the creation of the Brāhmaṇas, the Āraṇyakas, and the earliest Upaniṣads, the Bronze Age blended imperceptibly into the Iron Age, and a new culture was born from the fading remnants of India's magnificent past.[34] As small Indo-Āryan chiefdoms grew into larger kingdoms, a new sociopolitical order slowly evolved. By the third century BCE, the Āryas ruled India, and Sanskrit became the dominant language of politics, culture, and religion. During this time, Hinduism branched out simultaneously in several directions.

## Post-Vedic Hinduism

Building on Vedic knowledge, philosophers developed the six orthodox schools of thought, or *darśanas* ("ways of seeing"), which embodied their teachings in the form of aphoristic statements called *sūtras* ("threads"). Among the darśanas, the dualistic Sāṁkhya philosophy, attributed to the sage Kapila, offered a rational inquiry into the nature of reality and the mind and provided a philosophical basis for Patañjali's closely related Yoga, the science of meditation as a means to achieve the ultimate consciousness. The nondualistic (*advaita*) Vedānta philosophy was systematized in Bādarāyaṇa's Brahmasūtra (or Vedāntasūtra), based on Upaniṣadic teachings concerning the attainment of Self-knowledge.

Beginning around 300 BCE, new religious movements arose that emphasized devotion as a spiritual path. *Bhakti,* originally loyalty or dedication to a personal deity, soon grew into the attitude of intense love that continues to characterize the major devotional sects—Vaiṣṇava, Śaiva, and Śākta—of modern theistic Hinduism.

The Vaiṣṇava sect exalted Viṣṇu, formerly a minor solar deity in the Ṛgveda, to the status of supreme god. He became the universal guardian of the moral order (*dharma*), who assumes a human form (*avatāra,* literally "descent") whenever worldly conditions call for the restoration of righteousness. India's two great epics, the Rāmāyaṇa and the Mahābhārata, celebrate Viṣṇu's earthly incarnations in turn as Rāma and Kṛṣṇa. Part of the immense Mahābhārata, the Bhagavadgītā presents Kṛṣṇa's teachings as an all-embracing synthesis of the religious and philosophical thinking of the second century BCE, and its universality places it among the most widely-known Hindu scriptures.

The Śaiva sect similarly elevated Śiva to absolute supremacy. Originally, Śiva may have been a non-Āryan, possibly Harappan, deity assimilated around the second century BCE to the volatile Vedic storm-god Rudra, who ultimately may also be pre- or non-Vedic. To Śaivas, he is Mahādeva ("Great God"), the lord of yogis who embodies renunciation and destroys ignorance. He is also the transcendental Absolute, whose dynamic power is personified as Śakti, the divine consort.

The Śākta tradition reveres the Divine Mother as the universal creative power, the all-pervading source of change within and identical to the changeless reality. Here, Śakti is not the consort of Viṣṇu or Śiva, as the Vaiṣṇavas or Śaivas envision her, but their source, to whom they and all other gods are subordinate. The formless and immeasurable power that is Śakti can be conceptualized only in relation to her activity as the creator, sustainer, and destroyer of the universe. Accordingly, Śakti is Mahādevī, the Great Goddess, worshiped throughout India in various forms, beneficent and awesome, including the powerful Durgā and Kālī. Sir John Woodroffe, who wrote his authoritative studies on Śākta religion under the name of Arthur Avalon, observed that the worship of Śakti preserves the essential features of the ancient, widespread religion of the Mother Goddess, who was called by many names and venerated in many forms by the peoples of the remote past.[35]

Śākta religious practice is primarily, though not exclusively, Tantric, and the two traditions overlap but do not entirely coincide.[36] Tantra, which exists in Vaiṣṇava, Śaiva, and Śākta forms, is most broadly defined as a complex of ancient practices outside the Vedic sphere. Tantra evolved into a highly sophisticated philosophical nondualism that views the world as the projection and transformation of Śakti, the divine creative principle. This idea is inherent in the word *tantra* itself, which derives from a verbal root meaning "to extend, spread, be diffused." In the intransitive sense, what is extending is the divine reality itself, in a seamless continuum that encompasses both transcendence and immanence, infinity and finitude, being and becoming, spirit and matter.[37] In the transitive sense, what Tantra extends is knowledge of the divine reality. Accordingly, the word applies to a class of sacred writings, also called Tantras or Āgamas. Of unknown authorship and disputed age, the major Tantras are thought to be no older than the 12th or 14th centuries CE, although the practices they record have roots in pre-Buddhist times, some two thousand years earlier.[38] The nondualistic philosophy they present is based on the Upaniṣads, even though Tantra remains apart from the six darśanas of orthodox Brahmāṇical tradition.

As a spiritual practice (*sādhana*), Tantra aims at union with the Divine. In its Śākta form, it requires strict discipline, ritual purification, and devotion to the Divine Mother. Paradoxically, the instruments used to overcome the limitations of body, mind, and intellect are the body, mind, and intellect themselves. The aim is to break free from the ever-repeating cycle of birth, death, and rebirth by cultivating freedom from desire and detachment from the objects of sense perception. Ultimately, it is knowledge (*jñāna*) that leads to liberation.

With the gathering momentum of devotional theism in the fourth and fifth centuries CE, the Purāṇas emerged as a new class of sacred literature. The word *purāṇa* means "ancient," and the texts characteristically present a highly mythologized history of the universe through successive cosmic cycles. As the Purāṇas grew through the absorption of local histories and myths, non-Āryan popular traditions entered the prestigious realm of Sanskrit literature[39] as part of the ongoing process of assimilation that has marked Indian religion since time immemorial. Through colorful myths and allegories, the Purāṇas gave popular access to the abstract truths of the Vedas and Upaniṣads, and in doing so, harmonized the paths of jñāna and bhakti—of spiritual knowledge and devotion.

# THE DEVĪMĀHĀTMYA'S ORIGINS, STRUCTURE, AND CONTEXT

In the fifth or sixth century CE, the appearance of a unique text within the Purāṇic fold marked a defining moment in Indian religious history. The Devīmāhātmya, which is the primary text of the Śākta tradition, united many and diverse strands of Indian myth, cult practice, and philosophy spanning at least four millennia and created one great hymn of glorification that proclaimed an all-encompassing vision of the Great Goddess. It revealed her as the omnipotent yet all-compassionate Mother, who is at once the source of this perplexing universe, a protective and guiding presence, and the bestower of supreme knowledge and liberation. From northwest India, the Devīmāhātmya spread rapidly eastward to Bengal, where it became known as the Caṇḍī. By the ninth century CE it had spread throughout the southern subcontinent under the title of Śrī Durgāsaptaśatī ("Seven Hundred Verses to Śrī Durgā").

The Devīmāhātmya forms Chapters 81 through 93 of the Mārkaṇḍeyapurāṇa. In typical Purāṇic fashion, the sage Mārkaṇḍeya relates to his disciple Krauṣṭuki Bhāguri the history of the world through its cosmic ages (*manvantaras*). When Mārkaṇḍeya begins his account of the eighth manvantara, the Devī suddenly appears out of nowhere, becomes the focal point of the chapters that constitute the Devīmāhātmya, and then vanishes just as suddenly. Her absence from all other portions of the Purāṇa and the abrupt transitions immediately before and after the Devīmāhātmya point to the likelihood that it is an interpolation by a Śākta redactor rather than a part of the original text.[1] Three other facts strengthen that likelihood. Although the Purāṇas typically grew over time by accretion, the text of the Devīmāhātmya remained relatively fixed. Few manuscripts of the entire Mārkaṇḍeyapurāṇa are known, but many of the Devīmāhātmya survive and attest to its widespread popularity. The Purāṇas generated few commentaries, but the Devīmāhātmya inspired many.[2] From the beginning, it seems to have enjoyed an independent existence, and in all probability it arose independently as well

It probably was transmitted orally at first, but committed to writing not long afterward. The early Purāṇic literature belongs to the period of transition from an oral to a written culture, and the Devīmāhātmya exhibits the repetitive, formulaic quality consistent with the bardic style of the late preliterate period.

At the same time, the text is a compilation and synthesis of far older myths and traditions, skillfully integrated into a single narrative. It consists of three episodes based on previously known but formerly unassociated myths from Vaiṣṇava, Śaiva, and indigenous tribal sources, interwoven with Harappan and Vedic strands and refashioned to affirm the Devī's absolute supremacy and glory. Connecting the myths is a frame story, told by Mārkaṇḍeya, about a king, a merchant, and a sage. In turn the sage, named Medhas, becomes the narrator of the three myths describing the Devī's activity (*carita*) in vanquishing the forces that threaten the world order, personified as demons variously called *asuras, daityas,* or *dānavas.*

A myth should not be regarded as fiction simply because it does not describe a historical event. As the Platonic philosopher Synesius of Cyrene put it, "Myths are things that never happened, but always *are.*"[3] Indeed, a myth illustrates elusive truths that are difficult to express by more conventional means, precisely because it ventures beyond the realm of fact and into the realm of meaning. Open to multiple interpretations, a myth is valuable as a window through which one's experience of the world can be understood.[4] Through symbolism, it plumbs the deeper levels of the human psyche, and at one time myth may have functioned as an ancient form of psychology. Mythologist Joseph Campbell identified the four functions of myth as inspiring a sense of awe, explaining the origin and nature of the cosmos, supporting the social order, and awakening individuals to their own potential, especially in the spiritual domain.[5] We find all four functions at work in the Devīmāhātmya.

The Devīmāhātmya's three mythological narratives are allegories of outer and internal experience. Outwardly, the asuras symbolize the chaos or *adharma* that threatens cosmic stability or dharma. Inwardly, they symbolize the ego-based ignorance that plagues the human condition. The gods and the all-powerful Devī in her many aspects represent light and truth, and their clashes with the asuras symbolize the internal struggles that human beings face daily. Reflection on the myths' often gory details reveals an underlying psychological and spiritual wisdom.

If the battle sequences concentrate on the Devī's destructive side as the vanquisher of evil, the text's four sublime hymns emphasize her auspicious and protective qualities. Although integral to the narratives, the hymns are markedly different in quality. Writing in the mid-18th century, the commentator Bhāskararāya characterized the hymns as *dṛṣta* ("seen") rather than *kṛta* ("made"), thus conferring on them the exalted status of revealed knowledge generally accorded only to the Vedas.[6] Because of their surpassing beauty and devotional fervor, they are frequently chanted in ritual. These four hymns—the Brahmāstuti (DM 1.73–87), the Śakrādistuti (DM 4.3–27), the Aparājitāstuti (DM 5.9–82) and the Nārāyaṇīstuti (DM 11.3–35)—additionally speak of perennial, universal themes and have continued over the centuries to nourish philosophical thought.

## The King, the Merchant, and the Seer

The Devīmāhātmya begins with Mārkaṇḍeya relating how a virtuous king named Suratha suffers the loss of his kingdom, then rides off alone into the forest and comes upon the hermitage of Medhas, a holy man. Soon afterward, a merchant named Samādhi, dispossessed of his wealth and cast out by his greedy family, arrives at the forest retreat. Amid the beautiful, peaceful surroundings, the two of them expect to find tranquility but encounter instead their own inner turmoil, fueled by recurring thoughts of loss, betrayal, and attachment to what they have left behind. The king feels that as men of knowledge they ought to know better than to be so overcome with misery. Together they approach Medhas, who recognizes that by "knowledge" the king means awareness of the objective world and not a deeper understanding of the true nature of things. The sage's task will be to awaken his two disciples to a higher, spiritual awareness.

Medhas tells Suratha and Samādhi that, like everyone else, they are deluded by Mahāmāyā, the goddess who hurls even the so-called wise into the dark whirlpool of attachment. Having seized their minds, she binds them to this transitory existence (*saṁsāra*) and all its attendant woes.

Medhas explains that nothing in this world is as it seems to be. The world as perceived through the senses constantly deceives. Humans and animals alike share the ability to see, hear, smell, taste, and touch, but the faculties are differently attuned and developed according to species. To speak of sensory knowledge of the world is to describe only one's own experience, and since the world is experienced differently according to the capacity of each experiencer, there is no single empirical world that is the same for all living beings. Additionally, the knowledge gained through the senses is conditioned by the physical properties of time and space, causing things to appear not as they are in themselves, but as they seem in relation to everything else.

If a simple act of sensory perception can be so fraught with deception, are not the more complex issues of animal and human behavior even more likely to confound? Medhas observes that birds feed their young even while feeling the pangs of hunger, whereas humans raise their children with the expectation of future reward. Birds act out of instinct according to predetermined patterns. Humans, also possessing instinct, additionally have the capacity to reason and make choices, but those choices are most often driven by self-interest, desires, and expectations. The Devīmāhātmya classifies both instinctual and rational awareness as lower forms of knowledge, because neither has the ability to liberate. Living creatures are bound to the ever-repeating cycle of birth, death, and rebirth. Medhas instructs that Mahāmāyā creates the universe, then "seizes the minds of even the wise and draws them into delusion" (DM 1.55). But, he adds, she is also "the supreme knowledge and the eternal cause of liberation" (DM 1.58).

The delusion of which Medhas speaks is a basic fact of life. The Sanskrit word *moha* is translated variously as "delusion, bewilderment, distraction, infatuation, error, folly," but none of these is an adequate synonym for the total pattern of thinking that fails to recognize that things are not as they seem to be and instead accepts appearance as reality. The fundamental meaning of moha is "loss of consciousness," and its cause is *māyā,* another word with no English equivalent. Initially māyā denoted extraordinary or supernatural power, and later, magic or sorcery, sometimes in the negative sense of deception. In the later Upaniṣads and the contemporaneous Sāṁkhya and Vedānta philosophies, māyā took on metaphysical dimensions. The Devīmāhātmya's understanding of māyā is closest to that of the later Upaniṣads, where it appears as the divine power of self-concealment. What it conceals is the infinite consciousness that is Brahman. Now the definition of moha as loss of consciousness begins to make sense.

The Śvetāśvataropaniṣad equates māyā with *prakṛti* as the female energy by which Śiva, the Lord of Māyā, projects the universe (ŚU 4.9–10). This portrayal as

Śiva's female counterpart implies the personification of māyā as a goddess, and such a goddess is the first one encountered in the Devīmāhātmya. Her name, Mahāmāyā, means either "the great māyā'" or "she whose māyā is great." Either way it signifies immense power.

The king wants to know more about this goddess Mahāmāyā, and Medhas responds by relating the first of three stories. There will be three stories, because everything in the world has a beginning, a middle, and an end, over which the Devī presides as the universal creator, preserver, and destroyer. In the first episode (*carita*) she appears in her cosmogonic, world-creating aspect.

## Mahāmāyā

Long before the present creation, when the previous universe was dissolved into an endless primordial ocean, the blessed Lord Viṣṇu lay in deep meditative sleep. Suddenly, two demons named Madhu and Kaiṭabha sprang forth from the wax in his ears, intent on killing Brahmā, who sat on the lotus growing from Viṣṇu's navel. Desperately, Brahmā tried to awaken Viṣṇu but in vain, for the sleep that had settled over the supreme lord's eyes was the goddess Mahāmāyā herself. Brahmā extolled her with a hymn and asked her to release Viṣṇu from her spell. Awakening, Viṣṇu beheld the raging Madhu and Kaiṭabha and engaged them in combat for five thousand years until Mahāmāyā confounded them with pride. Having withstood the might of Viṣṇu himself, in their arrogance they decided to grant him a boon, but they realized their folly too late, for what Viṣṇu asked was to slay them then and there.

Comprising only one chapter, the story of Madhu and Kaiṭabha is a succinct reinterpretation of an earlier Vaiṣṇava myth found in the Mahābhārata and other sources. In the earlier accounts, Viṣṇu is the great hero and supreme lord who defeats the asuras through his own strength. In the Devīmāhātmya, the Devī is supreme, holding the sleeping Viṣṇu in her power until praised by Brahmā. When released, Viṣṇu battles Madhu and Kaiṭabha without victory until the Devī again intervenes. In the Vaiṣṇava versions, the asuras' pride arises as a consequence of their own enormous strength, but in the Devīmāhātmya, the deluding power of Mahāmāyā tricks the pair into sealing their own doom.[7] As retold, the myth establishes the Devī as the ultimate power in the universe, upon whom even the gods are dependent.

The brutish Madhu and Kaiṭabha are ultimately done in by their own arrogant stupidity, and the obvious message is that pride goes before a fall. Their destructive impulses, anger, and brute force represent the basest aspects of human nature. The demonic pair symbolize *tamas,* one of three fundamental energies (*guṇas*) pervading all creation. To combat this negative force, the Devī appears also in a tamasic manifestation as Mahāmāyā, "the dark goddess" (DM 1.89) who casts her veil of delusion and obscures the light of truth.

Brahmā's hymn (DM 1.73–87), with its focus on the Devī's tamasic, cosmogonic aspect, reveals deep insights into the nature of divine reality and the ever-changing physical universe. The initial verses establish the Divine Mother's ultimate transcendence and identify her as the creator, sustainer, and dissolver of the cosmos. She is both consciousness and creativity—the substratum of existence and the great deluding power that projects the world out of herself. She is the all-encompassing source of good and evil alike, both radiant splendor and terrifying darkness, yet ultimately she is the ineffable bliss beyond all duality.

The Devīmāhātmya, already having pointed out that nothing in this world is as it seems, explains the origination of the universe with the startling paradox that the world is created by an act of simultaneous self-concealment (*āvaraṇa*) and projection (*vikṣepa*). The supreme Devī's māyā veils her infinitude and causes the universe of name and form (*nāmarūpa*) to emanate from her limitless consciousness. "She is eternal, having the world as her form," says Medhas (DM 1.64). This verse is an unequivocal statement of Śākta nondualism and affirms an ontological continuity between undifferentiated divine reality and its manifestation as the material universe.

Next, the Devī is prakṛti (DM 1.78), usually translated as "primordial matter" or "nature." As a verbal noun that literally means "making at first," prakṛti does not signify inert, insentient matter but a dynamic process endowed with awareness. Latent within the unmanifest prakṛti are the three basic energies, the guṇas. During the cyclical periods when the universe is not manifest, the guṇas exist in a state of perfect equilibrium. When the Devī disturbs their balance, she produces a cosmic vibration, a manifestation of energy of which the approximate sound is OṀ. The activation of the guṇas is the first step in the differentiation within prakṛti—an early event in the cosmic process of transformation from potentiality to actuality.

The guṇas—called tamas, *rajas,* and *sattva*—are the three basic energies, and their complex interactions create the physical universe. Tamas is inertia. The Sanskrit word signifies physical or mental darkness, and the force it represents manifests as heaviness, dullness, ignorance, error, and negative human behavior. Rajas is activity. The word signifies intermediate dimness between darkness and light, and the force it represents manifests as restlessness, impurity, urgency, and passion. Sattva is balance. The word signifies something like "being-ness" or "truth-ness." Sattva is not reality itself, but it points toward reality; and its manifestations include light, calmness, purity, goodness, and wisdom. Tamas veils, sattva reveals, and rajas allows those two polarizing forces to interact. As the basic forces operative in the universe, the three guṇas determine everything from the structuring of physical matter to the subtleties of human behavior.

It is easy to regard inanimate mineral matter as devoid of consciousness and to regard plant life as limited in awareness, but to do so is to forget that everything consists of forms assumed by the supreme Śakti through her guṇas. Minerals are intensely tamasic, but their greatly obscured consciousness is observable in the consistency of their atomic and subatomic organization. At the other end of the observable spectrum is the sattva-steeped awareness of the seer who has experienced the Divine. The Devīmāhātmya speaks of all the universe, moving and unmoving, as divine manifestation in which nothing is devoid of consciousness.[8]

Matter, perceived as solid objects in space and time, is in fact a relatively stable form of energy, highly organized into systems of many kinds of subatomic particles or waves that are themselves made of still smaller quanta of energy. Overall, quantum physics and Śākta philosophy agree in viewing the physical universe as a manifestation of energy. Just as vibrating quanta of energy form ever more complex units of matter to produce the entire cosmos, so the three guṇas combine and recombine with increasing complexity to structure the material universe and its living beings. Scientists claim that the amount of energy in the universe is constant; late in the 19th century, Swami Vivekananda wrote that the Divine Mother is "the sum total of the energy in the universe."[9] While science continues to probe deeper for the ultimate simplicity—the perfect, unbroken symmetry before the beginning of creation, before matter crystallized out of energy—Śākta philosophy has known all along that the ultimate form of matter is energy and that the ultimate form of energy is consciousness.

Ādyā Śakti—the primordial power devoid of all duality—is the ultimate reality, an inconceivable formlessness that is neither female, male, nor neuter but is pure, undifferentiated being-consciousness-bliss (*saccidānanda*). Though without beginning, Ādyā Śakti is the beginning of all else. Śākta philosophy agrees with the Upaniṣads that Brahman and māyā, which it calls Śiva and Śakti, are one undivided reality; it is called Śiva when experienced as the unchanging ground of existence and Śakti when experienced as the dynamic power of becoming. This power of becoming (*māyāśakti*), which manifests as mind and matter, is the power through which the infinite changelessness dons the ever-changing veils of time and space and becomes a universe that is none other than the resplendent form of the formless (*śūnyasyākāra*), a universe wherein spirit, mind and matter are ultimately one.[10]

Although compiled from disparate sources, the Devīmāhātmya reveals a consistent philosophical basis, but later commentators have exercised wide latitude in attempting to reveal its secrets according to one philosophical position or another. The two greatest commentaries are the *Guptavatī* ("Confirming What is Hidden"), written around 1741 by Bhāskararāya, and the slightly earlier commentary of Nāgoji Bhaṭṭa. While Bhaṭṭa held in large part to the established practice of interpreting the Devīmāhātmya according to the Vedānta school, Bhāskararāya was the first commentator to write from the Tantric standpoint.

Although Śākta philosophy and the Advaita Vedānta of the eighth-century philosopher-saint Śaṁkarācārya are both nondualistic in agreeing that one reality underlies all diversity, they reach radically different conclusions about the nature of the world. For Śaṁkara, the world is neither real nor unreal. His nondualism posits an ontological hierarchy of the absolutely real or transcendental (*pāramārthika*), which is the nondual Brahman; the empirical (*vyāvahārika*), which is the objective universe of human experience, lying somewhere between absolute truth and complete falsity; and the apparent or illusory (*prātibhāsika*), which includes illusions, hallucinations, and dreams. According to the process known as sublation, a new experience disproves something formerly experienced as true. For example, a dream is revealed as unreal when the sleeper returns to the waking state. Similarly, the experience of the phenomenal, objective universe is sublated by the experience of Brahman, and the universe disappears. But because Brahman, the Absolute, cannot be sublated by any other experience, it is the ultimate and sole reality.

The absolute Brahman is *nirguṇa,* or without qualities, and according to Śaṁkara the universe is only a superimposition (*adhyāsa*) on that changeless reality. This doctrine, known as *vivartavāda,* explains the universe as merely a matter of mistaking one thing for another. The classic example is of seeing a rope in the semi-darkness and thinking it to be a snake. As long as the misperception lasts, the snake is very real to the perceiver, who reacts accordingly. But the snake and the fear of it vanish when the light reveals it to be a rope. In the same way, the empirical world vanishes with the experience of the infinite Brahman. Śaṁkara's philosophy does not regard the world as pure illusion but as a flawed experience of reality through māyā's veils of time and space, and this contigent reality exists only in the fleeting experience of it.

In contrast to Śaṁkara's doctrine of vivartavāda, Bhāskararāya's *Guptavatī* and the Devīmāhātmya articulate the doctrine of *pariṇāmavāda,* the world as an actual transformation of divinity. The classic analogy expressing this view is that of thread being woven into cloth. The cause (thread) is transformed into the effect (cloth) through a change of form but not of substance.[11] The Upaniṣads support the Śākta view of the universe as real. The Chāndogyopaniṣad's pronouncement, *Sarvaṁ khalvidaṁ brahma,* "Truly all this [universe] is Brahman" (ChU 3.14.1), continues, "From that all things originate, into that do they dissolve, and by that are they sustained." The Śvetāśvataropaniṣad affirms the identity of the Absolute, the relative, and the māyā that bridges them, and declares all three to be Brahman (ŚU 1.9, 12). Through a mystery beyond the mind's understanding, Śakti becomes the manifold universe even while Śiva remains unitary and transcendental, and divine reality encompasses both the experience of the whole and the partial within the whole. For the Śākta, everything exists in the infinite Śakti, even all limitations within her wholeness are but her other aspects.[12] In glaring contrast, for Śaṁkara the absolute reality of Brahman lies in its immutability, which admits to no possibility of the imperfection inherent in change.

In truth, no philosophy can take the human mind beyond the finitizing principle of māyā to encompass the infinite, all-transcending consciousness. One can accept Śaṁkara's position that the world is no more real than the snake misperceived in the rope, or one can accept the Śākta position that the unchanging One somehow transforms itself into the ever-changing many even while remaining one and unchanging. Either way, there is a threshold that reason cannot cross, where wisdom becomes silence, and inexpressible experience alone can reveal its truth.

Now what is the relationship of that supreme consciousness to the world of human experience? Without Self-realization, humans live, deluded, in a universe projected by Mahāmāyā, who is both "the great goddess and the great demoness" (DM 1.77). The universe is a kaleidoscope of limitless possibility, of breathtaking beauty and appalling horror, where life oscillates between pleasure and pain, happiness and misery, success and failure. In such a world, the necessity arises for making choices. If Medhas's initial characterization of the Devī in her tamasic aspect inspires philosophical contemplation on the nature of reality, his depiction of her in her rajasic aspect inspires the vision of a goddess actively involved in her creation. Here she has the twofold nature of a compassionate mother worthy of devotion and a protective warrior intent on the victory of good over evil. Medhas's second story, related in Chapters 2 through 4, forms the Devīmāhātmya's second carita.

## Mahiṣāsuramardinī

Long ago, the demonic forces of Mahiṣa, the buffalo demon, battled with the heavenly forces of Indra for 100 years and defeated the gods. Cast out of heaven, the dispossessed gods appealed to Viṣṇu and Śiva for help. Thereupon a great radiance issued first from Viṣṇu's angered face and then from Brahmā's and Śiva's. From all the other gods, light also came forth and united into a fiery goddess, to whom each god gave a weapon or adornment symbolic of his power. Thus arrayed, she laughed thunderously and defiantly until the very universe shook.

Hearing the disturbance, Mahiṣa and his demon hordes rushed to the scene and beheld the Devī Durgā in all her awesome glory. Millions upon millions of asuras attacked her, but she serenely cut through their weapons as if in play. Her exhaled breaths became her legions, and amid scenes of horrific carnage the Devī stood victorious.

Next, Durgā destroyed Mahiṣa's generals one by one until she faced the buffalo demon alone. With boundless anger he pawed the earth with his hooves, bellowed in rage and rent the clouds with his thrashing horns. Whenever Durgā struck him, he changed his form, from buffalo to lion to man to elephant and back to buffalo, evading her death-blows until she leapt upon him, pinned his neck underfoot, and pierced him with her spear. Then from his buffalo's mouth, Mahiṣa's hideous, true form emerged halfway, and the Devī Durgā beheaded him with a single stroke of her mighty sword.

In the centuries before the Devīmāhātmya's composition, the goddess Durgā emerged in the Śākta movement as one of the Devī's principal forms. She seems to be of indigenous origin, and many early references associate her with the Vindhya Mountains south of the Indus Valley, a region peopled by hostile tribes.[13] The word *durga* ("difficult of access") occurs in the Ṛgveda only as a masculine or neuter adjective or noun and never as a feminine name,[14] and this textual evidence suggests that Durgā was absorbed into the Vedic pantheon after the period of the Saṁhitās. She first appears as a goddess in Vedic literature in the Taittirīyāraṇyaka, which characterizes her as "the flaming one" connected to the power of Savitṛ and Agni, the gods of the sun and fire (TA 10.1).[15]

Early traces of Durgā's defining myth, concerning the slaying of the buffalo demon, are found in six statues and a terracotta plaque from the northwestern Indian state of Rajasthan. Dating from the middle of the first century BCE to the early fourth century CE, they illustrate the myth's climactic moment and depict Mahiṣāsuramardinī—Durgā as the slayer of the buffalo demon—as a goddess armed with trident and spear in combat with a buffalo. The plaque additionally shows a lion accompanying her.[16]

Although the myth's ultimate origin remains unknown,[17] circumstantial evidence places it in the extremely remote past. We recall that pre-Harappan images of a formidable goddess were found in Baluchistan in connection with those of a wild bull and have been interpreted as credible symbols of good conquering evil. Such an interpretation finds support in the work of archeologist Jacques Cauvin, who contends that the wild male bovine so terrified Neolithic people with its brute force and destructive ferocity that it became a universal symbol of evil, of the chaos that threatened the peaceful order of sedentary agricultural societies.[18] Without direct evidence it is impossible to ascribe such a remote origin to the story of Mahiṣāsura, but we cannot rule out the possibility that one of Hinduism's most captivating myths preserves a primeval cultural memory.

Later terracotta tablets from Harappa show a male figure killing a water buffalo in the manner described in the Devīmāhātmya, by pinning the head underfoot and thrusting a spear into the shoulder. This act takes place in the presence of the horned male deity, speculated to be proto-Śiva, seated in the yogic position.[19]

This evidence hardly suggests a direct connection with Durgā but becomes noteworthy in light of the oldest literary account of myth, preserved in the Mahābhārata. There Mahiṣa is slain by Śiva's son, Skanda (MBh 3.221).[20] In the Harivaṁśa, a later supplement to the Mahābhārata, Mahiṣa's slayer is given once as Śiva himself and three times as an unnamed goddess.[21] The Vāmanapurāṇa, thought to postdate the Devīmāhātmya, contains two accounts of the slaying, one associated with Skanda and one with Durgā.[22] Arising from yet undetermined origins, the myth remained for a long while in a state of flux as to whether Skanda, Śiva, or an unnamed goddess killed Mahiṣāsura, until its unequaled formulation in the Devīmāhātmya for the first time actually linked the names of Mahiṣa and Durgā.[23]

The argument for Durgā's antiquity becomes all the more compelling in light of her linkage to another ancient goddess, Vindhyavāsinī. This identification is consistent in two hymns interpolated into the Mahābhārata—the Durgāstava (in MBh 4.5) and the Durgāstotra (in MBh 6.22)—and in three hymns of the Harivaṁśa. Among the latter, Viṣṇu's Praise of Nidrā first extols Vindhyavāsinī for foiling Kaṁsa's plot to kill the infant Kṛṣṇa (HV 47.38–57). Then a later, fifty-eight-line addition to the hymn (HV Appendix I, No. 8) not only makes it clear that Vindhyavāsinī and Durgā are one and the same goddess but also identifies her in line 32 with Aditi, the universal mother of the Ṛgveda.[24] This is highly significant, considering that the references to Aditi in the Ṛgveda may well be the most ancient surviving records of any goddess in the Indian literary tradition.

Durgā's association with the Vaiṣṇava themes of the destruction of wickedness and the protection of virtue is another thread running through the Durgāstava and the Durgāstotra. The Durgāstava's hymnist is Yudhiṣṭhira, the dispossessed king whose situation resembles Suratha's. Significantly, the Durgāstotra, one of the earliest Sanskrit hymns to the Devī,[25] occurs immediately before the 18 chapters that form the Bhagavadgītā. Arjuna, about to engage in battle at Kurukṣetra, is counseled by Kṛṣṇa to recite the Durgāstotra in order to insure victory. Arjuna descends from his chariot and invokes the Devī as Kālī, Bhadrakālī, Caṇḍī, and Durgā, and by other names and epithets found scattered throughout the Devīmāhātmya. Together, Yudhiṣṭhira's ecstatic praise and Arjuna's invocation present a vision of Durgā as a dark and resplendent goddess, the destroyer of Kaiṭabha and Mahiṣāsura, worthy of worship by the Vedic gods. Endowed with all manner of weapons and adornments, she grants victory in battle and removes human burdens. Many are the boons she bestows on those who seek refuge in her. The two hymns share a multitude of themes, images, and epithets with the Devīmāhātmya, even entire, closely-corresponding passages, especially relating to the Devī's promises of protection and blessing.[26]

The strategic positioning of the Durgāstotra in the Mahābhārata forges a link between the Devīmāhātmya and the Bhagavadgītā. So does the forced enumeration of the Devīmāhātmya's text into seven hundred verses in order to conform to the Bhagavadgītā's similar number. Despite its alternative title, Śrī Durgāsaptaśatī ("Seven Hundred Verses to Śrī Durgā"), the Devīmāhātmya actually consists of fewer than six hundred full couplets (*ślokas*). To arrive at the requisite seven hundred, redactors have variously numbered some single lines, partial lines, and interlocutory phrases ("so-and-so said") as full ślokas. For wishing to draw such a parallel to the Bhagavadgītā, they must have had a compelling reason. Indeed they did. They wanted to equate the Devī Durgā's activity with the redemptive role of Śrī Kṛṣṇa in Vaiṣṇava religion.

The idea of divine intervention in worldly affairs belongs to the Vaiṣṇava tradition of the avatāra, or incarnate deity. In the Bhagavadgītā (BhG 4.6–8) Kṛṣṇa declares that whenever righteousness declines and evil proliferates, he is born into the world to protect the good, to destroy wickedness, and to re-establish the natural order, the dharma that upholds (*dhāryate*) the world. In the Mahābhārata, protective intervention is a role ascribed also to the Devī. On Kṛṣṇa's advice, Arjuna invokes Durgā with a hymn immediately before the battle of Kurukṣetra, whereupon she appears and assures victory. And just as the opening words of the Bhagavadgītā declare the field of Kurukṣetra to be a metaphor for the field of dharma—the battleground of human life with its perpetual conflict between good and evil—the battlefields of the Devīmāhātmya embody a parallel symbolism. To compare the Devīmāhātmya to the Bhagavadgītā is to reinforce the Devī's protective, redemptive role and her saving grace in the face of adversity. Whenever evil prevails over good and upsets the natural order, the Devī, who is the universal mother, protector, and salvific goddess, intervenes.

The second carita of the Devīmāhātmya has theological and practical dimensions in portraying the Devī as the salvific Durgā, and the story is intended for Suratha. Having lost his kingdom to evildoers, he can relate to the dispossessed gods; having ruled by divine authority, duty-bound to uphold the dharma, he can relate to its overturning. The heaven-storming asuras and the gods represent the good and evil tendencies that pervade the world in perpetual opposition. Mahiṣa's fury symbolizes the ego-based sense of attachment that plagues Suratha over his lost kingdom. The buffalo demon's behavior embodies the guṇa of rajas, the fiery, active energy that manifests as restlessness, desire, rage, and corrosive passion. The Devī also appears in her rajasic aspect, as the inherent splendor (*tejas*) of the male gods. And she is subordinate to none of them. Their individual strengths and virtues, which emerge from their bodies with fiery brilliance and coalesce into one supreme female form, are but facets of her own undivided might.

The episode of Durgā's triumph over evil is her defining moment, a myth so powerful that it has been celebrated in sculpture and painting for at least two thousand years. Beyond moral victory, the multilayered imagery of the myth has deeper psychological and spiritual implications. As a metaphor, Mahiṣa represents more than anger, however monumental. Whenever Durgā attacks, the buffalo demon eludes her deadly blows by using the protective shield of his changing forms. Until he reveals his true form, he remains elusive and seemingly unconquerable. In the same way, human delusion dons an array of guises to mask and protect an ego ruled by attachment, aversion, and deep-seated fear. Personal demons will continue to bedevil in one form or another until recognized for what they are. Of course, Mahiṣa's unwillingness to reveal himself stems from a sense of self-preservation, and Durgā forces the revelation by piercing his side with her spear, symbolizing the penetrating light of the higher knowledge. When Mahiṣa emerges in his true form, Durgā decapitates him with her sword, a metaphor for *viveka,* the ability to discern between the apparent and the real, the transient and the eternal.

The myth reveals an intimate connection between good and evil and the ego. The experience of duality and finite selfhood arises from moha, the limitation of consciousness. Without a nondualistic understanding, the presence of evil in the world remains a vexing question. Some dualistic religions seek a solution by acknowledging God as the source of good and inventing a devil as the source of evil, but in doing so they create the further problem of a diminished God, who is no longer the supreme being but one of two mutually-limiting adversaries. The simple fact is that good and evil coexist in the relative world and neither is possible without the other to define it. Practically and philosophically, evil is that which distances from the Divine, and good is that which leads toward it. As for the ego, when the Devī enters into her creation to experience it as her divine play (*līlā*), her infinite consciousness appears fragmented as finite centers in time and space that define everything in their experience in terms of "I, me, and mine" and their negative corollaries. Inevitably, the interests of one ego clash with those of another, and the need arises for moral choices between divisive egocentrism and the uniting power of selfless love. Durgā's slaying of Mahiṣāsura symbolizes the conquest of ego-based attachment and all its consequent pain. No wonder Mahiṣa's final expression, gazing up at his sword-wielding slayer, is one of rapt awe.

In the eloquent, richly detailed Śakrādistuti (DM 4.3–27) that follows, Indra and the other gods praise Durgā's supremacy and transcendence before elaborating on the meaning of Mahiṣa's slaying, which centers on the salvific nature of the Devī's power and on her unconditional compassion. Her purpose is to preserve the moral order, and to that end she appears as "good fortune in the dwellings of the virtuous and misfortune in the abodes of the wicked" (DM 4.5), granting abundant blessings and subduing misconduct. "Ever intent on benevolence toward all" (DM 4.17), she reveals even her vast destructive power as ultimately compassionate, for in slaying those enemies of the world who "may have committed enough evil to keep them long in torment" (DM 4.18), she redeems them with the purifying touch of her weapons so that they "may attain the higher worlds" (DM 4.19). Since good and evil exist only relative to each other, no evildoer meets with eternal damnation. In the end, all are assured of the Divine Mother's blessing.

The Devī's promise to return whenever she is remembered by the gods or humankind in times of distress prompts Medhas to announce that he has yet another story, and so begins the Devīmāhātmya's longest and most elaborate carita, which constitutes Chapters 5 through 13.

## The Devī—One and Many

Long ago, two arrogant asuras, the brothers Śumbha and Niśumbha, seized Indra's sovereignty over the three worlds, and once again the gods were dispossessed. The Devī had promised that whenever remembered in times of distress, she would appear and put an end to misfortune, and so the gods invoked her with praise.

She emerged in a resplendent form from the body of Śiva's consort, Pārvatī, and took up her abode in the Himālayas. Soon her captivating beauty caught the attention of Caṇḍa and Muṇḍa, Śumbha and Niśumbha's two servants, who reasoned that since their masters had already stolen everything of value from the gods, should they not also possess this most beautiful of goddesses? Śumbha sent his messenger, Sugrīva, to beguile the Devī to come to him and Niśumbha. But Sugrīva returned with a challenge, for the Devī had vowed long ago that whoever she married would first have to conquer her in battle.

Śumbha appointed the chieftain Dhūmralocana to bring her back by force, and after his failed attempt, Caṇḍa and Muṇḍa were sent to fetch her. The Devī saw them and their immense army approaching, and when she scowled, the frightful goddess Kālī sprang forth from her brow and slaughtered the demon hordes.

Next, Śumbha marshaled all the asura clans, and in turn the Devī evoked her śaktis, seven fierce goddesses who sprang forth from the bodies of the gods. From her own body the most terrifying śakti of all, Śivadūtī, came forth and sent the great Lord Śiva himself as a messenger to Śumbha and Niśumbha to warn them of the consequences of battle. The arrogant asuras took no heed, and fighting of unprecedented fierceness left in its wake a scene of gruesome slaughter.

While the surviving demons fled from the fury of the śaktis, the great asura Raktabīja strode onto the battlefield. Whenever a drop of his blood touched the ground, it grew into an asura of equal size and strength, and soon the Devī's hosts again battled countless foes. Terror seized the gods, but the Devī merely laughed while Kālī began to drink in the drops of blood and the asuras being born therefrom. As she consumed them, others did not arise. Finally the mighty Raktabīja, drained of blood, fell dead.

Then Śumbha and Niśumbha themselves battled with the Devī and her śaktis until Niśumbha, too, lay slain. In rage and grief, Śumbha reproached the Devī for relying on the strength of others, but she replied that the śaktis were but projections of her own power. Drawing them back into herself, she stood alone against him, and at the climax of battle, the two leapt to the sky and fought in midair until the Devī sent the great Śumbha crashing to the earth. When he lay dead, the sky cleared, the sun shone in glory, and the universe rested in luminous calm. The gods praised the Devī in a great hymn of thanksgiving, and she pledged her protection and blessing thenceforth to all who praise her with hymns, recite the destruction of the asuras, and worship her with devotion.

Of the Devīmāhātmya's three myths, the story of Śumbha and Niśumbha is the least attested in Sanskrit literature.[27] In all likelihood, it originated among aboriginal, goddess-worshiping peoples of north India who perpetuate their ancient traditions to the present time. Among those same peoples the legends of Kṛṣṇa as the beloved cowherd Gopāla first arose, and the few traces of Śumbha and Niśumbha in Sanskrit literature before the Devīmāhātmya appear in connection with Kṛṣṇa Gopāla's exploits, later absorbed into the Vaiṣṇava fold.[28]

From the same Vaiṣṇava milieu comes yet another myth, briefly alluded to in the Devīmāhātmya (DM 11.41–42): the story of Kṛṣṇa's birth and the role played in it by the goddess Vindhyavāsinī.

It had been foretold to the wicked king Kaṁsa that his sister Devakī would give birth to a child at whose hand he would die. Preparing to take birth as the child Kṛṣṇa, the great Lord Viṣṇu asked the goddess Yoganidrā (Mahāmāyā) to be born at the same time to the cowherd Nanda and his wife Yaśodā, and with the help of Yoganidrā's deluding power, the babies were switched at birth. When Kaṁsa rushed to Devakī's side to murder her newborn child, the baby escaped his grasp and assumed the goddess's eight-armed form. Telling Kaṁsa that his slayer had been born into the world, Yoganidrā flew off to the Vindhya mountains, where she is still worshiped as Vindhyavāsinī.

This myth demonstrates that the goddess Yoganidrā, or Mahāmāyā, belongs to a pre-existing tradition that was incorporated into the early Vaiṣṇava legends.[29] Likewise, hymns interpolated into the Mahābhārata and the Harivaṁśa invariably describe the Mahādevī, the Great Goddess, who incarnates to aid Viṣṇu, as abiding permanently in the Vindhya mountains—a designation that places her among non-Vedic tribal peoples of the natural wilderness.[30] However, Vindhyavāsinī's Vaiṣṇava association is not exclusive; the Matsyapurāṇa, one of the six Śaiva Purāṇas, considers her, Caṇḍikā, and Kālī as three manifestations of the Devī, each again connected with wild, mountainous regions.[31]

Today, Vindhyavāsinī's temple complex dominates the north-central Indian village of Vindhyācal (Uttar Pradesh). Just north of a pavilion that bears upon its marble walls the recently inscribed text of the Devīmāhātmya, an ancient and unprepossessing stone shrine houses the goddess. She stands upon a lion and gazes out through wide, silver eyes set in her black, birdlike face.[32] Her startling appearance recalls the avian-faced terracotta figurines from Harappa and Mohenjo-daro, which in turn look back to the still earlier goddesses with birdlike heads from Baluchistan, and from there the chain recedes ever farther back into the incomprehensibly remote past.

By the time the myth of Śumbha and Niśumbha attained definitive form in the Devīmāhātmya, the Devī had either replaced Kṛṣṇa Gopāla as their slayer or had been restored to a role that was originally hers. Additionally, the Devīmāhātmya's version of the myth contains details that signal a Śaiva influence, for example, the shift of locale from the Vindhyas to the Himālayas (Śiva's abode), the emergence of the Devī from the body of Śiva's consort, and the importance of Kālī in the narrative.

As described in the seventh chapter, Kālī has loosely hanging, emaciated flesh that barely conceals her bones. Gleaming white fangs protrude from her gaping, blood-stained mouth, framing her lolling red tongue. Red, too, are her eyes, which peer out from her black face. We can take this black, red, and white—the colors of tamas, rajas, and sattva—to indicate that Kālī is no subsidiary goddess but the supreme Mother of the Universe (Jagadambā), in whom the three guṇas reside. In short, she is the resplendent Devī in another, darker form.

Manifesting to confront Śumbha's escalating evil, she carries the skull-topped staff that traditionally accompanies her in battle.[33] This staff, also associated with shamans, supports Kālī's presumed origin among the tribal societies of India's mountainous regions. Although her ultimate origin remains shrouded in mystery, her dark skin may point back to the dark, fertile earth, and her dual aspects as the giver and taker of life point back to very ancient times. Conforming to her predominantly fearsome character, Kālī's early temples were situated at the edges of civilization, often near forests and cremation grounds.[34]

Her name comes from the feminine adjective *kālī,* meaning "dark" or "blue-black." It is probably related to the masculine noun *kāla* ("time"), which fits the concept of Kālī as ever-turning time, the relentless devourer who brings all things to an end. The name first appears in Sanskrit literature around 2,500 years ago in the Muṇḍakopaniṣad, where it identifies one of Agni's seven flaming tongues that devour the oblations of clarified butter in the Vedic sacrifice (MU 1.2.4). This is scarcely sufficient evidence to confirm or even to suggest that Kālī originated as a śakti of Agni, but it is noteworthy that fire dissolves matter back into energy—in the form of heat and light—just as Kālī, the destroyer, dissolves the material universe back into undifferentiated śakti. The same verse of the Upaniṣad designates another of Agni's seven tongues as Karālī ("formidable, dreadful, terrible, having a gaping mouth and protruding teeth"). This word appears twice in the Devīmāhātmya's final hymn to describe Kālī's terrifying mouth (11.21) and Bhadrakālī's flaming trident (11.26).

Kālī first appears unequivocally as a goddess in the Kaṭhaka Gṛhyasūtra, a ritualistic text from late Vedic times that places her among Vedic deities to be invoked with offerings of perfume during the marriage ceremony.

During the epic period, sometime after the fifth century BCE, Kālī makes a startling appearance in the Mahābhārata. When the Pāṇḍava brothers' camp is attacked one night by the sword-wielding Aśvatthāman, his deadly assault is seen as the work of "Kālī of bloody mouth and eyes, smeared with blood and adorned with garlands, . . . crowned and holding noose in hand." She, the Night of Death (Kālarātri), laughs derisively while binding men, horses, and elephants with her terrible snares of death (MBh 10.8.64–65).[35] Even though the passage goes on to describe the slaughter as an act of human warfare, it makes clear that the fierce goddess is ultimately the agent of death who carries off those who are slain.

In the 17th and 18th centuries, Kālī's characterization changed radically, when Bengali Tantrics and devotional poets such as Rāmprasād and Kamalākānta envisioned her as voluptuously beautiful and began to sing her praises as the loving, universal Mother and supreme metaphysical reality. That characterization of Kālī remains the predominant one today.

The eighth chapter of the Devīmāhātmya relates how the Devī multiplies her strength in the escalating battle by calling forth seven individual śaktis from the bodies of the male gods. The seven śaktis are known collectively as the *mātṛgaṇa* ("band of mothers"), the Saptamātṛkās ("Seven Little Mothers") or simply the Mothers. We learn from the Bṛhat Saṁhitā, a text contemporary with the Devīmāhātmya, that in the sixth century there existed a prevalent and powerful cult centered on a group of fierce goddesses, usually seven in number. The same text recommends that images of them should display the same identifying marks as the gods to whose names their own correspond. The abundant iconographic evidence from this period includes a sculptured panel from a temple to the Saptamātṛkās, portraying the seven goddesses accompanied by an inscription that invokes the benefits of their protective power. As in the Devīmāhātmya, the Mothers' function is to fight for the preservation of the world.[36]

But who are these Mothers? When we meet them in the Devīmāhātmya, they have already been absorbed into the Brāhmaṇical fold and considerably tamed, but they were not always considered so benevolent. Only in the century or two immediately preceding the Devīmāhātmya did they take on the role of battling demons, as they became increasingly identified with male deities,[37] and only then did they evolve into the differentiated forms recognizable as the seven śaktis described in our text. Before then, the seven appeared as uniform figures.[38]

Predating the Devīmāhātmya by about 500 years,[39] references to the Mothers in later strata of the Mahābhārata invariably link them to the war god Kārttikeya (Skanda) and describe them as exceedingly ferocious and bloodthirsty minor goddesses in whom, paradoxically, the impulses of motherhood are deeply ingrained.[40] Their number is often unspecified but implied to be very large, and they are portrayed not only as inauspicious but also as downright dangerous.[41] These goddesses are predators of children until Kārttikeya persuades them instead to assume a protective role. Nevertheless he concedes to them the right to torment the young until the age of sixteen! Their names, when given, do not yet correspond to the names in the Devīmāhātmya.[42]

Earlier still, the Mothers were an independent group of violent goddesses associated with the dangers of pregnancy and childbirth, infant mortality, and illnesses afflicting small children. Many such goddesses survive to this day in the folk religion of Indian villages, where they still receive blood offerings for their appeasement.[43]

Given ample evidence that features of the Indus-Sarasvatī civilization endure even today in Indian villages, if we look back two millennia or so before the references in the Mahābhārata, we discover that some of the Harappan stone seals bear the carved images of seven identical figures, all standing in a row, sometimes with hands joined. Clad in matching tunics, with hair in a braid and a bird's plume on the head, they display avian qualities in body and attire, but their faces are human.[44] Could these mysterious figures, peering at us across more than 4,000 years, be early representations of the Seven Little Mothers?

The Mahābhārata describes the Mothers as dark-skinned, speaking various languages, and inhabiting mountains and caves. Together, these traits suggest that the Mothers were present in the multi-ethnic diaspora of Indus-Sarasvatī emigrants, who resettled in remoter, peripheral regions after abandoning their doomed villages, towns, and cities.[45] Although the Brāhmaṇical culture that produced the Mahābhārata viewed the probably non-Āryan Mothers with suspicion, the Śākta author(s) of the Devīmāhātmya accorded them full legitimacy, fixing their identification with the Vedic and post-Vedic gods and then revealing them not as mere goddess-consorts but as individualized powers of the one Great Goddess.

As allegory, the myth of Śumbha and Niśumbha has particular immediacy, because the sphere of action is decidedly terrestrial rather than cosmic or celestial. The gods, distressed that the asuras have once more overturned the world order, invoke the Devī in a magnificent hymn, the Aparājitāstuti ("Praise to the Invincible Goddess," DM 5.9–82), which celebrates her immanence in the world as the consciousness that manifests in all beings.

Thereupon, the Devī appears on the bank of the Gaṅgā. Her effulgent manifestation, emerging from the body of Parvatī, embodies the guṇa of sattva, the energy of light, purity, peace, and goodness. Having already revealed her tamasic and rajasic aspects, she appears as sattvic and bewitchingly beautiful, although she will take on multiple and varied forms in the course of battle.

Śumbha and Niśumbha's traditional characterization as mountain demons further emphasizes the terrestrial locale, and of all the Devīmāhātmya's villains, they and their cohorts appear the most human. Individually, Śumbha represents the ego, and his younger brother represents its sense of attachment. They are central to the entire catalog of human failings and vices. The portrayal of Śumbha amid the glittering excess of his ill-gotten riches and powers is a sickening picture of corruption and materialism gone mad. The toadying Caṇḍa and Muṇḍa appeal to their master's immense vanity and inflame his lust with tempting descriptions of the Devī's captivating beauty. Courting the young goddess for Śumbha, the unctuous Sugrīva speaks with the intent to dissemble, and her refusal, citing a vow to marry whoever can conquer her in battle, establishes the pattern of challenge and counterchallenge that will drive the narrative's steady escalation from that point on.

When Śumbha orders Dhūmralocana to bring the Devī back "kicking and screaming" if need be, the dim-witted thug becomes a casualty of the proverbial violence that begets violence. Śumbha, now driven by unreasoning rage, sends Caṇḍa and Muṇḍa to reattempt Dhūmralocana's failed mission, whereupon the sattvic Devī evokes her fearsome manifestation, Kālī, who quickly slays the two servants and their army.

When Śumbha mobilizes for all-out war, the Devī multiplies her forces with seven fierce śaktis, evoked from the gods, and with her own śakti, the terrifying Śivadūtī. In counter-response there appears Raktabīja ("he whose seed is blood") with his amazing replicative ability. His red blood, symbolic of rajas, represents the awesome power of desire and mental restlessness. Just as each drop that falls to earth produces another asura, so does one desire or thought lead to another. Indulgence leads to insatiability, and the ghastly metaphor of Kālī lapping up the dripping blood symbolizes the sound principle that human desires and uncontrolled mental activity are best conquered if nipped in the bud.

Raktabīja's death marks the turning point. Henceforth the theme of escalating multiplicity reverses itself. One by one the outward manifestations of ego have been vanquished, and only its essence, represented by Śumbha and Niśumbha, remains against the Devī and her forces.

The prolonged battle with Niśumbha runs parallel to the Devī's victory over Mahiṣāsura. Both myths involve the demon's metamorphosis, the piercing by her spear, and the revelation of an inner being who is beheaded. When Niśumbha, symbolizing attachment, sprouts 10,000 grasping arms, his awful transmutation is not a graceful evasion like Mahiṣa's, but an act of ugly desperation. In both myths, the Devī's spear, representing insight, leaves the asura exposed and vulnerable. The mighty demon that emerges from Niśumbha's gaping chest wound calls for the Devī to stop, but in sādhana halfway measures simply won't do, and she annihilates him with her sword of knowledge.

Now only Śumbha, the naked ego, remains. When he reproaches the Devī for relying on the strength of others, she responds that the śaktis are only projections of her own power and recalls them into herself. Meeting in final combat, the lone Devī and Śumbha rise to the sky, signaling disengagement from the world. After the ultimate struggle, when Śumbha lies dead, the veil of individual nescience (*avidyā*) that obscures the indwelling Self is lifted. Metaphoric clouds disperse to reveal the brightly shining sun and beatific peace, the realization of infinite consciousness.

If the myth of Mahiṣāsura is intended for King Suratha, whose duty and interests lay in conquering evil and governing righteously, the third of Medhas's tales is intended for Samādhi, the merchant. With its imagery of material wealth and human passions, it resonates with his bitter experience of the vanity of riches and ephemeral pleasures and the folly of lamenting their loss. His goal is not to regain a kingdom but to renounce the world and attain liberation.

The Devīmāhātmya's final hymn, the Nārāyaṇīstuti (DM 11.3–35), comments on the foregoing action. Popularized through widespread liturgical use, it lauds the Devī in her universal, omnipotent aspect and also in the diverse expressions of her power. Once again pleased by the gods' praise, she renews her promise to confer well-being upon the world and to intervene whenever evil arises. In a fascinating sequence of verses (DM 11.40–55), she predicts five of her future incarnations, which in fact reveal their origins in humankind's remote past.

Chapter 12 is a *phalaśruti,* a conventional literary form that details the benefits of reciting or hearing a sacred text. Cast in the Devī's own words, it names specific blessings and protections and pronounces the Devīmāhātmya "the supreme way to well-being" (DM 12.7).

In the final chapter, Medhas resumes the thread of his original discourse, repeating that the Devī is both the binding ignorance (*avidyāmāyā*) and the liberating knowledge (*vidyāmāyā*). She alone is, and nothing exists apart from her. Medhas instructs the king and the merchant to take refuge in her. At this point (DM 13.6), Mārkaṇḍeya again becomes the narrator of the framing story and relates how the Devī appears to Suratha and Samādhi after three years of austerities. To each, she grants his fondest wish. Samādhi, who has grown wise and dispassionate toward the world, receives eternal liberation. The virtuous Suratha, who remains duty-bound, regains his earthly kingdom and receives the promise of rebirth as the *manu* named Sāvarṇi, who will rule over a future cosmic age (manvantara).

## The Limbs of the Devīmāhātmya

In the centuries following the Devīmāhātmya's composition, three *dhyāna*s ("meditations") were incorporated into the text before Chapters 1, 2 and 5 to signal the beginning of each carita. These brief meditations describe the three cosmic aspects of Śakti—the tamasic Mahākālī, the rajasic Mahālakṣmī, and the sattvic Mahāsarasvatī.[46] The dhyānas are thought to be a Tantric addition because of their carefully defined imagery, which facilitates the practice of visualized meditation.[47] Exactly when they were added is uncertain, but literary evidence points to the period before the ninth or, at the latest, before the 12th century.[48]

Around the 14th century a set of ancillary texts, the six *aṅgas* ("limbs"), gravitated toward the Devīmāhātmya.[49] The first three—the Devyāḥ Kavacam, Argalāstotra, and Kīlakastotra—are preparatory ritual texts, always chanted before the formal recitation of the Devīmāhātmya. The remaining three—the Prādhānika Rahasya, Vaikṛtika Rahasya, and Mūrtirahasya—deal with philosophy and formal worship (*pūjā*) and are optionally recited afterward.

Directly before and after the Devīmāhātmya itself, two ancient hymns are customarily chanted as a kind of auditory jewel box, symbolically to enclose it and separate it from the aṅgas. The Vedic Rātrisūkta ("Hymn to Night," ṚV 10.127) praises the starry night as the beautiful goddess Rātrī, who brings rest to all creatures; at the same time it asks for protection from predators that lurk in the darkness. The Vedic Devīsūkta ("Hymn of the Goddess," ṚV 10.125) is the Devī's own unequivocal revelation of herself as the Divine Mother and transcendent reality.

Since Tantra recognizes the word (*vāk*) as an actual manifestation of Śakti, it sees a correlation between the physical universe of form and the divine, formless reality. According to this view, the verses of the Devīmāhātmya are not mere poetry (śloka) but the actual embodiment of the divine presence (*mantra*), a power so great that Śiva himself is said to have restrained it "as if with a bolt" to prevent its intentional or unwitting misuse. Accordingly, the Devīmāhātmya is recited publicly in temples and also privately in homes, often by a paid professional, since proper recitation must be preceded by careful ritual preparation in order to gain access to that power, which then may be directed either to temporal or spiritual goals.

With the Devyāḥ Kavacam ("The Devī's Armor"), the reciter dons divine protection. The verses invoke the individual śaktis who inhabit various parts of the body, and the prayer insures the Devī's indwelling, protective presence. The Argalāstotra ("Hymn of the Bolt") is another series of invocations; all but three of its verses have the form of a *dhāraṇī,* a Tantric mantra that first praises a deity and then appeals for assistance.[50] In this case, the appeal is an unchanging refrain that requests contact with the indwelling divinity, the assurance of victory, glory, and the destruction of hostile forces. The Kīlakastotra ("Hymn of the Pin") is the pivot on which access to the Devīmāhātmya's limitless power hinges. Its language is deliberately obscure, lest its knowledge fall into the wrong hands, and its hidden key to the Devīmāhātmya's power is the reciter's attitude of complete surrender and selfless dedication to the Divine Mother.

If the function of the first three aṅgas is to assure the reciter's safe access to immense power, the purpose of the remaining three is to instruct in philosophy and ritual worship. The Rahasyas ("secrets") form a continuation of King Suratha's dialogue with Medhas and relate to Śakti's manifestations. Together, the three Rahasyas have been called the "earliest systematic statement of Śākta philosophy."[51]

The Prādhānika Rahasya ("The Secret Relating to Primary Matter") relates to the cosmogonic Devī of the first carita. Reaffirming the nondualism of the Upaniṣads and proclaiming the uncompromising unity of ultimate reality and its manifestation, the Prādhānika Rahasya considers how formless, singular consciousness assumes the forms of the ever-changing plural universe.[52] The Vaikṛtika Rahasya ("The Secret Relating to Transformation") explains that the supreme Devī's manifestation is a modification (*vikṛti*) from formless transcendence to perceptible form. The Mūrtirahasya ("The Secret Relating to Forms") elaborates on her incarnations as foretold in Chapter 11 of the Devīmāhātmya, describing their iconography and specifying the benefits of worshiping them. The final aṅga reaffirms the Devī's maternal beneficence and salvific power, often conjuring up telluric and agricultural images connected to the ancient Earth Goddess.

## About the Commentary

In the classical Indian sense, a commentary seeks to enlighten by arguing the fine points of a text from a particular philosophical position. Such commentaries are intended for people already well-versed in Hindu religion and philosophy.

Mine is not a commentary in that sense. Instead, it is meant for readers who may have little or no previous knowledge of Indian culture or Hindu thought. It draws broadly on diverse sources of information—religious, philosophical, scientific, or historical—that help to reveal the Devīmāhātmya's deeper levels of meaning. In the traditional manner it refers to the external authority of scriptures that would have been known to the author(s) of the Devīmāhātmya, particularly the Upaniṣads and Vedic hymns. But, departing from tradition, its approach relies heavily on the Devīmāhātmya's own internal evidence, revealed through analyzing the text and its structure as well as the derivations of key Sanskrit words. Despite the differences of method, this commentary arrives at conclusions completely in accord with the Śākta philosophy underlying the text. Its purpose is to promote a deeper understanding, not a novel one.

On one level, the Devīmāhātmya is an allegory of the spiritual journey; on another it is a blueprint of the soul. Much of the commentary is written in simple language, aimed at explaining the practical application of the Devīmāhātmya's teachings. Other portions, dealing with matters that may at first seem purely theoretical, but which are essential to a fuller understanding of the Devīmāhātmya's profound teaching, are unavoidably more technical. Some of the most difficult passages occur at the very beginning of the commentary in connection with the meditation on Mahākālī and the opening mantra invoking the Divine Mother as Caṇḍikā. After that, the commentary becomes much less daunting.

Making no claim to be a definitive interpretation, the commentary is only a guide to what can become a voyage of discovery. The Devīmāhātmya is no ordinary book. It can serve us equally in times of personal difficulty and decision, in moments when we look in rapt wonder at the beauty around us, or in those indescribable moments when the profound quiet of holiness reveals its presence. The deepest meanings of this great poem make themselves known only through direct experience, and such immediacy can only come from within.

## The Devīmāhātmya Today

In present-day Bengal, the autumn Navarātri is one of the most widely-celebrated religious festivals. Occurring in September or October, it coincides with the harvest season and carries associations of agricultural fertility.[53] The central deity worshiped is Durgā as Mahiṣāsuramardinī, the ten-armed goddess of golden complexion. Specially created for the occasion, the crowned, bejeweled, and garlanded image of the buffalo demon's slayer stands triumphant upon her lion while Mahiṣa lies below, emerging from his decapitated buffalo's body and regarding her with awestruck wonder.

While an air of festivity reigns amid the rhythms of pūjā, devotional singing, and the recitation of sacred texts, Navarātri is at heart a time for inner purification. For the first three days, devotees invoke Durgā—the warrior-Mother's destructive and protective aspect—to destroy the asuras within, the acknowledged personal shortcomings of fear, passion, selfishness, and anger. For the next three days, they worship her as the beneficent Lakṣmī and ask for sufficient prosperity along with the positive virtues of courage, tranquility, generosity, kindness, devotion, and the desire for liberation. During the following three days, they appeal to Sarasvatī for spiritual knowledge. The festival culminates on the tenth day, called Dasarā or Vijayā Daśamī. This day, sacred also to Vaiṣṇavas as a celebration of Rāma's victory over the demon-king Rāvaṇa—with help from the Devī[54]—is for Śāktas an occasion for joyous feasting. Spiritually, it commemorates the great and total victory, the realization that the individual soul is one with the Divine.[55]

Sixteen centuries after its composition, the Devīmāhātmya still shines as a beacon from a primordial age when men and women, enchanted by nature's beauty and abundance, yet terrified by its fierce, destructive power, honored the source of creation as the Great Mother. It enshrines many an ancient memory in the resounding cadences of its verses and continues to sing her glory. At the same time as the last open expressions of Goddess-centered religion were vanishing from the Western world, the Devīmāhātmya took shape on the more tolerant soil of India, where the religion of the Divine Mother flourished and continues to flourish. Even today, the great hymn of praise that is the Devīmāhātmya reveals to us an all-embracing vision of harmony between the Mahādevi's abiding earthly presence and the transcendental unity proclaimed by Hinduism's seers.

# THE ŚRĪ DURGĀSAPTAŚLOKĪSTOTRA

Besides full ritual chanting of the Devīmāhātmya in temples or on special occasions, less elaborate methods of recitation may be practiced on a daily basis. One of these is to recite the Devīmāhātmya continuously in a seven-day cycle: Chapter 1 on the first day; Chapters 2 and 3 on the second day; then successively Chapter 4; Chapters 5 through 8; Chapters 9 and 10; Chapter 11; and Chapters 12 and 13.[1]

Another method is to recite the text in a highly condensed form, known as the Śrī Durgāsaptaślokīstotra ("Song of Seven Verses to Śrī Durgā"), or simply as the Saptaślokī Durgā. This consists of those mantras in which the Devī's power is most concentrated: 1.55, 4.17, 11.10, 11.12, 11.24, 11.29 and 11.39. In a preface to the Saptaślokī Durgā, Śiva praises the Devī's accessibility and asks the means for accomplishing what is desired. Lovingly, the Devī reveals this song of praise, which she calls the Ambāstuti ("Hymn to the Mother"), saying it is the highest path to spiritual attainment:

ज्ञानिनामपि चेतांसि देवी भगवती हि सा ।
बलादाकृष्य मोहाय महामाया प्रयच्छति ॥ १ ॥

*jñāninām api cetāṁsi devī bhagavatī hi sā*
*balād ākṛṣya mohāya mahāmāyā prayacchati*

1. She, the blessed goddess Mahāmāyā, seizes the minds of even the wise and draws them into delusion.

दुर्गे स्मृता हरसि भीतिमशेषजन्तोः
स्वस्थैः स्मृता मतिमतीव शुभां ददासि ।
दारिद्र्यदुःखभयहारिणि का त्वदन्या
सर्वोपकारकरणाय सदार्द्रचित्ता ॥ २ ॥

*durge smṛtā harasi bhītim aśeṣajantoḥ*
*svasthaiḥ smṛtā matim atīva śubhāṁ dadāsi*

*dāridryaduḥkhabhayahāriṇi kā tvad anyā*
*sarvopakārakaraṇāya sadārdracittā*

2. Remembered in distress, you remove fear from every creature. Remembered by the untroubled, you confer even greater serenity of mind. Dispeller of poverty, suffering and fear, who other than you is ever intent on benevolence toward all?

सर्वमङ्गलमाङ्गल्ये शिवे सर्वार्थसाधिके ।
शरण्ये त्र्यम्बके गौरि नारायणि नमोऽस्तु ते ॥ ३ ॥

*sarvamangalamāngalye śive sarvārthasādhike*
*śaraṇye tryambake gauri nārāyaṇi namo 'stu te*

3. Salutation be to you, Nārāyaṇī, who are the good of all good, the auspicious one; to you who accomplish every intent; to you, the refuge, the all-knowing, shining Gaurī!

शरणागतदीनार्तपरित्राणपरायणे ।
सर्वस्यार्तिहरे देवि नारायणि नमोऽस्तु ते ॥ ४ ॥

*śaraṇāgatadīnārtaparitrāṇaparāyaṇe*
*sarvasyārtihare devi nārāyaṇi namo 'stu te*

4. Salutation be to you, Nārāyaṇī, who are intent on rescuing the distressed and afflicted that take refuge in you; to you, O Devī, who remove the suffering of all.

सर्वस्वरूपे सर्वेशे सर्वशक्तिसमन्विते ।
भयेभ्यस्त्राहि नो देवि दुर्गे देवि नमोऽस्तु ते ॥ ५ ॥

*sarvasvarūpe sarveśe sarvaśaktisamanvite*
*bhayebhyas trāhi no devi durge devi namo 'stu te*

5. O Devī, who exist in the form of all, who are the ruler of all, possessing all power, protect us from fears. O Devī Durgā, salutation be to you!

रोगानशेषानपहंसि तुष्टा
रुष्टा तु कामान् सकलानभीष्टान् ।
त्वामाश्रितानां न विपन्नराणां
त्वामाश्रिता ह्याश्रयतां प्रयान्ति ॥ ६ ॥

*rogān aśeṣān apahaṁsi tuṣṭā*
*ruṣṭā tu kāmān sakalān abhīṣṭān*
*tvām āśritānāṁ na vipannarāṇāṁ*
*tvām āśritā hy āśrayatāṁ prayānti*

6. When pleased you destroy all afflictions, but when displeased you thwart all aspirations. No calamity befalls those who have taken refuge in you, and they who resort to you become a refuge to others.

सर्वाबाधाप्रशमनं त्रैलोक्यस्याखिलेश्वरि ।
एवमेव त्वया कार्यमस्मद्वैरिविनाशनम् ॥ ७ ॥

*sarvābādhāpraśamanaṁ trailokyasyākhileśvari*
*evam eva tvayā kāryam asmadvairivināśanam*

7. O ruler of all, may you allay all the miseries of the three worlds and so, too, annihilate our enemies.

# Part II
# The Devīmāhātmya Translation and Commentary

# FIRST CARITA

## Meditation on Mahākālī

Oṁ. I revere Mahākālī, who holds in her hands the sword, discus, mace, arrow, bow, iron club, spear, sling, human head, and conch; who is three-eyed, adorned on all her limbs, and sparkling like a sapphire; who has ten faces and ten feet; and whom Brahmā extolled while Viṣṇu slept, in order to slay Madhu and Kaiṭabha.

# 1

## The Slaying of Madhu and Kaiṭabha

Oṁ. Salutation to Caṇḍikā.

1.1 Oṁ aiṁ. Mārkaṇḍeya said:

1.2 Sāvarṇi, who is Sūrya's son, is called the eighth manu. Listen while I relate the story of his birth

1.3 and of how, by Mahāmāyā's authority, he—the illustrious son of the sun god—came to be the lord of an age.

1.4 Long ago in the age of the manu Svarociṣa, there arose from the line of Caitra a king named Suratha, who ruled over the whole earth.

1.5 He looked after his subjects justly, as if they were his own children. But there were princes at that time who attacked the native hill tribes and became his enemies.

1.6 Though mightily armed and resolved to fight against them, he suffered defeat in battle, despite his enemies' inferior forces.

1.7 And so, with only his native province left to rule, he returned to his own city. There, powerful adversaries set upon him, the illustrious Suratha,

1.8 now bereft of strength. His ministers, mighty, corrupted, and disposed to evil, seized power and plundered the treasury, even there in his own city.

1.9 Thus robbed of his dominion, the king mounted his horse on the pretext of hunting and rode off alone into the dense forest.

1.10 He came upon the hermitage of Medhas, chief among the twice-born, and beheld a forest retreat, graced by the sage's disciples. There he saw beasts once wild now peacefully abiding.

1.11 Welcomed by the sage, he remained at the hermitage for some time, wandering here and there about the enclosure.

1.12 In that setting, self-centered concerns came to seize his mind, and he reflected:

1.13 I have left behind the capital that my ancestors governed before me. Are my perverse officials overseeing it justly or not?

1.14 My prized elephant, valiant and of unceasing prowess, has fallen into the hands of my enemies. I know not what comforts he'll now enjoy.

1.15 Those retainers of mine, constantly eager for favor, wealth, and feasting, now surely submit to other lords.

1.16 Their habitual squandering will soon deplete the wealth I so laboriously amassed.

1.17 While pondering those and other questions, the king caught sight of a lone merchant approaching the sage's hermitage.

1.18 "Who are you," he asked, "and what brings you here? Why do you look so sorrowful and dejected?"

1.19 Hearing the king speak in friendship, the merchant bowed respectfully and replied.

1.20 The merchant said:

1.21 "I am a merchant named Samādhi, born in a wealthy family. My wife and children grew wicked through avarice and cast me out.

1.22 Destitute of riches, wife, and children, my wealth taken from me, I have arrived in the forest, distressed and forsaken by trusted kinsmen.

1.23 Being here, I know not whether good fortune or ill has befallen my children, wife, and family.

1.24 At present is well-being or misfortune theirs at home?

1.25 How are my children? Is their behavior virtuous or vile?"

1.26 The king said:

1.27 "Those greedy sons, wife, and others who dispossessed you of your wealth—

1.28 why does your mind still cherish them?"

1.29 The merchant said:

1.30 "Even as you say it, this very thought occurs to me. But what can I do? My heart is not inclined to rancor

1.31 but still turns with affection to those who drove me away, scorning love for father, husband, and kinsman, out of lust for wealth.

1.32 I recognize this, O wise one. Still, I do not understand how my thoughts are drawn in love to my unworthy kinsfolk.

1.33 Because of them I sigh, overcome with despair.

1.34 What can I do, since the pain has failed to harden my heart?"

1.35 Mārkaṇḍeya said:

1.36 Then together they approached the sage,

1.37 that merchant named Samādhi and Suratha, the best of kings.

1.38 Having observed the respect that was the sage's due, the merchant and the king sat down to tell their stories.

1.39 The king said:

1.40 "Revered sir, I wish to ask you one thing. Please reply.

1.41 Without control of my thoughts, my mind is coming to grief.

1.42 I remain possessive toward my lost kingdom and all parts of the realm as if unaware that they are no longer mine. Venerable sage, how can this be?

1.43 And this fellow has been humiliated by his children and wife, deserted by his servants, and forsaken by his own people. Still he feels exceeding affection for them.

1.44 It is the same with me. We both are distressed to the utmost, held by attachment to things, even though we see their faults.

1.45 Venerable sir, how is it that we who should know better can be so deluded? Ours is the perplexity of those who are blind to right understanding."

1.46 The seer said:

1.47 "Illustrious king, through the perceptions of the senses, every living being has knowledge of the manifest universe. The objects of sense-perception reveal themselves in various ways.

1.48 Some creatures are blind by day, and others are blind by night. Some creatures see equally by day and night.

1.49 Truly, humans are endowed with the power of perception, but they are not alone, for cattle, birds, wild animals, and all other living creatures also perceive.

1.50 That awareness which humans have, birds and beasts possess also; and their awareness, humans have, too. In other ways also the two are similar.

1.51 Look at these birds. Though feeling the pangs of hunger, out of delusion they still busy themselves by dropping food into the beaks of their young.

1.52 Illustrious sir, humans long for offspring, surely expecting gratitude in return. Do you not see this?

1.53 In this very manner they are hurled into the whirlpool of attachment, the pit of delusion, by the power of Mahāmāyā, who produces the continuing cycle of this transitory world.

1.54 Do not be astonished. This same Mahāmāyā is Yoganidrā, the meditative sleep of Viṣṇu, the lord of the world. By her this world is deluded.

1.55 She, the blessed goddess Mahāmāyā, seizes the minds of even the wise and draws them into delusion.

1.56 She creates all this universe, moving and unmoving, and it is she who graciously bestows liberation on humanity.

1.57 She is the supreme knowledge and the eternal cause of liberation,

1.58 even as she is the cause of bondage to this transitory existence. She is the sovereign of all lords."

1.59 The king said:

1.60 "Revered sir, who is that goddess whom you call Mahāmāyā? How did she originate, and in what ways does she act?

1.61 And whatever her glory, this goddess, whatever her form and origin,

1.62 all that I wish to learn from you, who are supreme among the knowers of Brahman."

1.63 The seer said:

1.64 "She is eternal, having the world as her form. She pervades all this.

1.65 Yet she emerges in various ways. Hear it from me.

1.66 Although she is eternal, when she manifests to accomplish the purpose of the gods, she is said to be born in the world.

1.67 At the end of the cosmic day, when the universe dissolved into the primordial ocean, the blessed lord Viṣṇu stretched out on the serpent Śeṣa and entered into meditative sleep.

1.68 Then two fearsome asuras, the notorious Madhu and Kaiṭabha, issued forth from the wax in Viṣṇu's ears, intent on slaying Brahmā,

1.69 who was seated on the lotus that grew from Viṣṇu's navel. When he saw the raging asuras and the sleeping Viṣṇu,

1.70 Brahmā could think of nothing but to awaken him, and to that end he extolled Yoganidrā, who had settled over Viṣṇu's eyes

1.71 as his blessed sleep. The resplendent lord Brahmā extolled her who rules the universe, who sustains and dissolves it. He extolled her who is incomparable.

1.72 Brahmā said:

1.73 'You are the mantras of consecration to the gods and the ancestors. At your bidding they are uttered, and they are your very embodiment. You are the nectar of immortality, O imperishable, eternal one. Truly, you abide as the transcendent being,

1.74 yet in every moment you abide, inseparable and inexpressible, as the eternal source of all becoming. Indeed you are that. You are Sāvitrī, the source of all purity and protection; you are the supreme mother of the gods.

1.75 By you is this universe supported, of you is this world born, by you is it protected, O Devī, and you always consume it at the end.

1.76 You are the creative force at the world's birth and its sustenance for as long as it endures. So even at the end of this world, you appear as its dissolution, you who encompass it all.

1.77 You are the great knowledge and the great illusion, the great intelligence, the great memory and the great delusion, the great goddess and the great demoness.

1.78 You are primordial matter, differentiating into the threefold qualities of everything. You are the dark night of periodic dissolution, the great night of final dissolution, and the terrifying night of delusion.

1.79 You are radiant splendor; you reign supreme yet are unassuming; you are the light of understanding. Modesty are you, and prosperity, contentment, tranquillity and forbearance.

1.80 Armed with sword and spear, and with club and discus, waging war with conch, bow and arrows, sling and iron mace, you inspire dread.

1.81 Yet, you are pleasing, more pleasing than all else that is pleasing, and exceedingly beautiful. Transcending both highest and lowest, you are indeed the supreme sovereign.

1.82 Whatever exists, true or untrue, and wherever it may be, O soul of everything, you are the power of all that. How can I praise you?

1.83 By you, even he who creates, protects, and devours the world is subdued with sleep. Who here can praise you?

1.84 You have caused even Viṣṇu, Śiva, and me to assume our embodied forms. Who then can truly praise you?

1.85 Thus extolled, O Devī, may you with your exalted powers confound those unassailable asuras, Madhu and Kaiṭabha.

1.86 Let Viṣṇu, the lord of the world, be quickly awakened from his slumber

1.87 and be roused to slay the two great asuras.'"

1.88 The seer said:

1.89 "Praised thus by the creator to rouse Viṣṇu into slaying Madhu and Kaiṭabha, then and there the dark goddess

1.90 emerged from his eyes, mouth, nostrils, arms, heart, and chest, and appeared before Brahmā, who is born from the unmanifest.

1.91 And released by her, Viṣṇu, the lord of the world, arose from his serpent couch on the undifferentiated ocean and beheld

1.92 the evil-natured Madhu and Kaiṭabha, exceedingly strong and courageous, seeing red with anger and determined to devour Brahmā.

1.93 Then the blessed, all-pervading Viṣṇu rose up and fought with them in hand-to-hand combat for five thousand years.

1.94 And they, mad with the arrogance of power and confounded by Mahāmāyā,

1.95 exclaimed to him, 'Ask a boon from us!'

1.96 The blessed lord Viṣṇu said:

1.97 'Since you are pleased with me, so be it. I will surely slay both of you now.

1.98 What other boon is there to ask?'"

1.99 The seer said:

1.100 "Thus deceived, and beholding that the world consisted entirely of water, they addressed the lotus-eyed Viṣṇu, saying:

1.101 'Slay us where water does not flood the earth.'"

1.102 The seer said:

1.103 "'So be it,' said Viṣṇu, the wielder of conch, discus, and mace. Taking the two of them onto his lap, he cut off their heads with his discus.

1.104 Thus did the Devī herself appear when praised by Brahmā. Hear still more of her glory, which I will tell you."

# Chapter 1 Commentary

**Meditation on Mahākālī:** This brief meditation (dhyāna) invites us immediately to plunge into one of the most profound of all mysteries, the age-old question of how the universe came into being. The Hindu idea of creation differs from the naïve conception, popular in the West, that God called forth the world out of nothingness. To the Hindu mind, this idea of *creatio ex nihilo*—that something can come out of nothing—is illogical and absurd. Instead, according to the worldview of the Devīmāhātmya, the question to be posed is this: How does the One, which is eternal being-in-itself, manifest as the many? The question becomes an inquiry into the nature of the creative process itself, and the inquiry reveals that the creation of the universe is in fact a transition from potentiality into actuality. This truth is inherent even in the Sanskrit word for creation: *sṛṣṭi* literally means "emission" or "letting loose" from a latent to a manifest state.

Each of the Devīmāhātmya's three sections begins with a meditation on one of the supreme Devī's three primary forms. These forms—Mahākālī, Mahālakṣmī and Mahāsarasvatī—are not to be confused with her aspects as Kālī, Lakṣmī and Sarasvatī, goddesses of popular devotion who belong to a more immediate level of human experience.[1] Instead, each is an immensely more powerful, cosmic aspect (*vyaṣṭi*) of the Devī. The vyaṣṭis are the universal energies of inertia, dynamism, and luminosity—the three guṇas, known in Sanskrit as tamas, rajas, and sattva. In the phenomenal universe, they underlie all the subsequent activities of creation, sustenance, and dissolution.

At this early stage of differentiation, the pure guṇas are still unmanifest (*avyākṛta*) as causal energies. Though indescribable, they are conceived of as the four-armed forms of Mahākālī, Mahālakṣmī and Mahāsarasvatī. Through subsequent modification (vikṛti), these in turn become manifest forms with the same names. It is these that are described in the dhyānas as the ten-armed Mahākālī, the eighteen-armed Mahālakṣmī and the eight-armed Mahāsarasvatī. This imagery is intended to facilitate the Tantric technique of visualized meditation.

A physical image such as a sculpture or painting or a mental image visualized in meditation allows us to approach the Infinite through finite symbols and to interact with divinity. Such symbols correspond to psychological or spiritual truths, and every gesture, posture, color, or object associated with a deity stands for a particular attribute or power. A few symbols have universal significance, but others are esoteric, with meanings not readily obvious or easily understood. Not all symbols are invariable in meaning, and even the interpretations found in ancient sources such as the Purāṇas may differ among themselves. Later explanations of some symbols grow increasingly divergent, but even modern reinterpretations can convey valid new insights.[2]

Mahākālī, the Devī's tamasic aspect who presides over the first carita, has ten hands that symbolize the ten directions (the four cardinal points, the intermediate points, and the points above and below) and convey the idea of divine omnipresence. Her sword represents the knowledge that destroys ignorance by severing what is apparent and transitory from what is real and abiding. The discus is the constantly turning wheel of time, which inexorably destroys all that has name and form. According to the Varāhapurāṇa, the mace destroys unrighteousness (adharma). The Viṣṇupurāṇa interprets the bow as the tamasic aspect of ego and the arrows as the sensory and motor organs. Restraint or self-control is the general idea behind the iron bar. In the Devīmāhātmya's battle narratives, the Divine Mother's spear is a metaphor for the penetrating insight of spiritual awareness. The severed human head represents the vanquished ego and thus the triumph over the limitation of personality that obscures the infinite Self (ātman). The conch destroys ignorance; its auspicious sound symbolizes the power of awakening to divine awareness. Mahākālī's three eyes, witnessing past, present and future, symbolize omniscience. Her blue-black complexion, more than a mere reminder of her obscuring tamasic power, resembles the vast night sky and speaks of her infinitude.

**Invocation:** The mantra *Oṁ namaścaṇḍikāyai* ("Oṁ. Salutation to Caṇḍikā") invokes the Devī in her supreme, *samaṣṭi* form. Unknown in the Vedas, the name Caṇḍikā first appears in the Devīmāhātmya. Occurring there 29 times, it is second in frequency only to the term Devī itself.[3] Thus we see that the name is both of non-Vedic origin and of great importance.

Caṇḍikā means "the violent and impetuous one,"[4] whose anger and fierce passion, according to the commentator Bhāskararāya, inspire awe.[5] Nevertheless, this literal meaning should not limit our understanding of Caṇḍikā as only a fierce, horrific goddess. She is the ineffable Devī, whose many and varied manifestations in the course of the mythological narratives will reveal also a benign side that is maternal, protective, physically beautiful, and salvific.

Moreover, the *Guptavatī,* Bhāskararāya's great commentary on the Devīmāhātmya, boldly asserts that "Caṇḍī[kā] is the highest Brahman," the supreme nondual reality.[6] She is *saṁvit,* the pure, unitary consciousness that projects the three vyaṣṭis in the process of cosmic manifestation. In the language of the Śāktas, these energies are called, respectively, Mahākālī, Mahāsarasvatī and Mahālakṣmī.[7] This threefold differentiation, Bhāskararāya notes, is described in the Śvetaśvātaropaniṣad (ŚU 6.8) as Brahman's *icchā* ("will"), jñāna ("knowledge"), and *kriyā* ("action")—the divine will to create, the knowledge for doing so, and the action that carries out the intent. For Bhāskararāya, power (śakti) and the possessor of power (*śaktiman*) are one and the same, and the vyaṣṭis are non-different from the Devī's ultimate unity.[8] Accordingly, the name Caṇḍikā represents both the formless Absolute in itself (Ādyā Śakti, or nirguṇa Brahman in Vedantic terms) and that same reality in association with its inseparable, threefold power (the Devī's samaṣṭi form, or *saguṇa* Brahman). It is important to remember that this so-called aggregate (samaṣṭi) form, which is *triguṇa* ("consisting of the three guṇas"), is not the result of the combined energies of the vyaṣṭis; it is instead their source.[9]

The Prādhānika Rahasya, which is part of the earliest commentary on the Devīmāhātmya, describes the supreme Devī as *lakṣyālakṣyasvarūpā* ("with and without distinguishing characteristics") (PR 4). In essence, divine reality is both definable and indefinable—at once immanent and transcendent. In the 18th century this paradox was voiced by the Bengali poet Kamalākānta in the epithet *śunyasyākāra* ("the form of the formless"). Such utterances reflect the true sense of the mantra *Oṁ namaścaṇḍikāyai:* "Salutation to the absolute consciousness that manifests as the created universe."

**1.1:** Oṁ and *aiṁ* are not words in the ordinary sense but *bījas* ("seeds"). A bīja is the essential sound of a primary cause or principle from which something is produced. As a syllable of concentrated power with its own distinct vibration, a bīja is the essential component of any mantra. Oṁ, the first and greatest of all mantras, is the *mahābīja* ("great seed") that represents the absolute Brahman. It is the source of all other bījas. *Aiṁ,* the bīja of Mahāsarasvatī, proclaims that the Divine Mother's nature is pure consciousness.

In the opening scene of the Devīmāhātmya, the sage Mārkaṇḍeya relates to his disciple Krauṣṭuki Bhāguri the history of the world throughout its cosmic cycles. The setting is the present, or seventh age, and to explain what will come to pass in the eighth, Mārkaṇḍeya recounts the story of a king, a merchant, and a seer who lived long before, during the second age. From verse 1.46 onward, Medhas, the seer of Mārkaṇḍeya's tale, becomes the narrator and relates the Devīmāhātmya's three myths concerning the Divine Mother's activities. Mārkaṇḍeya returns as narrator in verse 13.6 to bring the Devīmāhātmya to its conclusion.

**1.2–3:** The purpose of Mārkaṇḍeya's story is to relate how Sāvarṇi will become the ruler of the eighth cosmic age through the authority of the Devī, here called Mahāmāyā. In Purāṇic cosmology, a period of cosmic manifestation, called a day of Brahmā, lasts 4,320,000,000 human years. This scheme need not be taken literally but does indicate the ancient Indian awareness of the vastness of time. A day of Brahmā is divided into fourteen ages (manvantaras), each with its own mythical progenitor and sovereign (manu). Although Sāvarṇi, the future manu, is described as the "son of the sun god" (→ 13.22),* he lived in the second manvantara as a mortal king named Suratha.

**1.4–34:** One of the functions of the Purāṇas is to chronicle the history of the ruling Āryan dynasties. Verses 1.4–16 present a brief account of Suratha's reign and establish his character as just and virtuous. Verses 1.17–25 introduce the merchant

* Arrows in verse citations indicate cross references within the commentary. Simple verse citations without arrows refer to the text of the Devīmāhātmya.

Samādhi and identify him also as a good and righteous man. Having suffered betrayal and loss, each of them seeks refuge in a holy man's forest retreat (*āśrama*). In the tranquil setting, Suratha continues to suffer mental and emotional turmoil over recurring thoughts of his lost kingdom. Samādhi, in his despair, fails to understand his own lingering feelings of love toward the family that betrayed him.

**1.35–38:** When the king, the merchant, and the seer meet, we recognize that they represent the three higher castes of Indian society. Medhas, a *brāhmaṇa*, belongs to the priestly class; Suratha, a *kṣatriya*, to the class of kings and warriors; Samādhi, a *vaiśya*, to the class engaged in trade or agriculture. In the traditional fourfold caste system, these three upper classes are called "twice-born," because their privileged access to the Vedas signifies an initiatory second birth. Such a privilege is not shared by the *śudra,* a member of the fourth, or servile, caste.

Additionally, the names Medhas, Suratha, and Samādhi identify Mārkaṇḍeya's characters as archetypal. The word *medhas* means "insight"; *suratha* means "he whose chariot is good"—a metaphor for the king's unimpeachable conduct; *samādhi* signifies union with the Divine—a fitting name for the merchant, who is poised to disentangle himself from worldly attachment.

**1.39–45:** The king's appeal to Medhas marks the first step of the spiritual journey that he and Samādhi are about to begin. Suratha confesses that feelings of possessiveness toward his lost kingdom torment him unceasingly and that the merchant's loving concern for the family that robbed and humiliated him persists. How can the two of them, who should know better, react so illogically? When the king declares, "Ours is the perplexity of those who are blind to right understanding," he assumes that he and Samādhi are possessed of superior knowledge, although vulnerable to the same pitfalls as those who are less wise. Medhas's task will be to show the king and the merchant how very wrong they are.

**1.46–50:** In order to distinguish between ordinary knowledge as the king understands it and higher, spiritual knowledge, Medhas begins with the example of sense-perception, or knowledge in its most concrete form. He points out that animals and humans alike have sensory awareness, although the faculties of perception differ according to genus and species. Despite those differences, both human awareness and nonhuman awareness are expressions of the same underlying consciousness.

**1.51–52:** In the more complex area of behavior, Medhas points out that birds ignore their own hunger for the sake of their young; but humans, hoping for future reward, harbor ulterior motives in begetting children. It is not that birds are altruistic and people are scheming. Birds act out of instinct, but humans possess the additional faculties of reason and will. What Medhas means to demonstrate is that even those forms of awareness that relate to behavior belong to the category of lower knowledge and are subject to the delusion (moha) inherent in the world.

**1.53:** If even the basic acts of seeing, hearing, tasting, smelling, and touching do not reveal an objective world as it really is but only our flawed experience of it, how much more fraught with confusion the world becomes when experienced through the additional filters of reason, emotion, memory, and will! Given imperfect data, our reason may easily draw the wrong conclusion, or it may take more than one path to different ends. Emotion colors everything. Memory is selective at best and rarely impartial. Will all too often arises from an ego motivated by self-interest, desire, or expectation. Since all knowledge as we understand it is thus relative and imperfect, we are, indeed, subject to delusion.

The cause of this delusion, says Medhas, is the goddess Mahāmāyā. That name, which occurs only in the first carita, can mean either that the Devī *possesses* great māyā or that she herself *is* the great māyā. Either way, māyā is the power that produces the cyclical flow (saṁsāra) of this ever-changing world. It is the power of self-concealment that imposes the interwoven limitations of time and space upon the infinite, absolute consciousness. And it is the power that projects the sense of personal identity, the ego, that beclouds the underlying unity of reality.

**1.54:** Medhas also refers to Mahāmāyā as Yoganidrā, another name of the Devī that occurs only in the first carita. Its meaning will soon become evident.

**1.55–58:** When Medhas says that not even the wise escape Mahāmāyā's deluding power, he is simply stating that nothing in this world is as it seems to be. Time and space distort our perceptions, and we know the universe not as it is but only as we individually experience it. For example, from our vantage point the moon appears to be much larger than the stars, but that is an illusion created by its proximity to the earth. The stars only appear tiny in comparison because they are so distant. Moreover, the starlight we see twinkling in tonight's sky has traveled through vast reaches of space over vast stretches of time, and the stars that emitted it may have ceased to exist millions of years ago. Medhas refers to this deluding goddess as "blessed" and reassures that Mahāmāyā has two aspects. As avidyāmāyā she is the veiling power that binds through the limiting sense of individuality, and as vidyāmāyā she is the liberating knowledge that breaks asunder every bond.

Finally, this passage marks the first appearance of two additional themes that will recur throughout the text: that of divine grace and that of the Devī's supremacy over all the male gods.

**1.59–64:** Two words in Medhas' statement, "She is eternal, having the world as her form. She pervades all this" (1.64), are particularly revealing. The adjective *nitya* ("eternal") originally meant "found inside of" or "innate." During the Ṛgvedic era, its usage expanded to connote "one's own, constant, permanent."[10] By the time of classical Sanskrit, *nitya* had acquired the meaning of "eternal," colored by the idea that eternity implies an interior, intrinsic and unchanging quality that is readily equated with the nondual Absolute.

The word *jagat* ("world"), from a verbal root meaning "to go," portrays the world as a realm of motion, life, and activity. Previously, verse 1.56 described the natural world with the poetic expression *carācaram* ("moving and unmoving"). To understand this imagery in terms of "animate and inanimate" would be to miss the point entirely. Those English terms, derived from the Latin *anima,* with its multiple connotations of air, breath, life, mind, and soul, imply a distinction between sentient beings and dead matter.

To the contrary, the Śākta worldview understands all material forms, "moving and unmoving," as emanating from divinity. Whether brilliantly shining like the sun, in constant motion like the wings of a hummingbird, or seemingly inert like an outcropping of granite, everything is pervaded by consciousness. When Medhas utters the words *nitya* and *jagat* in the same breath, he is saying in effect that the Devī is both the immutable ground of existence and the dynamic universe it supports.

**1.65–66:** The Devī manifests as the universe and pervades everything. "Yet she emerges in various ways," Medhas continues. Beyond taking form as the varied natural forces and objects of the material world, she manifests as personified goddesses, some of whom we shall meet in later chapters. She does so "to accomplish the purpose of the gods," whose function is to defend the cosmic order against the chaos wrought by demonic forces. But the Devī is in no way subservient to the gods; for whenever they fail, she herself, who is immeasurably more powerful, must intervene. She who manifests *as* this world (1.64) enters *into* this world (1.66). The universe becomes her sphere of activity, and that activity (carita) is the subject of the three tales Medhas now begins to relate.

**1.67–71:** According to Purāṇic cosmology, at the end of a *kalpa* or day of Brahmā, the manifest universe dissolves back into the causal, or potential, state. The traditional Vaiṣṇava symbolism for such an interim period represents the supreme god, Viṣṇu, in meditative sleep (*yoganidrā*), stretched out on the thousand-headed serpent Śeṣa, who floats on the undifferentiated ocean of potentiality.

Predating the Devīmāhātmya, an earlier and more elaborate account of the Madhu and Kaiṭabha myth, found in the Mahābhārata (MBh 3.194), extols Viṣṇu's blazing splendor and might and characterizes him as the eternal One, source of all and creator of the world. The lotus growing from his navel is as radiant as the sun. Brahmā himself, intimidated by the demons Madhu and Kaiṭabha, awakens the sleeping Viṣṇu, unaided, by shaking the lotus stalk.

This and other early Vaiṣṇava versions of the myth found in the epic literature make no mention of the Devī. In the Devīmāhātmya's retelling, only a trace of the original Vaiṣṇava outlook remains in verse 1.67, where Viṣṇu enters into yoganidrā presumably of his own volition. But note the change of emphasis three verses later. He is now in the power of the Devī, who as the goddess Yoganidrā has taken the active role of settling over his eyes. Viṣṇu is no longer omnipotent; instead it is the Devī who controls the universe in both its manifest and unmanifest states. Also, Brahmā's shaking of the lotus stalk is no longer the cause of Viṣṇu's awakening; instead, to release the sleeping god from Yoganidrā's spell, Brahmā must praise "her who rules the universe, who sustains and dissolves it. . . . who is incomparable" (1.71).

As for the demons, Hindu mythology recognizes various classes of malevolent beings. The terms *asura, daitya,* and *dānava* are often applied interchangeably to demons of the first order, whose shared characteristic is a perpetual, implacable hostility to the gods. These terms themselves shed light on the Hindu understanding of evil. In the Ṛgveda *asura* originally denoted a god, and its probable derivative, *sura,* also signified a god or sometimes the sun. But in later usage *asura* came to mean "demon," the dark half of the *asura/sura* pair. Similarly, the word *daitya* forms the dark half of a pair. Aditi, one of the most ancient Indian goddesses, is the mother of the solar deities, the Ādityas. Her name signifies "boundlessness, freedom, inexhaustible abundance." Her mirror-image is Diti, mother of the daityas, who represent the dark forces. The name of the dānavas, offspring of the demoness Danu, can conceivably be linked also to the word *dāna* ("cutting off, splitting, dividing"). From the lexical pairs *sura/asura* and *āditya/daitya* and from the semantic pair *daitya/dānava,* it becomes clear that the Divine is associated with boundlessness, wholeness, freedom, and light, and that the demonic implies limitation, separation, bondage, and darkness.

**1.72:** The brief statement "Brahmā said" announces the Devīmāhātmya's first hymn, the Brahmāstuti (1.73–87). Building upon the themes of Medhas's discourse and on the Madhu-Kaiṭabha myth, the hymn centers on the Devī's cosmogonic aspect, first celebrating her absolute and all-transcending nature, then extolling her threefold powers of creation, preservation, and destruction, which account for the universe as we know it.

**1.73–74:** In trying to express the inexpressible truth of how the One manifests as the many, the Brahmāstuti's first two verses use technical terms from Vedic ritual and Sanskrit prosody as metaphors. The translator's task in dealing with these extremely difficult verses is to preserve the immediacy and eloquence of the metaphors while conveying their broader meaning. Complicating the task are the Sanskrit terms themselves, which allow ample room for interpretation.

A literal translation would read:

> You are Svāhā. You are Svadhā. You are surely the *vaṣaṭkāra,* having sound as your essence. / You are the nectar, O eternal and imperishable one. You abide as the essence of the triple *mātrā.*
>
> You abide as the half mātrā, eternal, which cannot be uttered specifically. / You are indeed that; you are Sāvitrī; you are the supreme mother of the gods.

Unfortunately, such a translation makes little or no sense to most of us, unschooled as we are in the finer points of Vedic tradition.

In Vedic ritual, *svāhā* is the mantra of consecration intoned when an oblation to the gods is poured into the sacrifical fire; *svadhā* is the mantra that accompanies an oblation to the spirits of departed ancestors. Both mantras are sometimes personified as consorts of Agni, the fire god who conveys the ritual offerings to the gods.

During the ritual the priest who recites the sacrificial hymns utters the word *vaṣaṭ* to signal another priest to pour the oblation into the fire. The exclamation, reified as vaṣaṭkāra and personified as the deity Vaṣaṭkāra, is identified here with the Devī. In other words, it is truly through her agency that the sacrifice is carried out. In the broader scheme of things, she who is *svarātmikā* ("having sound as her essence") is also the agent of creation, because the universe is potential energy made manifest through the vibration of sound, or sacred speech.

The idea that creation proceeds from sound (*svara, śabda*) is not unique to Hinduism. Judaism and Christianity hold similar views on creation through the agency of the Word. In the first chapter of Genesis, the phrase "And God said . . . " signals in turn the creation of light, the heavens, the earth, and all living creatures. The Johannine Gospel proclaims the Word (Logos) as the creative force coeternal and consubstantial with God. Similarly, in the Ṛgvedic hymn known as the Devīsūkta (ṚV 10.125), the goddess Vāk ("Speech") proclaims herself to be both the supreme reality and the source of all becoming. One of most important Vedic goddesses, Vāk is often characterized as the all-pervading cosmogonic principle.[11]

The imagery now shifts from Vedic ritual to linguistic technicalities. In Sanskrit, a mātrā is a metrical unit representing the time required to pronounce a short vowel. Metaphorically the triple mātrā refers to OṀ, which consists of the three short vowels *a-u-m*. The vowel *a* resonates deep in the throat, and the vowel *u* carries the vibration forward, linking it to the mouth's foremost position, where the closed lips articulate the sound *m*. OṀ thus encompasses the entire apparatus of vocal production and is considered symbolic of the beginning, middle, and end of all things. As the triple mātrā, the Devī is Brahman's power of creation, preservation, and destruction; and because that power (śakti) and its possessor (śaktiman) are indistinguishable, the Devī is proclaimed here the supreme, nondual reality.

The half-mātrā, written in the Devanāgarī script as the dot (*bindu*) that nasalizes the preceding vowel, is unpronounceable by itself. Here it stands as a metaphor for the condensed state of power immediately before the actualization of the universe, the point of all possibility (bindu) from which the creation emanates. This elusive concept recently entered Western science when a refinement in Big Bang thinking, called the "cosmic inflation" theory, proposed that the entire universe popped out of a point with no content and no dimensions and instantaneously expanded to cosmic size in a miraculous event hinting at the agency of some higher force. Symbolizing the bindu, the source of all becoming, the half mātrā of Brahmā's hymn represents the all-pervasiveness of the divine presence, which remains inseparable from all experience yet inexpressible in ordinary thought or language. Taken together the symbolism of the triple mātrā and the half mātrā makes the fundamental Śākta point that the Devī is both the Absolute and the relative, the supreme reality and the source of all becoming.

Known in mythology as the wife of the creator god Brahmā, the goddess Sāvitrī, or Gāyatrī, is the personification of the Ṛgveda's most sacred verse, the Gāyatrī mantra: *Oṁ bhūr bhuvaḥ suvaḥ tat savitur vareṇyaṁ bhargo devasya dhīmahi dhiyo yo naḥ pracodayāt* ("May we meditate upon the splendor of the divinity, the supreme effulgence, and may That inspire our thoughts") (ṚV 3.62.10). She is the source of sacred knowledge, and this Gāyatrī mantra, her embodiment in sound, is considered the seed from which the Vedas sprang.

**1.75–76:** The creation, preservation, and dissolution of the universe are functions generally ascribed respectively to the gods Brahmā, Viṣṇu and Śiva. In keeping with the Śākta point of view, the Devīmāhātmya claims that these powers belong to the Devī alone.

Periodically created, sustained, and dissolved, this world or universe is referred to here by two common Sanskrit words. Each tells us something about the nature of the universe. *Jagat,* already discussed (→ 1.59–64), derives from a verbal root meaning "to go" and reveals the world as the realm of motion, life, and activity. *Viśva* ("all"), possibly from a root meaning "to pervade," carries the idea of inclusiveness and immensity, similar to the idea of wholeness and boundlessness evoked by the name of the Ṛgvedic goddess Aditi. Together *jagat* and *viśva* express the immense and ever-changing phenomenon of existence, played out against the immutable backdrop of pure being.

**1.77:** With sharp contrasts this verse characterizes the Devī as the supreme, liberating knowledge (*mahāvidyā*) of the changeless reality but also as the veiling power (mahāmāyā) that projects the world of our experience, as supreme insight (*mahāmedhā*) and unbroken continuity of memory (*mahāsmṛti*), but also as the deluding power (*mahāmohā*) that makes things appear as other than they truly are.

She is both the great goddess and the great demoness. The so-called Bombay recension of the text alters this startling phrase (*mahādevī mahāsurī*) to the less problematic *mahādevī maheśvarī* ("the great goddess, the great sovereign"), but that evades the essential point. By one interpretation, "the great demoness" implies that the Devī controls everything, negative as well as positive. After all, the text has established her as the supreme power of the universe. Still, the deeper, nondualistic understanding considers her the single source of all that is. We cannot dispute that both good and evil are present in the world, but we must understand that they exist only in a relative sense, because neither would be possible without the other to define it. As the source of both, the Devī encompasses—yet transcends—all duality.

**1.78:** The term usually translated as "primordial matter" or "nature" is *prakṛti,* a verbal noun that implies not inert, insentient matter but a dynamic process. Latent within the unmanifest prakṛti (*mūlaprakṛti* or māyāśakti) and existing in a state of perfect, nonactive equilibrium are the three basic energies or guṇas, called tamas, rajas, and sattva. When the Devī upsets their balance in the process of transformation from potentiality to actuality, there arises a bipolar tension in which tamas veils consciousness, sattva reveals it, and rajas becomes the force through which the one acts upon the other. Combining and recombining in patterns of ever-increasing complexity, the guṇas produce everything in the universe, from solid physical matter to fleeting human emotions.

Beyond saying that the Devī is "primordial matter, differentiating into the threefold qualities of everything," this verse tells us nothing more about the creative process. The later Prādhānika Rahasya and Vaikṛtika Rahasya offer two different, mythologically expressed scenarios of how the unmanifest becomes manifest. Both agree that the supreme Devī contains within herself the three guṇas, represented as the unmanifest four-armed Mahākālī, Mahālakṣmī, and Mahāsarasvatī. According to the Vaikṛtika Rahasya, these three unmanifest (avyākṛta) vyaṣṭis then assume the manifest (vikṛti) forms of the ten-armed Māhākālī, the eighteen-armed Mahālakṣmī, and the eight-armed Mahāsarasvatī, described in the Devīmāhātmya's three dhyānas. Such imagery can only hint at the inscrutable cosmic process by which the One projects itself as the manifold universe. In truth, there is no partition in nature; all is continuous.

Because they are Vaiṣṇava Tantric texts, the Rahasyas refer to the Devī in her supreme aspect not as Caṇḍikā but as Mahālakṣmī. They regard the unmanifest Mahākālī (tamas) and the unmanifest Mahāsarasvatī (sattva) as proceeding from—not coequal with—the unmanifest Mahālakṣmī, who they contend contains the power of all three guṇas. This creates a confusion in nomenclature, because in the Vaiṣṇava context the name Mahālakṣmī denotes the Devī's samaṣṭi form and not merely her purely rajasic vyaṣṭi form.

The three terms *kālarātri* ("dark night"), *mahārātri* ("great night") and *moharātri* ("night of delusion") all have "night" as their second element, which underscores the first carita's emphasis on the Devī's dark, tamasic quality. Beyond that, each term carries a specific meaning. In the mythical language of Purāṇic cosmology, a day of Brahmā is followed by a night of periodic dissolution (kālarātri) of equal length—4,320,000,000 human years—while Brahmā sleeps. Three hundred sixty such days and nights constitute a year of Brahmā, and Brahmā is said to live for one hundred years, a time span well in excess of three hundred trillion human years. After that, everything in the universe dissolves completely into the Absolute, and the correspondingly long period of dissolution is called the Great Night (mahārātri). Then the cycle of creation begins anew.

Creation has no absolute beginning, because the self-existent One alternates between states of potentiality and manifestation. In one sense, creation is an event marking the beginning of time-space, but in another sense it is an ongoing process that continues for as long as the universe endures. In the same way, dissolution, creation's inseparable companion, is not only a future event of cosmic catastrophe but also a continuous process inherent in the natural world. The passing of the seasons and the rhythms of the agricultural cycle, for example, demonstrate the interplay of life and death necessary for the continuance of the here and now. On the microcosmic level, matter in the form of ephemeral subatomic particles constantly crystallizes out of energy and dissolves back to its source, while in the vast macrocosm, over inconceivably long eons, galaxies are born, live, and die. The threefold process of interdependent creation-preservation-dissolution is Śakti's pulsating dance of existence.

The "terrifying night of delusion" (moharātri) differs qualitatively from the other night-based terms. It refers not to a lesser or greater unmanifest phase in the cosmic cycle but to the manifest state of nescience (avidyā) through which the vast majority of us experience the world, bound by the delusion of attachment and unaware of our own divinity. In short, it denotes the human condition.

**1.79:** After such dark imagery, Brahmā now extols the Devī with the attribute of dazzling light, both as perceptible splendor (śrī) and the metaphorical light of understanding. The many meanings of *śrī* include "light, luster, radiance, splendor, glory, beauty, grace, loveliness, prosperity, good fortune, wealth, majesty." Brahmā then names the positive, beneficial qualities that śrī engenders, often personified as goddesses in later Vedic literature. The word *puṣṭi,* translated in an abstracted sense as "contentment," originally related to the raising of livestock and the accompanying benefits of nourishment, prosperity, and well-being. Occurring frequently in the Vedas, the concept of puṣṭi preserves ties to India's age-old pastoral culture.

**1.80–81:** The contrast of opposites, illustrating the Devī's all-inclusiveness, continues here with imagery of the horrific and the benign. The dual portrayal of terrible and beneficent goddesses that was a feature of pre-Harappan and Harappan religion endures in the Devīmāhātmya. It reflects the universal fact of our dualistic perception of the universe. The weapons mentioned here are the same ones that appear in the dhyāna on Mahākālī, symbolizing her destructive power and the dread she inspires. The next verse praises her surpassing physical beauty. With these vivid contrasts we are dealing with a literary device known as a merism, which employs opposing pairs to imply totality. Another merism tells us that the Devī transcends "both highest and lowest," meaning everything. In other words, she is the Absolute.

In calling her the supreme sovereign (*parameśvarī*), Brahmā introduces the theme of divine omnipotence, continued in the next three verses.

**1.82–84:** The Devī's power is unequaled. She is said to subdue even Viṣṇu, "who creates, protects, and devours the world." That passage, which endows Viṣṇu with the triple functions of creation, protection, and destruction normally divided among Brahmā, Viṣṇu, and Śiva, once again reveals a trace of the Madhu and Kaiṭabha myth's Vaiṣṇava origin. But any idea of Viṣṇu's supremacy vanishes in the next breath, which alludes to the Devī's power over him as the sleep-inducing Yoganidrā. Moreover, she is said to cause even Brahmā, Viṣṇu, and Śiva to assume their embodied forms. So great is her glory that three times Brahmā asks if there is anyone at all who is capable of praising her.

**1.85–87:** Finally, the hymn pleads that Madhu and Kaiṭabha be killed. Note that Brahmā's petition has two parts: that the Devī confound the asuras and that she rouse the sleeping Viṣṇu to slay the demonic pair. The emphasis is clear: through her power, and not Viṣṇu's alone, will Madhu and Kaiṭabha be destroyed.

**1.88–1.103:** In the original myth as told in the Mahābhārata, for unexplained reasons, Viṣṇu, upon awakening, reacts with pleasure and offers the two asuras a boon. They are too proud to accept and instead respond with haughty laughter that *they* should grant *him* a boon. Viṣṇu assents and asks that the two of them should die by his hand. Since Madhu and Kaiṭabha, strangely, consider themselves devoted to truth and dharma, they must agree; but in a final attempt to save themselves, they impose the condition of being slain where space is uncovered. Viṣṇu finds such a place atop his own uncovered thighs, and lifting them there, he severs their heads.

The story unfolds very differently in the Devīmāhātmya. Responding to Brahmā's praise, Mahāmāyā, "the dark goddess" (*devī tāmasī*) emerges from Viṣṇu's recumbent figure, whereupon Viṣṇu arises and battles hand-to-hand with the asuras. After five thousand years the still undefeated Madhu and Kaiṭabha grow intoxicated with power. In their foolish arrogance they offer Viṣṇu a boon, because, as the text makes clear, they are "confounded by Mahāmāyā" (1.94). Note that the word *vimohitau* ("confounded") derives from the same source as *moha*. Of course, Viṣṇu is glad to oblige his strange combatants and makes the obvious request to slay them, adding, "What other boon is there to ask?" (1.98).

In what follows, the literary quality shows that great care was lavished on retelling this myth, however briefly it unfolds. Instead of simply trying to outwit Viṣṇu by asking to be slain where space is uncovered, as the asuras did in the Mahābhārata's account, here the battle of wits hinges on a pun. Realizing their fateful mistake, Madhu and Kaiṭabha survey the endless expanse of flood and ask to be killed where the earth (*urvī*) is not covered by water. In response Viṣṇu lifts them to his thighs (*ūrvī*) and slays them there.

Madhu and Kaiṭabha represent the ego in its most benighted, almost bestial, state. They attack Brahmā out of brute aggression for no reason other than that he is there. Their prowess in resisting Viṣṇu leads to self-aggrandizement, and eventually their hubris proves their undoing. The story serves as a cautionary tale that taking ourselves too seriously can have unforeseen and disastrous consequences. With this myth, Medhas illustrates the essential point made earlier that the human condition is the product of Mahāmāyā's deluding power.

**1.104:** The final verse links the first carita to the second. Medhas has another story to tell and bids the king and the merchant to listen.

# MIDDLE CARITA

## Meditation on Mahālakṣmī

OṀ. I revere Mahālakṣmī, who holds in her hands the prayer beads, ax, mace, arrow, thunderbolt, lotus, bow, waterpot, staff, lance, sword, shield, conch, bell, wine cup, trident, noose, and the discus Sudarśana; whose complexion is radiant like coral; who is seated on a lotus; and who is the destroyer of Mahiṣāsura.

# 2

## The Slaughter of Mahiṣāsura's Armies

2.1 Oṁ hrīṁ. The seer said:

2.2 "Long ago, when Mahiṣa was chief of the asuras and Indra was chief of the gods, there was a war between their forces for a full hundred years.

2.3 The valorous asuras vanquished the army of the gods, and after all were conquered, Mahiṣa became the lord of heaven.

2.4 Then led by Brahmā, the lord of beings, the defeated gods went to Viṣṇu and Śiva

2.5 and related in detail what had happened. The thirty gods told how Mahiṣāsura had wrought their defeat:

2.6 'He has usurped the authority of Sūrya, Indra, Agni, Vāyu, and Candra, and of Yama, Varuṇa, and all the others.

2.7 Cast out from heaven by the evil Mahiṣa, all the multitudes of gods wander over the earth as mere mortals.

2.8 We have related all that this foe of the gods has done, and we seek refuge in you. Be pleased to devise a means for his destruction.'

2.9 When Viṣṇu and Śiva heard the entreaties of the gods, they knit their brows in fury and contorted their faces,

2.10 whereupon a great radiance came forth from Viṣṇu's rage-filled countenance, and so, too, from Brahmā's and Śiva's.

2.11 And from Indra's body and from the bodies of all the other gods, a very great light issued, and it united and became one.

2.12 The gods saw before them a peak of light like a mountain, blazing brightly and pervading the sky in every direction with its flames.

2.13 Unequaled light, born from the bodies of all the gods, coalesced into a female form and pervaded the three worlds with its splendor.

2.14 From Śiva's light came that which formed the Devī's face. Yama's radiance formed her hair, and Viṣṇu's effulgence became her arms.

2.15 The moon god's soft light formed her breasts, and Indra's brilliance became her waist. Varuṇa's light became her legs, and earth's splendor formed her hips.

2.16 Her feet took shape from Brahmā's light and her toes from Sūrya's brilliance. From the Vasus' light her fingers formed and from Kubera's light, her nose.

2.17 From Prajāpati's lustre came her teeth, and from Agni's radiance her three eyes were born.

2.18 Dawn and dusk became her eyebrows, the wind god's splendor shaped her ears, and all else born of the other gods' light shone too as the auspicious Devī.

2.19 Then, beholding her who appeared from out of their amassed light, all those gods, tormented by Mahiṣa, rejoiced.

2.20 Then the gods bestowed on her their own weapons and adornments. From his trident Śiva drew forth another and gave it to her,

2.21 and Viṣṇu bestowed a discus spun out from his own. Varuṇa gave her a conch; and Agni, the eater of oblations, gave her a spear.

2.22 Vāyu, the wind god, presented a bow and two quivers filled with arrows. Extracting a thunderbolt from his own, Indra, the lord of the immortals,

2.23 the all-seeing one, gave it to her along with a bell from his elephant Airāvata. From his staff of death Yama produced another staff, and Varuṇa, the lord of waters, gave a noose.

2.24 Brahmā, the lord of beings, gave prayer beads and an ascetic's waterpot. Sūrya, the bringer of day, bestowed his rays of sunlight on all the pores of her skin;

2.25 and Kāla, the lord of time, presented a sword and shining shield. The ocean of milk bestowed a necklace of flawless pearls, ever-new garments,

2.26 a celestial crest-jewel, earrings, and bracelets, a radiant crescent-shaped ornament, armlets for all her arms,

2.27 a pair of shining anklets, a necklace beyond compare, and bejeweled rings for all her fingers.

2.28 Viśvakarman gave her a gleaming ax, weapons of all kinds, and impenetrable armor.

2.29 Garlands of unfading lotuses for her head and breast the ocean gave to her, and yet another magnificent lotus to grace her hand.

2.30 Himālaya, the lord of mountains, gave her a lion to ride upon and jewels of many kinds; and Kubera, the lord of wealth, presented a drinking vessel ever-brimming with wine.

2.31 Śeṣa, the lord of serpents, who supports this earth, gave her a garland of snakes, adorned with precious gems.

2.32 Honored also by the other gods with adornments and weapons, the Devī laughed thunderously and defiantly again and again.

2.33 She filled the entire sky with her terrible roar, and from the immeasurable din a great echo resounded.

2.34 All the worlds shook, and the oceans churned. The earth quaked, and the mountains heaved.

2.35 In joy the gods exclaimed, 'Victory!' to the lion-mounted Devī; and with bodies bowed in devotion, the sages praised her.

2.36 When the enemies of the gods saw the three worlds in upheaval, they readied all their forces for battle and rose up as one, with weapons held high.

2.37 'Aha! What is this?' Mahiṣāsura bellowed in wrath. Surrounded by countless asuras, he rushed toward the sound

2.38 and then beheld the Devī, who pervaded the three worlds with her radiance, bending the earth under her tread, scraping the sky with her diadem,

2.39 shaking all the nether regions with the resonance of her bowstring, and standing there, penetrating every direction with her thousand arms.

2.40 Thereupon, the battle began between the Devī and the enemies of the gods. Swords and missiles, hurled in every direction, lit up the quarters of the sky.

2.41 Mahiṣāsura's general, the great asura named Cikṣura, battled there, and Cāmara led cavalry, charioteers, elephant-drivers, and foot soldiers.

2.42 The great asura called Udagra commanded sixty thousand chariots, Mahāhanu gave battle with his ten million,

2.43 and the mighty Asiloman fought with forces fifty million strong. With sixty million Bāṣkala fought in the conflict.

2.44 Encircled by streaming multitudes of elephants and horses, Parivārita fought in that battle with ten million chariots,

2.45 and he who is called Biḍāla, with five billion chariots surrounding him, engaged in combat there.

2.46 Amid chariots, elephants, and horses, myriads of other great asuras battled with the Devī,

2.47 their countless chariots, elephants, and horses surrounding Māhiṣāsura there in the fray.

2.48 With lances and javelins, spears and clubs, swords and axes, and sharp-edged spears, they fought with the Devī.

2.49 Some hurled spears while others threw nooses; intent on killing her, they began an assault with their swords.

2.50 But she, the Devī Caṇḍikā, showered down all manner of weapons and cut through their armaments as if in play.

2.51 Praised by gods and seers, she remained serene, even while unleashing her weapons at the asuras' bodies.

2.52 Her lion-mount, shaking its mane in fury, stalked among the demon throngs as fire rages through a forest.

2.53 The sighs that Ambikā heaved while fighting became at once her legions by the hundreds and thousands.

2.54 They fought with axes, javelins, swords, and sharp-edged spears, and drawing strength from her power, they destroyed the demon hordes.

2.55 Some of her throngs beat war drums resoundingly, some blew conches, and others drummed upon tabors in their zest for battle.

2.56 Then the Devī, with her trident, club, and volleys of spears, with her swords and other weapons, slew great asuras by the hundreds

2.57 and brought down still more with the confounding din of her bell. Binding other asuras with her noose, she dragged them along the ground.

2.58 Her swordstrokes slashed others in two, while crushing blows from her mace brought still more down,

2.59 and those bludgeoned by her club vomited forth blood. Others fell to the ground, pierced through the chest by her trident.

2.60 Her steady stream of arrows made some on that battlefield resemble bristling porcupines, and those tormenters of the gods breathed their last.

2.61 Some had their arms severed, others their necks broken. The heads of others rolled, and still others had their bodies ripped apart.

2.62 Great asuras, their legs cut from under them, toppled to the ground. Some, severed lengthwise by the Devī, were left one-armed, one-eyed, one-legged.

2.63 While others there in the battle danced to the throbbing drums, those that she decapitated fell and rose again,

2.64 headless bodies, still grasping swords, spears, and lances in hand. 'Stop! Stop!' other great asuras cried out to the Devī.

2.65 Where that great battle raged, the earth was impassable with fallen chariots, elephants, horses, and corpses.

2.66 Torrents of blood, like mighty rivers, gushed from elephants, asuras, and horses there in the midst of the demon army.

2.67 In an instant, Ambikā led that vast legion of foes to its destruction, as quickly as fire consumes a heap of straw and wood.

2.68 And her lion, roaring thunderously and shaking its mane, prowled about in search of life-breath still issuing from the enemies' bodies.

2.69 So did the Devī's hosts wage war against the asuras. So also did the gods in heaven shower down flowers in praise."

# Chapter 2 Commentary

**Meditation on Mahālakṣmī:** The coral complexion of Mahālakṣmī, who presides over the second carita, identifies her as the Devī's rajasic vyaṣṭi; and her lotus throne, growing out of the mud but remaining immaculate, symbolizes spiritual purity and detachment from worldliness.

Mahālakṣmī holds in her eighteen hands the symbols of her attributes and powers. Six of them—the mace, arrow, bow, sword, conch, and discus—she shares with Mahākālī. As for the others, the prayer beads symbolize spiritual knowledge or devotion. The ax stands for the ignorance-destroying wisdom that severs worldly ties. The thunderbolt, associated with Indra and storm gods of other cultures, is a symbol of invincibility and illumination. Another natural symbol is the lotus, which in Hindu tradition represents the auspicious qualities of beauty, prosperity, peace, happiness, eternal renewal, purity, and spiritual unfoldment. The waterpot can signify either fertility and wealth or purification; through identification with ascetics it can also stand for renunciation. In connection with Mahālakṣmī its primary meaning is fertility and abundance. The staff is a symbol of discipline; the lance, of the penetrating power of knowledge; the shield, of protection. Among the divergent meanings of the bell, the one that best fits the Devīmāhātmya's narrative is the power to inspire fear in enemies. Its clear tone symbolizes the spiritual insight that dispels ignorance. The wine cup is linked to joy or bliss. Usually the trident's three points are said to represent the divine powers of creation, preservation, and destruction; alternatively they symbolize the destruction of time, space, and causation. The noose stands for worldly attachment. While in one sense representing a deity's powers, these weapons esoterically symbolize the internal functioning of human consciousness.[1]

**2.1:** *Hrīṁ,* known as the *śaktibīja* or *māyābīja,* signifies the Devī's all-pervasive being. In ancient times, the Vedic seers described Brahman as *saccidānanda*—being-consciousness-bliss absolute—a phrase not expressing three separate qualities but attempting to suggest something of the supreme reality that is unitary and indefinable. We can relate this Vedic locution to the Tantric bīja mantras that open the Devīmāhātmya's three caritas. As *aiṁ* (1.1) declares the Devī to be pure consciousness, *hrīṁ* (2.1) affirms her essential nature as absolute being. In the third carita, *klīṁ* (5.1) will proclaim that she is unconditional bliss. Together, the Tantric bīja mantras *aiṁ hrīṁ klīṁ* are another way of expressing the supreme reality.

By itself, the bīja *hrīm* stands as the Devī's supreme mantra, the Śākta equivalent of the Vedic Oṁ, the sound-form of the Absolute in herself, who is not different from her energy that gives birth to all creation.[2]

**2.2–8:** The impetuous, ill-tempered Mahiṣāsura, whose name means "buffalo demon," is the central demonic figure of the second carita. As told by Medhas, the story of his defeat at the hands of Durgā differs significantly from the only account known with certainty to predate the Devīmāhātmya. That version, found in the third book of the Mahābhārata, makes no mention of the Devī. Instead, during a prolonged battle between the gods, led by Indra, and the asuras, Mahiṣa emerges as a menacing but heroic figure. He scoops up a great mountain and hurls it down upon the gods, crushing the celestial hosts in vast numbers. Later, when he attacks Rudra (Śiva), the god refrains from killing him because of an earlier decree that Mahiṣa will meet his death at the hand of Skanda, who then hurls his blazing spear (*śakti*) and with a fatal blow splits open Mahiṣa's head.

In the Devīmāhātmya's retelling, which intertwines threads from several disparate Indian traditions, Mahiṣa is already the established chief of the asuras (2.2) when he defeats Indra—here called Puraṁdara ("destroyer of strongholds"). The epithet alludes to the power of Indra's thunderbolt to release life-giving rain from the clouds. Mahiṣa then becomes the lord of heaven (2.3). In Sanskrit the verse reads, *indro 'bhun mahiṣāsuraḥ* ("Mahiṣāsura became Indra"). To clarify, in the post-Vedic understanding, Indra is no longer the supreme deity nor even a specific individual god; the name designates instead the presiding position in the pantheon, just as the title *manu* designates an office occupied at various times by different individuals. The same is true of earthly kingship, and here Medhas intentionally draws a parallel between Indra's dispossession and Suratha's. The teaching of the second carita is intended specifically for the king.

The beginning part of the narrative (2.2–8) further reflects the transition from the old Vedic religion to the devotional sectarianism of Purāṇic times. When Brahmā leads the defeated gods to Viṣṇu and Śiva (2.4), the three deities named are those who form the Trimūrti of modern Hinduism. The group of thirty gods mentioned next (2.5) refers in rounded numbers to the thirty-three primary Vedic gods, seven of whom are named in the following verse. The bleak picture of multitudes of the old Vedic gods wandering dispossessed over the earth (2.7) illustrates the weakened state that leads them to appeal to the two great post-Vedic deities, Viṣṇu and Śiva, for refuge and deliverance (2.8).

**2.9–19**: Here we come to a nexus that joins two additional strands of Indian tradition to the already intertwining threads of Vedic religion and devotional sectarianism. This passage introduces the Śākta element in the person of the Devī and reveals also a connection to the Hindu law code known variously as the Manusmṛti, the Manusaṁhitā, or the Mānavadharmaśāstra.

This segment runs almost parallel to a portion of the Manusmṛti (MS 7.1–11) that explains how God creates a king to rule over humankind with justice and order, fashioning him from particles of the Vedic gods Indra, Vāyu, Yama, Sūrya, Agni,

Varuṇa, Candra, and Kubera. The first seven of these eight "lords of the gods" are the same ones named by the Devīmāhātmya in verse 2.6. In the same way as a king is formed from the lustre (tejas) of the gods and is a deity in human form,[3] the Devī Durgā emerges in fiery splendor from the bodies of the gods to assume a superior embodied form.

Although appearing to be modeled on the Manusmṛti, written around 200 CE, the Devīmāhātmya's account of Durgā's emergence does not imply that the goddess is a magnified version of royal power. In fact, the opposite is true. Royal power, with its obligation to uphold the dharma, is based on the divine model. What happens in the celestial sphere reverberates in earthly affairs. The seizure of Suratha's kingdom by wicked foes echoes the woeful dispossession of Indra and the other gods by Mahiṣa's demonic forces. In Purāṇic India, the accepted correspondence between divine and human affairs insured Durgā, the warrior goddess, a favored position among members of the kṣatriya caste, and under royal patronage her worship spread throughout the subcontinent.

The first sign of her appearance in our text comes when Viṣṇu, Śiva, and Brahmā contort their faces in fury and a great radiance (tejas) comes forth (2.9–10). Rage and brilliant light are both emblematic of the rajasic energy that predominates in the second carita's characterization of the Devī. Every verse describing her emergence (2.10–19) refers to the divine light as tejas. This term, derived from the verbal root *tij* ("to sharpen, to stir up, to excite"), can mean either the point of a flame, radiance, splendor, brilliance, lustre, magical power, spirit, or essence. Thus, we can understand tejas as an essential quality of brilliance with the power to excite or inspire. Tejas is a rajasic manifestation of spirit.

This radiance coalesces into a female form, said to be "born from the bodies of all the gods" (*sarvadevaśarīrajam*) (2.13). Are we to understand that the Devī is somehow derived from the male gods? The internal evidence of the Devīmāhātmya says no. In Chapter 1, Medhas tells us that the Devī is the sovereign of all lords (*sarveśvareśvarī*) (1.58), and Brahmā calls her "the supreme mother of the gods" (*devajananī parā*) (1.74), who wields the all-inclusive powers of creating, sustaining, and dissolving the universe (1.75–76). She causes even Brahmā, Viṣṇu, and Śiva to assume embodied form (1.84). Surely the supremely powerful mother of the gods cannot also be born from their bodies. In the phrase *sarvadevaśarīrajam,* the element *ja* means not only "born" or "descended from" but also "growing in, living at, belonging to, connected with." The tejas that emerges from the bodies of the gods is not their creation but the Devī's already indwelling presence.

In the subsequent verses (2.14–18) that detail the process of her materialization feature by feature, note that in no instance is the tejas that forms any part of her anatomy said to be born of the gods themselves, but only of their tejas. This distinction is important, because it implies that what coalesces into the Devī's magnificent form is actually her own power, previously fragmented among the various gods and now reuniting.

This idea is not original to the Devīmāhātmya. The Ṛgvedic Devīsūkta, presented in full in Part III, makes this same point. Vāk's repeated affirmations of supremacy in the later verses impart to her opening statement the impression that the gods are agents of her power.

Regarding the Devī's three eyes (2.17), "three-eyed" is a common figure of speech that signifies the ability to see past, present, and future—a metaphor for omniscience, also expressed visually in paintings and sculptures of Hindu deities. The god Agni, from whose radiance the Devī's three eyes take form, reappears four verses later. There he is called the "eater of oblations" (2.21) in an allusion to his role in the Vedic sacrifice, when, as the sacred fire, he consumes the offerings and conveys their essence to the gods and ancestral spirits.

**2.20–31:** In the language of metaphor, the weapons and adornments bestowed upon the Devī represent her diverse powers as already manifested through the gods. Note that the gods do not relinquish their weapons but give her duplicates extracted from them. In the same way as the gods do not relinquish their tejas, because all tejas belongs ultimately to the Devī, so do they not surrender their weapons but continue to act as conduits for the varied powers that are ultimately hers, even while those individualized powers reunite in the vastly more potent person of the Devī. In terms of the highest philosophical abstraction, this is a statement of the Śākta doctrine of simultaneous divine immanence and transcendence.

The powers itemized here correspond to seventeen of the eighteen attributes given in the dhyāna on Mahālakṣmī, and we can assume that the missing club (*gadā*) is included in the "weapons of all kinds" not specified (2.28). Besides the predominant martial symbols (and the slightly fewer than half that represent the benign qualities of creativity, knowledge, purification, and detachment), the recital of the gods' gifts includes adornments and clothing suggestive of feminine beauty and gentleness.

In the description of Durgā's fiery manifestation, we see two sets of intertwined images. One presents a mighty female goddess whose attributes encompass warlike ferocity, feminine beauty, and spiritual knowledge. The other, expressed in the language of nature, evokes solar effulgence, cool lunar light, earthly splendor, and the auspicious periods of dusk and dawn, when the mind is drawn to spiritual reflection. This connection to nature illuminates the meaning of the Devī's ever-new garments (2.25). We still speak of nature clothing herself in seasonal array, a metaphor that probably was not lost on the ancients. Under the crushing weight of centuries and millennia, once-great works built by human endeavor lie in ruin, while living nature abides ever glorious in its power of self-renewal. All this disparate imagery of the divine feminine, which flows from Vedic and various pre- or non-Vedic sources, merges here in Durgā's dazzling, syncretistic personality.

Verse 2.30 marks the first appearance of the lion, Durgā's *vāhana* ("vehicle"). In Hindu iconography, the vāhana is a deity's particular mount, emblematic of divine powers. The lion symbolizes either the Devī's ferocity or, according to the Vaikṛtika Rahasya, the principle of dharma (VR 30).

**2.32–39:** Durgā's ferocity dominates this passage's portrait of her immense power, which reverberates through the sky and sends shock waves throughout the earth. The natural imagery of sky, earth, and sea in tumult speaks of her awesome immanence, to which the gods react not with fear but with rejoicing. The asuras, in contrast, react with angry resistance and gird for battle while Mahiṣa bellows in wrath.

**2.40–49:** Judging by their suggestive names, the high-ranking demons in Mahiṣāsura's army are a colorful group. That impression endures in the exquisite Kangra Valley miniature paintings of the 18th century, which depict the asuras as monstrous and bizarre. Although the meaning of the name Cikṣura is uncertain, Cāmara has associations with the yak and suggests a bestial nature. The names of the Devī's adversaries here and in the following chapter connote either evildoing or physical unpleasantness. Mahāhanu means "large-jawed" and suggests coarseness. Asiloman is "sword-haired," and Bāṣkala possibly alludes to bellicosity. Parivārita, meaning "covered, concealed, veiled," indicates a mental state hemmed in by depressive thoughts, pictured here as his "streaming multitudes of elephants and horses." Biḍāla most likely suggests fetidness and therefore impurity.

**2.50–69:** For the first time, the name Caṇḍikā, which we encountered in the invocatory mantra, appears in the text itself, referring to the immense power of the Devī's ferocious but splendid form. Her power is so great that while the asuras resolutely attack, she remains serene, responding effortlessly to their exertions as if in play. Her allies mirror her own effortlessness. The lion, shaking his mane in rage, is compared to fire sweeping through a forest, an image of unimpeded energy. The Devī's legions (*gaṇas*), arising from her exhalations, likewise suggest a natural, effortless projection of power.

The word *līlā* literally means "play, sport, diversion, amusement," as well as "ease, facility, mere appearance, charm, elegance, loveliness." This simple term represents an important Indian philosophical concept: the phenomenal world does not follow a rigid, preordained course but at every moment is open to multiple creative possibilities. In contrast to this divine playfulness, Mahiṣa and his grim hosts are definitely not playing, any more than were Madhu and Kaiṭabha, who with a little help from Mahāmāyā took themselves too seriously and brought on their own downfall. Mahiṣa and his forces are deadly serious in combat, while the Devī Durgā, never in peril, remains calm and detached.

A second philosophical concept comes into play when we consider that the Devī's active expression as līlā is the reverse of her eternal immutability, described in the first carita by the word *nitya* (1.64–66). The second carita introduces līlā to make the point that the Devī is actively playing in the universe she projects out of her own being. Together the two terms tell us once again that Śakti, the divine energy-consciousness, is one, whether transcendent or actualized.

For all its ease, Durgā's power proves formidable when unleashed, and scenes of horrendous violence and grisly mutilation follow. Paradoxically, the awful carnage represents the victory of good over evil. While the Devī's gaṇas zestfully beat upon drums and blow conches (2.55), the asuras are drawn irresistibly into the dance of destruction (2.63–64). If we recall the earlier declaration that the Devī is "the great goddess and the great demoness" (1.77), we can interpret it here to mean that she has power over the gods *and* the demons, over the impulses of harmony and cooperation as well as the opposing forces of discord and divisiveness. In the gruesome dance of death that enthralls the asuras, we see that the pull toward divine unity is stronger than the impulse to pull away. Considering the dance metaphor further, we remember that in music one always speaks of dissonance resolving into harmony as the natural state of affairs. Ultimately it is the Devī who always wins.

Interestingly, the name Ambikā ("mother") first appears in connection with this gory battle scene (2.53, 2.67). After the terms Devī and Caṇḍikā, Ambikā is the third most frequent name in the Devīmāhātmya, occurring twenty-five times. Used also to address one's own mother or any other woman respectfully, it unequivocally affirms the Devī's maternal nature. Because its frequency and context run parallel to those of Caṇḍikā, Ambikā too refers to the Devī's all-powerful samaṣṭi form, the point being that the supreme Goddess is both horrific and benign.[4]

In late Vedic texts Ambikā appears in association with the emergent figure of Rudra-Śiva,[5] and in the Kāṭhaka recension of the Black Yajurveda her name designates the harvest season as the most productive—that is to say nurturing—time of the year.[6] The connection is clear: in addition to all her other attributes, Ambikā is the ancient Mother Goddess, associated with the earth and agricultural fertility.

# 3

## The Slaying of Mahiṣāsura

3.1 The seer said:

3.2 "Now when he saw the army being slaughtered, Cikṣura, the great asura general, went forth in fury to battle with Ambikā.

3.3 He rained showers of arrows on the Devī in the combat, just as a raincloud showers the summit of Mount Meru.

3.4 But easily shattering his volley, the Devī killed his steeds and charioteer with her arrows.

3.5 Like lightning, she slashed through his bow and high-flying banner. Having destroyed his bow, she wounded him in the limbs with her swift arrows.

3.6 With bow broken, chariot wrecked, and horses and charioteer slain, the asura, armed with sword and shield, rushed at the Devī.

3.7 First striking her lion on the head with his sharp-edged sword, he violently struck the Devī's left arm.

3.8 O king, as soon as the sword touched her, it shattered. Then, the great asura, his eyes red with rage, seized his blazing lance

3.9 and flung it at Bhadrakālī, as though he were hurling the very sun from the sky.

3.10 Seeing it approach, the Devī released her lance and shattered the great asura and his weapon into a hundred pieces.

3.11 When Mahiṣa's mighty general lay slain, Cāmara, the afflictor of the gods, advanced, mounted on an elephant.

3.12 He dispatched his spear toward the Devī. Quickly Ambikā's contemptuous outcry sent it hurtling powerless to the ground.

3.13 Seeing it fallen and shattered, the enraged Cāmara flung a lance, and that, too, she destroyed with her arrows.

3.14 Her lion then leapt up and, astride the elephant's forehead, engaged fiercely in direct combat with the enemy of the gods.

3.15 Struggling, the two fell from the elephant to the ground, still locked in dreadful combat.

3.16 In a flash the lion sprang skyward, then alighted and severed Cāmara's head with a single blow of its paw.

3.17 In the fighting the Devī assailed the asura Udagra with rocks and trees; and biting, punching, and slapping Karāla, she felled him, too.

3.18 Enraged, the Devī crushed Uddhata to a pulp with the blows of her mace. She killed Bāṣkala with her javelin and Tāmra and Andhaka with her arrows,

3.19 and with her trident the supreme three-eyed goddess slew Ugrāsya, Ugravīrya, and also Mahāhanu.

3.20 With her sword she struck Biḍāla's head from his body, and with her arrows she dispatched both Durdhara and Durmukha to the abode of death.

3.21 While his army thus met destruction, Mahiṣāsura terrified the Devī's hosts with his own buffalo form,

3.22 jostling some with his snout and pawing others with his hooves. Others he lashed with his tail and lacerated with his horns.

3.23 He toppled some of them to the ground with the unleashed force of his bellowing and wheeling about, and the blast of his breath brought still others down.

3.24 After destroying the great goddess's forces, Mahiṣāsura rushed forward to slay her lion. At that, Ambikā became enraged.

3.25 But Mahiṣāsura, great in valor, struck the earth angrily with his hooves, flung mountains skyward with his horns, and bellowed frightfully.

3.26 Under his frenzied wheeling, the trampled earth broke apart. Lashed by his tail, the ocean overflowed all around.

3.27 Thrashed by his horns, the clouds fragmented and dispersed. Tossed about on his blasting breath, mountains by the hundreds fell from the sky.

3.28 When she saw the great asura approaching, inflated with rage, Caṇḍikā aroused her wrath and prepared to slay him.

3.29 She threw her noose over him and bound him. Fettered thus in the fierce battle, the great asura left his buffalo form

3.30 and assumed the shape of a lion. No sooner had Ambikā severed his head than he appeared as a man with sword in hand.

3.31 Instantly, with her arrows the Devī cut him to shreds along with his sword and shield. Then he took the form of a great elephant

3.32 and dragged her mighty lion along with his trunk, but while he trumpeted loudly, the Devī chopped off his trunk with her sword.

3.33 Once more the great asura assumed his buffalo form and caused the three worlds, with all that is moving and unmoving, to tremble.

3.34 Angered, Caṇḍikā, the mother of the worlds, drank a divine potion, and with eyes reddened she laughed again and again.

3.35 The asura bellowed in return, intoxicated with his own might and valor, and with his horns he hurled mountains at Caṇḍikā.

3.36 Her volley of arrows reduced them to dust. Her face flushed with inebriation from the divine drink, and she addressed him excitedly.

3.37 The Devī said:

3.38 'Bellow, you fool, bellow for now while I drink this potion. After I have slain you, the gods will cheer in this very place.'"

3.39 The seer said:

3.40 "Having declared that, she leapt upon the great asura, pinned his neck down with her foot, and pierced him through with her spear.

3.41 Trapped there under the Devī's foot and crushed by her might, he emerged half-way in his true form from his buffalo mouth.

3.42 Half-revealed and fighting still, that great asura fell to the Devī, beheaded by her great sword.

3.43 Then crying out in alarm, the whole demon army perished, and all the divine hosts exulted.

3.44 Together with the great heavenly seers the gods praised the Devī, the celestial musicians sang, and throngs of cloud-nymphs danced."

# Chapter 3 Commentary

**3.1–20:** This chapter, which completes the battle narrative begun previously, falls into two halves, consisting of verses 1 through 20 and 21 through 44. The underlying theme of the first half is the ease with which Durgā and her lion counter the strenuous efforts of Mahiṣāsura's generals, whom they defeat one by one. This allegory tells us that the dharma which the Devī upholds is the natural state of affairs and that the asuras—the negative impulses arising from the ego—are in a sense swimming against the current.

Durgā is said to be as immune to attack as Mount Meru, a mythological mountain made of gold and gems that stands at the center of the world. The planets revolve around it, Brahmā dwells on its summit, and its slopes are home to the paradises of Viṣṇu and Kṛṣṇa. Gaṇgā is said in her heavenly descent to fall upon its peak and then flow downward to the earth. Durgā's unassailability is such that Cikṣura's swift, sharp arrows raining upon her pose no more of a threat than the gentle rain falling on the summit of the holy mountain (3.3).

Cikṣura is not so invulnerable, though. With lightning speed, Durgā's counterattack destroys his bow, chariot, horses, and driver. When the wounded asura strikes the Devī on the arm, the violent blow only shatters his sword, for she is indestructible. Cikṣura's eyes, red with rage, and his blazing lance, which he flings with great effort, "as though he were hurling the very sun from the sky," remind us of the rajasic quality of the struggle. But his heroic exertion is no match for the Devī, who with a single throw of her lance destroys him and his weapon (3.10). The battle with Cāmara (3.11–16) likewise confirms her effortlessness in combat.

In the next four verses (3.17–20) Mahiṣāsura's other mighty generals meet their destruction. Like those previously defeated (→ 2.40–49), these also have names that describe their repulsiveness: Karāla ("gaping-mouthed"), Uddhata ("arrogant, rude"), Tāmra ("oppressing"), Andhaka (morally "blind"), Ugrāsya ("fierce-faced"), Ugravīrya ("brutally strong"), Durdhara ("bearing evil"), and Durmukha ("foul-mouthed, abusive").

As for Durgā's characterization, twice this episode emphasizes her maternal nature by calling her Ambikā. Verse 3.9 introduces the name Bhadrakālī ("the auspicious dark one"). Although this goddess's historical background is sketchy, in the Kāṭhakagṛhyasūtra, Bhadrakālī appears as the benign or propitious aspect of Kālī invoked in household worship.[1] Today in the South Indian state of Kerala, Bhadrakālī is a simultaneously fierce and beautiful goddess—a wrathful warrior and a loving mother who blesses her children with fertility and prosperity.[2] Her modern portrayal with three eyes still conforms to the epithet "three-eyed" (*trinetrā*) in verse 3.19.

**3.21–44:** The chapter's second half contains Durgā's defining moment—her defeat of Mahiṣāsura, who is described here as a wrathful beast with formidable power (3.21–27). That description serves as an eloquent, cautionary metaphor, because Mahiṣa's anger jolts heaven and earth, and ruins everything in its path; not even the gentle clouds are immune to his pernicious fury. Such fury is a purely negative expression of rajas. To meet its challenge the Devī heightens her own rajas (3.24, 3.28), but while Mahiṣa's rage controls him, the Devī's is completely under her control. Now consider human anger, individually and collectively. Depending on the choices we make, it can manifest either as destructive rage or as the righteous indignation that counters evil.

In the combat, Mahiṣāsura undergoes a series of metamorphoses (3.29–33), and as long as he continues to mutate from buffalo to lion to man to elephant and back to buffalo, Durgā does not slay him. While this play goes on, her weapons appear ineffectual. Each time she delivers what should be a fatal blow, Mahiṣa eludes destruction by changing form. The buffalo demon becomes intoxicated by his own might, no doubt bolstered by his evasive ability, and in response Durgā drinks a potion that reddens her eyes and flushes her face with inebriation (3.34–36). Note again the rajasic symbolism. When she declares her intention to slay him (3.38), the final struggle begins in earnest. The text mirrors this change of attitude by three times employing the name Caṇḍikā (3.28, 3.34, 3.35) in connection with her wrathful determination to slay her adversary.

Durgā triumphs over Mahiṣa only when he is forced to reveal his true form. Her act of pinning down his neck underfoot is a potent metaphor, because even today in English to "pin down" means to find out, to ascertain or to determine. From this point on, there will be no more evasion. It is a psychological truth that an unidentified, underlying state of mental dis-ease can manifest within a range of dysfunctional behavior or even as physical symptoms without an apparent organic cause. In drastic cases of psychosomatic illness, there are accounts of blindness being "cured" by a cathartic experience such as faith healing, only to be replaced later by another impairment such as deafness or paralysis. Until the underlying cause is ascertained, the problem evades proper treatment.

That principle applies as much to behavioral and psychosomatic pathologies as to the normal, existential uneasiness that underlies and sometimes pollutes the conduct of our daily lives. Even though our ordinary conduct may be far from crossing over the line into pathology, as individuals we react irrationally to certain situations, repeating the same nonproductive patterns of behavior time and again. Until the true cause is pinned down, we remain subject to unsettling influences. Our mental states may mirror Suratha's and Samādhi's confusion and despair or Mahiṣāsura's overwhelming rage.

The symbology of the slaying (3.40–44) casts more light on the process of spiritual awakening. Durgā's piercing of Mahiṣa's side with her spear represents the penetrating light of understanding; it forces the demon to emerge in his real form.

Hindu teaching identifies "six passions" which are universal to human experience—desire, anger, greed, pride, jealousy, and delusion—along with other forms of ignorance, such as fear, shame, prejudice, and hatred. Like the protean Mahiṣāsura and his attendant demons, these present themselves in an interacting array and are exceedingly difficult to deal with until recognized for what they really are. Desire (*kāma*) is in the broadest sense any kind of longing for sensory gratification, material wealth, or power. Inherent in it is the sense of deficiency, limitation, or separation. Any desire is ultimately the desire for wholeness. When thwarted, it may turn to anger (*krodha*); paradoxically, when gratified it may become inflamed into greed (*lobha*)—excessive, insatiable want. Because the ego, by its very nature, remains deficient, no amount of gratification can fill the void. Additionally, fixation on the ego manifests as pride (*mada*), a sense of superiority that in turn can engender feelings of jealousy (*mātsarya*)—apprehensive resentment of the prestige, possessions, or good fortune of others. All these entangled passions thrive in the atmosphere of delusion (moha), which keeps us in denial of our true motivations, prevents us from seeing things as they really are, and keeps our awareness beclouded by a false and finite sense of self.

Durgā's decapitating sword of knowledge allows us to discern between what appears as finite and fleeting and what is infinite and abiding. In practical terms, it distinguishes between selfish, harmful impulses and the noble selflessness that promotes harmony and points toward unity. This allegory, directed at Suratha's concerns, hints at the theme of good and evil, which will be dealt with in the next chapter.

# 4

## Praise by Indra and the Other Gods

4.1 The seer said:

4.2 "When the Devī had struck down the brave but wicked Mahiṣāsura and his army of the gods' foes, Indra and the hosts of gods lifted their voices to her in praise, their heads bowed in reverence, their bodies made beautiful by the thrill of rapture.

4.3 'To the Devī, who spreads out this world through her own power and who embodies herself as all the powers of the hosts of gods; to Ambikā, who is worthy of worship by all the gods and great seers, we bow down in devotion. May she grant us that which is auspicious.

4.4 May she whose unequalled might and splendor even the blessed Viṣṇu, Brahmā, and Śiva are powerless to describe, may she, Caṇḍikā, be intent on protecting all the world and on destroying the fear of misfortune.

4.5 O Devī, we bow before you who are yourself good fortune in the dwellings of the virtuous and misfortune in the abodes of the wicked, intelligence in the hearts of the learned, faith in the hearts of the good, and modesty in the hearts of the high-born. May you protect the universe!

4.6 How can we describe this form of yours, which surpasses thought? And your abundant, exceeding valor that destroys evil? And your deeds in battle, O Devī, among all the throngs of gods and demons?

4.7 You are the cause of all the worlds. Though containing the triple forces of creation within yourself, you are untouched by any imperfection. You are unfathomable even to Viṣṇu, Śiva, and the other gods. You are the resort of all. You are this entire, manifold world and you are primordial matter, supreme and untransformed.

4.8 O Devī, you are the mantra of consecration whose utterance in all sacrifices brings satisfaction to the whole assemblage of gods, and you are the mantra which humans proclaim as the cause of satisfaction to the hosts of ancestral spirits.

4.9 O Devī, who are the cause of liberation and great, inconceivable austerities: sages yearning for liberation contemplate you with senses restrained, intent upon truth, with all faults cast off, for you are the blessed, supreme knowledge.

4.10 With sound as your essence, you are the treasury that holds the taintless Vedic hymns, sung to resound joyfully with your holy name. You are the blessed Devī, who embodies the three Vedas. Intent on conferring well-being, you are the supreme destroyer of pain in all the worlds.

4.11 O Devī, you are the intelligence by which the essence of all scriptures is understood. You are Durgā, the vessel free of attachments that takes one across life's difficult ocean. You are Śrī, the radiant splendor that abides in the heart of Viṣṇu. You are Gaurī, the shining goddess who abides with the moon-crowned Śiva.

4.12 Gently smiling, your shining face resembles the full moon's orb and is as pleasing as the lustre of the finest gold. Beholding it, how could Mahiṣāsura, even though enraged, be moved to strike it?

4.13 Still stranger was it, O Devī, that Mahiṣa did not perish the instant he beheld your wrathful face, reddened like the rising moon and scowling frightfully. For who can behold the enraged face of death and still live?

4.14 O Devī, who are supreme, be gracious to all creation, for when angered you can annihilate multitudes. We saw this the moment you brought Mahiṣāsura's vast power to an end.

4.15 Those to whom you are bounteous are honored among peoples, theirs are riches, theirs are glories, and their righteous acts know no limit. They indeed are blessed with devoted children, attendants, and wives.

4.16 One who is virtuous and ever mindful performs daily all righteous deeds, O Devī, and by your grace attains to heaven. Are you not, then, the giver of rewards in all the three worlds?

4.17 Remembered in distress, you remove fear from every creature. Remembered by the untroubled, you confer even greater serenity of mind. Dispeller of poverty, suffering, and fear, who other than you is ever intent on benevolence toward all?

4.18 The world attains happiness when you slay its foes, and though they may have committed enough evil to keep them long in torment, even as you strike down our enemies, O Devī, you think, May they reach heaven through death in battle with me.

4.19 Why does your mere glance not reduce all asuras to ashes? Because when assailed by your weapons and thus purified, even those adversaries may attain the higher worlds. Even toward them your intentions are most gracious.

4.20 If the intense light flashing frightfully from your sword or the glaring brilliance of your spearpoint did not blind the asuras' eyes, it was because you made them behold the moonlike radiance beaming from your face.

4.21 O Devī, your nature is to subdue the misconduct of the wicked. Others cannot equal your inconceivable grace, for even while your might destroys those who have wrested power from the gods, you show compassion toward those very foes.

4.22 To what may your prowess be compared? Where else is there beauty so ravishing, yet striking fear into enemies?

Where in the three worlds are compassion in heart and resolve in battle seen as they are in you, O beneficent Devī?

4.23 Destroying all foes, you have saved the three worlds. Slaying them at the battle-front, you led even those frenzied, hostile throngs to heaven, even while dispelling our fear of them. Salutations to you!

4.24 Protect us with your spear, O Devī, and protect us with your sword, O Ambikā. Protect us with the clangor of your bell and the resonance of your bowstring.

4.25 Guard us in the east and in the west, O Caṇḍikā. Guard us in the south and also in the north, O Īśvarī, by brandishing your spear.

4.26 With your gentle forms that move through the three worlds and with your surpassingly terrible ones, protect us and also the earth.

4.27 O Ambikā, with sword, spear, mace, and whatever other weapons your tender hands have touched, protect us on all sides.'"

4.28 The seer said:

4.29 "In that way the gods praised her who supports the worlds, honoring her with flowers that bloom in Indra's paradise and anointing her with perfumes.

4.30 Devotedly the assembled gods offered heavenly incense to her. Serene of countenance, she spoke to all the gods, who were bowed down in reverence.

4.31 The Devī said:

4.32 'All you gods, ask whatever you wish of me. Well pleased with your hymns, I will gladly grant it.'

4.33 The gods said:

4.34 'Since you, the glorious one, have slain our enemy, this Mahiṣāsura, all has been accomplished; nothing remains to be done.

4.35 But if you are to grant a blessing, O great sovereign, may you destroy our direst misfortunes whenever we remember you.

4.36 O you of spotless countenance, may you bring increased wealth, family, and success to whatever mortal shall praise you with these hymns.

4.37 Through your power of abundance, O Ambikā, be ever gracious unto us!'"

4.38 The seer said:

4.39 "O king, thus propitiated by the gods for the world's sake and for their own, Bhadrakālī said, 'So let it be,' and vanished from sight.

4.40 So is it told, O king, how she came forth long ago from the bodies of the gods, the Devī who desires the well-being of the three worlds.

4.41 I shall relate further how, for the destruction of Śumbha and Niśumbha and other wicked daityas, she appeared from the body of Gaurī,

4.42 the benefactor of the gods, for the protection of the three worlds. Hear me tell it. I shall relate it to you as it happened."

# Chapter 4 Commentary

**4.1–2:** To set the scene for the hymn that forms most of this chapter, the opening verses show the assembled gods bowing reverently in gratitude for the defeat of their enemies. While Indra leads the gods in praise, the ecstasy of their devotion causes their hair to stand on end.

The hymn (4.3–27) is known as the Śakrādistuti ("Praise by Indra and the Other Gods"), because Indra is called here by the name Śakra ("the powerful one"), an epithet derived from the verbal root *śak* ("to be able"), which is also the source of the word *śakti*.

Until now, the Devīmāhātmya's verses have been cast in the *anuṣṭubh* meter. Each verse (śloka) of this basic Sanskrit meter consists of two halves, and each half consists of two quarters of eight syllables. A full śloka contains thirty-two syllables. The regularity and directness of the anuṣṭubh meter create a repetitive, bardic quality well suited to epic and narrative texts. In contrast, most of the Śakrādistuti is composed in the elegant, fifty-six syllable *vasantatilakā* meter, which conveys a complex, rhythmic sinuosity when the hymn is sung. With a matching refinement of language, the eloquent Śakrādistuti is arguably the most beautiful of the Devīmāhātmya's four hymns.

**4.3:** The description of Ambikā, the Mother, spreading out this world as if in preparation for her divine play, is one of the text's loveliest images. This passage, *devyā yayā tatam idaṁ jagad*, is usually rendered as "to the Devī, who pervades this world." But that pallid statement of divine pervasiveness fails to express the true intent. The point was not missed in the translations by Pargiter[1] and Coburn,[2] who take the participle *tatam* in its primary, transitive sense of extending, spreading out, or expanding something. The distinction is important, because this reading emphasizes the active nature of the Devī's creative role. More than merely pervading what she has created, she takes a "hands-on" approach to it.

When we read that she "embodies herself as all the powers of the hosts of gods" and "is worthy of worship by all the gods and great seers," we recall Vāk's proclamations in the Devīsūkta: "I move through the gods of storm and light, through the gods of the heavens, through all the gods" and "I am foremost among those worthy of worship" (ṚV 10.125.1 and 3). The Devīmāhātmya's unequivocal statement of her self-embodiment as the gods' powers confirms that in her spectacular emergence from their tejas in the second chapter (2.10–19), she is not *created from* the gods' energies but *manifests through* them her own eternally independent power.

**4.4:** From the image of Ambikā, the loving but all-powerful mother, we pass to the image of a goddess whose glory even Brahmā, Viṣṇu, and Śiva cannot describe. Here called Caṇḍikā, she is more than the fierce, wrathful destroyer of evil implicit in that name; she is the transcendent reality beyond the comprehension of even the most powerful gods.

**4.5:** After two verses extolling her cosmic might, the next verse introduces five epithets relating to the sphere of human activity. They are *śrī*, *alakṣmī*, *buddhi*, *śraddhā*, and *lajjā*.

Śrī ("welfare, prosperity, abundance") and alakṣmī ("misfortune") form a pair relating to the reward or punishment of conduct that upholds or contravenes the natural moral order (dharma). The word *śrī*, found frequently in the Vedic Saṁhitās and Brāhmaṇas, denotes a deity's intrinsic radiance; it is often found in those texts in connection with the term *kṣatra*, the ruling power of the kṣatriya caste.[3] As a kṣatriya, King Suratha has the duty to defend the dharma, and the implication is that duty fulfilled has its rewards. Although śrī, in the present context, is an abstract quality with nevertheless material effects, Śrī is also a goddess of Āryan origin who became identified with the probably non-Āryan agricultural goddess Lakṣmī. The first literary record to identify Śrī and Lakṣmī as a single goddess is the Śrīsūkta. This hymn, appended to the Ṛgveda in late Vedic times, also marks the earliest known occurrence of the term *alakṣmī*.[4] The Śrīsukta makes clear that Śrī-Lakṣmī is all that alakṣmī is not. If the resplendent, generous goddess is the source of material bounty (gold, cattle, and horses), food, health, satisfaction, beauty, fame, and increase, then alakṣmī denotes the opposite: poverty and debt, hunger, disease, want, ugliness, anonymity, and misfortune.

The hymnist of the Śrīsūkta takes refuge in Śrī so that his ill fortune (alakṣmī) and illusion (māyā) may be driven away (ṚV Kh 2.6.5–6). The joint appearance of alakṣmī and māyā in a single breath jolts us back to Medhas's teaching that the deluding power of māyā is the cause of Suratha's, Samādhi's, and indeed everyone else's woe (1.53–55). Māyā is in some way linked to alakṣmī, and the explanation is simple. The paired terms *śrī/alakṣmī* reveal the same dichotomy of wholeness and fragmentation, of boundlessness and limitation, of abundance and scarcity, that we observe in other pairs that define good and evil, such as *asura/sura* and *āditya/daitya* (→ 1.67–71).

There is one other implication. Whether the Devī confers her blessings of abundance on the virtuous or visits misfortune on the wicked, she is simply upholding the dharma within the sphere of dualistic perceptions of right and wrong. Apart from the moral admonition that virtue is rewarded and evildoing is punished, an inescapable fact is that sometimes adversity is revealed through hindsight to be a blessing in disguise; even alakṣmī may not be considered intrinsically bad. The hymn will return to this important idea later.

However they appear to our practical, everyday sensibilities, good and evil are ultimately two inseparable sides of the same coin, polarized manifestations of the one reality as Mahādevī and Mahāsurī (1.77) or as śrī and alakṣmī (4.5). Without this nondualistic understanding, we would be hard put to resolve the glaring contradiction between the plea to the Devī Caṇḍikā to destroy the fear of misfortune (4.4) and her identification as misfortune itself in the very next verse! We might be forced to accept the distasteful possibility of trembling in fear before an inherently wrathful supreme being who demands constant placation.

But no. Let us observe that verses 4.3 through 5 all begin with praise and end with petition, and that they form a picture of a goddess who receives not appeasement but love. From the maternal Ambikā the gods request auspicious things (*śubhāni*); from the fierce Caṇḍikā they ask for the removal of the fear of misfortune (*aśubha*); and from the Devī of manifold attributes they ask again for protection. This pattern of praise and petition, repeated three times, speaks of a reciprocity between the Divine Mother and her children and reminds us that the second carita's main concern is her active, sustaining aspect within the world.

The three remaining epithets—buddhi, śraddhā, lajjā—are qualitatively different from the śrī/alakṣmī pair. As śrī and alakṣmī, the Devī governs external events that happen to people. As intelligence (buddhi) in the hearts of the learned, faith (śraddhā) in the hearts of the good, and modesty (lajjā) in the hearts of the high-born, she manifests as internal qualities found within human beings.

To understand what buddhi is, we need to know how a human being is constituted. Every person has a physical body (*sthūlaśarīra*), a subtle body (*sūkṣmaśarīra*) and a causal body (*kāraṇaśarīra*). The densest of the three, the physical, or gross, body has mass and is perishable. The subtle body consists of the vital force (*prāṇa*), physically apparent as breath, and the internal organ (*antaḥkaraṇa*), the seat of thought and feeling. Buddhi, *manas*, and *ahaṁkāra* are constituents of the antaḥkaraṇa. Buddhi is intellect, the determinative faculty of the mind, which categorizes the impressions received through the sense organs (*indriyas*) through manas, the cognitive faculty. Ahaṁkāra, the ego or I-consciousness, is the sense of individual identity, which makes the distinction between what it regards as "I" and "not-I." Some schools of Indian thought also include a fourth component, citta ("mind-stuff"), which is the repository of memory.

Buddhi, which forms and retains conceptions, is the instrument of discernment, doubt, determination, reason, and will. According to the famous metaphor of the Kaṭhopaniṣad, the body is the chariot, the sense organs are the horses, manas is the reins, buddhi is the charioteer, and the Self (ātman) is the lord of the chariot (KU 1.3.3–4). As the charioteer can possess varying degrees of competence, the individual buddhi can be more or less developed.[5] Still, of all human faculties, it remains the highest instrument of embodied consciousness (KU 1.3.10). Because of its proximity to the ātman, buddhi facilitates the flow of consciousness from the Absolute to the relative and in the opposite direction as well. Again according to the Kathopaniṣad, "The Self, hidden in all beings, does not [readily] shine forth but is seen by the seers of subtle things with the buddhi focused" (KU 1.3.12). Likewise, the Devīmāhātmya tells us that as intelligence the Devī dwells within the hearts of the learned (*kṛtadhīyāṁ*, "those of cultivated thought") as the potential power of divine revelation.

The idea of the Devī as faith in the hearts of the good cannot pass without comment, owing to the differing concepts of faith (śraddhā) in Eastern and Western religions. The East emphasizes experience; the West emphasizes belief. According to the Hindu view, merely saying, "I believe, I believe," will not whisk one into a state of salvation. At some point, doubt can even be a sign of healthy engagement in the quest for spiritual truth. Śraddhā is not blind acceptance but initially a working hypothesis of trust in the guru's teaching, an attitude to be cultivated along with prescribed practices, such as meditation and mantric repetition, which provide experience.

The Ṛgveda devotes an entire hymn (ṚV 10.151) to śraddhā, which is less a personified goddess than a principle containing the seeds of later personification in the Brāhmaṇas.[6] The hymn characterizes śraddhā as confidence on the part of worshipers that their sacrifices will produce results. Won by the yearnings of the heart (ṚV 10.151.4), śraddhā is invoked to render effectual the Vedic sacrifice.[7] The concluding phrase, "O śraddhā, endow us with belief," indicates that, for the Hindu, the conviction of belief is the product of experience carried out in trust. Śraddhā entails expectation and reveals once again a bridge of reciprocity between the human and the Divine.

The role of lajjā ("modesty") in spiritual awakening is self-evident. Modesty entails the lessening of ego and an outward expansion toward unity, just as its opposite—self-aggrandizement—only increases one's alienation from others—and from the limitless divine consciousness. Through Mahāmāyā's confounding power, the intoxication of self-importance brought about Madhu and Kaiṭabha's downfall. Through modesty, the beneficent Devī leads her children to greater harmony and awareness.

**4.6–7:** After a transitional verse that previews the theme of the warrior goddess, verse 4.7 marks a sudden return to the cosmogonic theme of the Brahmāstuti. "You are the cause of all the worlds," the gods proclaim. In this and the next four verses, the Śakrādistuti elaborates eloquently on ideas set forth with spare matter-of-factness in the earlier hymn.

Śākta philosophy recognizes the Devī as both the efficient and the material cause of the universe, the driving force and the substance of creation. The differentiation of the guṇas is a step away from timeless, perfect unity and toward the emergence of a polarized universe with all its potential for inevitable inequalities and conflicts. But even while the Devī is an all-pervasive presence within her often glorious, sometimes messy creation, she also remains ever perfect and apart from the imperfections and deficiencies of relative existence. She is at once this entire world composed of parts (*aṁśabhūtam*) and the primordial, undeveloped (avyākṛtā) and therefore supreme (*paramā*) prakṛti from which all things take form. That is the inscrutable mystery of being/becoming sung by an Upaniṣadic seer: "That [Brahman] is infinite, this [universe] is infinite. From out of the infinite [Brahman] emanates all [this universe], . . . yet the infinite [Brahman] alone remains" (BU 5.1.1). In the face of this mystery, the present verse again praises the Devī as unfathomable even to the great Hari (Viṣṇu), Hāra (Śiva), and the other gods.

She is the cause (*hetu*) of this world and also the resort (*āśraya*) of all. Here we observe a shift from the cosmic to the personal. Comparing the two Sanskrit terms, which occur strategically at the beginning and the midpoint of the verse, we see that *hetu* ("impulse, motive, cause, reason") suggests outward motion, or manifestation; and *āśraya*, from the verb *āśri* ("to adhere to, to join") implies uniting with the source. For the Devī and humans alike, the relationship is intensely personal.

**4.8:** This verse recalls the opening words of the Brahmāstuti, *tvaṁ svāhā tvaṁ svadhā* (1.73), but the lyrical elaboration over the terseness of the original statement adds a note of personal warmth. We learn that the Devī not only manifests as the sacrificial mantras but that through them she confers satisfaction. Again, this relates to the reciprocity inherent in the concept of śraddhā (→ 4.5).

**4.9:** If the Devī is the cause of all the worlds and the power that confers efficacy on the human activity of ritual worship, here she is also seen as the cause of liberation, an idea introduced in the first carita (1.56–57). Now we learn in greater detail that she is also the motivating power behind the conditions and practices for attaining that goal.

Comprehensive spiritual practice (sādhana) cannot succeed without the resolve to persevere. It means continually reining in the senses and consciously rejecting attitudes and actions that could obstruct progress. *Vrata*, translated here as "austerity," denotes variously a religious vow, an ascetic observance such as fasting or sexual abstinence, a devotional act or, broadly, an entire way of life.

Such a way of life was systematized in Patañjali's Yogasūtra, a philosophical and practical manual that predates the Devīmāhātmya by as much as seven centuries. Patañjali, who synthesized various yogic practices known in his time into a sādhana known as *rājayoga* ("the kingly path") or *aṣṭāṅgayoga* ("the eight-limbed path"), prescribed an eightfold practice for spiritual enlightenment.

First comes *yama*, the five ethical precepts of non-injury to others (*ahiṁsā*), truthfulness (*satya*), non-stealing (*asteya*), chastity (*brahmacarya*), and abstention from greed (*aparigraha*). These are to be observed in thought, word, and deed. These precepts differ radically in some respects from Vedic sacrificial practices, which has led some scholars to believe that they stem from an ancient monastic asceticism that may have been practiced in Harappan times.[8]

Next, having cast off all faults (as the Devīmāhātmya puts it), the aspirant needs to cultivate the five positive qualities of *niyama*: physical and mental purity, contentment, self-discipline (*tapas*, directing one's energy), study (reading holy texts and repeating sacred mantras), and devotion. In other words, applying body, mind, and heart to the task.

The first two limbs of yoga concern general dos and don'ts as preliminary requisites. The remaining six apply specifically to the practice of sitting for meditation. They are *āsana* (posture), *prāṇāyāma* (control of the breath), *pratyāhāra* (withdrawal of the mind from the objects of sense perception), *dhāraṇa* (concentration, literally "holding" the thought), dhyāna (actual meditation, which is profound reflection, defined as the unbroken flow of consciousness toward its object), and samādhi (a state of complete absorption in the Divine).

Not prescribing anything as systematic as Patañjali's rājayoga, the Devīmāhātmya nevertheless agrees with it in recognizing interior, purely mental forms of worship that involve feelings of devotion and control of the thought-waves that arise as modifications of pure consciousness. Additionally, later passages (12.9–13, 12.21–22, 13.9–12) introduce the externals of formal temple rituals, sacrifices, and pious acts. The outward acts of ritual worship, such as the offering of flowers, incense, lights, water, and perfume, along with mantric recitation and certain mental processes, are symbolic enactments that shape the consciousness of the worshiper and make it receptive to the experience of spiritual truth.[9]

For the Tantric practitioner (*sādhaka*), the physical body is not something to be despised, but a form and dwelling place of the Divine Mother and an instrument of liberation.[10] Within the body, Tantric physiology recognizes seven centers of awareness (*cakras*), represented as lotuses, five positioned along the spine from the base to the throat, and two more at the level between the eyebrows and at the top of the head. Lying coiled like a serpent in the lowest cakra is the indwelling Śakti, called *kuṇḍalinī*. While she sleeps there, the human being is fully awake to the physical world but oblivious to the spirit.[11] Śrī Rāmakṛṣṇa taught that when human consciousness is concerned only with physical survival, pleasure, and the exercise of power, the kuṇḍalinī dwells in the three lower cakras: the *mūlādhāra*, at the base of the spine; the *svādhiṣṭhāna*, at the level of the genitals; and the *maṇipūra*, at the navel. Spiritual awareness dawns, he said, when the kuṇḍalinī rises along the *suṣumnā*, the channel within the spine, to the *anāhata* cakra, at the heart level, where one experiences the awakening of love and the wonder and glory of something beyond the embodied self. Once the kuṇḍalinī reaches the *viśuddha* cakra, at the throat, the sādhaka becomes established in spiritual life, and there is no turning back. Henceforth, all thought is directed toward the Divine. At the *ājñā* cakra, between the eyebrows, one experiences *savikalpa* samādhi, wherein one sees the Divine, although a separation of worshiper and worshiped remains. Finally, in the *sahasrāra*, the thousand-petaled lotus at the crown of the head, *nirvikalpa* samādhi brings the realization of oneness with the formless Divine. In Tantric terms, Śakti is united with Śiva, and the material universe vanishes into the infinite, transcendental unity.[12]

Because of its highly esoteric nature, kuṇḍalinī yoga or anything resembling it is difficult to trace historically. There is no mention of it in the Devīmāhātmya. Nevertheless, the Śākta sādhana so minimally sketched in the text engages the aspirant at every level—physical and mental, gross and subtle—in the process of transformation from matter to spirit. The Devī, as the cause of such practice (vrata), is the means to attainment. As the blessed, supreme knowledge (*bhagavatī paramā vidyā*), she is the goal itself.

**4.10:** As Śaṁkarācārya, the greatest philosopher of Advaita Vedānta, noted in his commentary on the Brahmasūtra, the Vedas declare from the earliest times that the world comes forth from the Word (*śabda*, literally "sound").[13] "With sound as your essence" calls to mind the Vedic goddess Vāk, the creative Word through whom and from whom the universe comes into existence. According to Śākta philosophy, divine reality and its power of self-expression (vāk) are one and inseparable. To simplify an immensely complex subject, pure consciousness is unchanging, motionless, and therefore soundless (*aśabda*). That same reality as creative energy is dynamic, and its initial motion manifests as the vibration of sound (śabda).[14] Vāk or śabda—the terms are interchangeable[15]—assumes increasing degrees of manifestation in its descent from the motivating (causal) level of the initial creative ideation to the plane of the physical universe with its imperceptible (subtle) sound and its audible (gross) sounds of articulated speech. Recognizing an unbroken continuum through all levels of existence, Śākta Tantra regards mantra as the actual presence, or embodiment in sound, of a deity. In the broadest sense, śabda is the flow of consciousness from the One into the many.

The process by which the One manifests as the many through the creative Word is described in various ways by different philosophical and religious systems, which impose a profusion of synonymous or overlapping technical labels in order to delineate the successive stages of divine emanation. The important thing to remember is that these stages are not incremental steps at all but merely points along a continuum. In reality, divine consciousness remains indivisible as it flows along a seamless spectrum of being/becoming. Swami Brahmananda, a disciple of Śrī Rāmakṛṣṇa, put it simply: "Show me the line of demarcation where matter ends and spirit begins."[16] Throughout the apparent diversity of the universe abides the all-pervading unity, which is constant (nitya).

"You are the treasury that holds the taintless Vedic hymns" means that the Devī is the source of the eternal, most sacred Hindu texts. From her springs the Hindu tradition's highest authority. The word *veda* itself means "knowledge" in the sense of the liberating awareness that sees the divine reality as it is. The Vedas record that knowledge, revealed to ancient seers in states of deepest contemplation. The phrase "embodying the three Vedas" reflects the belief that the Ṛgveda, Yajurveda, and Sāmaveda are, respectively, the forms of Mahākālī, Mahālakṣmī and Mahāsarasvatī.[17] (The reference to three Vedas excludes the fourth and youngest, the Atharvaveda.) In no uncertain terms this verse expresses the Śākta correlation of divinity and mantras. The Devī is both the *source* of the sacred Vedic verses and their *manifestation*.

The phrase "sung to resound joyfully at the sound of your holy name" is a free rendering of "recited with delight over the *udgītha*." This term refers to a particular method of chanting the Sāmaveda's hymns of praise. In a general sense, the word *udgītha* also signifies OṀ, the highest name of divinity, approximating the sound of the primal vibration that initiates the birth of the universe.[18]

The second half of the verse shifts from how the Devī manifests *as* the world to how she acts *in* it. Through the power of the Vedas, which are an expression of her own supreme power, the beneficent Devī engages in conferring well-being and prosperity upon the world. Of course, in the polarized, relative universe, well-being has its inevitable companion, tribulation; but the verse reminds us that the merciful Divine Mother is also "the supreme destroyer of pain in all the worlds."

**4.11:** According to Indian grammarians, the subtle form of śabda is called *sphoṭa*, literally "bursting, opening, expansion." Sphoṭa is the eternal, indivisible, imperceptible energy underlying the gross śabda, the articulated sounds that make up words. It is sphoṭa that transmits the idea, which "bursts" or flashes on the mind when speech is heard (or read). Curiously, sphoṭa is manifested by the sounds of speech even while it manifests the meaning of speech. In the language of Śākta devotionalism, we find the same idea: the Devī is at once the source of the Vedas, their embodiment, and *the intelligence by which their essence is understood.* The word for "intelligence" used here is *medhā* ("knowledge"), which carries the connotations of insight and latent power[19]; the word for "essence" is *sāra*, which additionally means "power" or "energy." Again, what this describes is the unbroken flow of energy-consciousness.

In a sudden shift from the abstract, the remainder of this verse calls the Devī by three personal names: Durgā, Śrī, and Gaurī. This marks the first appearance in the text of the name Durgā, even though the entire second carita centers on Durgā's slaying of Mahiṣāsura, and even though an alternative title of the Devīmāhātmya is Śrī Durgāsaptaśatī ("Seven Hundred Verses to Śrī Durgā"). *Durgā* is Sanskrit for "difficult of access or approach," and the suggested analogy to a citadel or fortress underscores both her unassailability and her protectiveness. What she grants is refuge from durga, worldly adversity (literally, "rough going").[20] Like the names Ambikā and Caṇḍikā, the name Durgā relates to the Devī's supreme form.

The second quarter of this verse, "You are Durgā, the vessel free of attachments that takes one across life's difficult ocean," relates to a far older verse from the Ṛgveda in praise of Aditi (ṚV 10.63.10). There, in a long string of epithets, the ancient Great Mother is praised as incomparable Earth-and-Heaven (the shining totality of manifest creation as a personified deity), which in its goodness is well-protecting, granting secure refuge, and safely guiding. Aditi is then likened to a divine ship, well-fitted with oars, free of defects, and admitting no water. "Let us board this ship," sings the hymnist, "for our well-being."

We already know that *śrī* ("light, lustre, radiance, splendor, beauty") was originally the Vedic term for the inherent glory of any god or goddess. Later personified as a goddess, Śrī merged with Lakṣmī, Viṣṇu's beneficent consort, associated with fertility, growth, and abundance.

Contrasting with Śrī's solar brilliance is the gentler lunar resplendence of Gaurī ("white, yellowish, shining, beautiful"), otherwise known as Pārvatī, the benign wife of Śiva.

Appearing in rapid succession, Durgā, Śrī, and Gaurī—three names of Śākta, Vaiṣṇava, and Śaiva affiliation—together form a comprehensive vision of the Divine Mother that crosses sectarian lines and speaks of her universality and oneness.

**4.12–23:** The core segment of the Śakrādistuti concerns the battle with Mahiṣāsura and acts as a commentary on the two foregoing chapters. First it introduces the themes of evildoing (4.12), divine wrath (4.13–14), divine grace (4.15–17) and redemption (4.18), which it then intertwines in a repetitive summation (4.18–23). At face value, the twelve verses form a theological lesson on the relationship between human beings and a personified deity. On a deeper level the passage works as psychological or philosophical allegory. Both readings have much to teach us.

First we will consider the outward, or religious, meaning. How could Mahiṣāsura, even in his anger, bring himself to commit an act of violence toward the exquisitely beautiful, gently smiling Durgā (4.12)? While inviting us to contemplate the nature of evil, the question simultaneously defines evil as the profanation of anything that should be revered. The annals of history are strewn with accounts of such disregard for the sanctity of human life, human achievement, and the natural world. They record countless acts of slaughter, pillage, and persecution, which have claimed innumerable lives and toppled untold noble endeavors. Even today, we live with continual affronts to all we hold sacred: we witness terrorism, warfare, genocide, the cutting down of irreplaceable primeval forests, and the remorseless pollution of the very air, water, and earth upon which all life depends. How can we, like Mahiṣāsura, be moved to commit such acts, to condone an uncaring cruelty that inflicts physical and emotional violence upon the defenseless, corruption upon the innocent, disparagement upon the wise? In malevolent thoughts, hateful words, and injurious deeds, collective and individual evil is the human face of Mahiṣāsura's rage.

Inevitably, we see the Devī's face no longer gently smiling but wrathful. Note the rajasic imagery of her awful countenance, reddened like the rising moon (4.13). With this abrupt shift arises the question of why such a horrifying vision does not instantaneously destroy its beholder, for her destructive power is formidable and swift (4.14).

Before divulging the answer, the hymn draws our attention to the Devī's benevolent side. To those who live according to the dharma, she is generous with the blessings of material bounty, progeny, and honor. When remembered, she increases the righteous acts of the already righteous (4.15) and the mental serenity of the already serene. And she dispels the distress of those who live in poverty, suffering, and fear (4.17).

Even toward transgressors she is benevolent (4.18). This is the crux of the entire second carita, stated and restated in the next five verses (4.19–23) as if to make sure the point is not lost. The Divine Mother is benevolent toward the virtuous and the wicked alike. Her grace is unconditional, even though its expression may take dramatically different turns.

Why, then, does the horrific vision of divine wrath not destroy its beholder? Let us compare Mahiṣa's and the Devī's rage (4.12–13). We cannot equate the two. Mahiṣa's destructive rage is just that, destructive. The Devī's is righteous indignation on a cosmic scale. Her purpose is to restore happiness to the world (4.18) by subduing the misconduct of the wicked (4.21), a role that echoes Kṛṣṇa's dictum in the Bhagavadgītā: "Though I am unborn and imperishable, the lord of all creatures, controlling my own nature (prakṛti), I manifest myself by my own power (māyā). Whenever righteousness (dharma) declines and evil (adharma) rises up, I come forth to protect the good, to destroy the evildoers, and to establish righteousness. I am born in every age" (BhG 4.6–8).

When battling evil, the Devī confers her grace even upon evildoers (4.18–23). Instead of annihilating the wicked without hope of redemption, she purifies them by the touch of her weapons so that they may attain the higher worlds (4.19), even though they may have committed enough evil to keep them long in torment (4.18).

In the Hindu view, there is neither annihilation nor eternal damnation. Hell, and even heaven, are not places in which to spend eternity, but transitory states of punishment and reward between lives on earth. The Devī does not blind the asuras with the intense light flashing from her weapons, because she wants to reveal instead the salvific, moonlike radiance of her face (4.20)—another metaphor for the unconditional grace that excludes none. Whether chastening the wicked or blessing the righteous, her dual aspects evoke visions of incomparable strength, ravishing beauty, and infinite compassion. She is a fearsome warrior goddess intent on the victory of good over evil; she is also a loving mother worthy of trust and devotion. Either way, she is beneficent (4.22), because even her horrific aspect leads the wicked to redemption (4.23).

Beneath this theology of a personal goddess who intervenes in mundane affairs lie subtler psychological and philosophical truths. The battleground is an interior one of the human heart and mind, where conflicts rage daily between the polarities of right and wrong, love and hate, duty and pleasure. The Devī is the indwelling divine Self that calls us to the highest aspirations; the asuras represent everything that is selfish, ignorant, and destructive in the human ego.

"Virtue is its own reward," as the saying goes. A philosophical interpretation of verses 4.15 through 17 suggests that living in accordance with the dharma confers a sense of well-being and harmony with the larger universe. But what about transgression? Eventually there comes a day of reckoning, of recognizing the true nature and the consequences of one's misdeeds.

The first carita of the Devīmāhātmya understands the universe as an emanation of divine consciousness, functioning intelligently at every level. According to this impersonal view, the instrument of justice operative in the universe is the law of cause and effect, known as *karma*. Simply put, no good deed goes unrewarded and no evil deed escapes unpunished. But karma is splendidly more complex than that. *Karma* ("act, action, deed") refers equally to an individual action (mental, verbal, or physical), its consequence, and cumulative effect. Each action generates a reaction that becomes in turn the cause of another action, forging a karmic chain that becomes the imprisoning power of saṁsāra. Because every action creates a mental impression (*saṁskāra*), and those impressions accumulate into ingrained tendencies, our actions determine what we become.

Karma determines not only what we become but what happens to us. In this web of cause and effect are interwoven different kinds of karma. *Prārabdha* ("commenced") karma, being already activated, governs what happens to us in the present lifetime as the result of actions in past lives. It is beyond our control, like an arrow that has already been shot. Internally, it governs habitual, compulsive, or self-willed activity; externally it operates through the agency of other people or forces of nature to deliver the consequences of past actions. *Sañcita* ("gathered up") karma is the latent aggregate of deep impressions created either in this life or a previous one. It has yet to be activated but remains dormant during the present life, like arrows in a quiver. Karma that comes to fruition in this lifetime as the result of actions also performed during the present life is called *āgāmi* ("coming up"). The terms *āgāmi* and *kriyamāṇa* ("being done") are sometimes used interchangeably, although there are technical differences between the two. Kriyamāṇa karma more specifically pertains to what we do in the present moment. Of course, even in the present moment our actions are likely to be influenced by underlying mental impressions—those programmed patterns of response created by ourselves in this and previous lifetimes, which form our character. But the present moment offers the freedom either to follow the existing impressions or to cultivate new ones, in other words, to determine our destiny. Kriyamāṇa karma is within our control. Some would interpret this freedom of choice as an expression of divine grace.

When misfortune strikes, we suffer the consequences of previous actions. "What did I ever do to deserve this?" we may lament, but later we may talk about a "blessing in disguise." The most painful lessons are often the most instructive. Physical or emotional suffering may awaken us to the preciousness of life, adversity may inspire heroic resolve, and the hurts inflicted upon us may awaken us to compassion for others. Chastened and purified, we grow in character and behold our world with new insight and wonder. Seeing the Devī about to strike the final blow, Mahiṣa is overcome with rapt awe at the recognition of her salvific grace. This powerful metaphor means that whenever the higher Self defeats the baser impulses within us, we become open to greater awareness.

In theistic language, a god or goddess is said to possess the power to mitigate the painful consequences of karma through divine grace. In an impersonal, philosophical sense, we can understand grace as the higher awareness (jñāna) that reveals the world in its true light and severs our attachments, thereby lessening our pain and dispelling the shadows of fear. Whichever interpretation we choose, the Devīmāhātmya instructs that grace is unconditional and withheld from none (4.18, 4.21).

The theistic, devotional approach allows us to draw a parallel between the Devīmāhātmya and the Bhagavadgītā. Telling Arjuna to perform every action as an offering to him, Kṛṣṇa expounds the same themes of unconditional grace, mitigation of karma, and universal liberation: "Thus shall you be freed from good or evil consequences, the bonds of your actions. Steadfast on the path of renunciation, liberated shall you come to me. I am alike to all beings; to me none are hateful or dear. But those who worship me with devotion are in me, and I in them. If even an evildoer worships me with utter devotion, he should be regarded as good, for he is rightly resolved. Quickly he becomes righteous and attains eternal peace. O [Arjuna], know that my devotee shall never perish" (BhG 9.28–31).

To sum up, evil can be defined as intentionally injurious and profaning. It inevitably invites punishment, just as virtue invites reward, either through the direct agency of a personal deity or through an impersonal, intelligent process called karma. Divine justice and divine blessing alike purify and open us to greater awareness of the divine reality that is in the end benevolent toward all.

**4.24–27:** Reverting to the anuṣṭubh meter, the Śakrādistuti's last four verses assume a vastly different character from the main portion of the hymn. Changing from an outpouring of praise, these last verses are a formula to ward off evil. First the maternal Ambikā's specific powers of protection are invoked, then the fierce Caṇḍikā and the mighty Īśvarī ("sovereign, ruler," the feminine form of "lord") are called upon to guard the four cardinal directions. Next entreated are the Devī's fierce and gentle forms in the celestial, atmospheric, and terrestrial realms, and finally the whole panoply of her powers is invoked for all-inclusive protection.

**4.28–30:** Like verses 4.1–2 before the hymn, these three also serve to frame an especially sacred portion of the Devīmāhātmya. The reverence that the gods show the Divine Mother with offerings of flowers, perfumes, and incense reflects elements of the Hindu ritual worship even as it is practiced today.

**4.31–37:** The recurring theme of reciprocity between the Devī and her creation takes shape here as a dialogue between her and the gods, whom she is ready to reward. When they say that with the slaying of Mahiṣāsura nothing remains to be done, they mean that for now all is well. Note that they leave open the possibility that evil may rise up again. In fact, its resurgence is a foregone conclusion as long as the universe exists, and they would like the assurance of future help for themselves and for "whatever mortal shall praise you with these hymns," referring to the four hymns of the Devīmāhātmya.

**4.38–42:** The inclusion of humans in the gods' request indicates a new direction for the third carita. In the first carita, Medhas's cosmically remote tale of Madhu and Kaiṭabha centered on Mahāmāyā's tamasic, deluding power. In the second carita, Medhas presented Durgā, the slayer of Mahiṣāsura, as an example of the Devi's rajasic power. Addressing the king's concerns, he pointed out the link between heaven and earth, drew a comparison between divine and royal power, and illustrated the human responsibility of upholding the dharma. In the third carita, Medhas will tell how the sattvic Devī, as the slayer of Śumbha and Niśumbha, confers spiritual liberation. This most elaborate story of all, comprising several distinct episodes, will be meant for the merchant, and its orientation will be decidedly terrestrial and human.

The Devī's third, sattvic, manifestation emerges from the body of Gaurī. The adjective *gauri* means "white, yellowish, brilliant, shining, beautiful." Its feminine form is also the name of the Divine Mother. All instances of this name/epithet in the Devīmāhātmya refer to the Devī's supreme form. The Śakrādistuti hymns her as "Gaurī, [the shining goddess] who abides with the moon-crowned Śiva" (4.11), thus identifying her with Pārvatī or Śakti. The Aparājitastuti tells us that she is the eternal one who sustains the universe (5.10). According to the Nārāyaṇīstuti she is all-knowing (11.10). Omniscience equates her with infinite consciousness, which is self-luminous and shining (gauri).

The second carita described Durgā as manifesting through the fiery splendor that emerged from the bodies of the gods. From other evidence in the Devīmāhātmya and on the authority of the Vedic Devīsūkta, we understand that those gods are but differentiated and fragmented aspects of her own power. In the third carita Medhas will describe the Devī's direct manifestation from herself. The important point to be made is her essential unity, and the third carita will make that abundantly clear.

## FINAL CARITA

### Meditation on Mahāsarasvatī

OṀ. I worship the incomparable Mahāsarasvatī, who holds in her lotus-like hands the bell, trident, plough, conch, mace, discus, bow and arrow; who is effulgent like the moon shining at the edge of a cloud; who is the support of the three worlds; and who came forth from the body of Gaurī to destroy Śumbha and other asuras.

# 5

## The Devī's Conversation with the Messenger

5.1 Oṁ klīṁ. The seer said:

5.2 "Long ago, grown arrogant with power, the asuras Śumbha and Niśumbha seized Indra's sovereignty over the three worlds and his share of the sacrifices.

5.3 In like manner they usurped the authority of the sun and the moon, and that of Kubera, Yama, and Varuṇa—the lords of wealth, death, and the ocean.

5.4 They seized the wind god's power and Agni's functions. The gods were defeated, deposed, and driven out.

5.5 Stripped of their powers and cast out by those two great asuras, all the gods remembered the invincible Devī.

5.6 'She granted us a boon, saying, "Whenever you remember me in times of distress, from that very moment I will put an end to all your worst calamities."'

5.7 With that in mind, the gods went to Himālaya, the lord of mountains, and there praised the Devī, who is Viṣṇumāyā.

5.8 The gods said:

5.9 'Salutation to the Devī, to the great Devī. Salutation always to her who is auspicious. Salutation to her who is the primordial cause, to her who is gracious. With minds intent, we bow down to her.

5.10 Salutation to her who is terrible. To Gaurī, the eternal, shining one; to her who sustains the universe, salutations again and again. Salutation always to her who is moonlight, who has the form of the moon and is blissful.

5.11 We bow to her who is auspicious beauty. We make salutations again and again to her who is prosperity and attainment. Salutations again and again to her who is the fortune and misfortune of kings, to Śarvāṇī, the consort of Śiva.

5.12 Salutation always to Durgā, who takes us through difficulties, who is the creator and indwelling essence of all, who is right knowledge, and who also appears dark as smoke.

5.13 We bow down to her who is at once most gentle and most fierce. Salutations to her again and again. Salutation to the support of the world. To the Devī, who is creative action, salutations again and again.

5.14–16 To the Devī, who in all beings is called Viṣṇumāyā, salutation to her, salutation to her, salutation to her again and again.

5.17–19 To the Devī, who in all beings is seen as consciousness, salutation to her, salutation to her, salutation to her again and again.

5.20–22 To the Devī, who abides in all beings in the form of intelligence, salutation to her, salutation to her, salutation to her again and again.

5.23–25 To the Devī, who abides in all beings in the form of sleep, salutation to her, salutation to her, salutation to her again and again.

5.26–28 To the Devī, who abides in all beings in the form of hunger, salutation to her, salutation to her, salutation to her again and again.

5.29–31 To the Devī, who abides in all beings in the form of shadow, salutation to her, salutation to her, salutation to her again and again.

5.32–34 To the Devī, who abides in all beings in the form of power, salutation to her, salutation to her, salutation to her again and again.

5.35–37 To the Devī, who abides in all beings in the form of thirst, salutation to her, salutation to her, salutation to her again and again.

5.38–40 To the Devī, who abides in all beings in the form of forgiveness, salutation to her, salutation to her, salutation to her again and again.

5.41–43 To the Devī, who abides in all beings in the form of order, salutation to her, salutation to her, salutation to her again and again.

5.44–46 To the Devī, who abides in all beings in the form of modesty, salutation to her, salutation to her, salutation to her again and again.

5.47–49 To the Devī, who abides in all beings in the form of peace, salutation to her, salutation to her, salutation to her again and again.

5.50–52 To the Devī, who abides in all beings in the form of faith, salutation to her, salutation to her, salutation to her again and again.

5.53–55 To the Devī, who abides in all beings in the form of loveliness, salutation to her, salutation to her, salutation to her again and again.

5.56–58 To the Devī, who abides in all beings in the form of good fortune, salutation to her, salutation to her, salutation to her again and again.

5.59–61 To the Devī, who abides in all beings in the form of activity, salutation to her, salutation to her, salutation to her again and again.

5.62–64 To the Devī, who abides in all beings in the form of memory, salutation to her, salutation to her, salutation to her again and again.

5.65–67 To the Devī, who abides in all beings in the form of compassion, salutation to her, salutation to her, salutation to her again and again.

5.68–70 To the Devī, who abides in all beings in the form of contentment, salutation to her, salutation to her, salutation to her again and again.

5.71–73 To the Devī, who abides in all beings in the form of mother, salutation to her, salutation to her, salutation to her again and again.

5.74–76 To the Devī, who abides in all beings in the form of error, salutation to her, salutation to her, salutation to her again and again.

5.77 To her who presides over the elements and the senses, and is ever present in all beings, to the all-pervading Devī, salutations again and again.

5.78–80 To her who pervades this entire world and abides in the form of consciousness, salutation to her, salutation to her, salutation to her again and again.

5.81 Praised long ago by the gods for fulfilling their desires and likewise honored daily by the lord of the gods, may Īśvarī, the source of all good, create happiness and prosperity for us, and may she destroy our misfortunes.

5.82 Tormented by arrogant daityas, we gods now honor her, the supreme power. With bodies bowed down in devotion, at this moment we remember her who destroys all afflictions.'"

5.83 The seer said:

5.84 "O king, while the gods were thus engaged in praise and adoration, Pārvatī came to bathe in the waters of the Gaṇgā.

5.85 She who is fair of countenance asked the gods, 'Whom are you praising?' From her own body an auspicious form emerged and replied:

5.86 'This hymn is an appeal to me by those whom the daitya Śumbha cast out, by the assembled gods whom Niśumbha defeated in battle.'

5.87 And since Ambikā came forth from Pārvatī's bodily form, she is glorified in all the worlds as Kauśikī.

5.88 Thereupon, Pārvaṭī became black. Thus known as Kālikā, she makes her abode in the Himālayas.

5.89 Then Caṇḍa and Muṇḍa, two servants of Śumbha and Niśumbha, beheld Ambikā's captivating beauty.

5.90 And they told Śumbha, 'O great king, an unknown woman, surpassingly beautiful, dwells illuminating the Himālayas.

5.91 Nowhere has anyone ever seen such supreme beauty. May you learn who that goddess is and take possession of her, O lord of asuras!

5.92 She abides there, a jewel among women, fairest of limb, casting her radiance in all directions. O chief of daityas, surely you must behold her!

5.93 Master, whatever gems and jewels, elephants, horses, and other riches exist in the three worlds, all those now enhance your dwelling.

5.94 From Indra you have taken Airāvata, the jewel among elephants, and also the celestial coral tree and the horse Uccaiḥśravas.

5.95 Taken from Brahmā, this wondrous jewel among chariots, yoked with swans, stands here in your courtyard.

5.96 Seized from Kubera, the lord of wealth, is his treasure. And the lord of the ocean has relinquished his garland of unfading lotuses.

5.97 Varuṇa's umbrella, which showers down gold, now stands in your house along with this best of chariots, which once was Prajāpati's.

5.98 Master, you have taken Yama's spear, which grants departure from this life. Varuṇa's noose is among your brother's possessions.

5.99 To Niśumbha belong all manner of gems born of the sea. And to the two of you, Agni has given garments purified by his own fire.

5.100 Thus, O chief of daityas, you have appropriated all things of value. Why then do you not seize this jewel among women for yourself?'"

5.101 The seer said:

5.102 "On hearing these words of Caṇḍa and Muṇḍa, Śumbha sent the great asura Sugrīva as a messenger to the Devī.

5.103 Instructing him, he said: 'Go to her and speak such words on my behalf that she will be delighted and will quickly come to me.'

5.104 Sugrīva went there to the resplendent, craggy place where the Devī dwelt and spoke honeyed words to her in unctuous tones.

5.105 The messenger said:

5.106 'O Devī, in the three worlds Śumbha, the lord of daityas, is the supreme sovereign. I am his messenger. I have come here to your presence, sent by him

5.107 who has conquered all the enemies of the daityas and whose command is never resisted in the dwellings of the gods. Hear what he says:

5.108 "All the three worlds are mine, and the gods submit to my will. I enjoy each one's share of the sacrifices, every one of them.

5.109 Indeed I possess all the finest gems in the three worlds, and I have taken Airāvata, the jewel among elephants and Indra's mount.

5.110 The immortal gods, bowed down in reverence, offered me Uccaiḥśravas, the jewel among horses, born from the churning of the milk ocean.

5.111 And whatever else is precious among the gods and celestial beings, all that is mine, O fair one.

5.112 We think of you, O goddess, as the jewel among women in the world, which indeed you are. Come to us, for we take pleasure in all the finest things.

5.113 Choose either me or my valiant younger brother, Niśumbha, for with your flashing eyes you are truly a jewel.

5.114 By taking me you will obtain dominion beyond compare. With reasoning mind, consider this well and become my wife.""'"

5.115 The seer said:

5.116 "Thus addressed, the Devī smiled inscrutably. The blessed, auspicious Durgā, who supports the universe, spoke.

5.117 The Devī said:

5.118 'You have spoken the truth; there is nothing false in what you have said. Śumbha is the ruler of the three worlds, and so also is Niśumbha.

5.119 But how can I go back on my word? Hear of the vow I once made out of foolishness:

5.120 He alone who conquers me in battle, who removes my pride, who equals my strength in the world, will become my husband.

5.121 Therefore let Śumbha or the great asura Niśumbha come here. Why delay? Having conquered me, let him take my hand in marriage.'

5.122 The messenger said:

5.123 'You are arrogant, O Devī. Speak not so in my presence. What man in the three worlds surpasses Śumbha and Niśumbha?

5.124 Even against the other daityas, all the gods cannot stand face to face in battle, O Devī. How then can you, who are one woman alone?

5.125 Indra and all the other gods could not resist Śumbha and the other demons in battle. How will you, a woman, go forth and confront them?

5.126 As I have said, go to Śumbha and Niśumbha's side. Suffer not the indignity of being dragged there by your hair.'

5.127 The Devī said:

5.128 'So must it be. Śumbha is mighty and Niśumbha is exceedingly heroic, but what can I do? My rash vow was made long ago.

5.129 Go back and tell the chief of asuras exactly what I have said. And let him do what is fitting.'"

# Chapter 5 Commentary

**Meditation on Mahāsarasvatī:** Mahāsarasvatī, who presides over the third carita, is the Devī's sattvic aspect. She has eight hands, which hold the symbols of her powers. In common with Mahākālī or Mahālakṣmī, she holds the bell, trident, conch, mace, discus, bow and arrows. Only the plough is new, and its obvious symbolism relates to agricultural fertility. But metaphorically, the plough furrows through the individual consciousness, creating auspicious impressions and allowing seeds of wisdom to be sown. Although only implied, Mahāsarasvatī's complexion is white, signifying the sattva guṇa and its properties of purity and knowledge. The wonderful imagery that compares her beauty to that of moonlight shining at the edge of a cloud also expresses her gentle, auspicious nature.

**5.1:** The bīja *klīṁ* signifies the Devī's essential nature as pure bliss (*ānanda*). As noted previously, the Tantric bīja mantras that open the three caritas—*aiṁ, hrīṁ* and *klīṁ*—equate the Divine Mother, or Śakti, with saccidānanda—infinite being-consciousness-bliss—expressed by the Vedic bīja mantra OṀ. Thus the three caritas of the Devīmāhātmya reflect in turn the Mother's three essential qualities.

**5.2–4:** Once again the asuras, who represent the forces of chaos—the antithesis of order (ṛta, dharma)—seize what is rightfully the sovereignty of the gods. In the previous carita when Mahiṣa made himself the lord of heaven, we may assume that he also appropriated the gods' shares of earthly sacrifices and their wealth, although this material theft is not mentioned. To the contrary it is specified, elaborately so, in the third carita. Here the gods' circumstances after the depradations of the asuras Śumbha and Niśumbha parallel the situation of the merchant Samādhi, whose family stole all his material wealth. Even as the myth of Mahiṣāsura is directed to the king, whose concerns as a sovereign ruling by divine right bridge the celestial and earthly realms, the story of Śumbha and Niśumbha is intended for the merchant, a common man whose involvements with business, wealth, and family belong entirely to this world.

Unlike the myths of Madhu and Kaiṭabha or Mahiṣāsura, the story of Śumbha and Niśumbha is seldom mentioned in Sanskrit literature before the time of the Devīmāhātmya.[1] In all likelihood Śumbha and Niśumbha belonged originally to a mythic tradition of northern, non-Aryan, nonliterate pastoral tribes for whom the supreme divinity was the Great Goddess in both fierce and maternal aspects.[2] At some later date they became associated with the story of the cowherd boy, Kṛṣṇa

Gopāla.[3] A passage in the Harivaṁśa concerning the birth of Kṛṣṇa identifies them as mountain demons who will be slain by the goddess Nidrā Vindhyavāsinī,[4] an incident also alluded to in the Devīmāhātmya (11.41–42).

**5.5–7:** Dispossessed and driven out from heaven, the Vedic gods, instead of appealing to Viṣṇu and Śiva as they did before, appeal directly to the Devī. Recalling her promise to intervene whenever remembered in times of misfortune (4.32–35), they proceed to Himālaya, the greatest mountain, and praise her there. This mountainous site is not the Vindhyas, as one might expect, given that wild region's association with Śumbha and Niśumbha. Instead, the locale shifts to the more civilized Himālayan region associated with Śiva and signals a move away from the localized goddess Vindhyavāsinī toward a universalized understanding of the Devī.[5]

The gods appeal to her as Viṣṇumāyā (5.7), a name unknown in Vedic or epic texts.[6] Its obvious meaning, at least from the Vaiṣṇava Tantra standpoint, is that she is the Śakti of Viṣṇu, and in support the Kālikāpurāṇa defines Viṣṇumāyā as that which makes everything manifest or unmanifest through the guṇas.[7] However, the name also resonates with the name Yoganidrā, employed earlier in the Devīmāhātmya to express the Devī's own supreme power (1.54, 1.70–71), for it was that goddess, closely associated with Vindhyavāsinī, who had settled over Viṣṇu's eyes as his meditative sleep. From the Śākta point of view, Viṣṇumāyā, therefore, is the one who subjects even Viṣṇu to her power.[8]

**5.8:** This verse announces the Aparājitāstuti ("Hymn to the Invincible Devī," 5.9–82). This hymn is a great celebration of the Devī's immanence, praising her various aspects from the formless abstraction of supreme power to specific forms assumed by that power. Thus, every form offers the possibility of a tangible way to relate to the Divine. Although celebrating her immediacy, the Aparājitāstuti is the Devīmāhātmya's only hymn to address the Divine Mother in the third person. Perhaps the more reverential tone is intended to impress upon us the Devī's awe-inspiring majesty as she reveals herself in and through her creation.

The thinking behind this hymn shows a spiritual kinship to the ecstatic fourth, fifth, and sixth chapters of the Śvetāśvataropaniṣad, another outpouring in praise of divine immanence, which beholds divinity as fire, the sun, the moon, and the starry firmament; as woman, man, youth, and maiden; and as a host of natural images such as the dark blue butterfly, the green parrot with red eyes, the thundercloud, and the seasons. According to the Upaniṣad, the source of this creation is the blissful one (*śiva*), who assumes various forms (*anekarūpa*) and remains hidden in all creatures (*sarvabhūteṣu gūḍha*) (ŚU 4. 14–15), having brought everything forth from its own nature (*svabhāva*) (ŚU 5.5).

The Aparājitāstuti is a treasury of divine names and epithets. Many of them individually carry a host of associations and ideas, and the English language lacks the equivalent terms to express the fullness of the Sanskrit original.

**5.9:** Although the opening line contains the names Mahādevī (the feminine form of Mahādeva, an epithet of Śiva) and Śivā (the feminine form of *śiva,* "auspicious"), there is no specific attempt here to identify the Devī as Śiva's consort. The line should be approached purely and simply as a salutation to the Great Goddess (Mahādevī) who is auspicious (śivā) in her own right.[9]

In the second line the gods bow to her who is prakṛti, the divine energy which manifests as the universe. Moreover, she is *bhadrā* ("gracious, auspicious, favorable"), and the linking of the two terms creates a positive view of a world that simultaneously emanates from and is pervaded by the Divine Mother.

**5.10:** The Devī is also *raudrā* ("violent, impetuous, fierce, wild, inauspicious"). This adjective derives from the name of Rudra, a Vedic storm god once connected to Indra and especially to Agni and, in post-Vedic times, absorbed by Śiva, who originally may have been a non-Āryan deity. The name derives from the verbal root *rud,* meaning "to howl," and the adjective here expresses the frightening destructiveness of the Devī's terrible aspect.

The verse is quick to remind us, however, that she is also nityā, self-existent and constant. The ever-changing circumstances of the physical universe, however violent they may appear at times, take place against the eternal changelessness of divine reality, the reality that is gaurī, the shining, self-luminous consciousness, and also *dhātrī,* the support of the world.

In India, where the blazing heat of the sun can be brutal, moonlight is looked upon as cool and soothing. Likening the Devī to moonlight and saying that she herself has assumed the form of the moon emphasizes her benign aspect. She is indeed *sukhā*, bestowing happiness, pleasure, delight, and comfort in our lives. However, the apparent redundancy of this line—that she is moonlight and has the form of the moon—remains puzzling until we realize that it embodies a more profound truth. We find the explanation in the Devīgītā, written probably between the 13th and 16th centuries and incorporated into the 12th-century Devībhāgavatapurāṇa.[10] Here the moon/moonlight metaphor reappears in connection with the analogies of the sun and its brilliance and the classic fire and its heat to express the inseparability of consciousness and its power (DG 2.5).[11] The Devīmāhātmya uses the lunar imagery to explain the absolute identity of Śakti as pure consciousness with Śakti as creative power. A deceptively simple, poetic phrase becomes the expression of ultimate nondualism.

**5.11:** The usage of *kalyāṇī* ("auspicious, beautiful, lovely") in the Ṛgveda commonly denotes feminine beauty, and other Vedic texts link the word to themes of agricultural productivity and the nurturing cow. In one instance, the Atharvaveda declares Kalyāṇī the immortal one who becomes born as the manifold diversity of human life.[12] Not surprisingly, the present verse links her auspiciousness to *vṛddhi* ("growth, prosperity") and *siddhi* ("attainment").

Although she appears as the good fortune of kings, the second line cautions that she also appears as their misfortune, an obvious reference to worldly responsibility and the consequences of good and evil actions (→ 4.5). The terms previously used in the Śakrādistuti were *śrī* and *alakṣmī.* Here, they are *lakṣmī* and *nairṛtī.* The latter derives from Nirṛti, the name of an abstract but nonetheless terrifying

Vedic goddess. Because she personified adversity, calamity, infertility, disease, and destruction and presided over death, she was the focus of propitiatory rituals.[13] The noun *nirṛti* ("decay") derives from the verb *nirṛ,* meaning "to separate, to disjoin," illustrating that whatever is subject to decay and dissolution is separate from the whole. Nirṛti is the opposite of the related word *ṛta,* which signifies the universal moral order. Once again, we see that chaos and cosmos, asura and deva, evil and good, reflect the underlying principles of fragmentation and wholeness. Elsewhere in the Mārkaṇḍeyapurāṇa, outside the chapters that form the Devīmāhātmya, Nirṛti appears as the daughter of Adharma and Hiṁsā (Unrighteousness and Injury); she in turn gives birth to Naraka and Bhaya (Torment and Fear). Again, we are reminded of the intimate connection and fluid boundary between evil-doing and misfortune.

The present verse begins with an invocation of the auspicious Kalyāṇī and ends with one of Śarvāṇī, Śiva's consort and destructive power at the end of a cosmic cycle. Encompassing the benign and the terrible, it reminds us that the same Divine Mother who sustains life and makes it joyful also calls it into dissolution.

**5.12:** Earlier we saw that Durgā's name means "difficult of access or approach" and suggests her unassailability and protective nature against worldly adversity or durga, which literally means "rough going" (→ 4.11). The compound *durgapārā* means "she who takes across (rescues, saves, protects from) difficulties." Note how beautifully the first line resounds: *durgāyai durgapārāyai sārāyai sarvakāriṇyai.* It means that Durgā, who sees us through the worst of circumstances, is also the essence (*sārā*) and the maker or doer (*kāriṇī*) of all things, in other words the Divine Mother who herself appears *as* and acts *in* the universe.

*Khyāti* ("she who makes known") and *kṛṣṇā* ("she who is dark") refer to her dual powers of revelation and obscuration, of liberation and bondage. Emphasizing the latter, *dhūmrā* ("she who is smoky, dark") refers to the veiling power of avidyāmāyā.

**5.13:** The first line restates the final idea of verse 5.11, that the same Great Goddess who sustains life also calls it into dissolution. She is most gentle (*atisaumyā*) and most fierce (*atiraudrā*). The adjective *saumyā* conjures up visions of the moon's cool serenity, and *raudrā* evokes the tempest's fierce howling—starkly contrasting images from nature that declare the polarity of a benign yet terrifying deity.

The five introductory verses (5.9–13) of the Aparājitāstuti proceed from an opening statement of divine transcendence to the recognition that the Devī dwells in and acts through all that exists. She is both the world's support (*jagatpratiṣṭhā*) and the creative action (*kṛti*) that animates it.

**5.14–16:** The hymn's central portion (5.14–76) consists of the well-known litany of twenty-one nearly identical ślokas, of which nineteen differ from one another only by one word. In each case that word is the initial element of the compound ending with *-rūpeṇa,* meaning "in the form of . . . " Each such word is a feminine noun expressing an attribute or personified abstraction of divinity. The tendency to personify abstract qualities, found earlier in the Ṛgveda, may be far older, since people of prehistoric times are thought to have observed the phenomena of their surroundings and then formulated philosophical abstractions, which in turn became personified as deities.[14] By the time of the Devīmāhātyma, what originally may have been considered multiple divinities had come to be understood as diverse powers of one supreme deity.

The Aparājitāstuti unites in a single litany a dazzling series of such personified attributes, which we would consider both "positive" and "negative," for such is the nature of the world we experience. Each epithet makes a self-contained statement, yet in relation to one another they reveal a broader picture. Since recitation of the hymn allows no time to contemplate those relationships, what we sense instead is the incantatory, cumulative effect of the words.

The peculiar numbering of this sequence, which counts each śloka as three, serves in part to extend the Devīmāhātmya's total number of verses to seven hundred in conformity with the alternate title, Śrī Durgāsaptaśatī ("Seven Hundred Verses to Śrī Durgā"). Because each of the ślokas contains the salutation *namastasyai* uttered three times, some interpreters consider the salutations as directed to the Devī's tamasic, rajasic, and sattvic aspects. This interpretation is convincing in all instances only if we consider that on the level of observable phenomena nothing exists in a pure guṇa state but is the result of the mixing of all three guṇas in complex patterns. Thus, an attribute like intelligence (buddhi), while predominantly sattvic by nature, can be tinged with any of the three guṇas. Sattvic buddhi is directed to the attainment of higher, spiritual knowledge; rajasic buddhi is concerned with secular knowledge; tamasic buddhi is directed to nefarious ends.

This view of the triple salutation conforms to the twice-stated instruction of the Vaikṛtika Rahasya that the Aparājitāstuti is to be chanted in worship of the Divine Mother's supreme form, who contains the three guṇas within herself (VR 7 and 23).

Alternatively, the threefold nature of the salutation may refer to the divine presence in all three planes of actualized existence—the causal (motivating), the subtle (psychical) and the gross (physical). It is important to remember here that these planes are not spatial realms but states of consciousness. Considering that the Aparājitāstuti is a hymn of divine immanence, it ought to recognize that everything in the empirical universe has a subtle (*sūkṣma*) and a causal (*para*) dimension behind its gross (*sthūla*) manifestation and that all three exist in potential form even within the undifferentiated Viṣṇumāyā.

Hindu tradition supports either approach. The three-guṇa reading reflects the Sāṁkhya model of the universe, with its emphasis on the elements of creation. The three-plane reading reflects the understanding of the Upaniṣads as to how the universe contains causal, subtle, and gross levels of existence.

The Devī, "who in all beings is seen as Viṣṇumāyā," is the creative power that is inseparable from and ultimately one with the self-luminous Absolute. Viṣṇumāyā is a threefold power, consisting of tamasic *āvaraṇaśakti* (the power that conceals the transcendental unity of the divine Self), rajasic *vikṣepaśakti* (the projecting power that sustains the universe), and sattvic *jñānaśakti* (the liberating power of knowledge).[15] Containing the perfectly balanced, unactivated guṇas, Viṣṇumāyā is the unmanifest Śakti, whose subsequent progression from the One to the many anticipates modern science's Big Bang.

**5.17–19:** We can define *cetanā* as a state of awareness that has emerged from absolute and unchanging consciousness (cit or *saṁvit*) and developed the distinction between subject and object. Cetanā is both percipient and perceptible, and it not only signals a cosmic event in the unfurling of creation but also abides within each individual as the causal body (kāraṇaśarīra), also known as the sheath of bliss (*ānandamayakośa*). It is the veil of nescience (avidyā) covering the self-luminous ātman and appearing to limit the infinite consciousness. In the state of dreamless sleep, when there is no longer any awareness of the four outer sheaths (the physical body, life-breath, sense perception, and mental activity), the ānandamayakośa alone remains to conceal the infinitude of the divine Self. Without it, we would attain enlightenment every time we fell into deep sleep.

**5.20–22:** Buddhi, the instrument of intelligence, discerns, doubts, determines, reasons, and wills. Although it is a limited manifestation of consciousness, it is the highest faculty of the human mind and possesses the potential power of divine revelation. According to the Kathopaniṣad, "The Self, hidden in all beings, does not [readily] shine forth but is seen by the seers of subtle things with the buddhi focused" (KU 1.3.12).

**5.23–25:** In Chapter 1, Medhas identifies Mahāmāyā with Yoganidrā, "who had settled over Viṣṇu's eyes as his blessed sleep." That passage (1.70–71) makes a clear connection between nidrā ("sleep") and Yoganidrā, who it says is the ruler, sustainer, and dissolver of the universe. She is the power that projects form out of her own formlessness. She deludes all creatures by limiting their awareness and perpetuating cyclical existence (saṁsāra). When the Devī is said to abide in all beings in the form of sleep, that refers to her cosmic aspect as the creator of the physical universe.

Within the individual, sleep is one of three possible states of embodied consciousness. In dreamless sleep (*suṣupti*) there is no awareness of the world, the body, the mind, or the ego. This state is not unconsciousness, for everything that exists is a form of consciousness; instead, it is a state marked by the cessation of thought. In the dream state (*svapna*) the mind acts, but independently of the body and the exterior world. In waking (*jāgrat*) the mind experiences the physical world. These three states of consciousness correspond to the causal, subtle, and gross planes. They exist as finite forms of awareness distinct from the infinite, transcendental consciousness called Brahman or *turīya* ("the fourth").

The metaphor of sleep used to express the duality of knowledge and nescience—of absolute and partial consciousness—is also found in verse 21 of the Durgāstotra. That hymn from the Mahābhārata proclaims that of the various kinds of knowledge, Durgā is herself the knowledge of Brahman, and as the great sleep (*mahānidrā*) she is the knowledge of embodied creatures.[16]

**5.26–28:** So far, the litany section of the hymn has dealt with consciousness in progressively more differentiated forms. At some point along the continuum of being/becoming, we passed imperceptibly into the realm of the physical universe. The attributes of the next sixteen verses become ever more specific or reified, and we are more likely to experience them as they appear to us rather than to regard them as expressions of the one consciousness which, in reality, they are.

The theme of hunger (*kṣudhā*) occurs in the Devīsūkta, where Vāk reveals that: "Through me alone every mortal lives [literally, "eats food"] who sees and breathes and hears what is said, not knowing that he abides in me" (ṚV 10.125.4). In the same spirit, Viṣṇu, in the Harivaṁśa, hymns the Devī Nidrā ("Sleep") as "the hunger of all creatures."[17]

Hunger has a concrete meaning to all life forms, whether they possess the intellect to reflect upon it or merely respond to it instinctively. It is a primary motivation that sustains physical life. When our hunger is satisfied, we say we are full, and significantly, the Sanskrit word for "full," *pūrṇa,* is the key to the higher understanding of this verse. *Pūrṇa* is an epithet of the Absolute, which is complete in itself: "That [Brahman] is infinite (pūrṇam), this [universe] is infinite (pūrṇam). From out of the infinite [Brahman] (pūrṇāt) emanates all [this universe] (pūrṇam), . . . yet the infinite [Brahman] (pūrṇam) alone remains" (BU 5.1.1). As physical hunger signifies lack in the material realm, existential hunger is similarly a state of incompleteness, of being cut off (*diti*) from the fullness of divine reality (Aditi). As hunger abiding within all creatures, the Devī keeps us in the embodied state, separated from our true wholeness and bound (*dita*) by māyā's limitations.

**5.29–31:** *Chāyā* means "shade" or "shadow." In the physical universe it is a visible manifestation of tamas that results from the blockage of light. Metaphorically, chāyā is the blockage of the light of pure consciousness by the veiling power of Mahāmāyā. The shadow thus cast is the material universe, which is nothing less than the formless Devī appearing as form. We must remember that she is the shadow, that which casts the shadow, and the light—the universe, its cause, and its divine source.

**5.32–34:** The word *śakti* means "power, ability, strength, energy." As a common noun, *śakti* also means the power of any male god, often personified as his consort. (We shall meet several such śaktis in the course of Medhas's narrative.) When capitalized, Śakti is the singular, ultimate power, regarded as feminine.

Everything in the universe is nothing other than the Divine Mother herself, shining vibrantly in every form. The Kaṭhopaniṣad teaches that the sun, the moon, the stars, lightning, and fire do not shine by their own light, but by Brahman's: "That shining, everything shines" (KU 2.2.15). In Śākta terms, we might say, "She shining, everything shines."

**5.35–37:** Thirst (*tṛṣṇā*), like hunger (5.26), has a gross form involved in sustaining physical life, and a metaphoric meaning: a thirst for life itself, that is to say a longing to enjoy the objects of sense. Recalling the triple salutation of this and the other verses that form the body of this hymn, we can consider that sattvic thirst is the desire for ennobling experiences that convey a sense of the sacred; rajasic thirst is the desire for excitement; and tamasic thirst could be sexual lust, which is the mind's most intensive identification with physical matter.

**5.38–40:** While tṛṣṇā, particularly in its rajasic and tamasic forms, sustains bondage, *kṣānti* ("forgiveness, patience") is one of several auspicious attributes named in the hymn that have the opposite effect.

The opposite of forgiveness is resentment, which reinforces the initial mental impression (saṁskāra) of a wrong done to us. With sustained ill will, the cumulative mental energy causes the saṁskāra to develop into a *vāsanā,* a persistent tendency or character trait. The antidote for this kind of bondage is forgiveness, or letting go. Severing the attachment to our own hurt feelings, we experience in forgiveness a liberating sense of expansion beyond ourselves. Moreover, forgiveness plays a healing role in three different ways, regarding the harm we have done to others, the harm others have done to us, and the harm we do to ourselves. Forgiveness releases us from the past and opens our lives to renewal.

**5.41–43:** The word *jāti* ("order") comes from the root *jan,* meaning "to be born, to come into existence." Jāti is one's own form of existence as determined by birth—the genus, species, or class to which each thing belongs. Acorns produce oak trees, humans give birth to babies, and each creature brings forth according to its own kind.

A look at the world around us reveals an order in which we can infer the presence of an intelligence at work. Organic life forms (plants and animals) are composed of cells, and those cells, like inorganic forms (minerals), are composed of molecules. Molecules are made of atoms, which are highly organized systems of still smaller particles or waves, acting in an orderly fashion. The author(s) of the Devīmāhātmya did not have the electron microscopes, particle accelerators, or the developed mathematics that allow modern scientists to study the quantum universe, but they did have the intuitive knowledge that divine intelligence operates in and through everything.

On the level of ordinary experience, jāti functions as a differentiating but also ordering power. The world is filled with forms of every conceivable shape, size, color, or other quality, and ideally everything should coexist harmoniously. Accordingly, some Indian philosophers recognize jāti as an abstract universalizing principle, because the Divine Mother's universe necessarily has to partake of and reflect her own nature.

**5.44–46:** Earlier, we noted the significance of lajjā as the diminution of ego (→ 4.5). This important attribute of modesty occurs in all four of the Devīmāhātmya's hymns and in the Mahābhārata's two hymns to Durgā as well. The Durgāstotra additionally links modesty with good fortune and intelligence (verse 56),[18] a triad repeated in Viṣṇu's Praise of Nidrā in the Harivaṁśa (verse 54).[19] Such recurring connections suggest a traditional understanding that the Divine Mother smiles upon those who act wisely.

**5.47–49:** *Śānti* ("peace") is a welcome condition in the often conflict-ridden world. Spiritually, śānti is the inner peace that comes with the higher knowledge that lessens and ultimately frees us from attachment to the physical body, sensory experiences, and ever-shifting states of mind. It is evenness of mind in happiness and sorrow. In the Harivaṁśa, Śānti is personified as the daughter of Śraddhā, the subject of the next verse.

**5.50–52:** Śraddhā ("faith") was understood originally as confidence on the part of the Vedic worshipers that their sacrifices would produce results, and that the trust thus engendered would lead to the strength of unwavering conviction. Since śraddhā entails expectation, it forges a bridge of reciprocity between the human and the Divine (→ 4.5).

**5.53–55:** *Kānti* means "beauty," and particularly feminine beauty or loveliness. We experience beauty in countless ways—in nature, in art and music, in human thoughts and deeds—and in every such experience the Devī is revealing herself and inspiring wonder. Beauty is the Divine Mother's way of reminding us of her presence. How often we speak of "truth, goodness, beauty" all in the same breath. That is because beauty is a gift of divine grace. Together with the other auspicious qualities named in this hymn, such as forgiveness, modesty, compassion, and contentment, loveliness belongs to a class of the Devī's manifestations that signify an expansion of consciousness and reveal glimpses of the larger divine reality.

**5.56–58:** *Lakṣmī* ("good fortune") is the Divine Mother's gift of abundance and happiness. The Durgāstotra (verse 56) links good fortune with modesty and intelligence and suggests a further connection between them and dharma.[20] In the Devīmāhātmya, the Śakrādistuti also links lakṣmī and dharma in calling the Devī "good fortune in the dwellings of the virtuous" (4.5).

**5.59–61:** The term *vṛtti* ("activity") allows for more than one interpretation. In the physical world (*jagat*, literally "that which moves"), we perceive vṛtti as the constant motion and change in all things. Even something as seemingly inert as a stone teems with activity, as electrons orbit the nuclei of its atoms. Beyond the physical motion of the material plane lies the subtler activity of the mental plane. And so, within human consciousness, vṛtti is defined as a thought wave or modification of the mind, an impulse of energy that flows out through the senses and makes knowledge of the exterior world possible. Behind the subtle vṛtti that makes the outer world manifest through perception lies the motivating impulse of the causal dimension. As the cause of differentiated thought-forms that arise from the undifferentiated ocean of consciousness, vṛtti and moha share a parallel, which is to say limiting, function.

However, unlike moha, which only keeps us in delusion, vṛtti can be harnessed to lead us toward enlightenment. In the Yogasūtra, Patañjali declares with startling simplicity, "Yoga is the control of activity in the mind" (*yogaś cittavṛttinirodhaḥ*) (YS 1.2). He defines yoga as the restraint (*nirodha*) of the thought waves (vṛttis) in the field of consciousness (citta), which encompasses the functions of manas, buddhi, and ahaṁkāra. Patañjali distinguishes between vṛttis that increase our ignorance and bondage and those that foster knowledge and freedom. In his prescribed sādhana, harmful thought-waves are first neutralized by intentionally raising their opposites, replacing "bad" thoughts with "good" ones. Then even the "good" thought-waves must be stilled in order to experience the infinite consciousness beyond all form.

**5.62–64:** The physical universe is a manifestation of consciousness. In order for the universe to remain in a manifest or actualized state, continuity is necessary. That continuity is provided by the particular form or modification of consciousness known as *smṛti* ("memory").

The universe of our experience is a relative universe, in which all parts exist in relation to all other parts. The process by which we experience our existence in the world is relational, and therefore all empirical knowledge is relational. Without the continuity of memory, the intellect could not function, because it could not relate anything to anything else. It would be devoid of all content except the immediate object of perception, which it would be powerless to interpret. Even the basic process of recognition would be impossible, because recognition, which follows directly upon perception, is experience associated with memory.[21] Without the underlying continuity of memory, none of the intellectual processes could function; the buddhi could not categorize, relate, compare, infer, or determine. In short, the universe of our experience would no longer be possible.

Memory also functions apart from perception when its object is the revived impression of a previous experience.[22] In that sense, memory bridges past and present; again, it provides continuity. This idea finds support in verse 44 of the Durgāstāva, which praises the Devī as knowledge, continuity, and mind.[23]

The word *smṛti* has a second meaning. The Hindu scriptures belong to two classes: *śruti* ("what is heard" or divinely revealed) and smṛti ("what is remembered" or of human origin). The Vedas alone are śruti; everything else is considered smṛti and is authentic insofar as it conforms to the Vedas. The smṛti texts are repositories of social customs, moral and religious observances, cultural traditions, and spiritual disciplines. They include the law codes, the Sūtras, the epics (Mahābhārata and Rāmāyaṇa), the Purāṇas and the Tantras.

**5.65–67:** *Dayā* ("compassion") is one of eight epithets in the litany that deal with the Divine Mother's auspicious manifestations, the others being forgiveness (5.38), modesty (5.44), peace (5.47), loveliness (5.53), faith (5.50), good fortune (5.56), and contentment (5.68). Four of them—the virtues of forgiveness, modesty, contentment and compassion—imply a lessening of ego or individual ignorance. The other four are more in the general nature of blessings bestowed upon people.

Compassion can be defined as any action that diminishes the suffering of others. For the Hindu, it embraces not merely a sympathetic attitude but a commitment to active service. It is a quintessentially divine quality, and when reflected in human behavior, it opens us to the Divine.

**5.68–70:** With the other auspicious epithets, *tuṣṭi* ("contentment") shares the common quality of expanded awareness. In the material world, we understand contentment as satisfaction or the fulfillment of desires, but that describes only its gross or tamasic form, and such contentment is fleeting, indeed. The higher contentment signals a sense of fullness arising from the cessation of desire. It distances us from the driving sense of lack that inevitably arises when consciousness is associated with the ego. This higher contentment is the Divine Mother's gentle reminder that the true Self wants for nothing.

**5.71–73:** It is easy to understand that when the Devī abides in all beings as mother (*mātṛ*), she takes form as the female of the species, who gives birth and who in the more highly evolved life forms nurtures and displays maternal affection. It is the mother alone who wraps spirit in matter, and all mothers of all creatures thus replicate the process of the universal Divine Mother, who gives birth to the universe of name and form. Because male children are also her creations, ultimately they are not different from her, either. She dwells in every one of us, and her indwelling presence is a constant reminder that we are never alone. Moreover, that connection is so intimate that within all embodied beings, male and female alike, the Mother's divine radiance abides as the true Self.

**5.74–76:** At the end of this ecstatic litany, the final verse may come as a shock, for we are told that this same Devī abides in everything in the form of error (*bhrānti*)! When understood, this is no cause for worry, but merely the hymn's way of coming full circle. The Divine Mother is, we remember, Viṣṇumāyā (5.14), who obscures her self-luminous, infinite consciousness in order to project the world. Because the consciousness that animates and illumines us as individuals is fragmented, limited, and imperfect, we do not experience the Devī's shining fullness directly; instead we see her manifestation through the kaleidoscope of delusion (moha). We experience this sometimes dark, sometimes dazzling world only because the Devī abides in the form of error.

The English word *error* (from Latin *errare*) and the Sanskrit *bhrānti* (from *bhram*) both derive from verbs meaning "to wander." A secondary meaning of *bhram* is "to waver, to be perplexed, to err." We can understand that error is simply a wandering away from the truth, a misreading of reality that takes the finite parts for the infinite whole. The form that such error takes, the false premise upon which our unenlightened worldly existence is based, will be revealed at the very core of Medhas's teaching by way of this final narrative concerning the demons Śumbha and Niśumbha.

**5.77–80:** How do we experience the universe just described? Through the Devī herself, who pervades and presides over the instruments of consciousness and the elements of which the senses and their objects are composed. The Devī herself is pure consciousness, which is both the source and, when modified, the manifestation of the perceptible world. Though translated here as "consciousness," the term *citi* more accurately means "the thinking mind." Citi is not the absolute consciousness (cit), but the Absolute's ideational energy (*sṛṣṭikalpanā*) that brings about the world-process.[24] The Devī abides in her creation as creative consciousness, pervading the entire world (jagat) that is ever in motion.

**5.81–82:** At this point the hymn shifts momentarily into the forty-eight-syllable *vaṁśastha* meter, probably to distinguish the petitionary nature of the final two verses from the laudatory nature of the rest. These verses also prepare for a return to the narrative, wherein the gods will appeal to the Devī, who earlier promised to intervene whenever misfortune should arise.

**5.83–88:** The mention of the Gaṇgā establishes the sphere of action as right here on earth. Coming to bathe in the holy river, the Devī first appears to the gods as Pārvatī, portrayed less as Śiva's consort than as an independent and supreme deity in her own right. (When Śiva appears later in the narrative, he is decidedly subordinate to her.)

When Pārvatī asks the gods, "Whom are you praising?" an auspicious (śivā) form emerges from her own body and replies, "This hymn is an appeal to me." This lovely manifestation, we are told, is glorified as Kauśikī, because she came forth from Pārvatī's bodily form (*kośa*). In the first and second caritas, the Devī appeared in tamasic and rajasic aspects; now she manifests in sattvic form. As soon as she emerges, Pārvatī darkens and is henceforth known as Kālikā, or Kālī, who will play a major role in the course of events. This play of light and dark illustrates graphically the Devī's dual nature of bright auspiciousness and dark terror.

**5.89–100:** Mahiṣa was the only demon of the previous myth to be well characterized, while his attendant generals remained little more than colorfully descriptive names. In the elaborately drawn, multiple episodes of the Śumbha-Niśumbha myth, the demons possess fully developed and very human personalities.

First we meet the toadying servants, Caṇḍa and Muṇḍa, who bring news to Śumbha of a beautiful goddess whose radiance illuminates the Himālayas. Playing upon Śumbha's vanity, they flatter him with an account of his riches and powers, all stolen from the gods and adding up to sickening excess when concentrated in the asura's hands. If Śumbha possesses all that, Caṇḍa and Muṇḍa ask, should he not also possess the fairest of goddesses?

**5.101–121:** His lust inflamed at the thought of the beautiful maiden, Śumbha sends Sugrīva to court her. The messenger, who represents deceit and hypocrisy, knows full well that his fine words intend to mislead. The Devī knows it, too, and ironic humor colors their exchange. With "honeyed words" spoken "in unctuous tones," Sugrīva glorifies his hideous master by boasting of the asura's dazzling wealth and power. Note the irony when the Devī pretends to take his words at face value, saying, "You have spoken the truth; there is nothing false in what you have said" (5.118). Sugrīva's attempt at beguilement represents the seductive nature of the world. As Medhas earlier alerted the king and the merchant, behind the glittering façades of material wealth and temporal power, things are not as they seem.

Even the marriage proposal strikes us as odd, because Śumbha's exact words, transmitted through the messenger, are: "Choose either me or my valiant younger brother, Niśumbha. . . ." (5.113). The significance of this becomes clear only much later, when we discover exactly what Śumbha and Niśumbha symbolize (→ 9.4–41).

In response, the Devī issues a challenge, citing a vow to wed only him who conquers her in battle. This initiates an escalating series of challenges and counterchallenges that drive the narrative to its climax.

**5.122–129:** Piqued at the Devī's refusal, Sugrīva changes his tone from seductive to confrontational. Insultingly, he asks how she, a mere woman alone, can hope to defy Śumbha and Niśumbha, against whom even the gods are powerless. And he threatens her with the humiliation of being dragged away by her hair! This conversation ends very differently than it began, and the Devī's bemused playfulness stands in marked contrast to Sugrīva's increasing bluster. It is the same playfulness we saw previously when she serenely met Mahiṣa's demon army head on. All the demons—Madhu and Kaiṭabha, Mahiṣa, and those we have yet to meet—represent human vices, weaknesses, and failings, and without exception they take themselves very seriously. The Devī is blissfully beyond such silly and ultimately self-defeating posturing. Once again, she voices her challenge to Śumbha, and with her last words, "let him do what is fitting," the chapter closes on a note of ominous expectation.

# 6

## The Slaying of Dhūmralocana

6.1 The seer said:

6.2 "On hearing the Devī's words, the messenger was filled with indignation. He returned to the king of the daityas and related everything in great detail.

6.3 On hearing his messenger's report, the asura king grew enraged and said to Dhūmralocana, the chieftain of the daityas:

6.4 'Dhūmralocana, hasten with your army and bring that vile woman here by force, dragging her by the hair, kicking and screaming.

6.5 If anyone rises up to save her, even a god or other celestial being, he is to be slain.'"

6.6 The seer said:

6.7 "Commanded thus by Śumbha, the daitya Dhūmralocana quickly set off, accompanied by sixty thousand asuras.

6.8 And when he saw the Devī stationed on the snowy mountain, he thundered, 'Come to the presence of Śumbha and Niśumbha.

6.9 And if her highness will not come in gladness to my master now, then I will take her by force, dragging her by the hair, kicking and screaming.'

6.10 The Devī said:

6.11 'You who are sent by the lord of the daityas are mighty yourself and accompanied by your army. If you take me by force, what can I do to you?'"

6.12 The seer said:

6.13 "Thus addressed, the asura Dhūmralocana rushed at her. Thereupon, with a contemptuous outcry, Ambikā reduced him to ashes.

6.14 The great army of asuras, now provoked, rained sharp arrows, spears, and axes upon Ambikā.

6.15 Then the lion, the Devī's mount, angrily shook its mane. Emitting a terrifying roar, it fell upon the demon army.

6.16 With blows of its paws, it slew some daityas and crushed others in its jaws. And it trampled other great asuras under its hind legs.

6.17 With its claws, the lion tore into the entrails of some and beheaded others with the stroke of a paw.

6.18 It tore the arms and heads off others still, and tossing its mane, it lapped up the blood from the bellies of others.

6.19 In an instant that noble, infuriated lion which bore the Devī wreaked destruction on all that army.

6.20 When he heard that the Devī had slain the asura Dhūmralocana and that her lion had destroyed his entire army,

6.21 Śumbha, the king of daityas, shook with rage. His lower lip quivering, he commanded the two great asuras, Caṇḍa and Muṇḍa:

6.22 'Caṇḍa! Muṇḍa! Go there with immense forces, and bring her here at once,

6.23 seizing her by the hair or tying her up. But if you hesitate to do this, then let all the asuras with all their weapons strike her down in battle.

6.24 When that vile woman has been wounded and her lion slain, seize her, bind her, and bring her here without delay!'"

# Chapter 6 Commentary

**6.1–9**: At news of the Devī's refusal of marriage, Śumbha flies into a rage. Suddenly the ardently desired "jewel among women" (5.92, 5.100) becomes "that vile woman" (6.4). The word used is *duṣṭā,* rendered by previous translators as "shrew" (Pargiter, Jagadīśvarānanda), "wicked woman" (Coburn, Sharma), "wretch of a woman" (Śivānanda), "proud lass" (Siddhināthānanda), and "naughty one" (Satyānanda). *Duṣṭā* definitely conveys the idea of sexual impurity and is applied to adulteresses and other women of loose morals. There is no doubt that Śumbha's intention is to be insulting, although not excessively so, and any stronger English term would be inappropriate here.[1]

This would be a classic case of sour grapes, except that Śumbha is bent on possessing the beautiful Devī by any means, even if that means having her taken by force and slaying anyone who attempts to intervene. To that end he dispatches Dhūmralocana ("the smoky-eyed one"), whose name aptly describes the dim-witted thug whose vision is clouded, metaphorically, by the smoke of ignorance. Remember that the Aparājitāstuti employs *dhūmrā* as an epithet of the Devī (5.12) in reference to the obscuring power of her māyā, which is, of course, the source of the asura's ignorance. Note Dhūmralocana's sarcasm when he addresses the Devī with the deferential "her highness" (*bhavatī*) and in the next breath threatens her with force (6.9).

**6.10–19:** The Devī's reply (6.11) seems innocent enough, but when Dhūmralocana suddenly rushes at her, she instantaneously destroys him with an outcry of contempt, the sound *huṁ*. Understanding only the rule of force, Dhūmralocana quickly falls victim to the proverbial violence that begets violence.

Previously, sound has been associated with the divine creative power; here it represents destructive might. Such a show of strength is mere play for the Devī, and when she unleashes her lion to wreak havoc upon Dhūmralocana's accompanying forces, sixty thousand strong, we are reminded of the similarly effortless destruction of Mahiṣa's army in the second chapter.

**6.20–24:** Śumbha is angered to the point of losing self-control. His lower lip quivers with rage as he next sends Caṇḍa and Muṇḍa and an immense army to reattempt Dhūmralocana's failed mission. In his desperation to possess the Devī, the asura no longer cares whether "that vile woman" be delivered unharmed or beaten into submission (6.23–24). He simply wants to possess her. Similarly, thwarted human ambition breeds intemperance, and the goal becomes success at any cost. On that note, the Devīmāhātmya's shortest chapter ends.

# 7

## The Slaying of Caṇḍa and Muṇḍa

7.1 The seer said:

7.2 "Headed by Caṇḍa and Muṇḍa, the daityas' fourfold army of elephants, charioteers, cavalry, and infantry went forth at Śumbha's command, brandishing weapons.

7.3 They saw the Devī smiling gently, seated upon her lion atop the great, golden peak of the highest mountain.

7.4 Seeing her, they contrived to carry her off. While some approached with swords drawn and bows poised in readiness,

7.5 Ambikā cried out angrily against those foes, and in wrath her face turned as black as ink.

7.6 From her scowling brow, Kālī sprang forth, frightful of countenance and armed with sword and noose,

7.7 bearing a strange skull-topped staff, adorned with a garland of skulls, and clad in a tiger's skin. Her emaciated flesh appalling,

7.8 her mouth gaping, her lolling tongue horrifying, her sunken eyes glowing red, she filled the four quarters of the sky with her roars.

7.9 Swiftly falling upon the great asuras in that army, she slew and devoured those hosts of the gods' foes.

7.10 Attacking the rear guard and seizing the elephants with their drivers, warriors, and bells, she flung them into her mouth with a single hand.

7.11 In like manner, she tossed the cavalry with its horses and the charioteers with their chariots into her mouth and ground them furiously between her teeth.

7.12 She seized one asura by the hair and another by the throat. Crushing another underfoot, she slammed yet another against her breast.

7.13 The weapons and great missiles the asuras hurled she caught in her mouth and ground angrily between her teeth.

7.14 All that army of mighty and evil-natured asuras she ravaged, devouring some and beating others severely.

7.15 She struck down some with her sword and battered others with her skull-topped staff. Other asuras met their destruction between her gnashing teeth.

7.16 When Caṇḍa saw the entire army of asuras swiftly struck down, he rushed at the terrifying Kālī.

7.17 With a formidable deluge of arrows, that great asura engulfed the glowering Kālī while Muṇḍa hurled discuses at her by the thousands,

7.18 myriad discuses that entered her mouth as so many solar orbs vanishing into the denseness of a cloud.

7.19 With a terrifying roar, Kālī laughed in fury, her fearsome teeth gleaming within her ghastly mouth.

7.20 Mounting her great lion, the Devī rushed at Caṇḍa, seized him by the hair, and severed his head with her sword.

7.21 Seeing Caṇḍa slain, Muṇḍa attacked her. She pushed him to the ground and struck him in fury with her sword.

7.22 Seeing Caṇḍa and also the most valorous Muṇḍa slain, the remaining army panicked and fled in all directions.

7.23 And Kālī, grasping the heads of Caṇḍa and Muṇḍa, approached Caṇḍikā. Mingling fierce, loud laughter with her words, she said:

7.24 'I here present to you Caṇḍa and Muṇḍa as two great offerings in the sacrifice of battle. You yourself shall slay Śumbha and Niśumbha.'"

7.25 The seer said:

7.26 "When she saw those two great asuras, Caṇḍa and Muṇḍa, brought before her, the auspicious Caṇḍikā spoke these playful words to Kālī:

7.27 'Because you have overpowered Caṇḍa and Muṇḍa and delivered them to me, you, O Devī, will henceforth be known in the world as Cāmuṇḍā.'"

# Chapter 7 Commentary

**7.1–8:** As the bloodthirsty demon army approaches the resplendent Devī seated on the mountaintop, the epic magnificence of the scene signals a momentous event. We are not kept long in anticipation. Suddenly the Devī's gentle smile melts to ink-black wrath, and from her scowling brow springs forth the formidable goddess Kālī. Previously, Durgā emerged as a great radiance from the scowling faces of Viṣṇu, Śiva, and the other gods (2.9–13). This time, in a complete reversal, Kālī emerges as utter blackness from the radiant form of the sattvic Ambikā-Kauśikī, who had only recently come forth from the body of Pārvatī, leaving her darkened and renamed Kālikā, "the black one" (5.85–88). We've been given a graphic vision of the Devī's power of inexhaustible metamorphosis.

Kālī is not merely a secondary emanation of the Devī, as this passage might lead us to think. According to the understanding that developed in later centuries, she is the supreme Devī herself in another form, with multiple aspects of her own. Śrī Rāmakṛṣṇa remarked that, in many household shrines, Kālī is worshiped as Śyāmā, the tender dispeller of fear and granter of boons. In times of natural disasters, she is invoked as the protective Rakṣākālī. As Śmaśānakālī, the embodiment of destructive power, she haunts the cremation grounds in the company of howling jackals and terrifying female spirits, and as Mahākālī she is the formless Śakti who is not different from the Absolute.[1] At the Dakṣiṇeśvar Temple, where Śrī Rāmakṛṣṇa served as priest, Kālī is revered as the beautiful Bhavatāriṇī ("redeemer of the universe").

**7.9–22:** In the violent and grisly battle that ends with the slaughter of Caṇḍa and Muṇḍa, Kālī's favored method of destruction is to pulverize her enemies between her teeth, warranting mention three times in rapid succession (7.11, 7.13, 7.15). The image of grinding teeth brings to mind a turning millstone that crushes grain into flour, and from there it is not a large leap to the revolving wheel of time (*kālacakra*), which metaphorically grinds all things to dust. The name Kālī is the feminine form of the adjective *kāla,* meaning "dark" or "blue-black." This is probably related to the masculine noun *kāla* ("time"), an epithet of Śiva. As his śakti, or power, Kālī is ever-turning time, the relentless devourer who brings all things to an end. Note also the cosmic imagery of the myriad discuses hurled by Muṇḍa that disappear into her mouth "as so many solar orbs vanishing into the denseness of a cloud" (7.17–18).

**7.23–27:** Viṣṇu's slaying of Madhu and Kaiṭabha in the first chapter hinged on a pun (→ 1.88–1.103). There is word-play again in connection with the slaying of Caṇḍa and Muṇḍa when Kālī, delivering the heads of the demon pair to the auspicious Caṇḍikā-Ambikā as trophies of battle, is given the nickname Cāmuṇḍā. Historically, Cāmuṇḍā appears to have been a non-Āryan goddess who was assimilated to Kālī, and this passage in the Devīmāhātmya marks her initial appearance in Sanskrit literature.[2] Even today temple images of Cāmuṇḍā in Bhubaneśvar and Jajpur (Orissa) portray the goddess as emaciated, with protruding bones and fierce, round eyes bulging from their sunken sockets. The Jajpur Cāmuṇḍā bares her teeth, and her four hands hold cleaver, spear, skull-cup, and human head (*muṇḍa*).[3]

Why does Cāmuṇḍā leave the task of slaying Śumbha and Niśumbha to the auspicious Caṇḍikā herself? In the destruction of Caṇḍa and Muṇḍa we saw her violent, horrific aspect in action, just as in ordinary life drastic, heavy-handed means are sometimes necessary to defeat evil. But in the final battle for enlightenment, it is the Devī's sattvic power that rends the veil of nescience and grants the liberating vision. What we have here is a scene of the Devī talking to herself, as it were, since all her forms are but her own projections. She will make that fact clear before her final confrontation with Śumbha.

A deeper understanding of Cāmuṇḍā emerges from the Navārṇamantra, a nine-syllable Tantric mantra, which the 18th-century commentator Bhāskararāya considered as important as the Devīmāhātmya itself in the worship of the Devī.[4] This mantra, *aiṁ hrīṁ klīṁ cāmuṇḍāyai vicce,* begins with the three bījas that together identify the Devī as pure being (sat), consciousness (cit), and bliss (ānanda). In the Navārṇamantra the customary salutation (*namaḥ*) is unspoken but understood, and the name Cāmuṇḍā in the dative case (*cāmuṇḍāyai,* "to Cāmuṇḍā") occupies a pivotal position. While interpretations of this mantra are highly esoteric and often contradict one another in detail, they all agree that it is Cāmuṇḍā who severs the knot of ignorance, cuts through the illusion of duality, and reveals the Absolute. Although the Navārṇamantra, like any other Tantric mantra, cannot be understood, let alone translated, in a strictly semantic sense, it is generally interpreted as a prayer to the immanent-yet-transcendent Devī for the highest knowledge, which grants release from all limitation.

# 8

## The Slaying of Raktabīja

8.1 The seer said:

8.2 "After Caṇḍa was killed, Muṇḍa slain, and the vast armies annihilated, the lord of asuras

8.3 burned with rage. His reason overcome, Śumbha ordered the marshaling of all the demon hosts:

8.4 'Now let the daitya clans with all their troops go forth, the eighty-six Udāyudha and the eighty-four Kambu families, together with their forces.

8.5 Let the fifty Koṭivīrya families and the hundred Dhaumra clans depart at my command.

8.6 So also at my command, let the Kālaka, Daurhṛda, Maurya, and Kālakeya asuras set out in haste, armed for battle.'

8.7 Having issued his orders, Śumbha, the despotic lord of asuras, went forth, attended by many thousands of mighty troops.

8.8 Seeing that most formidable army approach, Caṇḍikā filled the space between earth and sky with the resonance of her bowstring.

8.9 Thereupon her lion emitted a deafening roar, O king, and Ambikā heightened the noise with her clanging bell.

8.10 Kālī drowned out the din of bowstring, lion, and bell, filling every direction with terrifying howls from her gaping mouth.

8.11 Hearing the tumult, the enraged demon armies closed in on the Devī, her lion, and Kālī from all four sides.

8.12 O king, at that very moment, to insure the well-being of the supreme gods and to annihilate their adversaries, surpassingly brave and powerful

8.13 śaktis, the gods' embodied powers, sprang forth from the bodies of Brahmā, Śiva, Skanda, Viṣṇu, and Indra, mirroring the form of each. They approached Caṇḍikā.

8.14 Whatever that god's form was, whatever his adornments and his mount, in that very form his śakti went forth to combat the asuras.

8.15 In a celestial chariot drawn by swans, Brahmā's śakti came forth with prayer beads and waterpot in hand. She is called Brahmāṇī.

8.16 Māheśvarī arrived astride a bull, holding the finest trident, wearing great serpents for bracelets, and adorned with the crescent moon.

8.17 Ambikā, having the war god's form and riding a fine peacock, came forth as Kaumārī with spear in hand to fight against the daityas.

8.18 Likewise the śakti Vaiṣṇavī, mounted on Garuḍa, approached holding conch, discus, mace, bow, and sword.

8.19 The śakti of Hari, who bears the unique form of the sacrificial boar, came forward as Vārāhī in that boarlike aspect.

8.20 Nārasiṁhī, resembling Viṣṇu's embodiment as a man-lion, arrived there, scattering the constellations with the toss of her mane.

8.21 Thousand-eyed like Indra, and in like manner with thunderbolt in hand, Aindrī arrived riding on the lord of elephants.

8.22 Then Śiva, surrounded by those śaktis of the gods, said to Caṇḍikā, 'Let the asuras quickly be slain for my satisfaction.'

8.23 Thereupon from the Devī's body there issued forth Caṇḍikā's own terrifying śakti, savage in her fury and howling like a hundred jackals.

8.24 And she, the unvanquished one, said to Śiva of dark, matted locks, 'Go, my lord, as my messenger to Śumbha and Niśumbha.

8.25 Say to those two arrogant dānavas, Śumbha and Niśumbha, and to the other dānavas assembled there for battle:

8.26 "Indra must regain the three worlds, the gods must again enjoy the sacrificial oblations, and you must return to the nether world if you wish to live.

8.27 But if through the conceit of strength you are desirous of battle, then come and let my jackals be satiated with your flesh!"'

8.28 Since the Devī appointed Śiva himself as messenger, she has come to be known in this world as Śivadūtī.

8.29 Hearing Śiva declare the Devī's words, the great asuras were filled with indignation and went to where Kātyāyanī stood.

8.30 At the outbreak of battle, the gods' adversaries, arrogant in their anger, rained torrents of arrows, spears, and lances upon the Devī.

8.31 And she, with great arrows shot from her resounding bow, playfully split asunder their hurtling arrows, lances, spears, and axes.

8.32 Kālī roamed about the battlefront, slashing her enemies to shreds with her spear and crushing them with her skull-topped staff.

8.33 And Brahmāṇī, wherever she went, left her enemies sapped of strength, disabled by the holy water sprinkled from her waterpot.

8.34 Māheśvarī slew the daityas with her trident; so, too, did Vaiṣṇavī with her discus, Kaumārī with her spear, and the wrathful

8.35 Aindrī with her thunderbolt. Daityas and dānavas, torn asunder, fell by the hundreds, discharging torrents of blood upon the earth.

8.36 They fell, scattered by blows from Vārāhī's boarlike snout, pierced through the chest by her tusks, and ripped apart by her discus.

8.37 Nārasiṁhī, tearing other great asuras apart with her claws and devouring them, roamed about the battlefield, filling the sky with her roars.

8.38 Dazed by Śivadūtī's violent laughter, the asuras fell to the ground, and she devoured those fallen ones.

8.39 When the enemy troops saw the enraged band of Mothers crushing the mighty asuras by diverse means, they fled.

8.40 Seeing the remaining daityas flee, tormented thus by the band of Mothers, the great asura Raktabīja went forth in anger to do battle.

8.41 Whenever a drop of blood fell from his body to the ground, an asura of like measure would rise up from the earth.

8.42 With club in hand the great asura fought with Indra's śakti. Then Aindrī struck Raktabīja with her thunderbolt.

8.43 Blood streamed in torrents from the stricken asura, and from that blood rose up warriors of identical form and might.

8.44 As many drops of blood fell from his body, so many beings of equal valor, strength, and courage arose,

8.45 and those who sprang up from his blood battled there with the Mothers ever more fiercely, hurling the most formidable of weapons.

8.46 When the Devī's thunderbolt struck Raktabīja's head, blood flowed again, and from it asuras were born by the thousands.

8.47 In the combat Vaiṣṇavī attacked the lord of asuras with her discus, and Aindrī beat him with her mace.

8.48 Blood flowed from the cuts of Vaiṣṇavī's discus, and therefrom great asuras of equal measure arose by the thousands and filled the world.

8.49 Kaumārī with her spear, Vārāhī with her sword, and Māheśvarī with her trident struck the great asura Raktabīja,

8.50 and he, the mighty, rage-filled daitya, struck all the Mothers one by one with his club.

8.51 Out of the blood that streamed upon the earth from the relentless wounds of spear, lance, and other weapons, asuras sprang up by the hundreds,

8.52 and those demons born from this one demon's flowing blood pervaded all the world. Utter terror seized the gods.

8.53 Caṇḍikā burst into laughter at their despair and said to Kālī, 'O Cāmuṇḍā, open wide your mouth

8.54 and quickly drink in the drops of blood from my weapons' blows and the great asuras born therefrom.

8.55 Roam about on the battlefield and devour the great demons sprung from Raktabīja. So shall this daitya, drained of blood, go to his destruction.

8.56 As you consume those fierce asuras, others shall not arise.' Having spoken thus, the Devī attacked Raktabīja with her lance,

8.57 while Kālī avidly lapped up his blood. Raktabīja turned upon Caṇḍikā with his club,

8.58 but his cudgel blows caused her not even the slightest pain. From his beaten body blood flowed copiously

8.59 in every direction, and Cāmuṇḍā engulfed it with her mouth. And within her mouth those great asuras who sprang into being from the flow,

8.60 those she now devoured, even while drinking Raktabīja's blood.

8.61 The Devī assailed Raktabīja with lance, thunderbolt, arrows, swords, and spears while Cāmuṇḍā drank his blood.

8.62 O king, battered by that array of weapons and drained of blood, the great asura Raktabīja toppled to the ground.

8.63 The gods attained immeasurable joy, O king, and the band of Mothers born from them danced about, intoxicated with blood."

# Chapter 8 Commentary

**8.1–7:** Śumbha loses all reason upon news of the second failed mission and the loss of his two servants. Overpowered by lust and rage, he marshals the vast numbers of his demonic hosts, clan by clan: the Udāyudha ("with upraised weapons"), the Kambu ("plunderer"), the Koṭivīrya ("eminently brave"), the Dhūmra ("smoky"), the Kālaka ("dark, black"), the Daurhṛda ("evil-hearted, villainous"), the Maurya (possibly "destroyer"), and the Kālakeya, also expressing darkness. This mobilization is the next step in the steady escalation.

**8.8–10:** At this point the Devī's opposing forces consist of the lovely Cāṇḍikā-Ambikā, her lion, and the horrific Kālī. Here the text employs various forms of sound to express divine power: the bowstring's resonance, the lion's roar, the clanging of the bell, and—drowning them all out—Kālī's bloodcurdling howls. "Filling every direction" signifies divine omnipresence.

**8.11–21:** As the enraged asura throngs circle round, the Devī multiplies her forces. She calls forth seven śaktis or individual energies from the bodies of the male gods (8.13). Each śakti, personified as the god's female counterpart, displays the specific signs of the corresponding deity: his form, adornments, weapons, and vehicle.

From Brahmā emerges Brahmāṇī, riding in a swan-yoked chariot and personifying sattvic, purifying power. In Hindu tradition the swan (*haṁsa*) possesses the ability to separate milk from water, metaphorically to distinguish what is true and abiding from what is impermanent and fleeting. When repeated many times over, *haṁsa, haṁsa, haṁsa*. . . is perceived in reversal as the mantra *so 'haṁ, so 'haṁ, so 'haṁ*. . . , meaning "I am that," "I am Brahman." Brahmāṇī's prayer beads symbolize *japa* (repetition of the mantra) and therefore contemplation of the Divine. The waterpot, symbolizing wealth, fertility, and immortality,[1] also contains her power of purification in the form of holy water.

Māheśvarī is the feminine derivative of Maheśvara ("Great Lord"), an epithet of Śiva as the destroyer of ignorance and the lord of yogis. She appears riding the bull Nandi, a symbol of dharma, who stands on the four legs of truth, purity, compassion, and generosity.[2] Māheśvarī is bedecked with Śiva's traditional symbols: the trident (signifying creation, preservation, and dissolution), serpents (symbolizing immortality, fertility, regeneration, and the eternal cycle of time),[3] and the crescent moon (symbolizing passing time, measured by the lunar waxing and waning).[4]

Kaumārī is the śakti of Śiva's son Kumāra (Skanda), the war god represented as a beautiful youth. As his power, she challenges the spiritually ignorant to battle and thus offers the opportunity for inner growth. Her peacock, Paravāṇi, represents alternatively the glory of the manifest universe or the bewitching power of avidyāmāyā.[5] What distinguishes the two readings is merely a difference of attitude regarding the world.

Viṣṇu contributes three śaktis to the group of seven. First comes Vaiṣṇavī, the śakti of his supreme form, who emerges mounted on the fabulous bird Garuḍa and holds the symbols of conch, discus, mace, bow, and sword. Traditionally, Viṣṇu has ten avatāras or earthly incarnations, which follow an evolutionary progression through the forms of fish, tortoise, boar, man-lion, dwarf, the ax-wielding Paraśu Rāma, the Rāma of the Rāmāyaṇa, Kṛṣṇa, the Buddha, and the yet to be born Kalki, whose arrival will mark the end of the present *yuga,* or world-age. Vārāhī is the śakti of Viṣṇu's third or boar incarnation. The ferocious Nārasiṁhī, half-woman and half-lioness, symbolizes the awakening of human consciousness within the physical (animal) body. Whatever it may have meant to the author who conceived it, for us the image of constellations being scattered by the toss of Nārasiṁhi's mane reflects with rare poetry that human consciousness is not limited to the confines of the physical body and surrounding environs, but soars through the power of imagination to the realm of the stars.

Aindrī, like the all-seeing Indra, has a thousand eyes, wields the thunderbolt (*vajra*) that represents strength, and rides upon the elephant Airāvata, an imposing mount for the chief of the Vedic gods. The scholar Thomas B. Coburn notes that Aindrī and the names of the other śaktis, except for Brahmāṇī, are not feminine versions of the male names but derivative forms that mean "belonging to" or "proceeding from." He suggests the reason, especially in Aindrī's case, may be to break with the earlier mythological concept of goddess-as-consort in order to express the idea of goddess-as-power. In the Ṛgveda and throughout the epic period, Indra's consort is well known as Indrāṇī. The name Aindrī, first found in the Devīmāhātmya, refashions her identity as independent from her previous role of divine spouse.[6]

Just as we understand the radiance (tejas) of the male gods from which the Devī's form coalesced (2.9–19) to represent not their own individual powers but her power inherent in them, here, too, we should regard the śaktis not as the gods' own powers but as diverse manifestations of the one Śakti. She herself makes this point clear later on, when she identifies the śaktis as projections of her own power. When they withdraw, it is not back into the gods from whom they emerged, but directly into her (10.5–8).

**8.22–28**: The Śākta view of the Devī as superior to and independent of the male gods becomes abundantly clear when Śiva, who so far seems to have had the role of a bystander, finds himself surrounded by the seven śaktis and makes the unexpected remark, "Let the asuras quickly be slain for my satisfaction." This is not just puzzling, but presumptuous. At least the Devī finds it so, because immediately from her body steps forth her own śakti, more terrifying than all the others. Here called Aparājitā ("the unvanquished one"), this śakti orders Śiva himself to deliver an ultimatum to Śumbha and Niśumbha! Note the symmetry here with Śumbha's employment of Sugrīva as a messenger. Accordingly, this immensely powerful śakti is also named Śivadūtī ("she whose messenger is Śiva," 8.28). The point of this name, and of the incident that prompted it, is that no god, however powerful, is superior to the power (śakti) of the Divine Mother.

**8.29–39:** Inevitably another battle breaks out after the asuras confront the Devī, here called Kātyāyanī. Later described as gentle-faced and adorned with three eyes (11.25), Kātyāyanī was probably the family goddess of the Āryan sages known as the Kātyas. The name reveals her Vedic credentials, although her three eyes suggest a later Śaiva influence.[7] Sources earlier than the Devīmāhātmya, notably the Durgāstotra and Aniruddha's hymn from the Harivaṁśa, equate her with Durgā. The Vāmanapurāṇa describes her incomparable effulgence as shining throughout the world. Without question, the name Kātyāyanī is equivalent to the names Durgā, Caṇḍikā, and Ambikā in signifying the Devī's supreme form.

Once again, the Devī makes a playful, effortless assault on the asuras. While she remains serene and seemingly above the fray, the śaktis engage more intensively in the battle, each according to her unique abilities. The contrast between the fierce Kālī and the lovely Brahmāṇī is especially instructive. Kālī's energy is shown as raw and brutal as she slashes and batters away (8.32). Brahmāṇī, on the other hand, demonstrates a gentler power. Call it conscience or innate goodness. We have all been on the verge of doing something we know to be wrong, when an inner voice appeals to our higher sensibility and restrains us. That nobler impulse is symbolized by the sprinkling of Brahmāṇī's holy water, which leaves her enemies—and our disgraceful urges—sapped of strength (8.33).

Verse 8.39 refers to the seven śaktis collectively as the mātṛgaṇa ("band of mothers"). Known also as the Saptamātṛkās ("Seven Little Mothers"), or simply as the Mothers, these fierce goddesses fight for the preservation of the world.[8] Although they are extremely ancient in origin and originally quite different in character, the allegory of the Devīmāhātmya presents them as individualized and internalized powers in the sādhaka's struggle for spiritual enlightenment.

**8.40–52:** When the demon Raktabīja strides onto the battlefield in the wake of the fleeing demons, he simultaneously makes his first appearance in Sanskrit literature.[9] His very name ("he whose seed is blood") identifies him as a force to be reckoned with, for whenever a drop of his blood falls to earth, another demon of equal size and strength springs up. Although only one of Śumbha's retainers, he possesses immense power—enough to warrant as much attention in the text as the chief asura, Mahiṣa, did in the second carita. The account of each one's battle scene runs to twenty-three verses.

The Mothers' attacks fail to kill him but only draw the blood from which countless other asuras proliferate until utter terror seizes the gods (8.52). Note the symmetry between their terror and the fear that earlier gripped the asuras who fled from the wrathful Mothers (8.39).

**8.53–63:** Caṇḍikā only laughs at the gods' despair, because even this fierce battle is nothing but her divine play. Ever in control, she instructs the gruesome Cāmuṇḍā-Kālī to drink the drops of Raktabīja's blood as they fall, and soon the asura lies dead.

Allegorically, Raktabīja's amazing replicative ability and the rajasic redness of his blood symbolize the almost unstoppable power of desire. Here we must make the distinction that not all desire is evil. Like everything else in the universe, desire comes in many colors, depending on the particular mixture of the three guṇas. The Devī herself takes form as desire, expressed by the metaphor of thirst in the Aparājitāstuti (5.35–37). But the kind of desire Raktabīja represents is not the divine thirst to experience the joys of the creation, but an aggressive, perverted grasping that stems from the ego's aching, existential deficiency. Such desire never remains satisfied for long, and the more it is gratified, the more it proliferates. The ghastly image of Kālī lapping up the copious flow of Raktabīja's blood, which swarms with nascent demons, illustrates graphically that desire is best dealt with before it gets out of hand. Here Kālī's destructive power manifests as a protective, beneficial force.

Esoterically, Kālī's slaying of Raktabīja relates to consciousness at a broader and deeper level. Raktabīja's replicative power symbolizes the working of the mind, whose every wave (vṛtti) gives rise to others. The battle with the Mothers recalls Patañjali's instruction to counter negative thought-waves with their opposite. Much to our dismay, just as a conscious attempt to "think good thoughts" often results in arousing our awareness of their opposite (for such is the nature of our dualistic mode of thinking), the Mothers' attacks only draw more blood and create more demons. Patañjali's advice is to counter negative thought-waves with positive ones and then to relinquish identification with both. According to Śākta sādhana, here is where Cāmuṇḍā-Kālī comes in. Cāmuṇḍā is the power of concentrated awareness that leads to the awakening of spiritual consciousness, and her slaying of Raktabīja symbolizes that awakening through the destruction or cessation of the vṛttis.[10] The grisly scene of Raktabīja's destruction illustrates the meaning of the Navārṇamantra (7.23–27): that Cāmuṇḍā is the Divine Mother acting to grant passage from the relative to the Absolute. She alone is the liberating knowledge that stills the vṛttis and brings union with the Divine.

While the gods rejoice at Raktabīja's defeat, the Seven Little Mothers revel in a blood-intoxicated dance that preserves the distant memory of their primordial, violent nature.

# 9

## The Slaying of Niśumbha

9.1 The king said:

9.2 "Wonderful is this, revered sir, that you have told me about the Devī's glorious deed in slaying Raktabīja.

9.3 I wish to hear more about what Śumbha and the wrathful Niśumbha did after Raktabīja was killed."

9.4 The seer said:

9.5 "After Raktabīja was killed and the others slain in battle, Śumbha and Niśumbha fell into unparalleled rage.

9.6 Seeing that his mighty army was being slaughtered, Niśumba was overcome with fury and rushed forward with the best of his demon forces.

9.7 In front of him, behind him, and on both sides, great asuras, their lips compressed in anger, advanced to slay the Devī.

9.8 Having battled the Mothers, Śumbha, mighty in valor and surrounded by his forces, came forward in fury to attack the Devī.

9.9 Fierce fighting erupted between them, and like two thunderclouds, Śumbha and Niśumbha rained down torrents of arrows on the Devī.

9.10 Caṇḍikā intercepted them with her own volley of arrows and struck the demon chiefs in the limbs with a stream of weapons.

9.11 Niśumbha, seizing his sharpened spear and shining shield, struck the lion, the Devī's magnificent mount, on the head.

9.12 Her lion assaulted, the Devī swiftly cut through Niśumbha's superb sword with her razor-sharp arrow and through his shield, emblazoned with eight moons.

9.13 His shield and sword broken, the asura hurled his spear, and as it came toward her, that, too, the Devī cut in half with her discus.

9.14 Blustering with rage, the dānava Niśumbha seized his lance, and as it came flying, the Devī crushed it with a blow of her fist.

9.15 Then swinging his club, Niśumbha flung it at Caṇḍikā. The Devī's trident reduced it to ashes.

9.16 After wounding the onrushing demon chief with ax in hand, the Devī forced him to the ground with a volley of arrows.

9.17 When he saw Niśumbha, his brother of fearsome strength, lying fallen on the ground, Śumbha moved forward, greatly enraged, to slay Ambikā.

9.18 Standing in his chariot and holding aloft magnificent weapons, he shone forth and filled the entire sky with his eight incomparable arms.

9. 19 While she watched him approach, the Devī sounded her conch, set off an unbearable reverberation with her bowstring,

9.20 and filled the firmament with the ringing of her bell, which sapped the strength of the assembled demon armies.

9.21 Then the lion filled every direction with great roars that caused even the elephants' mighty prowess to falter.

9.22 Kālī sprang skyward and alighted, pounding the earth with her two hands. The noise drowned out all the previous sounds.

9.23 Śivadūtī laughed loudly and menacingly. When the asuras grew terrified at the sounds, Śumbha flew into a monstrous rage.

9.24 Ambikā cried out for him, that evil-natured one, to stop, and the gods cheered her on to victory from their positions in the sky.

9.25 But Śumbha approached and hurled a fearsome, flaming spear, an oncoming mass of fire that the Devī's own firebrand warded off.

9.26 Śumbha's leonine roar pervaded the space between heaven, earth, and the netherworld, but the Devī's violent thunderclap drowned it out, O king.

9.27 The Devī split Śumbha's flying arrows with sharp arrows of her own, and likewise he split hers, each discharging arrows by the hundreds and thousands.

9.28 Then the enraged Caṇḍikā pierced Śumbha with her lance. Wounded, he fainted and fell to the ground.

9.29 Meanwhile Niśumbha, regaining consciousness, seized his bow and shot arrows at the Devī, Kālī, and the lion.

9.30 And then, creating ten thousand arms for himself, the daitya chief, that son of Diti, engulfed Caṇḍikā with ten thousand discuses.

9.31 Thus provoked, the glorious Durgā, who destroys adversity and afflictions, cut through his discuses and missiles with arrows of her own.

9.32 Niśumbha, surrounded by his demon army, swiftly seized his club and rushed at Caṇḍikā to kill her.

9.33 Instantly she split the onrushing Niśumbha's club with her keen-edged sword. He grasped his lance,

9.34 and as he approached with weapon in hand, Caṇḍikā pierced him, the afflictor of the gods, through the heart with a swiftly hurled spear.

9.35 From his heart's gaping wound came forth another mighty and valorous being, who shouted for the Devī to stop.

9.36 Bursting into derisive laughter, she severed his head with her sword, and the figure who had thus emerged fell to the ground.

9.37 The lion then devoured the asuras whose necks it had crushed with its fearsome fangs, while Kālī and Śivadūtī devoured others.

9.38 Great asuras perished, pierced through by Kaumārī's spear; others shrank away from the water sanctified by Brahmāṇī's mantras.

9.39 Others fell, ripped open by Māheśvarī's trident; some lay on the ground, smashed by the blows of Vārāhī's snout.

9.40 Dānavas were cut to pieces, some by Vaiṣṇavī's discus and others by the thunderbolt discharged from Aindrī's fingertips.

9.41 Some asuras perished, some fled from the great battle, and others were devoured by Kālī, Śivadūtī, and the lion."

# Chapter 9 Commentary

**9.1–3:** The word *māhātmya,* which is an element of the title Devīmāhātmya, appears in the text for the first time in verse 9.2 and will recur several times in Chapter 12. Derived from *mahātman* ("having a noble nature"), *māhātmya* is an abstract noun meaning "magnanimity, majesty, exaltedness." By extension, it came to denote a kind of literary composition that glorifies the "distinctive greatness" of a deity, a sacred place, or anything else worthy of veneration.[1]

**9.4–41:** In a long battle sequence, the Devī fights one-on-one first with Niśumbha, then with Śumbha, and again with Niśumbha. At the end, Niśumbha is slain, and Śumbha lies unconscious. To understand the nature of this battle, we need to know exactly what Niśumbha represents, but by chapter's end, the slain asura still remains an indistinct personality. The structure of the battle affords an important clue, however. The vacillation, wherein one brother is disabled only as the other rises up again, hints at the intimate connection between the two. At the beginning of the next chapter, which forms a seamless continuation of the narrative, we learn that Niśumbha was to Śumbha "as dear to him as life itself" (10.2). If we recall also Śumbha's puzzling marriage proposal, made through the messenger, that the Devī choose either him or his valiant younger brother, Niśumbha (5.113), we see again an extreme intimacy. From this, we can deduce that if Śumbha is the ego (ahaṁkāra), Niśumbha is its tag-along sibling, the persistent, clinging sense of attachment (*mamatva*, *mamatā*).[2] Niśumbha is as dear to Śumbha as life itself, because the ego cherishes its attachment to body, mind, possessions, and all the other adjuncts that shape its identity.

In Sanskrit, such an adjunct is called an *upādhi,* meaning variously a defining attribute, a limiting qualification, a substitute, anything that may be taken for something else, appearance mistaken for reality. The ego's sense of identity derives from the totality of a human being's upadhis: physical appearance, demeanor, likes and dislikes, family roles and relationships, relationships outside the family, and societal roles involving gender, profession, nationality, religious affiliation, and whatever else makes each one of us unique. While Śumbha represents the subjective ego-awareness itself (I-ness), Niśumbha symbolizes the attachment to all its objective attributes (me-ness and my-ness). The Devī's battle with the asura brothers is the infinite spirit's struggle with the finite ego's persistent, borrowed sense of personal identity. Ego and attachment are almost inextricably iinked, and when one brother is knocked out, the other rises up again.

Niśumbha, gloriously arrayed, represents attachment to fame, influence, wealth, possessions, and the identity they confer. His shield emblazoned with eight moons is a sign of personal identity. But in the end, all that is of little value; the final meaning of *upādhi* is not "defining attribute" but "appearance mistaken for reality." That point is made when Niśumbha, in all his splendor, is knocked senseless to the ground. Even so, he rises up again in horrifying desperation, a monster with ten thousand arms, grasping as it were at the countless pieces of his individuality that, in truth, are worthless tokens of his separation from the Infinite. The Devī shatters them all.

Then with her spear, she penetrates his heart. Sometimes spiritual awakening dawns only after the experience of great pain, a severe wounding of the heart. The suffering of the king and the merchant over their worldly losses is that pain of mamatva ("my-ness"), or attachment (1.42, 44). Now Niśumbha's essence appears from his heart's gaping wound, still reluctant to let go, pleading for the Devī to stop, but exposed and defenseless before her sword of knowledge. She slays him, and with Niśumbha destroyed, only Śumbha remains.

# 10

## The Slaying of Śumbha

10.1 The seer said:

10.2 "Seeing the lifeless body of Niśumbha, the brother who was as dear to him as life itself, and seeing his forces being slaughtered, the enraged Śumbha spoke these words:

10.3 'O Durgā, who are corrupt with the arrogance of power, do not show your pride here, for though you are haughty, you fight depending on the strength of others.'

10.4 The Devī said:

10.5 'I am alone here in the world. Who else is there besides me? Behold, O vile one! These are but projections of my own power, now entering back into me.'

10.6 Thereupon all those goddesses, led by Brahmāṇī, merged into the Devī's body. Then Ambikā alone remained.

10.7 The Devī said:

10.8 'I have now withdrawn the many forms I inhabited here, projected by my power. I stand alone. Be resolute in combat.'"

10.9 The seer said:

10.10 "Then a horrific battle broke out between the two of them, the Devī and Śumbha, while all the gods and asuras looked on.

10.11 With showers of arrows, sharp weapons, and terrifying missiles, the two met again in a combat that frightened all the world.

10.12 The wondrous weapons that Ambikā now unleashed by the hundreds, the daitya chief deflected with defensive strikes.

10.13 And the magic missiles that he hurled, the supreme Devī shattered playfully with fierce cries of contempt.

10.14 Then the asura covered her with hundreds of arrows. Provoked, the Devī discharged her arrows and split his bow.

10.15 His bow broken, the daitya chief took up his spear, but even as it rested in his hand, the Devī cut through it with her discus.

10.16 Then, grasping his sword, emblazoned with a hundred moons, the supreme lord of the daityas rushed at the Devī.

10.17 As he advanced, Caṇḍikā broke his sword with sharp arrows shot from her bow, and also his shield that shone as the sun's rays.

10.18 His steed slain, his bow broken, his chariot wrecked, the daitya grasped his fearsome mace, intent on destroying Ambikā.

10.19 With sharp arrows, she shattered the onrushing Śumbha's mace. Still, he rushed at her with fist upraised.

10.20 The daitya chief slammed his fist down on the Devī's heart, and she struck him on the chest with her palm.

10.21 Struck by that blow, the demon king fell to the ground. At once, he rose up again,

10.22 and springing upward, he seized the Devī and ascended high into the sky. There in mid-air Caṇḍikā battled with him.

10.23 In the sky, the daitya and Caṇḍikā fought hand to hand as never before, to the astonishment of saints and sages.

10.24 And after prolonged combat, Ambikā snatched him up, swung him around, and flung him to the earth.

10.25 Striking the ground, the evil one immediately raised his fist and ran forward, desirous of destroying Ambikā.

10.26 The Devī thrust her spear through his chest and threw that onrushing lord of all demonic creatures to the ground.

10.27 Pierced through by the Devī's weapon, his life-breath gone, he fell to the ground, shaking all the earth together with its oceans, islands, and mountains.

10.28 When the evil one was slain, all the universe became calm, regaining its natural order, and the sky cleared.

10.29 The flaming clouds of portent that formerly gathered now subsided, and rivers again flowed along their courses when Śumbha fell slain.

10.30 All the hosts of gods were overjoyed when he lay slain, and the celestial musicians sang sweetly.

10.31 Others sounded their instruments, and throngs of heavenly nymphs danced. Favorable winds blew, and the sun shone in glory.

10.32 The sacred fires glowed peacefully, and the sounds born of the four directions faded away."

# Chapter 10 Commentary

**10.1–8:** The key to understanding the entire third carita lies in the first six verses of Chapter 10. Note that Śumbha addresses the Devī as Durgā (10.3), a reminder that his brother's slayer is the same supreme goddess who vanquished Mahiṣāsura. With the many names used to refer to her—Devī, Caṇḍikā, Ambikā, Kālī, and a profusion of others—it is easy to forget that the Devī is indeed one. Śumbha has forgotten. In chiding her for depending on the strength of others, he only betrays his ignorance, a refusal to recognize the unity of all existence. The Devi reveals that she is one without a second, saying, "I am alone here in the world. Who else is there besides me?" (10.5). Following this proclamation of divine unity, which has been called the *mahāvākya,* or great dictum, of the Devīmāhātmya,[1] she explains that all the goddesses who fought beside her—Kālī, Śivadūtī, and the Mothers—are but projections of her power, as are all the other forms she inhabits (10.8).

Still, Śumbha, as the individual ego, can never reach beyond Mahāmāyā's deluding veil, which limits consciousness to the dimensions of time and space and creates the sense of separate but impermanent selfhood. Until Mahāmāyā lifts that veil, the truth of infinite being is beyond comprehension.

The structure of the third carita reveals a pattern of parallel challenge, counterchallenge, and escalation. The initial antagonism involves only the Devī and Sugrīva, then the Devī and Dhūmralocana. When Caṇḍa and Muṇḍa are sent to capture her, she multiplies her strength by calling forth Kālī, who defeats the two servants and earns the nickname Cāmuṇḍā. When Śumbha mobilizes the asura clans, the Devī calls forth the Seven Little Mothers and Śivadūtī. Then the self-replicating Raktabīja brings the escalation to a climax with the countless asuras born from his blood. His defeat signals the de-escalation that ends with the Devī finally facing Śumbha alone (10.8).

The parallelism suggests that just as Kālī, the Mothers, and Śivadūtī are multiple manifestations of the one Devī, the asuras we have met along the way are Śumbha's—the ego's—projections. Are we to conclude that the Devī and Śumbha are equals? Not at all. The Divine Mother is infinite consciousness, and everything in the universe is her projection—even Śumbha. He is a bit of finite awareness whose subsequent manifestations symbolize human weaknesses and failings, the further fragmentations of something that is already partial and imperfect. Caṇḍa and Muṇḍa are the ego's self-aggrandizing and lust-inciting capacities. They drive Śumbha's crazed desire to possess the Devī's lovely physical form, and they flatter him with an account of his own dazzling wealth and power, which, stolen from the gods, is not really his at all. The messenger Sugrīva represents the ego's capacity for guile in attempting to have its way, and when that fails, Dhūmralocana steps in as the abject ignorance that resorts to brute force. Raktabīja stands for desire pathologized as rampant greed, which befouls the whole world with its presence; and Niśumbha is the sense of attachment that makes all the others possible. He occupies the closest position to ego itself. In these all-too-human asuras we recognize our own faults and shortcomings.

The slaying of Niśumbha is qualitatively different from the Devī's previous conquests. Earlier Dhūmralocana, Caṇḍa, and Muṇḍa attempted to capture the Devī by physical force, just as in the first carita Viṣṇu's struggle against Madhu and Kaiṭabha involved brute strength until Mahāmāyā outwitted the asura pair. In each struggle, tamas is the predominant guṇa. Rajas becomes foremost in the battle with Mahiṣa, whose rage is fueled by desire, and in the conflict with Raktabīja, who embodies desire out of control. Since Niśumbha symbolizes the more abstract sense of attachment, the battles with him and his brother Śumbha are existential struggles to be won only by higher forms of spiritual insight through the Devī's sattvic power. The struggle with Śumbha is the most rarefied and difficult of all, because the ego, the motivating force behind all the other asuras, is extremely elusive. In total, the battle scenes teach that sādhana involves every dimension of who we are, from our gross (physical) and subtle (mental) components, involving actions and attitudes, to the causal ignorance that masks our true nature.

**10.9–27:** For the first time in any battle scene, the weapons—both the Devī's and the asura's—are described as *divya,* translated here as "wondrous" (10.12) and "magic" (10.13). Of course, when the Devī revealed herself as the source of the various gods' powers in the second chapter, it goes without saying that those, too, displayed a divine quality. But the specific mention here of the weapons as divya (from the same source as *deva, devī,* and English *divine*) indicates a spiritual struggle well beyond the realm of day-to-day existence. This is confirmed again when the combatants metaphorically rise above the earth and fight in midair (10.22) until Śumbha is defeated (10.27).

**10.28–32:** The figure of Niśumbha taught us that we define ourselves by how we look, what we own, what we do, and what others think of us. Even after his defeat, even after the ego is stripped of all its identifying marks, the sense of individuality still hangs on in the person of Śumbha. Why? Because he still clings to the idea that he is a separate and unique entity. It is not unknown in deep meditation to feel oneself slipping into a still deeper state and to pull back for fear of losing one's identity or maybe even one's own existence. But in truth, to let the ego slip away is to relinquish a smaller identity for an unimaginably greater one; in misreading reality, we have also misread ourselves. The "death of ego" marks the passage from ever-changing becoming into pure being.

The Devīmāhātmya expresses this enlightenment with the beatific image of a universe restored to perfect order (10.28–32). It presents a lovely picture of calm and clarity, wherein everything is exactly as it should be, but those poetic images fall far short of expressing the soul's release into inexpressible infinitude. Earlier, the Devīmāhātmya itself admitted this inability when it extolled the divine reality as surpassing thought (4.6) and "unfathomable even to Viṣṇu, Śiva, and the other gods" (4.7).

Mystical experience—the immediate, unmediated knowledge of the Divine—cannot be described, but that has not discouraged people of all times and places from attempting to describe the ineffable with the cultural metaphors available to them. Hindus call it saccidānanda ("being-consciousness-bliss") or pūrṇa ("full"), referring to its absolute wholeness. Buddhists employ the negative imagery of *śūnyatā* ("emptiness"), because it is devoid of all form. Kabbalistic Jews use the term *Ein Sof* ("there is no end") to allude to the infinite Absolute beyond all qualities. Christians speak of "the peace that passeth all understanding." In the third century the Neoplatonist mystic Plotinus described the soul's return to its source as "the flight of the alone to the Alone." In our present age, we might prefer the psychological objectivity of "unitive dimension of being" or the philosophical abstraction of "ultimate reality." In the Śvetāśvataropaniṣad, a text the author(s) of the Devīmāhātmya surely knew, the sage addresses his disciples as "children of immortal bliss" and declares, "I have known the unchanging, primeval One, the indwelling Self of all, everywhere present and all-pervading, whom the wise declare to be free from birth and eternal" (ŚU 3.21).

# 11

## Hymn to Nārāyaṇī

11.1 The seer said:

11.2 "After the Devī had slain the great asura chief, Indra and the other gods, led by Agni, praised Kātyāyanī for granting their wishes. With hopes fulfilled, their faces beamed.

11.3 'O Devī, who remove the sufferings of those who take refuge in you, be gracious. Be gracious, mother of the entire world. Be gracious, ruler of all. Protect the universe, O Devī, who are the ruler of the moving and the unmoving.

11.4 You alone are the sustaining power of the world, for you abide in the form of the earth. By you, who exist in the form of water, all this universe prospers, O Devī of unsurpassable strength.

11.5 Of boundless might, you are Viṣṇu's power, the source of all, the supreme māyā. Deluded, O Devī, is all this universe. In this world, you alone, when pleased, are the cause of liberation.

11.6 All forms of knowledge are your aspects, O Devī, as are all women in the world. By you alone, the Mother, is this world filled. What praise can be sung to you who are beyond praise?

11.7 O Devī, who have become all things, who bestow enjoyment and liberation—when you are praised, what words, however excellent, can extol you?

11.8 Salutation be to you, Devī Nārāyaṇī, who abide as intelligence in the hearts of all beings, granting heavenly reward and final liberation.

11.9 Salutation be to you, Nārāyaṇī, who bring change as the moments of ever-passing time, who are the power at the cessation of the universe.

11.10 Salutation be to you, Nārāyaṇī, who are the good of all good, the auspicious one; to you who accomplish every intent; to you, the refuge, the all-knowing, shining Gaurī!

11.11 Salutation be to you, Nārāyaṇī, who are the power of creation, sustenance, and destruction; who are eternal; who are the source and embodiment of the threefold energy.

11.12 Salutation be to you, Nārāyaṇī, who are intent on rescuing the distressed and afflicted that take refuge in you; to you, O Devī, who remove the suffering of all.

11.13 Salutation be to you, Nārāyaṇī, who assume the form of Brahmāṇī, riding in a swan-yoked chariot, O Devī, and sprinkling sanctified water.

11.14 Salutation be to you, Nārāyaṇī, who have the form of Māheśvarī, bearing trident, moon, and serpent, and riding a mighty bull.

11.15 Salutation be to you, Nārāyaṇī, who have the form of Kaumārī, the faultless one attended by peacock and cock, and bearing a great spear.

11.16 Salutation be to you, Nārāyaṇī, who have the form of Vaiṣṇavī, holding the supreme weapons of conch, discus, mace, and bow. Be gracious!

11.17 Salutation be to you, Nārāyaṇī, auspicious one, who have Viṣṇu's boarlike form, grasping a great, formidable discus and uplifting the earth with your tusks.

11.18 Salutation be to you, Nārāyaṇī, who in the ferocious form of the man-lion are intent on killing the daityas and protecting the three worlds.

11.19 Salutation be to you, Nārāyaṇī, who are adorned with diadem, great thunderbolt, and thousand-eyed radiance; to you, O Aindrī, who took the demon Vṛtra's life-breath!

11.20 Salutation be to you, Nārāyaṇī, who in the form of Śivadūtī, of frightful visage and piercing shrieks, slew the mighty demon army.

11.21 Salutation be to you, Nārāyaṇī, whose mouth bares its terrifying teeth and whose neck is adorned with a garland of skulls; to you, O Cāmuṇḍā, destroyer of Muṇḍa!

11.22 Salutation be to you, Nārāyaṇī, who are good fortune, modesty, great knowledge, faith, prosperity, satisfaction to the ancestral spirits, constancy, the great night, and the great illusion.

11.23 Salutation be to you, Nārāyaṇī, most excellent Sarasvatī, who are intelligence and well-being, the divine consort and the dark one, ever constant. Be gracious, O you who are supreme!

11.24 O Devī, who exist in the form of all, who are the ruler of all, possessing all power, protect us from fears. O Devī Durgā, salutation be to you!

11.25 May this gentle face of yours, adorned with three eyes, protect us in every way. O Kātyāyanī, salutation be to you!

11.26 May your terrible, flaming trident, exceedingly sharp and destroying all asuras, protect us from dread. O Bhadrakālī, salutation be to you!

11.27 May your bell that destroys the daityas' life-force and fills the world with its ringing protect us from all evils, O Devī, even as a mother protects her children.

11.28 May your sword, smeared with the mire of asuras' blood and fat and blazing as the sun's rays, be for our welfare. O Caṇḍikā, we bow to you!

11.29 When pleased, you destroy all afflictions, but when displeased, you thwart all aspirations. No calamity befalls those who have taken refuge in you, and they who resort to you become a refuge to others.

11.30 O Devī, multiplying your own form into many, you have wrought destruction on the mighty asuras who hate righteousness. O Ambikā, who else can accomplish that?

11.31 Who other than you abides in all forms of learning, in the sacred texts that are lights of understanding, in the primordial wisdom of the Vedas? Yet who else confounds this universe in the darkest abyss of attachment?

11.32 Where malevolent beings and venomous serpents lurk, where enemies and thieves abound, where forest conflagrations rage, there and even in mid-ocean you stand and protect the universe.

11.33 O ruler of the universe, you protect the universe. You are the essence of all things, and you support all that is. All kings must praise you, O revered one, and those who bow to you in devotion become the refuge of all.

11.34 Be gracious, O Devī. Even as you have destroyed the asuras, protect us always from the fear of enemies. May you subdue the evils of all the worlds and great disasters born of ominous portents.

11.35 To those who bow down to you, be gracious, O Devī, who remove the afflictions of all and who are worthy of praise by the dwellers of the three worlds. Confer your boons upon the worlds.'

11.36 The Devī said:

11.37 'O hosts of gods, I am the giver of boons. Whatever blessing is your heart's desire, choose that, and I will grant it for the welfare of the world.'

11.38 The gods said:

11.39 'O ruler of all, may you allay all the miseries of the three worlds and so, too, annihilate our enemies.'

11.40 The Devī said:

11.41 'When the twenty-eighth cycle in the age of the manu Vaivasvata has come, two other great asuras, also named Śumbha and Niśumbha, will arise.

11.42 Then shall I be born in the home of the cowherd Nanda, brought forth from Yaśodā's womb; and dwelling in the Vindhya Mountains, I shall destroy the two asuras.

11.43 Again, having incarnated on earth in a surpassingly horrific form, I shall slay the demons descended from Vipracitti.

11.44 Upon devouring those fierce asuras, my teeth will become red like pomegranate flowers.

11.45 Thereafter, in praise of me, the gods in heaven and the humans in the mortal realm will forever call me Raktadantikā.

11.46 Again, when no rain has fallen for a hundred years and there is no water on earth, then praised by sages, I shall appear, but not born of a womb.

11.47 Since I shall behold the sages with a hundred eyes, humankind will glorify me as Śatākṣī.

11.48 Causing the rains to fall, O gods, I shall support the entire world with life-sustaining vegetables brought forth from my own substance.

11.49 Thus shall I be celebrated on earth as Śākambharī,

11.50 and then also shall I slay a great asura called Durgama and thus come to be celebrated as the Devī Durgā.

11.51 Again, when I have assumed a terrible form in the Himālayas, I shall destroy malevolent beings for the protection of the sages.

11.52 Then all the sages, with bodies bowed, will praise me. Thus shall I come to be celebrated by the name of Bhīmadevī.

11.53 When a demon called Aruṇa wreaks great havoc in the three worlds, then shall I assume form as a swarm of countless bees

11.54 and slay the great asura for the welfare of the three worlds. Thus will people everywhere extol me as Bhrāmarī.

11.55 And so, whenever danger arises from demonic sources, I shall descend and bring about the complete destruction of enemies.'"

# Chapter 11 Commentary

**11.1–2:** By way of introduction to the fourth and final hymn, the Nārāyaṇīstuti (11.3–35), Indra and the other gods, this time led by Agni, approach the Devī in a spirit of thanksgiving. Here she is called Kātyāyanī (→ 8.29), a name used interchangeably with Caṇḍikā, Ambikā, and Durgā to denote her all-powerful aspect, presiding over the functions of creation, preservation, and destruction.[1]

**11.3:** Along with the preceding verse, the first four verses of the Nārāyaṇīstuti (11.3–6) and six near the end (11.29–34) are in a meter called *upajāti,* which has forty-four syllables per śloka. Like the elegant vasantatilakā meter of the Śakrādistuti, it imparts an eloquence to the exalted praise of the verses that frame the main body of the hymn. Reverting to the anuṣṭubh meter, the hymn's central portion (11.7–28), like that of the Aparājitāstuti, has the character of a litany.

The Nārāyaṇīstuti has other features in common with the preceding hymns. Like the Śakrādistuti, it comments on the action of the foregoing narrative, and with all three other hymns it shares common language and themes. In a sense, it is a summation of all that has gone before, and on that comprehensiveness rests its reputation as a central statement of Śākta theology and devotion.[2]

The opening verse concisely presents the themes of divine intervention (as removal of suffering), divine motherhood, sovereignty, and protection. The order of presentation progresses from the personal and immediate relationship with the Devī, who offers refuge and alleviates suffering, to the cosmic understanding that she is the mother of the universe, who rules over all that is moving and unmoving.

**11.4:** The themes here are support and nurture. The word *ādhāra* means both a physical support or substratum and a sustaining power. Since the verse also specifies that the Devī abides in physical form as the earth (*mahī*, having the connotation of ground, soil, or land), *ādhāra* is best understood as the energy that supports it.

Because the Devī exists in the form of water (*ap*), everything thrives (*āpyāyate*). Although the two Sanskrit words are unrelated (the verb deriving from *pyai,* "to swell, increase, overflow"), their alliteration and the coincidental connection of water and overflowing make for powerful imagery grounded in the world of nature. The much earlier Ṛgvedic hymns repeatedly refer to the Āpaḥ goddesses, "the Waters," as "our mothers." Semipersonified as spirits of the primeval water, these plural goddesses were identified with the universal principle of motherhood.[3] According to one hymn, before heaven and earth came into being, the Waters received the primal germ that contained the gods, all gathered together (ṚV 10.82.5–6). Even in later Vedic texts, which explore the idea of water as the basis of all fertility, the Āpaḥ goddesses retained their original connection to natural phenomena.

Combining the imagery of earth and water, the Nārāyaṇīstuti's second verse preserves primordial memories of the Mother Goddess as the earth itself and as the waters that cause it to bring forth its abundance. It praises the energy supporting this life-sustaining power of heaven and earth as the Devī's unsurpassable strength.

**11.5:** Next, the hymn celebrates māyā as both the deluding power that binds (avidyāmāyā) and the power that leads to the knowledge that liberates (vidyāmāyā). This single verse summarizes a longer passage (1.53–58) in which Medhas explains how Mahāmāyā, Viṣṇu's meditative sleep (yoganidrā), hurls people "into the whirlpool of attachment (mamatā, literally "my-ness") and "seizes the minds of even the wise and draws them into delusion." Yet, "it is she who graciously bestows liberation on humanity."

In the earlier passage, Medhas calls Mahāmāyā "the meditative sleep *of* [Viṣṇu,] the lord of the world" (*yoganidrā jagatpateḥ*) (1.54). The Aparājitāstuti employs the epithet Viṣṇumāyā, the deluding power *of* Viṣṇu (5.14–16). Both expressions carry the idea of possession, even though in the first instance Viṣṇu is clearly subject to the Devī's power at that point in the story. The present verse makes a subtle but significant departure with the term *vaiṣṇavī śaktiḥ,* which does not mean power as Viṣṇu's possession (that would be *viṣṇoḥ śaktiḥ* or *viṣṇuśaktiḥ*, but power in the Devī's own right, *operative through* but not necessarily *belonging to* Viṣṇu. The distinction may seem hairsplitting, but the broader implication is not. Even as māyā, the Devī is supreme (*paramā*).

By her the entire universe is deluded (*sammohita*). Some translations of this verse render the adjective as "enchanted,"[4] or "bewitched,"[5] and given that the third carita's general focus is on the sattvic Devī, the idea of her enchanting beauty is reasonable. Monier-Williams's *Sanskrit-English Dictionary* defines *sammohita* in both negative and conceivably positive terms as "stupefied, bewildered, fascinated, enraptured." But *sammohita* derives from *sammuh,* to which the same dictionary ascribes only the pejorative connotations of stupefaction, bewilderment, confusion, perplexity, and unconsciousness. In the overall context of Medhas's discourse on the reason for the king's and the merchant's misery (1.53–55), to which the present verse clearly alludes, the likely rendering of *sammohita* is "deluded."[6]

The same Mahāmāyā is, when gracious, the cause of liberation in this very world (11.5). The adjective *prasanna,* meaning either "gracious" or "pleased," leaves open the question of whether liberation is freely bestowed or earned. When the Śakrādistuti praises the Devī as "good fortune in the dwellings of the virtuous and misfortune in the abodes of the wicked" (4.5), it intimates that in this world of cause and effect we earn the consequences of our actions. Yet that same hymn extols her compassion even toward the wicked, whose misconduct she subdues (4.21). Thus we learn that the Mother operates through both principles. Similarly, Śrī Rāmakṛṣṇa answered the perennial philosophical question of grace and self-effort with the simple but profound teaching that the breeze of divine grace is always blowing and one needs only to set the sails of the mind to catch it.

The intimate relationship between grace and self-effort is further borne out by the adjective *prasanna* itself. It derives from the verb *prasad,* meaning either "to settle down, to become clear or calm" or "to become satisfied, pleased, or gracious." The former meaning reminds us of Patañjali's teaching that enlightenment follows upon the restraint of thought-waves in the field of consciousness (YS 1.2). For the restless, finite mind to open itself to the calm of infinite awareness, effort is necessary, but without the underlying constancy of divine consciousness in the first place, all effort would be futile. As with the concept of śraddhā (→ 4.5), we see an element of interaction between the human and the Divine. The word *prasanna,* with its range of meaning, validates equally the jñāni's self-effort in stilling the thought waves of the mind and the bhakta's intimate partaking of the Mother's love, which we may call divine grace.

**11.6:** "All forms of knowledge are your aspects" relates to ideas expressed earlier: "you are the light of understanding" (1.79), "you are the treasury that holds the taintless Vedic hymns" (4.10), and "you are the intelligence by which the essence of all scriptures is understood" (4.11). Śakti is pure consciousness (cit) and contains within herself all possible modifications of consciousness, which include the manifold forms of knowledge. The supreme, absolute knowledge (*vidyā*) is unitary, but this verse speaks of "knowledges" in the plural (vidyāḥ), referring to the relative or lower forms of knowledge that include all branches of learning: the sciences, philosophy, politics, agriculture, medicine, commerce, and every other intellectual or practical skill.

The laud that all women are her aspects and by her alone is this world filled echoes the Devī's abiding presence in the form of mother, incarnate not only in all women but in every creature (→ 5.71–73).

The rhetorical question, "What praise can be sung to you who are beyond praise?" recalls the Brahmāstuti's similar utterances (1.82–84), designed to suggest divine ineffability.

**11.7:** Switching to the anuṣṭubh meter, which will continue through verse 11.28, the hymn now assumes the character of a litany.

"O Devī, who have become all things" echoes Medhas's teaching that she has the world as her form (1.64). This is an unequivocal statement of pariṇāmavāda, the doctrine that the multiplicity we experience as the universe is an actual transformation of the ultimate unity and not merely an appearance. Just as clay is transformed into a pot through a change of form but not of substance, or as thread is woven into cloth, the Divine Mother herself takes form as her creation. In this point the nondual Śākta philosophy differs from Śaṁkarācārya's Advaita Vedānta, which embraces vivartavāda, the doctrine that the created universe is not a transformation but only an appearance—neither real nor wholly unreal—superimposed on the sole reality of the immutable Brahman.

The Śākta philosophy considers the physical universe—called *virāj*, the Devī's cosmic body—to be the supreme intellect permeating the aggregate of gross forms; in other words, consciousness manifest as matter. The term *virāj* (literally, "ruling far and wide, excellent, splendid") derives from a root meaning "to rule, shine, be beautiful, be eminent" and underscores the miraculous nature of the creation and its inherent worth. If we concede that the universe is "just māyā," we should do so with the Śākta understanding that māyā is nothing less than the creative aspect of divinity. Śākta nondualism proclaims that the natural universe, however imperfect in our experience, is "absolutely saturated in the Divine."[7] It is a point that the Devīmāhātmya makes emphatically: "She is eternal, having the world as her form" (1.64).

The other idea, which follows naturally and inevitably upon the doctrine of *pariṇāma* and which bears enormous weight, is contained in the eight-syllable compound, *bhuktimuktipradāyinī.* Its modest appearance belies its significance and leaves us wondering whether our author(s) found it so obvious as to warrant little more attention than that. For in that single expression lies a key to understanding the whole of the Devīmāhātmya.

The first element (*bhukti,* "worldly enjoyment") is implicit in earlier passages such as verse 4.15, which specifies the pleasures of honor, wealth, love and progeny that the propitious Devī bounteously bestows *in* this world. But its dramatic juxtaposition to the second element (*mukti,* "release"), signifying eternal liberation *from* this world, causes us to regard both in a new light.

We recall that the framing story concerns a king and a merchant who have each suffered betrayal and loss. The resulting inner turmoil follows them into the peaceful forest retreat of a holy man, who exposes the nature of their suffering by relating three stories of similarly dispossessed gods, evil demons, and the always-triumphant Devī. The first story reveals that she is the supreme reality who manifests as the universe. Perceived through our own veiled awareness, this universe appears polarized, filled with the clashing dualities of light and darkness, pleasure and pain, right and wrong, good and evil. The second story, through the example of Durgā's defeat of Mahiṣāsura, instructs the king how to live in the world, rewarded with the enjoyments that result from virtuous conduct. The third story, relating the destruction of Śumbha and Niśumbha, teaches the world-weary merchant how to break the bonds of saṁsāra and attain mukti, realization of the infinite, ever-blissful Self.

But for the king, there is a caveat. The word *bhukti* derives from the same verbal root, *bhuj* ("to enjoy, use, consume"), as the noun *bhoga,* which broadly encompasses enjoyment, eating, sexual pleasure, feeding upon, ruling over, and experiencing pleasure *or pain.* Bhukti, although world-affirming, carries the implicit warning that in the relative universe, where opposites define each other, to reach for one is to embrace both. Mukti, to the contrary, is world-transcending. The expression *bhuktimuktipradāyinī* tells us that the dazzling splendor of the universe is here for us to enjoy, but we must play by the rules, the dharma. Even then, the very fact of living an embodied existence leaves us subject to the inescapable processes of birth, growth, maturation, decline, death, and rebirth. The only way to escape the wheel of saṁsāra is to return to the ineffable source of the world's bewitching wonder. Finally, one who is enlightened (*prabuddha,* literally "awakened") recognizes that the Divine Mother is both nature and spirit[8] and that bhukti and mukti belong to a single consciousness.[9] The Devī presents both options, and the choice is ours.

Like the preceding verse, this one ends with the rhetorical question of how the ineffable Devī can be extolled.

**11.8:** The expression *buddhirupeṇa* ("in the form of intelligence") occurred in the Aparājitāstuti (5.20–22) and carries the identical meaning here. The first line of the present verse merely restates the idea more eloquently.

The theme of heavenly reward arose previously in the Śakrādistuti (4.18 and 23), and the commentary on those verses explained that in the Hindu cosmology, heavens and hells, like the earth, belong to the relative plane of existence and are no more than transitory states of reward or punishment.

The final phrase, *nārāyaṇi namo 'stu te* ("salutation be to you, Nārāyaṇī"), serves as the refrain of the next fifteen verses. Nowadays, the name Nārāyaṇī is regarded as an epithet of Viṣṇu's consort, Lakṣmī. It is the feminine form of Nārāyaṇa, which the Manusmṛti applies to Brahmā, but which the Mahābhārata applies to Viṣṇu and his avatāra, Kṛṣṇa. Nārāyaṇa signifies universal consciousness, inhabiting all forms: human beings, animals, and plants; mountains, rivers, and forests; the sun, the moon, and the distant stars.[10] The name is a compound of *nara* ("man, human being") and *ayana* ("going, walking, path, progress, place of refuge"), meaning that Nārāyaṇa (or, in this case, the Divine Mother Nārāyaṇī) is the ultimate resting place or goal of all humanity.[11]

**11.9:** "The moments of ever-passing time" refers not only to the constant change or transformation (pariṇāma) inherent in the time-space continuum but also and more specifically to the relentless, destructive power of time, which brings the universe to periodic dissolution within the never-ending cosmic cycle.

**11.10:** *Sarvamaṅgalamāṅgalye* means "to [you who are] the good of all good" (or "the auspiciousness of all that is auspicious"). Beneath the surface of all that is auspicious, the Divine Mother is the very essence of auspiciousness. She herself is Śivā, the auspicious one.

She is addressed as *sarvārthasādhike,* because she fulfills every aim or purpose (*artha*). Human life has four such aims (*puruṣārthas*): kāma (fulfillment of desire), artha (acquisition of wealth), dharma (fulfillment of duty), and *mokṣa* (liberation). Some spiritual teachers like to reorder the puruṣārthas as dharma-artha-kāma-mokṣa, because placing dharma first guarantees that righteousness will be the guiding principle for all the rest. Note that dharma, kāma, and artha relate to worldly life (bhukti) and that mokṣa is liberation (mukti) (→ 11.7). This distinction mirrors the difference between Suratha's concerns, which remain this-worldly and centered on the first three aims, and Samādhi's single remaining goal, which is spiritual liberation. Recognizing that, we see that the expressions *sarvārthasādhike* and *bhuktimuktipradāyinī* are virtually synonymous.

As *śaraṇyā,* the Divine Mother grants shelter and protection from all fears and dangers; in suggesting an unassailable place of refuge, the epithet is closely related in meaning to the name Durgā. *Tryambakā* ("three-eyed") refers to divine wisdom and omniscience, and *gaurī* or Gaurī (→ 4.38–42) denotes pure, shining consciousness.

This highly significant verse is older than the rest of the Nārāyaṇīstuti, being identical to the final verse of the Vedic Śrīsūkta, whose eight concluding ślokas were appended to the original hymn probably in Brāhmaṇic or Upaniṣadic times.[12]

**11.11:** As the universal power, the Devī Nārāyaṇī encompasses the threefold energies of creation, preservation, and destruction, generally personified in the Hindu pantheon as the gods Brahmā, Viṣṇu, and Śiva. These ultimately are not separate deities but different aspects of the one Īśvara ("Lord"), the transcendent Brahman associated with its inseparable power, variously called māyā, śakti, or prakṛti. But according to Śākta theology, the powers of creation, preservation, and destruction (*sṛṣṭisthitivināśāḥ*) belong to the Devī alone (→ 1.75–76), and all three functions are not merely singular events in the cosmic life cycle but interconnected processes in the daily, ongoing life of the natural world (→ 1.78).

The supreme Ādyā Śakti is *sanātanī* ("eternal, perpetual, permanent, primeval"), the uncaused cause of all things. Because the three guṇas are inherent within her, she is their source (*guṇāśrayā*); and because she projects and becomes the universe through the differentiated energies of those same guṇas, she is also their embodiment (*guṇamayā*). This same kind of circularity arose earlier in connection with the Devī's characterization as both the source and manifestation of intelligence (→ 4.10 and 4.11) and expresses once again the Śākta understanding of the seamless unity of being/becoming.

**11.12:** The Divine Mother, who is all-compassionate, comes quickly to the rescue of those who turn to her in times of calamity. This verse offers an eloquent, personalized expression of the same theme previously met in verses 4.17 and 11.3.

**11.13–19:** This passage praises the Seven Little Mothers in their original order of appearance in the eighth chapter, mostly repeating the initial descriptions (8.12–21) but amplifying the information about Vārāhī and Aindrī. The Purāṇic allusion to Vārāhī's lifting up the earth on her tusks symbolizes the power of physical sustenance (11.17).[13] Aindrī's slaying of Vṛtra (11.19) is a Śākta reinterpretation of a Ṛgvedic myth concerning the drought demon Vṛtra, who withheld the heavenly waters from creation. When the thunderbolt of the storm god Indra breached the drought demon's strongholds—a metaphor for clouds—the waters poured down upon the earth to fill the rivers and make the land fertile.[14] Indra's role in releasing the rain thus assures the earth's ability to sustain life. The Devīmāhātmya refashions this ancient myth by ascribing Vṛtra's destruction to the female śakti, Aindrī, who is the source of Indra's empowerment.

**11.20–21:** These verses extol the Divine Mother's terrifying forms as the bloodcurdling Śivadūtī and the crone-like Cāmuṇḍā, who is Kālī as the slayer of Caṇḍa and Muṇḍa as well as of Raktabījā (→ 8.53–63). Her destructive power, which annihilates evil, is praised through the symbolism of her devouring mouth;

but in the next breath, the garland of skulls adorning her neck and symbolizing the letters of the Sanskrit alphabet becomes a metaphor for creative power, relating her to Vāk, the Ṛgvedic feminine face of the supreme reality.

**11.22:** The first line of this verse enumerates auspicious qualities seen in the previous hymns: good fortune (4.5, 5.11 and 5.56), modesty (1.79, 4.5, and 5.44), great knowledge (1.77), faith (4.5 and 5.50), prosperity (1.79), the mantra *svadhā* (1.74 and 4.8), and constancy (*dhruvā* is synonymous with *nityā* in 1.73 and 5.10).

But in a dramatic shift the next line returns to darker epithets from the Brahmāstuti: kālarātri, the great night (→ 1.78) and Mahāmāyā, the great illusion (→ 1.77), both relating to tamasic power. This passage illustrates the impossibility of translating Sanskrit terms that have no English equivalent. For lack of anything better, we follow Pargiter, Jagadīśvarānanda, and Coburn in rendering *mahāmāyā* as "great illusion," even though that is somewhat misleading. The Śākta philosophy does not understand māyā as illusion in the sense of mere appearance or unreality (→ 1.53–58) but as the experience in time and space of self (ego) and not-self, rather than the experience of the undifferentiated wholeness of Self (ātman).[15] If, in the present passage, the inadequacy of language forces us to accept the definition of māyā as "illusion," then we should think of it as the illusion of separation. And we should never forget that in the Śākta understanding, both experiences, the partial and the full, are real.[16]

**11.23:** Contrasting the benign and the terrifying, the first line continues the imagery of the preceding verse, but the second line turns petitionary immediately before the refrain. This pattern of praise and petition characterizes the next five verses as well.

Sarasvatī, who is named in the text only once, is an ancient aspect of the Devī, recognized since early Vedic times. Her name means "abundantly flowing," and she was venerated first as the deified Sarasvatī River, believed to originate in the celestial realm. In the later Vedic age, she was understood as the flow of thought into the great, shining sea of consciousness[17] and repeatedly identified with Vāk.[18] As such, Sarasvatī-Vāk represents the intelligent power pervading creation. Even today she is revered as the beneficent goddess of knowledge and the arts.

In the present verse, Sarasvatī is readily identified with intelligence (medhā) and well-being (*bhūti*), although the latter word, denoting also prosperity and wealth, can be linked as easily to Lakṣmī. The epithet *bābhravi* derives from Babhru, a name the Mahābhārata applies variously to Kṛṣṇa-Viṣṇu or Śiva. Ostensibly, it denotes the śakti associated with one or the other of those gods, and its proximity to *tāmasi* ("O dark one") suggests a more likely connection with Śiva. Thus, the multiple names and epithets seem to associate the Devī with Brahmā, Viṣṇu, and Śiva, and suggest once again that the Divine Mother transcends sectarian boundaries. For a verse that begins with the idea of divine wisdom, this would be a fitting theme.

**11.24:** The appeal to Durgā as existing in the form of all reminds us of the Śākta acceptance of pariṇāmavāda, the doctrine that the Mother transforms herself into her creation, a position that Medhas expressed when he said that the world is her form (1.64). Praising her sovereignty and possession of all power, the verse establishes her universal supremacy. Asking for protection from fear, it echoes a similar request in the Śakrādistuti (4.4).

**11.25–28:** The Divine Mother's portrayal as gentle, terrible, and protective, together with the mention of specific weapons, creates in these four verses a parallel to the final four verses of the Śakrādistuti (4.24–27). In both hymns, the mantras are intended to ward off evil. At the end, the contrast of bright and dark seen above (11.22–23) is artfully transformed into a symbol of victory, as the Devī's sword (right knowledge), smeared with the asuras' gore (ignorance), blazes with the light of truth.

**11.29:** Marking a return to the upajāti meter, with which the hymn began, this verse rephrases the Śakrādistuti's assertion that the Devī is "good fortune in the dwellings of the virtuous and misfortune in the abodes of the wicked" (4.5), tying the consequences to divine pleasure or displeasure. The Devī's ability to thwart all aspirations when displeased stirs memories of the fearsome Vedic goddess Nirṛti, alluded to in the Aparājitāstuti (→ 5.11).

A new idea appears in the second half of the verse, where the Devī's power to grant refuge is said to work indirectly through the agency of those who have taken refuge in her.

**11.30:** Summarized in a single brief verse are the three overarching themes that successively dominate the three divisions of the Devīmāhātmya: first, that the Divine Mother is the One who projects the many; second, that she intervenes in this world to destroy evil; and third, that she alone is capable of granting liberation.

"Multiplying your own form into many" has repeated illustrations throughout the text. In the battle with Mahiṣa's army Durgā multiplies her powers by heaving the sighs that become her legions (2.53). In the confrontations with Śumbha and Niśumbha, she first summons Kālī from her scowling brow (7.6), then the Seven Little Mothers from the bodies of the gods (8.12–13), and finally Śivadūtī from her own form (8.23). Brahmā's hymn calls her the supreme reality (1.73) that differentiates (1.78) and abides as the soul of everything (1.82), an idea taken up by the subsequent hymns and the Prādhānika and Vaikṛtika Rahasyas. In Chapter 10, the process is reversed when the Devī tells Śumbha, "I am alone here in the world. . . . These [śaktis] are but projections of my own power, now entering back into me" (10.5). Beyond the allegory lies the metaphysical truth that the One becomes many while still and ever remaining one.

The second theme initially appeared when Medhas explained to Suratha and Samādhi that although the Devī is eternal (transcending the universe of time, space, and causation), she manifests in the world to accomplish the purpose of the gods—to uphold the cosmic and moral order (1.66). The theme of divine intervention is inseparable from the fact that struggles inevitably arise in the world of multiplicity.

We have seen time and again that the Devī always wins, for she is the supreme, ultimate, and only power in the universe. No one other than she can accomplish what she does, for the destruction of ignorance is synonymous with spiritual liberation, the predominant theme of the third carita.

**11.31:** Previously, the text linked the Devī to Vedic knowledge, calling her "the treasury that holds the taintless Vedic hymns, . . . the blessed Devī, who embodies the three Vedas" (4.10) and "the intelligence by which the essence of all scriptures is understood" (4.11). The Nārāyaṇīstuti repeats that she "abides in all forms of learning, in the sacred texts that are the lights of understanding, in the primordial wisdom of the Vedas." This insistent motif seeks to integrate the Devī's many non-Vedic forms into the hallowed Vedic tradition by identifying her with the supreme knowledge.

Yet, immediately following the imagery of dazzling light and soaring consciousness, this verse plunges into the abyss. Determined to affirm simultaneously the Mother's Vedic credentials and the unshakable, primal conviction that the Devī has her benign and terrible sides, the author characterizes her as Mahāmāyā, the great deluder who casts her dark spell of attachment over the universe. Since this last idea is phrased as a rhetorical question, the intent is once again to express the uniqueness of her power.

**11.32–35:** Many details relating to the Devī's protective role will be elaborated in Chapter 12, of which these verses are a foretaste. The specific language of this passage is not original to the Devīmāhātmya but drawn from older hymns, such as the Mahābhārata's Durgāstava and Durgāstotra.

The euphony of verse 11.33, which cannot be duplicated in English, warrants mention. Note the alliterative use of the element *viśva* ("all, universe"), appearing six times, and the similarity of *bhavatī* ("[you who are] worthy of adoration" or "revered one") and *bhavanti* ("[they] become").

To mark the end of the hymn and the transition back to narrative, verse 11.35 reverts to the standard anuṣṭubh meter.

**11.36–39:** The exchange between the Divine Mother and the gods runs parallel to the corresponding passage following the Śakrādistuti (4.31–37). In each instance, she offers a boon, and the gods respond. But there are differences as well. In the fourth chapter, the gods answer that with the defeat of Mahiṣāsura nothing remains to be done; still, they ask that the Devī intervene whenever future misfortune arises and that she bestow her abundance on any mortal who praises her with the hymns of the Devīmāhātmya. In Chapter 11, the gods' request is simply that she annihilate their enemies and allay the misery of the three worlds.

**11.40–42:** The Devī's prediction of her future manifestations in the world (11.40–55) builds upon Medhas's earlier declaration that although she is the eternal reality who embodies herself as the universe and pervades it, she emerges also in other ways (1.65). When she manifests specifically to uphold or restore the dharma ("to accomplish the purpose of the gods"), she is said to be born in the world (1.66). For a fuller understanding of the remarkable passage that follows, we must look to the

Mūrtirahasya ("The Secret Relating to Forms"), the last of the Devīmāhātmya's six aṅgas.

The problematical nature of the first prediction concerns the fact that having just slain Śumbha and Niśumbha, she announces that two other asuras of the same names will arise (11.41–42). It is important to remember that the framing story of Medhas, Suratha, and Samādhi takes place in the second manvantara, more than a billion and a half years ago according to mythological reckoning, and that Medhas began his story of Śumbha and Niśumbha with "long ago," placing it in a still more remote past. In that account, the Devī predicts the future Śumbha and Niśumbha, who will arise at the time of Kṛṣṇa's birth in the seventh manvantara. Her prediction is of future events that from our vantage point have already come to pass.

That solves one vexing problem but creates a different problem for the commentator. We have used Vindhyavāsini as powerful circumstantial evidence to trace Durgā's origin to the Neolithic period and to tie the origin of the demons Śumbha and Niśumbha to the non-Āryan peoples of north India among whom the legends of Kṛṣṇa's boyhood also arose. Here mythology and history collide, since we have attributed all the information surrounding the later Śumbha and Niśumbha to the original pair of demons. Admittedly, this does not stand up to rational scrutiny, but in the often convoluted and contradictory realm of Indian mythology, which disseminates in protean fashion, we can never hope to correlate myth and history. Our conflation of the identically named pairs of demons may in fact reflect more the historical development of the myth than its mythological truth.

Those reservations aside, we recall that when Viṣṇu planned to incarnate as Devakī's son, Kṛṣṇa, it was foretold that the infant would be killed by his wicked uncle, Kaṁsa. In order to thwart him, Viṣṇu persuaded Yoganidrā (Mahāmāyā) to be born simultaneously to Yaśodā. When the babies were switched and Kaṁsa attempted to dash Devakī's child against the paving stones, the baby assumed the goddess's eight-armed form and flew away to the Vindhya mountains, where she is still worshiped as Vindhyavāsinī.

The Mūrtirahasya, showing its Vaiṣṇava orientation, offers a radically different portrayal of this goddess born to Nanda and Yaśodā. It makes no mention of her dwelling-place in the Vindhyas, even though the Devīmāhātmya certainly does. Instead, it calls her Bhagavatī Nandā, implying a more beneficent deity than the bloodthirsty Vindhyavāsinī, and describes her not as black and bird-headed but as brilliant like the finest gold, magnificently ornamented, and identified with Viṣṇu's auspicious consort, variously named Indirā, Kamalā, Lakṣmī, and Śrī (MR 1–3).

Despite its gentler characterization, which is neither confirmed nor contradicted by the Devīmāhātmya, the Mūrtirahasya is essential for understanding the remainder of the Devī's prediction. The text of the Devīmāhātmya is ambiguous about how many future incarnations are meant. It seems to mention seven goddesses: the dweller in the Vindhyas (11.42), Raktadantikā (11.45), Śatākṣī (11.47), Śākambharī (11.49), Durgā (11.50), Bhīmādevī (11.52), and Bhrāmarī (11.54). The commentator Bhāskararāya agrees with this enumeration.[19] But the Mūrtirahasya reduces the number to five by stating outright that Śatākṣī, Śākambharī, and Durgā are one goddess (MR 15). That there are five manifestations is clearly understood by comparing the parallel structures of the Mūrtirahasya and the corresponding passage of the Devīmāhātmya.

**11.43–45**: After Vindhyavāsinī comes a particularly dreadful incarnation who slays the demonic sons descended from an asura named Vipracitti. In devouring them, her teeth become stained red with blood, and she is called Raktadantikā ("having blood-stained teeth"). Since the Mūrtirahasya and the other aṅgas became associated with the Devīmāhātmya around the 14th century, they reflect later Tantric developments possibly unknown to the author(s) of our text. That said, the Mūrtirahasya characterizes Raktadantikā as totally red in complexion, hair, eyes, teeth, tusks, nails, clothing, adornments, and weapons. As early as Paleolithic times, red was a symbol of life and fertility. Moreover, Raktadantikā is as red as the inside of a pomegranate, another symbol of fertility frequently connected with the Mother Goddess.[20] She is indeed terrifying, but to her devotees she is as faithful as a wife is to a husband, and she allays all fear. Broad as the earth and with mountainous breasts, she is a maternal goddess who satisfies all desires. She is known also as the Red Cāmuṇḍā or Yogeśvarī ("ruler of [divine] union") (MR 4–11).

**11.46–50:** The third manifestation is called Śatākṣī, Śākambharī, or Durgā, and the question of how she manifests claims our attention. We note that Vindhyavāsinī was born of Yaśodā's womb (11.42), although under supernatural circumstances. Raktadantikā's manner of manifestation remains unspecified; the text merely employs the participle *avatīrya* ("having descended, having become incarnate"), which neither confirms nor denies biological birth. Śākambharī specifically comes into being not born of a womb (*ayonijā*) (11.46). The reason is that she is the earth.

The nurturing Śākambharī is associated with fertile soil and vegetation. After a hundred years without rain, as Śatākṣī ("the hundred-eyed"), she pours her tears upon the drought-stricken earth, filling the rivers, reviving vegetation, and causing the land to bring forth all manner of edible plants.[21] The Mūrtirahasya's insistence that Śākambharī and Śatākṣī are the same goddess signifies a union of the earth's dark, fertile soil and the life-giving rain that falls from the sky. Śākambhari-Śatākṣī is the ancient Vedic Dyāvāpṛthivī by another name.

But the five-verse account of Śākambharī is not without difficulties. Most translators render *āvṛṣṭeḥ* (11.48) as "until the rain comes," but that reading makes no sense if Śākambharī and Śatākṣī are the same goddess. The Sanskrit is ambiguous, because the ablative *āvṛṣṭeḥ* can mean either a separation from the rain (a period of drought) or "proceeding from the rain," "because of the rain," or "after the rain." Among previous translators, only Pargiter grasped the logic of the context and rendered *āvṛṣṭeḥ* as "during a period of heavy rain."

The Mūrtirahasya describes Śākambharī as blue, with blue eyes, full breasts, a deep navel, and a slender waist with three ripples of skin, perhaps signifying furrows. One of her four hands holds a cornucopia of flowers, sprouts, roots, and various fruits and vegetables, signifying the abundance of her physical, nurturing presence as the earth itself. Hence, her name Śākambharī, which means "bearing vegetables" or "nourishing with herbs." Fulfilling every desire and removing every fear, she is renowned also as the hundred-eyed Śatākṣī and as Durgā. Subduing the wicked and dispelling all difficulties, she is known also as Umā, Gaurī, Satī, Caṇḍī, Kalikā, and Pārvatī, all names of the Goddess associated with Śiva (MR 12–16).

**11.51–52:** Historically, Bhīmādevī was an important goddess of the Himālayan region. Her mountain shrine, as described in the seventh century CE, was a place of pilgrimage, where devotees from all over India fasted and prayed before her image, a naturally occurring likeness in dark blue stone. Her name means "the fearsome goddess." As mentioned in the Devīmāhātmya, Bhīmādevī assumes a terrifying form in the Himālayas and kills malevolent beings for the protection of sages. She appears to be a fierce aspect of Tārā, one of the ten Mahāvidyās, who represent personifications of Śakti that reveal the knowledge of Brahman.[22] The Hindu Tārā is not to be confused with the usually gentle Tārā of Tibetan Buddhism, who represents compassion.[23] Instead, she is closely identified with Kālī[24] and described in the Mūrtirahasya as blue, with shining teeth and tusks and plump breasts. In her four hands she holds a glittering scimitar, a small drum, a severed head, and a drinking vessel. A solitary warrior goddess who grants desires, she is also known as Kālarātri.

**11.53–54:** Finally, in order to vanquish a demon named Aruṇa, the Devī takes form as Bhrāmarī. The name, which shows a connection to bees, belongs to an incarnation that the Mūrtirahasya describes as glittering, variegated, and bejeweled, surrounded by an impregnable circle of light and holding in her hand a swarm of multicolored bees. The aṅga also calls her "the great pestilence," which is at variance with her usual Tantric connection with sexual arousal.[25] Her description as either a great bee or as surrounded by a swarm of bees ties in with the common symbolism of the bee as sexual desire in Indian erotic literature.[26]

**11.55:** The Devī ends her remarkable recital with a general pledge of protection whenever demonic forces threaten. Summing up, we are struck by the atavistic nature of her predicted incarnations. These are aspects of the Goddess that hark back to very ancient times. Vindhyavāsinī connects her to fertility through the imagery of birds, whose eggs are an enduring and universal symbol of life and renewal; Śākambharī-Śatākṣī, to the productive union of earth and rain; Raktadantikā, to nature's death-dealing ferocity; Bhīmādevī, possibly to the terrifying menace of darkness; and Bhrāmarī, either to swarming pestilence or the sexual allure that spurs the generation of new life.

# 12

## The Promise of Blessings

12.1 The Devī said:

12.2 "I shall without doubt destroy every misfortune of those who with collected mind will praise me always with these hymns.

12.3 Those who recite the destruction of Madhu and Kaiṭabha, the killing of Mahiṣāsura, and the slaying of Śumbha and Niśumbha

12.4 with singleness of mind on the eighth, fourteenth, and ninth days of the lunar fortnight, and those who listen with devotion to this supreme poem of my glory

12.5 will have no evil befall them, nor any misfortunes arising from wrongdoing. For them there will be neither poverty nor separation from loved ones,

12.6 nor danger from enemies, robbers, or kings. Nor at any time will danger arise from weapons, fire, or flood.

12.7 Therefore this poem of my glory is to be recited by those of concentrated mind and heard always with devotion, for it is the supreme way to well-being.

12.8 May this glorification of mine put to rest all misfortunes born of pestilence, and also the three kinds of calamity.

12.9 Where it is always and rightly recited in my sanctuary, that place shall I never abandon. There my presence is abiding.

12.10 In the offering of oblations, in worship, in the fire ceremony, and in the great festival, all these deeds of mine are to be proclaimed and heard.

12.11 When offerings are made in worship, with or without proper knowledge, I shall receive them gladly and also the fire oblation performed in like manner.

12.12 At the great annual worship which is performed in the autumn season, those who hear this poem of my glory and are filled with devotion

12.13 will be freed by my grace from all afflictions and endowed with wealth, grain, and progeny. Of this there is no doubt.

12.14 Hearing of my glory, my auspicious manifestations, and my prowess in battles, they become fearless.

12.15 For those who hear my glorification, their adversaries go to utter destruction. Well-being comes to them, and their families rejoice.

12.16 For those troubled by nightmares or the ill-boding of stars, at rituals for averting evil this poem of my glory should always be heard.

12.17 It causes misfortunes and evil portents to subside, and it turns nightmares into sweet dreams.

12.18 It pacifies children overcome by seizures, and wherever discord divides, it best restores friendship.

12.19 It is unsurpassed in diminishing the might of all evil-doers. Truly its recitation brings about the destruction of fiends, ghosts, and ghouls.

12.20 This entire glorification of mine draws one near to me.

12.21 As by the offerings of finest cattle, flowers, gifts, incense, perfumes, and lights, made day and night for a year;

and as by the feeding of Brāhmaṇas, by oblations, by consecrated water;

12.22 and as by diverse other propitiations and offerings; so also by hearing the recital of my auspicious deeds am I pleased.

12.23 When heard, this poem of my glory removes impurities and grants freedom from disease. The relating of my births confers protection from evil spirits.

12.24 Since it recounts my deeds in battle, crushing the wicked daityas, when heard, it dispels all fear of enemies.

12.25 Praises uttered by you and the Brāhmanical seers and by Brahmā himself produce an auspicious mind.

12.26 When in a forest, or on a lonely road, or surrounded by a forest fire, when encircled by robbers in a desolate place or seized by enemies,

12.27 when stalked by lions and tigers or wild elephants in the jungle, when imprisoned or sentenced to death by a wrathful king,

12.28 when in a wind-tossed boat on the mighty sea or assailed by hurtling weapons in the midst of battle,

12.29 when caught in dreadful straits or tormented with agony, whoever remembers these deeds of mine is freed from danger.

12.30 By my power, lions and beasts, robbers and enemies flee far away from one who remembers these deeds of mine."

12.31 The seer said:

12.32 "Having spoken thus, the blessed Caṇḍikā, fierce in valor, vanished from the sight of the gods.

12.33 Their enemies struck down, the gods were delivered from affliction. They reclaimed their own dominions as before, and all partook of their shares in the sacrifices.

12.34 As for the daityas, after the Devī had slain in battle those two enemies of the gods—Śumbha, the afflictor of the world, terribly fierce and unequaled in prowess,

12.35 and Niśumbha, great in valor—the rest of them returned to the netherworld.

12.36 Thus, O king, does the blessed Devī, though eternal, manifest again and again for the protection of the world.

12.37 By her this universe is deluded. She herself brings forth everything. Entreated, she bestows right knowledge; propitiated, she bestows prosperity.

12.38 O king, by her all this universe is pervaded, by Mahākālī, who takes form as the great destroyer at the end of time.

12.39 At that time, she herself is the great destroyer. Existing from all eternity, she herself becomes the creation. She, the eternal one, sustains all beings.

12.40 In times of well-being she is indeed good fortune, granting prosperity in the homes of humankind. In times of privation, she exists as misfortune, bringing about ruin.

12.41 And so, praised and worshiped with flowers, incense, perfumes, and the like, she grants wealth, progeny, and a pure mind established in righteousness."

# Chapter 12 Commentary

**12.1–30:** Most of Chapter 12 is in the form of a phalaśruti, a conventional listing of the merits and benefits of reciting or hearing a sacred text. Here the Devī herself instructs that her māhātmya is to be recited and heard with a collected mind (12.2, 12.4, 12.7). Full, unwavering attention is essential to all forms of sādhana, including ritual worship and meditation, and must be given likewise to singing the Divine Mother's praises. Besides attentiveness, devotion is paramount (12.4, 12.7, 12.12).

The text recommends the times and places for recitation: on certain auspicious days during the lunar month (12.4), during the great autumn festival (12.10, 12.12), and in the Devī's sanctuary (12.9). Historically, temples to Durgā were well-established by the sixth century CE.[1] What the text adds to our knowledge is that recitation of the Devīmāhātmya draws the divine presence to those places and renders them holy (12.9). The great autumn festival (12.10, 12.12) also was well-established by the time of the Devīmāhātmya. Either it is an ancient prototype of the modern, autumn Navarātri, or the present-day festival is its direct continuation, a harvest celebration with roots in the agricultural cycle. Of this there can be no doubt; even the yellow complexion of the Durgā images made for the occasion call to mind the golden fields of ripened wheat and rice glowing in the autumn sunlight. The description of formal pūjā, accompanied by the recitation of the Devīmāhātmya, and the sacrificial *homa* fire (12.10), applies to the Durgā Pūjā today as well as then. During this festival period it is highly likely that worship then, as now, took place in the temples as well as in private dwellings, for the text makes a concession to those not skilled in the arts of worship and sacrifice, saying that even acts imperfectly performed will be gladly received (12.11).

At the same time, the recitation of the text alone is as pleasing to the Devī as lavish offerings, ritual worship, and the observance of other religious duties (12.21–22). The verses, or mantras, themselves have the power to draw the reciter or hearer toward divinity (12.20), to remove impurities (12.23), and to produce an auspicious mind (12.25). The māhātmya is thus "the supreme way to well-being" (12.7).

When properly recited or heard, the Devīmāhātmya provides access to its inherent power. Even as the sacred verses draw the individualized consciousness toward the universal consciousness, the Devī's energy proceeding through the sacred words destroys every misfortune (12.2) so that no evil will befall her devotees (12.5). Because it protects from "misfortunes arising from wrongdoing" (12.5), the Divine Mother's power over the law of karma is a manifestation of her grace. The text confirms that her devotees "will be freed by my grace from all afflictions" (12.13), among them poverty and separation from loved ones (12.5).

The six dangers listed in verse 12.6 are of two kinds: those arising from human agency (enemies, robbers, kings, and weapons), and those arising from natural disasters (fire and flood). These are two categories within the "three kinds of calamity," which the māhātmya is said to put to rest (12.8). The three categories are defined as *adhibhautika* (stemming from the actions of others in the objective world external to oneself), *adhidaivika* (concerning the gods or divine agency operating through material objects—the so-called "acts of God," such as earthquakes, fires, and floods), and *adhyātmika* (concerning oneself, such as physical illness, mental distress, and self-inflicted suffering).

This triad affects our physical as well as our psychological well-being. In regard to the body, the recitation of the text wards off "misfortunes born of pestilence" (12.8) and childhood seizures (12.18), and it "grants freedom from disease" (12.23). Additionally, it protects against physical threats (12.6, 12.26–30), including those from natural disasters, wild animals, warfare, crime, and societal injustice. These last-mentioned verses are extraordinarily rich in material found in earlier hymn texts, and we find that verses 12.26 through 28 actually quote from those sources: the Ṛgvedic Rātrī Khila, the Durgāstotra, the Durgāstava, and Viṣṇu's Praise of Nidrā from the Harivaṁśa. Most pervasive is the reference to forests, usually characterized in the earlier hymns as "dreary" to emphasize the dangers lurking therein. What distinguishes the concluding passage (12.26–30) from other portions of the phalaśruti is its exclusive emphasis on danger within the physical environment. Based on much older texts, which indicate that those ideas were widely attested and even standardized, this final portion of the phalaśruti proper is obviously of very ancient origin.

The verses of the phalaśruti that deal with psychological or nonphysical dangers are not found in those earlier sources. Verses 12.13 through 15, after emphasizing the positive material benefits of wealth, grain, and progeny, turn to the question of fear in general; they connect the Devī's prowess in battle and the destruction of enemies to fearlessness, well-being, and rejoicing. The linkage of the allegorical victories, representing psychological and spiritual growth, and the resulting fearlessness recurs in verse 12.24. Concerning more specific forms of mental well-being, it is said that the recitation or hearing of the text "turns nightmares into sweet dreams" (12.17), relieves anxiety caused by the ill-boding of stars and other evil portents (12.16–17), and nullifies the influence of evil spirits (12.19, 12.23). Blaming psychological discomfort (as well as actual misfortune) on adverse astrological influences or demonic possession may seem quaint in light of modern science, which has identified other causes of anxiety or dysfunctional behavior and developed other methods of treatment; nevertheless, the power of spiritual healing has a validity that science is increasingly willing to acknowledge.

Looking outward to the societal sphere, wherever discord erupts within human relationships, recitation of the Devīmāhātmya is said to effect reconciliation (12.18). The Devīmāhātmya's benefits thus apply to all areas of human existence and endeavor, promoting social harmony and justice, physical health and safety, and psychological and spiritual wholeness.

**12.31–35:** Medhas now returns once more to the scene of the gods assembled before the Devī. Having vanquished Śumbha and Niśumbha and having restored the natural order, Caṇḍikā vanishes from sight.

**12.36–41:** Medhas now finishes the discourse he began in the first chapter. Through the three myths, he has fulfilled the king's wish to know everything about the Devī (1.60–62). Everything has been an elaboration of verse 1.66: "Although she is eternal, when she manifests to accomplish the purpose of the gods, she is said to be born in the world." Now he brings the narrative full circle: "Thus, O king, does the blessed Devī, though eternal, manifest again and again for the protection of the world" (12.36). The remaining verses (12.37–41) summarize the major points that the eternal Devī takes form as the creation, sustains for a time the drama of life within a universe polarized between enchantment and terror, and then dissolves it all back into undifferentiated, self-luminous bliss.

# 13

## The Granting of Boons to Suratha and the Merchant

13.1 The seer said:

13.2 "Thus have I related to you, O king, this supreme glorification of the Devī:

13.3 Such is the splendor of the Devī, by whom the world is upheld, and such is the knowledge fashioned by the blessed Viṣṇumāyā.

13.4 By her are you and this merchant and other thoughtful people deluded, just as others have been and will be deluded.

13.5 O great king, take refuge in her, the supreme sovereign. When worshiped, she truly confers enjoyment, heaven, and final liberation on humanity."

13.6 Mārkaṇḍeya said:

13.7 Hearing his words, Suratha the king bowed in reverence to the illustrious seer of steadfast austerities.

13.8 Despondent over excessive attachment and the loss of his kingdom, he went at once to practice austerities, O great sage, and so did the merchant,

13.9 that they might obtain a vision of the Mother. The king and the merchant settled on a riverbank and engaged in spiritual practice, chanting the supreme hymn to the Devi.

13.10 When they had fashioned an earthen image of her on the riverbank, the two of them worshiped the Devī with flowers, incense, fire, and libations of water.

13.11 Now fasting, now restraining their senses, with minds constant in concentration, they made offerings sprinkled with the blood of their own bodies.

13.12 When they had worshiped her in this way with self-restraint for three years, Caṇḍikā, the support of the universe, was well pleased. She appeared before them and spoke.

13.13 The Devī said:

13.14 "That which you desire, O king, and you, the delight of your family,

13.15 receive all that from me. Well pleased, I will grant it."

13.16 Mārkaṇḍeya said:

13.17 Thereupon the king chose a kingdom imperishable even in another lifetime and also his own kingdom here, to be reclaimed by force from his enemies' control.

13.18 And then the wise merchant, dispassionate in mind, chose that knowledge which severs attachment from "I" and "mine."

13.19 The Devī said:

13.20 "In a few days, O king, you will reclaim your own kingdom.

13.21 When your enemies are slain, thenceforth it will assuredly be yours.

13.22 And after your death you will obtain another birth from the sun god Vivasvat.

13.23 Dwelling on earth, you will become the lord of the age, the manu named Sāvarṇi.

13.24 And the boon that you, O best of merchants, desire,

13.25 that do I grant you. The knowledge that leads to final liberation shall be yours."

13.26 Mārkaṇḍeya said:

13.27 When she had given each his desired boon, the Devī, lovingly praised by both of them, vanished at once.

13.28 Thus, having received the Devī's boon, Suratha, the best of sovereigns will obtain birth from the sun god and will become the manu named Sāvarṇi,

13.29 will become the manu named Sāvarṇi. Klīṁ Oṁ.

The Devīmāhātmya of seven hundred verses is concluded.

Oṁ tat sat Oṁ

# Chapter 13 Commentary

**13.1–4**: For one last time, Medhas repeats that the Devī makes possible the functioning and sustenance of the universe (13.3). She does this through the knowledge (vidyā) she creates. Here *vidyā* refers not to the uncreated, eternal knowledge but to relative knowledge, which consists of the modifications of the supreme, undifferentiated consciousness as effected by Mahāmāyā. Such knowledge allows human beings to experience the phenomenal universe.

**13.5:** Medhas enjoins the king to surrender himself to Mahāmāyā. His last words are that she confers bhoga ("enjoyment," meaning also the experience of either pleasure or pain), *svarga* ("abode of light," meaning heavenly reward), and *apavarga* ("completion," meaning emancipation from bodily existence, final beatitude [→ 11.7]). In short, the sum total of experience, in the relative or the absolute state, rests in the Devī.

**13.6–11:** At this point Mārkaṇḍeya returns as the primary narrator and brings the framing story to an end.

When they take their leave of Medhas, the king and the merchant go off to a riverbank and engage in intensive sādhana (13.9–11). They chant the supreme hymn to the Devī (the Ṛgvedic Devīsūkta) and fashion an earthen image, probably much like those still made in India for the autumn Durgā Pūjā. The other details of worship and austerities, except for the offering of human blood, also relate to modern practice. Fasting means not only restraint of physical nourishment but also of anything taken in through the senses, for in the broadest meaning, "food" includes all sensory and intellectual impressions gathered from without. Minimizing food involves not only physical asceticism but also the calming of the mind through the control of everything that stimulates it.

**13.12–18:** The Devī Caṇḍikā appears to the king and the merchant and offers each a boon. Although it is not stated in the text, the king realizes that running away was a cowardly act, unbefitting his status as a kṣatriya. Having failed to fulfill his duty, he asks for a second chance by reclaiming his earthly kingdom, followed by the reward of an imperishable kingdom in a future existence. He is not ready to relinquish his desires and merge with the Divine but wants to live righteously, in harmony with the dharma. The merchant Samādhi, on the other hand, realizes the folly of seeking wealth and position and of lamenting their loss. Grown wise and dispassionate, he asks for the liberating knowledge that dissolves the ego and its bondage.

**13.19–29:** The Devī promises that the king will fight bravely and regain his earthly kingdom. After his death, the sun god, Vivasvat, will grant him rebirth as Sāvarṇi, the manu of the eighth manvantara. And Samādhi, through knowledge, will attain samādhi, union with the Absolute. In this final scene, the Devī appears exactly as characterized in verse 11.7 of the Nārāyaṇīstuti: as the bestower of worldly enjoyment and final liberation (bhuktimuktipradāyinī).

"She who has become all things" exists from all eternity and takes form as the creation (12.39). All that is finite exists in the infinite Śakti, who is at once the nondual reality and the kaleidoscopic universe that is the resplendent form of the formless. The Devīmāhātmya's all-embracing vision sees the whole of being and becoming as one reality, for Mother is everything and everything is Mother.

Oṁ tat sat Oṁ.

# Part III
# The Aṅgas

# INTRODUCTION TO THE AṄGAS

Around the 14th century, a set of six ancillary texts, or aṅgas ("limbs"), became associated with the Devīmāhātmya. The first three aṅgas—the Devyāḥ Kavacam, Argalāstotra, and Kīlakastotra—are preparatory prayers and incantations employed in the Devīmāhātmya's ritual recitation. The remaining three—the Prādhānika Rahasya, Vaikṛtika Rahasya, and Mūrtirahasya—deal with cosmogony and formal worship and are optionally recited afterward. Besides these, two Vedic hymns—the Rātrisūkta and the Devīsūkta—are customarily chanted immediately before and after the text of the Devīmāhātmya itself. In recognizing the Word (vāk) as an actual manifestation of Śakti, Śākta Tantra correlates the physical universe with the divine reality from which it flows. Accordingly, the words of the Devīmāhātmya are not merely poetry (śloka), but the actual embodiment of divine power (mantra). This power Śiva himself is said to have restrained "as if with a bolt" to prevent its intentional or unwitting misuse. Formal recitation, performed according to elaborate and strictly defined ritual practices involving physical and mental preparation, affords access to that power, which may be directed toward either temporal or spiritual ends.

# देव्याः कवचम्

## DEVYĀḤ KAVACAM

ॐ नमश्चण्डिकायै

Oṁ. Salutations to Caṇḍikā.

मार्कण्डेय उवाच ।

Mārkaṇḍeya said:

ॐ यद्गुह्यं परमं लोके सर्वरक्षाकरं नृणाम् ।
यन्न कस्यचिदाख्यातं तन्मे ब्रूहि पितामह ॥ १ ॥

1. Oṁ. That which is the supreme secret in this world, affording every protection to humankind, which is not told to anyone—tell me that, O Grandsire.

ब्रह्मोवाच ।

Brahmā said:

अस्ति गुह्यतमं विप्र सर्वभूतोपकारकम् ।
देव्यास्तु कवचं पुण्यं तच्छृणुष्व महामुने ॥ २ ॥

2. There is a most hidden secret, O wise one, beneficial to all beings—the holy armor of the Devī. Hear of it, O great sage.

प्रथमं शैलपुत्रीति द्वितीयं ब्रह्मचारिणी ।
तृतीयं चन्द्रघण्टेति कूष्माण्डेति चतुर्थकम् ॥ ३ ॥

3. First, she is called Śailaputrī; second, Brahmacāriṇī; third, Candraghaṇṭā; fourth, Kūṣmāṇḍā.

पञ्चमं स्कन्दमातेति षष्ठं कात्यायनी तथा ।
सप्तमं कालरात्रिश्च महागौरीति चाष्टमम् ॥ ४ ॥

4. Fifth, she is called Skandamatā; sixth, Kātyāyanī; seventh, Kālarātri; eighth, Mahāgaurī.

नवमं सिद्धिदात्री च नवदुर्गाः प्रकीर्तिताः ।
उक्तान्येतानि नामानि ब्रह्मणैव महात्मना ॥ ५ ॥

5. And ninth, she is Siddhidātrī. The nine Durgās are revealed; the noble Brahmā has spoken their names.

अग्निना दह्यमानास्तु शत्रुमध्यगता रणे ।
विषमे दुर्गमे चैव भयार्ताः शरणं गताः ॥ ६ ॥

6. When consumed by fire or surrounded by enemies in battle, when seized by fear in adversity or crisis, those who take refuge in the Devī

न तेषां जायते किञ्चिदशुभं रणसङ्कटे ।
आपदं न च पश्यन्ति शोकदुःखभयङ्करीम् ॥ ७ ॥

7. will have nothing inauspicious befall them amidst the danger of battle, nor will they know any misfortune that brings grief, suffering or dread.

यैस्तु भक्त्या स्मृता नित्यं तेषां वृद्धिः प्रजायते ।
ये त्वां स्मरन्ति देवेशि रक्षसि तान्न संशयः ॥ ८ ॥

8. Those who remember her always with devotion will surely win success. O supreme Devī, you protect those who remember you. Of that there is no doubt.

प्रेतसंस्था तु चामुण्डा वाराही महिषासना ।
ऐन्द्री गजसमारूढा वैष्णवी गरुडासना ॥ ९ ॥

9. Standing upon a corpse is Cāmuṇḍā; seated on a buffalo is Vārāhī; mounted on an elephant is Aindrī; seated on Garuda is Vaiṣṇavī.

नारसिंही महावीर्या शिवदूती महाबला ।
माहेश्वरी वृषारूढा कौमारी शिखिवाहना ॥ १० ॥

10. Nārasiṁhī is great in valor; Śivadūtī is great in might. Mounted on a bull is Māheśvarī, and borne on a peacock is Kaumārī.

लक्ष्मीः पद्मासना देवी पद्महस्ता हरिप्रिया ।
श्वेतरूपधरा देवी ईश्वरी वृषवाहना ॥ ११ ॥

11. Seated upon a lotus, with lotus in hand, is Lakṣmī, the goddess beloved of Viṣṇu. And the sovereign Devī who is borne on a bull, pure white is the form she possesses.

ब्राह्मी हंससमारूढा सर्वाभरणभूषिता ।
इत्येता मातरः सर्वाः सर्वयोगसमन्विताः ॥ १२ ॥

12. Brāhmī, adorned with all her jewels, rides upon a swan. These, then, are all the Mothers, all united together,

नानाभरणशोभाढ्या नानारत्नोपशोभिताः ।
श्रेष्ठैश्च मौक्तिकैः सर्वा दिव्यहारप्रलम्बिभिः ॥ १३ ॥

13. arrayed in bejeweled splendor, adorned with all manner of gems: all with strands of the most excellent pearls and magic-bearing pendants,

इन्द्रनीलैर्महानीलैः पद्मरागैः सुशोभनैः ।
दृश्यन्ते रथमारूढा देव्यः क्रोधसमाकुलाः ॥ १४ ॥

14. with great blue sapphires and splendid rubies. Riding in chariots the goddesses appear, bristling with anger

शङ्खं चक्रं गदां शक्तिं हलं च मुसलायुधम् ।
खेटकं तोमरं चैव परशुं पाशमेव च ॥ १५ ॥

15. and bearing conch, discus, mace, spear, plough, and club; shield, lance, and ax and noose,

कुन्तायुधं त्रिशूलं च शार्ङ्गमायुधमुत्तमम् ।
दैत्यानां देहनाशाय भक्तानामभयाय च ॥ १६ ॥

16. pike, trident, and mighty bow—weapons to destroy the demons' bodies and to dispel the devotees' fears.

धारयन्त्यायुधानीत्थं देवानां च हिताय वै ।
नमस्तेऽस्तु महारौद्रे महाघोरपराक्रमे । १७ ॥

17. Indeed, for the well-being of the gods, they bear weapons in this manner. Salutations be unto you, great fierce one of mighty and awesome courage.

महाबले महोत्साहे महाभयविनाशिनि ।
त्राहि मां देवि दुष्प्रेक्ष्ये शत्रूणां भयवर्धिनि ॥ १८ ॥

18. O you of great might and great resolve, annihilating fear, protect me, O Devī, who are difficult for our enemies to behold, for you increase their dread.

प्राच्यां रक्षतु मामैन्द्री आग्नेय्यामग्निदेवता ।
दक्षिणेऽवतु वाराही नैर्ऋत्यां खड्गधारिणी ॥ १९ ॥

19. May Aindrī guard me in the east, and Agnidevatā in the southeast; may Vārāhī defend me in the south, and Khaḍgadhāriṇī in the southwest.

प्रतीच्यां वारुणी रक्षेद्वायव्यां मृगवाहिनी ।
उदीच्यां पातु कौबेरी ईशान्यां शूलधारिणी ॥ २० ॥

20. May Vāruṇī protect me in the west, and Mṛgavāhinī in the northwest; may Kaumārī protect me in the north, and Śūladhāriṇī in the northeast.

ऊर्ध्वं ब्रह्माणी मे रक्षेदधस्ताद्वैष्णवी तथा ।
एवं दश दिशो रक्षेच्चामुण्डा शववाहना ॥ २१ ॥

21. May Brahmāṇī guard me above, and Vaiṣṇavī below. In this way, may Cāmuṇḍā, riding upon a corpse, guard the ten directions.

जया मामग्रतः पातु विजया पातु पृष्ठतः ।
अजिता वामपार्श्वे तु दक्षिणे चापराजिता ॥ २२ ॥

22. May Jayā stand in front of me, and Vijayā stand behind; Ajitā on my left, and Aparājitā on my right.

शिखां मे द्योतिनी रक्षेदुमा मूर्ध्नि व्यवस्थिता ।
मालाधरी ललाटे च भ्रुवौ रक्षेद्यशस्विनी ॥ २३ ॥

23. May Dyotinī guard my topknot. May Umā abide atop my head, and Mālādharī on my forehead. May Yaśasvinī guard my eyebrows.

नेत्रयोश्चित्रनेत्रा च यमघण्टा तु पार्श्वके ।
त्रिनेत्रा च त्रिशूलेन भ्रुवोर्मध्ये च चण्डिका ॥ २४ ॥

24. May Citranetrā abide in my eyes, and Yamaghaṇṭā in my nose. May Trinetrā protect me with her trident, and Caṇḍikā dwell between my eyebrows.

शङ्खिनी चक्षुषोर्मध्ये श्रोत्रयोर्द्वारवासिनी ।
कपोलौ कालिका रक्षेत् कर्णमूले तु शङ्करी ॥ २५ ॥

25. May Śaṇkhinī abide between my eyes, and Dvāravāsinī upon my ears. May Kālika guard my cheeks, and Śaṇkarī protect within my ears.

नासिकायां सुगन्धा च उत्तरोष्ठे च चर्चिका ।
अधरे चामृताबाला जिह्वायां च सरस्वती ॥ २६ ॥

26. And may Sugandhā protect my nostrils. May Carcikā abide on my upper lip, Amṛtābālā on my lower lip, and Sarasvatī on my tongue.

दन्तान् रक्षतु कौमारी कण्ठदेशे तु चण्डिका ।
घण्टिकां चित्रघण्टा च महामाया च तालुके ॥ २७ ॥

27. May Kaumārī guard my teeth, and Caṇḍikā my throat. May Citraghaṇṭā guard my uvula, and Mahāmāyā abide in my palate.

कामाक्षी चिबुकं रक्षेद्वाचं मे सर्वमङ्गला ।
ग्रीवायां भद्रकाली च पृष्ठवंशे धनुर्धरी ॥ २८ ॥

28. May Kāmākṣī guard my chin, Sarvamaṅgalā my voice, Bhadrakālī the nape of my neck, and Dhanurdharī my spine.

नीलग्रीवा बहिः कण्ठे नलिकां नलकूबरी ।
स्कन्धयोः खड्गिनी रक्षेद् बाहू मे वज्रधारिणी ॥ २९ ॥

29. May Nīlagrīvā abide outside my throat, and Nalakūbarī within. May Khaḍginī guard my shoulders, and Vajradhāriṇī my arms.

हस्तयोर्दण्डिनी रक्षेदम्बिका चाङ्गुलीषु च ।
नखाञ्छूलेश्वरी रक्षेत् कुक्षौ रक्षेन्नरेश्वरी ॥ ३० ॥

30. May Daṇḍinī guard my hands; may Ambikā abide in my fingers. May Śūleśvarī guard my nails, and Nareśvarī my abdomen.

स्तनौ रक्षेन्महादेवी मनःशोकविनाशिनी ।
हृदये ललिता देवी उदरे शूलधारिणी ॥ ३१ ॥

31. May Mahādevī guard my chest, and Śokavināśinī my mind. May the Devī Lalitā abide in my heart, and Śūladhāriṇī in my stomach.

नाभौ च कामिनी रक्षेद् गुह्यं गुह्येश्वरी तथा ।
मेढ्रं रक्षतु दुर्गन्धा पायुं मे गुह्यवाहिनी ॥ ३२ ॥

32. May Kāminī guard my navel, Guhyeśvarī my private parts, Durgandhā my penis, and Guhyavāhinī my anus.

कट्यां भगवती रक्षेदूरू मे मेघवाहना ।
जङ्घे महाबला रक्षेत् जानू माधवनायिका ॥ ३३ ॥

33. May Bhagavatī guard my hips, Meghavāhanā my thighs, Mahābalā my shanks, and Mādhavanāyikā my knees.

गुल्फयोर्नारसिंही च पादपृष्ठे तु कौशिकी ।
पादाङ्गुलीः श्रीधरी च तलं पातालवासिनी ॥ ३४ ॥

34. May Nārasiṁhī abide in my ankles. May Kauśikī guard my heels, Śrīdharī my toes, and Pātālavāsinī the soles of my feet.

नखान् दंष्ट्रकराली च केशांश्चैवोर्ध्वकेशिनी ।
रोमकूपेषु कौमारी त्वचं योगीश्वरी तथा ॥ ३५ ॥

35. May Daṁṣṭrakarālī guard my toenails, and Ūrdhvakeśinī my hair. May Kaumārī abide in my pores, and Yogīśvarī protect my skin.

रक्तमज्जावसामांसान्यस्थिमेदांसि पार्वती ।
अन्त्राणि कालरात्रिश्च पित्तं च मुकुटेश्वरी ॥ ३६ ॥

36. May Pārvatī guard my blood, bone-marrow, lymph, flesh, bones, and fat. May Kālarātri guard my intestines, and Mukuṭeśvarī my bile.

पद्मावती पद्मकोशे कफे चूडामणिस्तथा ।
ज्वालामुखी नखज्वालामभेद्या सर्वसन्धिषु ॥ ३७ ॥

37. May Padmāvatī guard my lungs, and Cūḍāmaṇi my phlegm. May Jvālāmukhī protect the luster of my nails, and Abhedyā dwell in all my joints.

शुक्रं ब्रह्माणी मे रक्षेच्छायां छत्रेश्वरी तथा ।
अहङ्कारं मनो बुद्धिं रक्षेन्मे धर्मधारिणी ॥ ३८ ॥

38. May Brahmāṇī guard my semen, and Chatreśvarī my shadow. May Dharmadhāriṇī protect my ego, mind, and intellect,

प्राणापानौ तथा व्यानमुदानं च समानकम् ।
वज्रहस्ता च मे रक्षेत् प्राणान् कल्याणशोभना ॥ ३९ ॥

39. and likewise my breath, elimination, digestion, nervous system, and body heat. May Vajrahastā, who sparkles with auspicious beauty, guard these, my vital forces.

रसे रूपे च गन्धे च शब्दे स्पर्शे च योगिनी ।
सत्त्वं रजस्तमश्चैव रक्षेन्नारायणी सदा ॥ ४० ॥

40. May Yoginī abide in taste, form, smell, sound, and touch; and may Nārāyaṇī ever guard my knowledge, action, and desire.

आयू रक्षतु वाराही धर्मं रक्षतु पार्वती ।
यशः कीर्तिं च लक्ष्मीं च सदा रक्षतु वैष्णवी ॥ ४१ ॥

41. May Vārāhī protect the span of my life; may Pārvatī protect my virtue; may Vaiṣṇavī protect always my honor, reputation, and prosperity.

गोत्रमिन्द्राणी मे रक्षेत् पशून् रक्षेच्च चण्डिका ।
पुत्रान् रक्षेन्महालक्ष्मीर्भार्यां रक्षतु भैरवी ॥ ४२ ॥

42. May Indrāṇī guard my stable, and Caṇḍikā my herds. May Mahālakṣmī protect my children, and Bhairavī, my wife.

धनेश्वरी धनं रक्षेत् कौमारी कन्यकां तथा ।
पन्थानं सुपथा रक्षेन्मार्गं क्षेमङ्करी तथा ॥ ४३ ॥

43. May Dhaneśvarī guard my wealth, and Kaumarī, my virgin daughter. May Supathā guard my way, and Kṣemaṅkarī also.

राजद्वारे महालक्ष्मीर्विजया सतत स्थिता ।
रक्षाहीनं तु यत् स्थानं वर्जितं कवचेन तु ॥ ४४ ॥

44. May Mahālakṣmī dwell at my gate, and Vijayā be ever abiding. That which remains excluded and wanting for protection by this armor,

तत्सर्वं रक्ष मे देवि जयन्ती पापनाशिनी ।
सर्वरक्षाकरं पुण्यं कवचं सर्वदा जपेत् ॥ ४५ ॥

45. all that protect, O Devī, who conquer and destroy all evil. At all times should one invoke this holy armor that affords all protection.

इदं रहस्यं विप्रर्षे भक्त्या तव मयोदितम् ।
पादमेकं न गच्छेत् तु यदीच्छेच्छुभमात्मनः ॥ ४६ ॥

46. This secret have I revealed, O wise one, by reason of your devotion. If one seeks his own well-being, he should not take a single step

कवचेनावृतो नित्यं यत्र यत्रैव गच्छति ।
तत्र तत्रार्थलाभश्च विजयः सार्वकालिकः ॥ ४७ ॥

47. unclothed by this armor, wherever he goes. Everywhere he will attain his ends, victorious, at all times.

यं यं चिन्तयते कामं तं तं प्राप्नोति निश्चितम् ।
परमैश्वर्यमतुलं प्राप्स्यते भूतले पुमान् ॥ ४८ ॥

48. Whatever desire he contemplates, that will he surely obtain. That man will attain unequaled supremacy on this earth.

निर्भयो जायते मर्त्यः संग्रामेष्वपराजितः ।
त्रैलोक्ये तु भवेत्पूज्यः कवचेनावृतः पुमान् ॥ ४९ ॥

49. That mortal will become fearless and unvanquished in battles. The man clad in this armor is to be worshiped in the three worlds.

इदं तु देव्याः कवचं देवानामपि दुर्लभम् ।
यः पठेत्प्रयतो नित्यं त्रिसन्ध्यं श्रद्धयान्वितः ॥ ५० ॥

50. This armor of the Devī is difficult for even the gods to obtain. He who recites it always at dawn, noon, and dusk, intent on devotion and possessed of faith,

दैवीकला भवेत्तस्य त्रैलोक्ये चापराजितः ।
जीवेद्वर्षशतं साग्रमपमृत्युविवर्जितः ॥ ५१ ॥

51. attains a portion of the Divine and remains unconquered in the three worlds. He will live for a full hundred years, untouched by sudden or accidental death.

नश्यन्ति व्याधयः सर्वे लूताविस्फोटकादयः ।
स्थावरं जङ्गमं चैव कृत्रिमं चैव यद्विषम् ॥ ५२ ॥

52. All his ailments will vanish—skin infections, eruptions, and the like—along with all manner of natural poisons and those of human artifice,

अभिचाराणि सर्वाणि मन्त्रयन्त्राणि भूतले ।
भूचराः खेचराश्चैव कुलजाश्चौपदेशिकाः ॥ ५३ ॥

53. all spells, incantations, and magical charms in the world. Those creatures that go upon the earth, move through the air, and dwell in water, be they induced by others,

सहजा कुलजा माला डाकिनी शाकिनी तथा ।
अन्तरिक्षचरा घोरा डाकिन्यश्च महारवाः ॥ ५४ ॥

54. self-arisen or family-born; the ḍākinī, the śākinī, and such: the terrible, howling ḍākinīs that move through the atmosphere,

ग्रहभूतपिशाचाश्च यक्षगन्धर्वराक्षसाः ।
ब्रह्मराक्षसवेतालाः कूष्माण्डा भैरवादयः ॥ ५५ ॥

55. the spirits that possess, fiends and apparitions, ghosts, demons, and ghouls, the undead, spirits of terror, and the like,

नश्यन्ति दर्शनात्तस्य कवचेनावृतो हि यः ।
मानोन्नतिर्भवेद्राज्ञस्तेजोवृद्धिः परा भवेत् ॥ ५६ ॥

56. all those perish at the sight of him who is clad in this armor. The king will hold him in high regard, and the spreading of his glory will know no bounds.

यशोवृद्धिर्भवेत् पुंसां कीर्तिवृद्धिश्च जायते ।
तस्मात् जपेत् सदा भक्तः कवचं कामदं मुने ॥ ५७ ॥

57. Increased renown will be his, and his fame will be exalted. For this reason, the devotee should always recite the wish-fulfilling armor, O wise one.

जपेत् सप्तशतीं चण्डीं कृत्वा तु कवचं पुरा ।
निर्विघ्नेन भवेत् सिद्धिश्चण्डीजपसमुद्भवा ॥ ५८

58. Having first done this, he should recite the Caṇḍī of seven-hundred verses. Without interruption he should accomplish his recital of the Caṇḍī.

यावद्भूमण्डलं धत्ते सशैलवनकाननम् ।
तावत्तिष्ठति मेदिन्यां सन्ततिः पुत्रपौत्रिकी ॥ ५९ ॥

59. As long as the earth's globe, with its mountains, forests, and groves, endures, so long will his continuity through sons and grandsons last on this earth.

देहान्ते परमं स्थानं सुरैरपि सुदुर्लभम् ।
प्राप्नोति पुरुषो नित्यं महामायाप्रसादतः ॥ ६० ॥

60. At death this person, through Mahāmāyā's grace, will attain the supreme, eternal state, greatly difficult for even the gods to reach.

तत्र गच्छति गत्वासौ पुनश्चागमनं नहि ।
लभते परमं स्थानं शिवेन समतां व्रजेत् ॥ ६१ ॥

61. He will go there, and having gone shall surely not return. He will attain the supreme state and with the Absolute will merge.

# Devyāḥ Kavacam Commentary

To recite the Devyāḥ Kavacam ("Armor of the Devī"), or Kavaca, is to don its protection. The verses invoke individual śaktis who together represent the full array of the Devī's protective energies residing in the human body.

**1–2:** Mārkaṇḍeya, assuming the role of disciple, asks Brahmā to reveal the supreme secret. The god replies that such hidden knowledge exists in the form of the Devī's indwelling presence.

**3–5:** Brahmā first reveals the names of Durgā's nine aspects. Śailaputrī ("daughter of the mountain peak") denotes her purificatory power as the deified Gaṅgā, flowing from the Himālayas. Brahmacāriṇī ("the one who moves in Brahman") denotes her dynamic power, Śakti. Candraghaṇṭā ("she whose bell is like the moon") emphasizes benign creativity. Kūṣmāṇḍā, derived from the word for a plump gourd, represents fertility. Skandamātā is the mother of the war god, Skanda. Kātyāyanī represents the Devī's supreme form, containing the three guṇas. Kālarātri ("black night") indicates her power of cosmic dissolution. In total contrast, Mahāgaurī ("great shining one") signifies the dazzling light of knowledge. Finally, Siddhidātrī designates the Mother's power to grant supreme spiritual attainment.

**6–8:** Listing some of the benefits of taking refuge in the Devī, this passage closely resembles the phalaśruti of the Devīmāhātmya's twelfth chapter.

**9–18:** The Mothers enumerated here do not correspond to the seven of the Devīmāhātmya plus Śivadūtī and Cāmuṇḍā. The Kavaca names eleven.

**19–22:** This section invokes divine protection in the ten directions and to the reciter's front, back, left, and right. The names of the divine energies and their meanings are: Aindrī (Indra's śakti), Agnidevatā ("deity of fire"), Vārāhī (the śakti of Viṣṇu in his boar incarnation), Khaḍgadhāriṇī ("sword-wielder"), Vāruṇī (the śakti of Varuṇa, the Vedic god of the sea), Mṛgavāhinī ("deer-rider"), Kaumārī (the śakti of Kumāra, god of war), Śūladhāriṇī ("spear-bearer"), Brahmāṇī (the consort of Brahmā, embodying creative power), Vaiṣṇavī (the śakti of Viṣṇu), Cāmuṇḍā (Kālī as the bridger of transcendental and relative consciousness), Jayā ("victory"), Vijayā ("triumph"), Ajitā ("unconquered"), and Aparājitā ("invincible").

**23–38:** The protective energies are invoked throughout the body, starting at the crown of the head and working downward. The topknot refers to the tuft of hair on the top of the head; in pūjā the bīja *hrīṁ* is linked to it as the protecting and invoking mantra. As written, the aṅgas would have been recited by married males of the higher castes, and some verses refer specifically to the male body or to masculine societal roles. If the reciter is female, she is free to make the necessary alterations in the references to male genitalia and reproductive function in verses 32 and 38. Similarly, in verses 42 and 43, a married female would change "wife" to "husband," and a celibate monastic of either gender would substitute "devotion" for "wife," and "disciples" for "children."[1]

The names of the powers usually have an obvious bearing on the body part or function specified. They are: Dyotinī ("brilliant"), Umā (another name of Pārvatī, linked by some philologists to ancient Semitic or Dravidian terms for "mother"), Mālādharī ("garland-wearer"), Yaśasvinī ("renowned"), Citranetrā ("clear-eyed"), Yamaghaṇṭā ("holder of the bell of restraint"), Trinetrā ("three-eyed"), Caṇḍikā ("violent, impetuous"), Śaṅkhinī ("possessor of the conch"), Dvāravāsinī ("dweller at the portal"), Kālikā ("black"), Śaṅkarī ("causing prosperity"), Sugandhā ("fragrant"), Carcikā (referring to the repetition of a word in reciting the Veda), Amṛtabālā ("drop of nectar"), Sarasvatī ("flowing"), Kaumārī ("maidenly, virginal"), Citraghaṇṭā ("clear-sounding"), Mahāmāyā ("great deluding power"), Kāmākṣī ("she whose soul is love"), Sarvamaṅgalā ("all-auspicious"), Bhadrakālī ("auspicious Kālī"), Dhanurdharī ("bow-bearer"), Nīlagrīvā ("blue-necked"), Nalakūbarī (perhaps a feminine counterpart of Nalakūbara, the son of Kubera), Khaḍginī ("possessor of the sword"), Vajradhāriṇī ("bearer of the thunderbolt"), Daṇḍinī ("possessor of the staff"), Ambikā ("Mother"), Śūleśvarī ("ruler of the spear"), Nareśvarī ("ruler of humankind"), Mahādevī ("Great Goddess"), Śokavināśinī ("destroyer of anguish"), Lalitā ("playful"), Śūladhāriṇī ("spear-bearer"), Kāminī ("goddess of love"), Guhyeśvarī ("sovereign of secrets"), Durgandhā ("ill-smelling"), Guhyavāhinī ("tortoise-rider"), Bhagavatī ("blessed"), Meghavāhanā ("cloud-rider"), Mahābalā ("she of great strength"), Mādhavanāyikā ("mistress of Viṣṇu"), Nārasiṁhī (the śakti of Viṣṇu's incarnation as a man-lion), Kauśikī (the Devī's sattvic aspect, who emerged from Pārvatī's kośa, or physical sheath), Śrīdharī ("bearing splendor"), Pātālavāsinī ("the dweller below"), Daṁṣṭrakarālī ("she of terrifying fangs"), Ūrdhvakeśinī ("she whose hair stands on end"), Kauberī (the śakti of Kubera, the Vedic god of wealth), Yogīśvarī ("sovereign of ascetics"), Pārvatī (Śiva's divine consort in her beneficent aspect), Kālarātri ("dark night," referring to the Devī's world-destroying power), Mukuṭeśvarī ("sovereign of the crown"), Padmāvatī (a name of Lakṣmī, associated with the lotus), Cūḍāmaṇi ("crest-jewel"), Jvālāmukhī ("flame-faced"), Abhedyā ("unbreakable"), Brahmāṇī (Brahmā's consort), Chatreśvarī ("possessor of the royal parasol"), Dharmadhāriṇī (upholder of righteousness).

**39:** The generic term for the life force is *prāṇa* ("breath"), but prāṇa has five functions. More specifically, the term *prāṇa* denotes respiration; *apāna* governs elimination; *samāna* effects digestion, the assimilation of nutrients, and the circulation of the blood; *vyāna*, pervading the body, governs the nervous system, speech, and conscious action; *udāna* regulates growth and body heat.[2] The protective śakti is Vajrahastā ("she who holds the thunderbolt in hand"). Similarly, three śaktis invoked in verses 36 and 37 afford divine protection over the three bodily humors of Ayurvedic medicine: *pitta* (bile, of which the chief quality is heat), *vāta* (wind, represented in the text by the lungs), and *kapha* (phlegm, of which the chief quality is cold).

**40:** The five senses—taste, sight, smell, hearing, and touch—are protected by Yoginī. The three guṇas—sattva, rajas, and tamas—can be taken as metaphors for knowledge (jñāna), action (kriyā), and desire (icchā), relating to the universal fact that human beings think, act, and feel. The śakti is Nārāyaṇī, the Devī as the ultimate goal of all humanity.

**41:** This verse deals with life span, the conduct of life, and the rewards of living in accordance with the dharma. The three guardian powers are cited previously in the Kavaca.

**42–43:** Invoked to watch benevolently over the reciter's material wealth, family, and the conduct of his life are Indrāṇī, Caṇḍikā, Mahālakṣmī, Bhairavī ("frightful"), Dhaneśvarī ("lady of wealth"), the previously cited Kaumārī, Supathā ("she whose path is good"), and Kṣemaṅkarī ("giver of safety").

**48–61:** The concluding section, in the form of a phalaśruti, details the this-worldly and spiritual benefits of reciting the Kavaca. Verses 53 through 56 present a list of supernatural entities against which the text affords protection: the *ḍākinī* (a flesh-eating female attendant of Kālī), the *śākinī* (a fierce attendant of Durgā), the *grahabhūta* (a spirit that possesses), the *piśāca* (the vilest of demons, according to the Ṛgveda), the *yakṣa* (a harmless ghost or apparition), the *gandharva* (usually a celestial musician, but sometimes a malevolent, disembodied spirit), the *rakṣasa* (a demon that haunts cemeteries and harasses human beings), the *brahmarākṣasa* (the ghost of a brāhmaṇa who led an unholy life), the *vetāla* (a vampire or spirit inhabiting a corpse), the *kūṣmāṇḍa,* and the *bhairava* (kinds of frightening demons that accompany Śiva). Ending on a positive note, the Kavaca promises that the devotee who recites it will proceed from a position of highest honor in this world to the supreme goal of union with the Divine.

# अर्गलास्तोत्रम्

## ARGALĀSTOTRA

ॐ नमश्चण्डिकायै

Oṁ. Salutation to Caṇḍikā.

मार्कण्डेय उवाच ।

Mārkaṇḍeya said:

ॐ जय त्वं देवि चामुण्डे जय भूतापहारिणि ।
जय सर्वगते देवि कालरात्रि नमोऽस्तु ते ॥ १ ॥

1. Oṁ. Be victorious, O Devī Cāmuṇḍā; be victorious, destroyer of demons; be victorious, all-pervading Devī; Kālarātri, salutations be unto you!

जयन्ती मङ्गला काली भद्रकाली कपालिनी ।
दुर्गा शिवा क्षमा धात्री स्वाहा स्वधा नमोऽस्तु ते ॥ २ ॥

2. Victorious be the auspicious Kālī, Bhadrakālī, adorned with skulls. Gracious be Durgā, the patient upholder of earth. Svāhā, Svadhā, salutations be unto you!

मधुकैटभविध्वंसि विधातृवरदे नमः ।
रूपं देहि जयं देहि यशो देहि द्विषो जहि ॥ ३ ॥

3. Salutations to you who, granting a boon to Brahmā, brought Madhu and Kaiṭabha to ruin. Give the form, give the victory, give the glory, kill the enemies.

महिषासुरनिर्नाशि भक्तानां सुखदे नमः ।
रूपं देहि जयं देहि यशो देहि द्विषो जहि ॥ ४ ॥

4. Salutations to you who ordained Mahiṣāsuras destruction, O giver of happiness to your devotees. Give the form, give the victory, give the glory, kill the enemies.

धूम्रनेत्रवधे देवि धर्मकामार्थदायिनि ।
रूपं देहि जयं देहि यशो देहि द्विषो जहि ॥ ५ ॥

5. O Devī, slayer of Dhūmralocana, bestower of righteousness, pleasure, and wealth; give the form, give the victory, give the glory, kill the enemies.

रक्तबीजवधे देवि चण्डमुण्डविनाशिनि ।
रूपं देहि जयं देहि यशो देहि द्विषो जहि ॥ ६ ॥

6. O Devī, destroyer of Raktabīja and slayer of Caṇḍa and Muṇḍa: give the form, give the victory, give the glory, kill the enemies.

निशुम्भशुम्भनिर्नाशि त्रैलोक्यशुभदे नमः ।
रूपं देहि जयं देहि यशो देहि द्विषो जहि ॥ ७ ॥

7. Salutations, O destroyer of Niśumbha and Śumbha and cause of goodness in the three worlds; give the form, give the victory, give the glory, kill the enemies.

वन्दिताङ्घ्रियुगे देवि सर्वसौभाग्यदायिनि ।
रूपं देहि जयं देहि यशो देहि द्विषो जहि ॥ ८ ॥

8. O Devī, at whose feet we bow, bestower of all well-being; give the form, give the victory, give the glory, kill the enemies.

अचिन्त्यरूपचरिते सर्वशत्रुविनाशिनि ।
रूपं देहि जयं देहि यशो देहि द्विषो जहि ॥ ९ ॥

9. O you of inconceivable form and deeds, destroyer of all foes; give the form, give the victory, give the glory, kill the enemies.

नतेभ्यः सर्वदा भक्त्या चापर्णे दुरितापहे ।
रूपं देहि जयं देहि यशो देहि द्विषो जहि ॥ १० ॥

10. O Aparṇā, dispelling the distress of those who bow to you always in devotion; give the form, give the victory, give the glory, kill the enemies.

स्तुवद्भ्यो भक्तिपूर्वं त्वां चण्डिके व्याधिनाशिनि ।
रूपं देहि जयं देहि यशो देहि द्विषो जहि ॥ ११ ॥

11. O Caṇḍikā, destroying the disease of those who praise you with devotion; give the form, give the victory, give the glory, kill the enemies.

चण्डिके सततं युद्धे जयन्ति पापनाशिनि ।
रूपं देहि जयं देहि यशो देहि द्विषो जहि ॥ १२ ॥

12. O Caṇḍikā, ever battling, victorious destroyer of vice; give the form, give the victory, give the glory, kill the enemies.

देहि सौभाग्यमारोग्यं देहि देवि परं सुखम् ।
रूपं देहि जयं देहि यशो देहि द्विषो जहि ॥ १३ ॥

13. Grant good fortune and health, O Devī, grant supreme happiness. Give the form, give the victory, give the glory, kill the enemies.

विधेहि देवि कल्याणं विधेहि विपुलां श्रियम् ।
रूपं देहि जयं देहि यशो देहि द्विषो जहि ॥ १४ ॥

14. O Devī, confer virtue, bestow abundant success. Give the form, give the victory, give the glory, kill the enemies.

विधेहि द्विषतां नाशं विधेहि बलमुच्चकैः ।
रूपं देहि जयं देहि यशो देहि द्विषो जहि ॥ १५ ॥

15. Lay waste my adversaries, create immense strength in me. Give the form, give the victory, give the glory, kill the enemies.

सुरासुरशिरोरत्ननिघृष्टचरणेऽम्बिके ।
रूपं देहि जयं देहि यशो देहि द्विषो जहि ॥ १६ ॥

16. O Ambikā, whose feet are polished by the crest-jewels of gods and demons; give the form, give the victory, give the glory, kill the enemies.

विद्यावन्तं यशस्वन्तं लक्ष्मीवन्तञ्च मां कुरु ।
रूपं देहि जयं देहि यशो देहि द्विषो जहि ॥ १७ ॥

17. Endow me with knowledge, fame, and prosperity. Give the form, give the victory, give the glory, kill the enemies.

देवि प्रचण्डदोर्दण्डदैत्यदर्पनिषूदिनि ।
रूपं देहि जयं देहि यशो देहि द्विषो जहि ॥ १८ ॥

18. O Devī, destroying the pride of demons with your fearsome long arm; give the form, give the victory, give the glory, kill the enemies.

प्रचण्डदैत्यदर्पघ्ने चण्डिके प्रणताय मे ।
रूपं देहि जयं देहि यशो देहि द्विषो जहि ॥ १९ ॥

19. O Caṇḍikā, destroyer of the pride of raging demons; to me who am bowed down, give the form, give the victory, give the glory, kill the enemies.

चतुर्भुजे चतुर्वक्त्रसंस्तुते परमेश्वरि ।
रूपं देहि जयं देहि यशो देहि द्विषो जहि ॥ २० ॥

20. O four-armed Devī, supreme sovereign, praised by the four-faced Brahmā; give the form, give the victory, give the glory, kill the enemies.

कृष्णेन संस्तुते देवि शश्वद्भक्त्या सदाम्बिके ।
रूपं देहि जयं देहि यशो देहि द्विषो जहि ॥ २१ ॥

21. O Devī, eternal mother, praised by the dark Viṣṇu with constant devotion; give the form, give the victory, give the glory, kill the enemies.

हिमाचलसुतानाथसंस्तुते परमेश्वरि ।
रूपं देहि जयं देहि यशो देहि द्विषो जहि ॥ २२ ॥

22. O supreme sovereign, who are praised by Pārvatī's great lord Śiva; give the form, give the victory, give the glory, kill the enemies.

इन्द्राणीपतिसद्भावपूजिते परमेश्वरि ।
रूपं देहि जयं देहि यशो देहि द्विषो जहि ॥ २३ ॥

23. O supreme sovereign, who are worshiped with pure love by Indrāṇī's lord; give the form, give the victory, give the glory, kill the enemies.

देवि भक्तजनोद्दामदत्तानन्दोदयेऽम्बिके ।
रूपं देहि जयं देहि यशो देहि द्विषो जहि ॥ २४ ॥

24. O Devī Ambikā, awakening boundless joy in your devotees; give the form, give the victory, give the glory, kill the enemies.

भार्यां मनोरमां देहि मनोवृत्तानुसारिणीम् ।
रूपं देहि जयं देहि यशो देहि द्विषो जहि ॥ २५ ॥

25. Grant me a wife who is pleasing and like-minded; give the form, give the victory, give the glory, kill the enemies.

तारिणी दुर्गसंसारसागरस्याचलोद्भवे ।
रूपं देहि जयं देहि यशो देहि द्विषो जहि ॥ २६ ॥

26. O redeemer, who are the unmoving source of this difficult ocean of existence; give the form, give the victory, give the glory, kill the enemies.

इदं स्तोत्रं पठित्वा तु महास्तोत्रं पठेन्नरः ।
सप्तशतीं समाराध्य वरमाप्नोति दुर्लभम् ॥ २७ ॥

27. Having recited this hymn, one should then recite the great hymn of seven hundred verses. Having accomplished that, he will obtain that which is most precious and difficult to attain.

# Argalāstotra Commentary

The Argalāstotra ("Hymn of the Bolt") is a series of incantations in the form of a dhāraṇī, a Tantric mantra that first praises a deity and then, in the imperative mode, appeals for assistance.[1] In this case, the appeal is an invariable refrain: "Give the form, give the victory, give the glory, kill the enemies." For its raw, incantatory insistence, my translation retains that literal wording, even though the sound is awkward and the meaning obscure. *Rūpa* means "beauty" as well as "form," and what the reciter asks is that the Divine Mother reveal her indwelling presence as the beauty of Self-knowledge. Next the refrain requests the assurance of success in spiritual endeavor, in other words, victory over the deluding power of māyā. With such victory should come glory—a state of spiritual bliss—as well as the destruction of all forces hostile to the sādhaka's efforts.

Thematically, almost every verse of this aṅga has its counterpart somewhere in the Devīmāhātmya, and the resemblances are self-evident. The first seven verses address the Devī by familiar names and refer specifically to the major asuras destroyed in the course of the three caritas. A few other points warrant explanation:

**10:** The name Aparṇā alludes to a myth in which the Devī took birth as Himavat's daughter and practiced the austerity of complete fasting in order to win Śiva as a husband. Its literal meaning is "not even having leaves [for food]." Alternatively, Aparnā ("without leaves [for clothing]") suggests the total freedom symbolized by Kālī's nakedness.

**18:** In English we speak of "the long arm of the law," and it is tempting to regard the Sanskrit *dordaṇḍa* ("long arm," from *dos*, "forearm," and *daṇḍa*, "staff") as a similar metaphor for the Devī's function as the upholder of dharma.

**20–23:** The "four-armed Devī" no doubt refers to the unmanifest, triguṇā Mahālakṣmī, the supreme Śakti, worshiped alike by the great creator, preserver, and destroyer gods of theistic Hinduism as well as by Indra, chief of the old Vedic gods.

**25:** As with the Kavaca, if the reciter is a married woman or a celibate monastic, "wife" may be replaced by either "husband" or "companion."

**27:** The "great hymn of seven hundred verses" is the Devīmāhātmya.

# कीलकस्तोत्रम्

# KĪLAKASTOTRA

ॐ नमश्चण्डिकायै

Oṁ. Salutations to Caṇḍikā.

मार्कण्डेय उवाच ।

Mārkaṇḍeya said:

ॐ विशुद्धज्ञानदेहाय त्रिवेदीदिव्यचक्षुषे ।
श्रेयःप्राप्तिनिमित्ताय नमः सोमार्धधारिणे ॥ १ ॥

1. Oṁ. To him whose body is pure knowledge, whose divine eyes are the three Vedas; to him who is the cause of attaining the supreme, salutations to [Śiva] who wears the half-moon.

सर्वमेतद्विजानीयान्मन्त्राणामपि कीलकम् ।
सोऽपि क्षेममवाप्नोति सततं जप्यतत्परः ॥ २ ॥

2. Whoever would understand all this, the key to the verses [of the Devīmāhātmya], and is ever intent on reciting [them] shall surely succeed.

सिद्ध्यन्त्युच्चाटनादीनि कर्माणि सकलान्यपि ।
एतेन स्तुवतां देवीं स्तोत्रवृन्देन भक्तितः ॥ ३ ॥

3. All actions for thwarting adversity succeed for those who sing the Devī's praises with this multitude of verses in succession.

न मन्त्रो नौषधं तस्य न किञ्चिदपि विद्यते ।
विना जप्येन सिद्ध्येत्तु सर्वमुच्चाटनादिकम् ॥ ४ ॥

4. Without this recitation there is no spell, or medicine, or anything else that will succeed in thwarting all adversity.

समग्राण्यपि सेत्स्यन्ति लोकशङ्कामिमां हरः ।
कृत्वा निमन्त्रयामास सर्वमेवमिदं शुभम् ॥ ५ ॥

5. [But with recitation] all will succeed. When Hara [Śiva] created this uncertainty in the world, he also ordained this entire auspicious [Devīmāhātmya].

स्तोत्रं वै चण्डिकायास्तु तच्च गुह्यं चकार सः ।
समाप्नोति स पुण्येन तां यथावन्निमन्त्रणाम् ॥ ६ ॥

6. And he made secret this very hymn to Caṇḍikā. [The reciter] reaches her through holiness in order that she may be pleased and accept his appeal.

सोऽपि क्षेममवाप्नोति सर्वमेव न संशयः ।
कृष्णायां वा चतुर्दश्यामष्टम्यां वा समाहितः ॥ ७ ॥

7. Without doubt, he who meditates with full concentration on the fourteenth or eighth days of the dark lunar fortnight attains complete well-being.

ददाति प्रतिगृह्णाति नान्यथैषा प्रसीदति ।
इत्थं रूपेण कीलेन महादेवेन कीलितम् ॥ ८ ॥

8. He gives [devotion to the Devī], [and] he receives [her grace]. In no other way is she pleased. And so, Mahādeva [Śiva] secured [the Devīmāhātmya] as if with a pin.

यो निष्कीलां विधायैनां चण्डीं जपति नित्यशः ।
स सिद्धः स गणः सोऽथ गन्धर्वो जायते ध्रुवम् ॥ ९ ॥

9. Whoever constantly recites this Caṇḍī properly, with the restraint removed, surely becomes a perfected being, a divine attendant, even a celestial singer.

न चैवापाटवं तस्य भयं क्वापि न जायते ।
नापमृत्युवशं याति मृते च मोक्षमाप्नुयात् ॥ १० ॥

10. And when he goes about, no danger arises anywhere. Never is he subject to untimely death, and at death he will attain liberation.

ज्ञात्वा प्रारभ्य कुर्वीत ह्यकुर्वाणो विनश्यति ।
ततो ज्ञात्वैव सम्पूर्णमिदं प्रारभ्यते बुधैः ॥ ११ ॥

11. Knowing [all this] and having commenced [this practice], one should perform [the recitation of the Devīmāhātmya]. Not doing so, one perishes. Knowing so, the wise devote themselves to this [which brings] complete fulfillment.

सौभाग्यादि च यत्किञ्चिद् दृश्यते ललनाजने ।
तत्सर्वं तत्प्रसादेन तेन जप्यमिदं शुभम् ॥ १२ ॥

12. Beauty, charm, and whatever other auspicious qualities are seen in women, all those are by [the Devī's] grace. For that reason this auspicious [Devīmāhātmya] should be recited.

शनैस्तु जप्यमानेऽस्मिन् स्तोत्रे सम्पत्तिरुच्चकैः ।
भवत्येव समग्रापि ततः प्रारभ्यमेव तत् ॥ १३ ॥

13. Even when this hymn is recited softly, its success is resounding, its fulfillment is complete. Therefore one should proceed.

ऐश्वर्यं तत्प्रसादेन सौभाग्यारोग्यमेव च ।
शत्रुहानिः परो मोक्षः स्तूयते सा न किं जनैः ॥ १४ ॥

14. Sovereignty, prosperity, health, the destruction of enemies, and supreme liberation are indeed by her grace; why should people not praise her?

चण्डिकां हृदयेनापि यः स्मरेत् सततं नरः ।
हृद्यं काममवाप्नोति हृदि देवी सदा वसेत् ॥ १५ ॥

15. One who always remembers Caṇḍikā in his heart attains his fondest desire; in his heart the Devī shall forever dwell.

अग्रतोऽमुं महादेवकृतं कीलकवारणम् ।
निष्कीलञ्च तथा कृत्वा पठितव्यं समाहितैः ॥ १६ ॥

16. At first Mahādeva imposed the restraint of this pin. Freed from that restraint, [the Devīmāhātmya] is to be recited by those whose minds are fixed in meditation.

# Kīlakastotra Commentary

The Kīlakastotra ("Hymn of the Pin") holds the bolt (*argalā*) in place and keeps the Devīmāhātmya's power under lock and key, as it were, lest it should fall into the wrong hands and be misused. For that reason, its language is intentionally obscure, elliptical, and grammatically ambiguous, allowing for considerable latitude in interpretation. According to esoteric tradition, the Kīlaka's true meaning will duly be revealed to the aspirant who is spiritually prepared to receive it.[1]

What is this secret meaning? Verse 8 begins, "He gives, he receives," followed by "in no other way is she pleased." Only by self-surrender in complete devotion can the practitioner be receptive to the Devī's grace. This brief dictum recalls the idea of reciprocity between the human and the Divine implied in the Devīmāhātmya (4.5; 5.50), and one can also infer from it the obstructive role of the ego in blocking the flow of grace.

"Destruction of enemies" in verse 14 should be taken in the metaphorical sense as the slaying of inner demons, the ego's ignorance and evil tendencies that spill their poison out into the world. Related to this is "thwarting adversity" (*uccāṭana*) in verses 3 and 4. The Sanskrit term can mean either ruining an adversary, using magic to stop another person from performing certain actions, eradicating something, or driving away a pernicious influence. Since causing harm to others is incompatible with spiritual advancement, *uccāṭana* has to be understood here as the mental eradication of internal forces that obstruct right knowledge. Similarly, "sovereignty" in verse 14 ultimately refers to power not over others but over one's lower self, the ego.

The person who surrenders to the Devī with complete devotion receives her protective grace in this life and liberation afterward (verse 10). Compare the Nārāyaṇīstuti's teaching on worldly enjoyment and final liberation in the Devīmāhātmya (11.7). There is no reason not to be devoted to the Devī, who is the source of all good, declares the Kīlaka (verse 14). In the same way that the Devīmāhātmya promises that she comes to those who remember her (4.35; 5.6), the Kīlaka reveals that the Devī dwells always in the heart that remembers her. The secret, the key, is to devote heart and mind to her. As she proclaims in the Devīmāhātmya, "This entire glorification (māhātmya) of mine draws one near to me. Therefore this poem of my glory is to be recited by those of concentrated mind and heard always with devotion, for it is the supreme way to well-being" (12.20; 12.7).

# रात्रिसूक्तम्

## RĀTRISŪKTA

ॐ रात्री व्यख्यदायती पुरुत्रा देव्यक्षभिः ।
विश्वा अधि श्रियोऽधित ॥ १ ॥

1. Oṁ. The goddess Night, approaching, illumines every direction with her eyes. She has put on all her glories.

ओर्वप्रा अमर्त्या निवतो देव्युद्वतः ।
ज्योतिषा बाधते तमः ॥ २ ॥

2. The immortal goddess has filled the world's breadth, heights, and depths with her light. She drives away the darkness.

निरु स्वसारमस्कृतोषसं देव्यायती ।
अपेदु हासते तमः ॥ ३ ॥

3. The approaching goddess follows upon her sister, Dawn, at whose coming the darkness likewise departs.

सा नो अद्य यस्या वयं नि ते यामन्नविक्ष्महि ।
वृक्षे न वसतिं वयः ॥ ४ ॥

4. Now she is upon us: at her coming we go to rest as birds to their nest in a tree.

नि ग्रामासो अविक्षत नि पद्वन्तो नि पक्षिणः ।
नि श्येनासश्चिदर्थिनः ॥ ५ ॥

5. The villagers have gone to rest, and so, too, all the creatures that walk or fly, even the ravenous hawks.

यावया वृक्यं वृकं यवय स्तेनमूर्म्ये ।
अथा नः सुतरा भव ॥ ६ ॥

6. Ward off the she-wolf and the wolf, ward off the thief, O wave of darkness, and be easy for us to pass through.

उप मा पेपिशत्तमः कृष्णं व्यक्तमस्थित ।
उप ऋणेव यातय ॥ ७ ॥

7. For now, the palpable blackness crushes down upon me. O Dawn, collect it dutifully.

उप ते गा इवाकरं वृणीष्व दुहितर्दिवः ।
रात्रि स्तोमं न जिग्युषे ॥ ८ ॥

8. As you would accept a precious herd of cattle, O daughter of heaven, O Night, accept this hymn, offered as if to a conqueror.

# Rātrisūkta Commentary

At face value, the Rātrisūkta ("Hymn to Night" [ṚV 10.127]) is a glorious nature poem in praise of the deified night, described as a beautiful goddess whose many eyes are the stars that illumine every quarter. Her approaching darkness causes people, animals, and birds to seek rest. But there are predators, animal and human alike, that lurk in that darkness. Against them the hymn appeals for protection and easy passage through the night until, as surely as the crushing blackness engulfs the earth like a wave, Night's sister, Dawn (Uṣas), heralds the returning light of day.

This earliest hymn to the goddess Rātri reveals her benevolent and terrifying faces, but a later gloss appended to the Ṛgveda immediately after the Rātrīsūkta concentrates on her auspicious, restful, and protective nature. That text, the Rātrīkhila, presents many themes found later in the Devīmāhātmya and employs the same epithets and entire verses that are markedly similar. Four times in three verses it refers to the personified Night as Durgā (ṚV Kh 4.2.5, 12, 13).[1] In Vedic worship, Rātri was closely identified with Vāk, Sarasvatī, and Aditi, who were considered one and the same goddess, the supreme deity further identified with Durgā.[2]

From a metaphysical standpoint, Rātri represents the obscuring māyā, the power that simultaneously projects the world and envelops it in spiritual darkness. Yet, as surely as night follows day, Rātri's sister, Uṣas, heralds the approaching light. The Devī's inseparable faces—the night of duality that deceives and the illuminating light of dawn that points toward enlightenment—represent in turn the ignorance and falsehood of ordinary human awareness, and the blissful knowledge of Brahman.[3] With darkness comes fear, for what dangers may lurk there unseen? For no small reason the Devīmāhātmya calls Mahāmāyā "the terrifying night of delusion" (1.78), referring to the embodied human state. Nevertheless, we must not forget that the dark goddess merely veils her own light, for beyond ignorance and knowledge she is self-luminous consciousness.[4]

# देवीसूक्तम्

## DEVĪSŪKTA

ॐ अहं रुद्रेभिर्वसुभिश्चराम्यहमादित्यैरुत विश्वदेवैः ।
अहं मित्रावरुणोभा बिभर्म्यहमिन्द्राग्नी अहमश्विनोभा ॥ १ ॥

1. OṀ. I move through the gods of storm and light, through the gods of the heavens, through all the gods. I uphold the lords of day and night, the sovereign of the atmosphere, the god of fire, and the benevolent celestial guardians.

अहं सोममाहनसं बिभर्म्यहं त्वष्टारमुत पूषणं भगम् ।
अहं दधामि द्रविणं हविष्मते सुप्राव्ये यजमानाय सुन्वते ॥ २ ॥

2. I bear the nectar of immortality. I support the creator of living beings, the protector of the universe, and the gracious lord of prosperity. I bestow wealth on those who prepare the sacrifices and offer the oblations with an attentive mind.

अहं राष्ट्री सङ्गमनी वसूनां चिकितुषी प्रथमा यज्ञियानाम् ।
तां मा देवा व्यदधुः पुरुत्रा भूरिस्थात्रां भूर्यावेशयन्तीम् ॥ ३ ॥

3. I am the sovereign in whom all the auspicious gods are united. Shining with consciousness, I am foremost among those worthy of worship. The gods diffuse me in every direction, my presence abiding in many places and revealed in manifold ways.

मया सो अन्नमत्ति यो विपश्यति यः प्राणिति य ईं शृणोत्युक्तम् ।
अमन्तवो मां त उपक्षियन्ति श्रुधि श्रुत श्रद्धिवं ते वदामि ॥ ४ ॥

4. Through me alone all mortals live who see and breathe and hear what is said, not knowing that they abide in me. Hear me as I speak the truth to you.

अहमेव स्वयमिदं वदामि जुष्टं देवेभिरुत मानुषेभिः ।
यं कामये तं तमुग्रं कृणोमि तं ब्रह्माणं तमृषिं तं सुमेधाम् ॥ ५ ॥

5. I myself proclaim this, which is pleasing to gods and men alike: I make mighty whomever I wish, I make him devout and open his eyes to right understanding.

अहं रुद्राय धनुरा तनोमि ब्रह्मद्विषे शरवे हन्तवा उ ।
अहं जनाय समदं कृणोम्यहं द्यावापृथिवी आ विवेश ॥ ६ ॥

6. For the god who puts evil to flight, I draw the bow, that his arrow may strike down the hater of devotion; such is the fervor I stir within that man. Through heaven and earth I extend.

अहं सुवे पितरमस्य मूर्धन् मम योनिरप्स्वन्तः समुद्रे ।
ततो वि तिष्ठे भुवनानु विश्वोतामं द्यां वर्ष्मणोप स्पृशामि ॥ ७ ॥

7. At the summit of creation, I bring forth the heavens. My creative power flows from amid the waters of the infinite ocean. Thence I spread through all the worlds and touch yonder heaven with my vastness.

अहमेव वात इव प्रवाम्यारभमाणा भुवनानि विश्वा ।
परो दिवा पर एना पृथिव्यैतावती महिना सं बभूव ॥ ८ ॥

8. I breathe forth like the wind, setting all the worlds in motion. So great have I become in my splendor, shining far beyond heaven and earth.

# Devīsūkta Commentary

The hymnist of the Devīsūkta (ṚV 10.125) is Āmbhṛṇī, the daughter of a Vedic sage. Inspired with the knowledge of the Self, she becomes the seer through whom the goddess Vāk proclaims her own glory. To appreciate the full import of this remarkable hymn, we must keep in mind that Vāk, Sarasvatī, and Aditi are one and the same goddess, the source of all powers of heaven and earth. The Bṛhaddevatā, a large work that explains the deities of the Ṛgvedic hymns, further identifies this supreme goddess with Durgā (BD 2.79).[1] Reinforcing that identity, the text of the Devīmāhātmya itself specifies that when Suratha and Samādhi worshiped on the river bank, they chanted the Devīsūkta (13.9). The Devī whom the king and merchant addressed is none other than the primeval Great Goddess who spoke through Āmbhṛṇī, the Ṛgveda's female seer.

The Devīsūkta belongs to the most highly-developed phase of early Vedic philosophical thought, which leans increasingly toward metaphysical inquiry. Its archaic language presents a number of difficulties, not the least of them a pervasive use of ordinary words in a metaphorical sense. Because the associations for many words employed as symbols of other things are lost on us today, literal translation tends to obscure the meaning that would have been obvious to the original hearers. The foregoing translation interprets the meaning behind the metaphors. A more literal version follows below, along with explanatory comments.

**1:** "I go about with the Rudras, the Vasus, I with the Ādityas and also with the All-Gods. I uphold both Mitra and Varuṇa, I both Indra and Agni, I the Aśvins." The verb *carāmi* means variously "I go," "I move," or "I act." It comes from the verbal root *car*, which implies movement in space and time and relates to the dynamic nature of Śakti. The names of the gods occur in the instrumental case, which denotes either accompaniment or agency. It is quite possible to read this verse as either "I go about with the gods" or "I work through the gods." Given that the speaker is the supreme Devī, it makes better sense to think of the gods as agents of her power than to consider her their mere traveling companion; it is logically consistent with the rest of the hymn to understand her as the indwelling presence that empowers the gods. The translation replaces the names of the Vedic deities, which no longer have meaningful immediacy, with their functions, because the realities of storm, sunlight, and nature's luminosity cannot fail to communicate. The term *viśvadevas* is especially ambiguous, because it means either "all the gods" or, alternatively, "the All-Gods," a particular but vaguely defined class of sky deities.

**2:** "I uphold the Soma to be pressed, and I [uphold] Tvaṣṭṛ, Pūṣan, [and] Bhaga. I grant wealth to the attentive sacrificer who offers oblation, who presses [the Soma]." The juice of the sacred *soma* plant played a significant role in Ṛgvedic ritual because of its mind-altering, ecstasy-inducing properties. Offered to the gods and ingested by the priests, soma was highly prized as the nectar of immortality. Its use died out by Brāhmaṇic times, and its identity was lost, although its recently proposed identification with *Amanita muscaria*, the fly-agaric mushroom, is highly persuasive.[2] In later mythology soma became connected with the moon, which was thought to be the receptacle of *amṛta*, the nectar of immortality. In the metaphoric language of the Ṛgveda, soma also represents the infinite ocean of bliss and creative energy, which is identical to the Devī's ultimate being as Ādyā Śakti. For the Devī to say in the Devīsūkta that she supports that which is her very nature is to proclaim that she is the self-existent One and the womb of all possibility.[3] Similarly, she supports (and acts through) the deities or divine energies that fashion the forms of life, sustain them, and grant prosperity and well-being.

**3:** "I am the queen, who gathers treasures together, the conscious (or knowing) one, first among those worthy of worship. The gods have diffused me in many directions, being in many places and made known in various ways." In the Ṛgveda the word *vasu*, generally translated here as "treasures," has the primary meaning of "gods," and especially the luminous sky deities. "Wealth" or "property" is another legitimate reading, but the reference to wealth in the preceding verse uses another word, *draviṇa*. The context of the present verse supports the reading of "gods," among whom the Devī, the supreme consciousness, is foremost. Precisely through those gods, who are but facets of her power, is the all-pervading divine energy-consciousness spread throughout the world in many ways.

**4:** "Through me he eats food, who sees, who breathes, who hears what is spoken. Knowing it not, they dwell beside me. Hear me tell you that which is worthy of faith." Here, eating is a metaphor for living, the embodied experience that entails metabolic processes, movement, perception, cognition, and all other functions of human intelligence, except for the higher awareness that the Devī is the source of them all. To become awakened to that supreme truth is the purpose of sādhana, for which righteous living is a prerequisite. Yet even those who are unaware of the divine presence are sustained by the Mother's grace.[4]

**5:** "I myself proclaim this, which is esteemed (or welcomed) by gods and men. Whomever I wish (or love), him I make mighty, him [I make] a brāhmaṇa, a seer, a man of good understanding." The terms *brāhmaṇa, seer*" and *man of good* (or clear) *understanding* represent, in the broadest possible sense, people who are awakened in turn to devoutness, divine vision, and spiritual knowledge.

**6:** "I draw the bow for Rudra, that his arrow may strike down the hater of devotion. I rouse [the wise] man to fervor (or battle); I penetrate heaven and earth." Rudra should be thought of as a manifestation of the Devī's own energy, and his bow as a metaphor for right intent, shooting the arrows of thought that destroy the obstacles to the higher knowledge that connects the human to the Divine. The person roused to excited action is the awakened votary of the previous verse, and the action both pertains to and proceeds from inner states of awareness. The word *battle* can also be understood as a debate between sages; such rhetorical contests were common in Vedic times as a means of arriving at spiritual truth.[5] At the end of the verse, the subject shifts abruptly to the Devī's all-pervasiveness.

**7:** "At the summit of this world, I give birth to the father; my womb is in the midst of the waters, in the ocean. Thence I extend through all worlds and reach up to yonder sky with my greatness." The father is the sky or heaven, and the Devī's womb (yoni), sometimes translated as "origin" or "home," is her creative power, inherent in the metaphoric waters of the ocean, which symbolizes infinite being-consciousness. From this emanates the whole of the universe, pervaded by the same divine consciousness from which it originates. As in the Devīmāhātmya, the Divine Mother is both source and manifestation.

**8:** "I blow forth like the wind, resolutely commencing all worlds. Beyond heaven, beyond this earth, to such an extent have I become in my glory." Here Vāk likens her energy to the wind, breathing forth all the forms of creation. Yet, even in her all-pervading immanence, she surpasses the limits of the wide world and the vaulted heavens, for ultimately, she is the transcendent Absolute.

# प्राधानिकं रहस्यम्

## PRĀDHĀNIKA RAHAṢYA

राजोवाच ।

The king said:

ॐ भगवन्नवतारा मे चण्डिकायास्त्वयोदिताः ।
एतेषां प्रकृतिं ब्रह्मन्प्रधानं वक्तुमर्हसि ॥ १ ॥

1. OṀ. Blessed one, you have told me about Caṇḍikā's manifestations. Be pleased, O knower of what is sacred, to speak of their essential nature.

आराध्यं यन्मया देव्याः स्वरूपं येन च द्विज ।
विधिना ब्रूहि सकलं यथावत्प्रणतस्य मे ॥ २ ॥

2. Accepting my reverence, O twice-born, tell me everything of the Devī's true being, and by what manner, by which ritual I am to worship.

ऋषिरुवाच ।

The seer said:

इदं रहस्यं परममनाख्येयं प्रचक्ष्यते ।
भक्तोऽसीति न मे किञ्चित्तवावाच्यं नराधिप ॥ ३ ॥

3. This is the supreme secret, and it is said that it should not be divulged. But look how devoted you are! There is nothing I would not tell you, O king.

सर्वस्याद्या महालक्ष्मीस्त्रिगुणा परमेश्वरी ।
लक्ष्यालक्ष्यस्वरूपा सा व्याप्य कृत्स्नं व्यवस्थिता ॥ ४ ॥

4. First and foremost is Mahālakṣmī, who holds the three forces of creation. She is the supreme sovereign. She is both defined by form and indefinably formless; having manifested in every way, she abides in everything.

मातुलिङ्गं गदां खेटं पानपात्रं च बिभ्रती ।
नागं लिङ्गं च योनिं च बिभ्रती नृप मूर्द्धनि ॥ ५ ॥

5. She holds a citron, mace, shield, and drinking vessel. On her head, O king, she bears a serpent, liṅga, and yoni.

तप्तकाञ्चनवर्णाभा तप्तकाञ्चनभूषणा ।
शून्यं तदखिलं स्वेन पूरयामास तेजसा ॥ ६ ॥

6. Her complexion is the color of molten gold, and like molten gold, her ornaments shine. She filled the entire void with her radiant light.

शून्यं तदखिलं लोकं विलोक्य परमेश्वरी ।
बभार परमं रूपं तमसा केवलेन हि ॥ ७ ॥

7. Seeing the entire universe a void, the supreme sovereign conceived a surpassing form through her power of tamas.

सा भिन्नाञ्जनसंकाशा दंष्ट्राङ्कितवरानना ।
विशाललोचना नारी बभूव तनुमध्यमा ॥ ८ ॥

8. She became a woman, shining black like collyrium, teeth glistening in her lovely mouth, her eyes wide, her waist slender,

खड्गपात्रशिरःखेटैरलंकृतचतुर्भुजा ।
कबन्धहारं शिरसा बिभ्राणा हि शिरःस्रजम् ॥ ९ ॥

9. her four hands adorned with sword, drinking-cup, head, and shield, her neck garlanded with strands of headless torsoes and a necklace made of skulls.

सा प्रोवाच महालक्ष्मीं तामसी प्रमदोत्तमा ।
नाम कर्म च मे मातर्देहि तुभ्यं नमो नमः ॥ १० ॥

10. The dark one, this fairest of women, asked Mahālakṣmī, “Mother, give me my names and deeds. Salutations to you again and again.”

तां प्रोवाच महालक्ष्मीस्तामसीं प्रमदोत्तमाम् ।
ददामि तव नामानि यानि कर्माणि तानि ते ॥ ११ ॥

11. Mahālakṣmī answered her, the dark one fairest among women, “I give you the names [you will be known by] and the actions [you will perform].

महामाया महाकाली महामारी क्षुधा तृषा ।
निद्रा तृष्णा चैकवीरा कालरात्रिर्दुरत्यया ॥ १२ ॥

12. Mahāmāyā, Mahākālī, Mahāmārī, Kṣudhā, Tṛṣā, Nidrā, Tṛṣṇā, Ekavirā, Kālarātri, Duratyayā—

इमानि तव नामानि प्रतिपाद्यानि कर्मभिः ।
एभिः कर्माणि ते ज्ञात्वा योऽधीते सोऽश्नुते सुखम् ॥ १३ ॥

13. these are your names, and their meanings will be revealed by your actions. Understanding your actions through them, whoever reflects on them will attain happiness.”

तामित्युक्त्वा महालक्ष्मीः स्वरूपमपरं नृप ।
सत्त्वाख्येनातिशुद्धेन गुणेनेन्दुप्रभं दधौ ॥ १४ ॥

14. O king, when she had spoken to her thus, Mahālakṣmī, through her surpassingly pure power known as sattva, assumed another unequaled form, lustrous like the moon.

अक्षमालाङ्कुशधरा वीणापुस्तकधारिणी ।
सा बभूव वरा नारी नामान्यस्यै च सा ददौ ॥ १५ ॥

15. She became an exquisite woman, holding prayer beads and goad, vīṇā, and book. And to her Mahālakṣmī gave names:

महाविद्या महावाणी भारती वाक् सरस्वती ।
आर्या ब्राह्मी कामधेनुर्वेदगर्भा च धीश्वरी ॥ १६ ॥

16. Mahāvidyā, Mahāvāṇī, Bhāratī, Vāk, Sarasvatī, Āryā, Brāhmī, Kāmadhenu, Vedagarbhā and Dhīśvarī.

अथोवाच महालक्ष्मीर्महाकालीं सरस्वतीम् ।
युवां जनयतां देव्यौ मिथुने स्वानुरूपतः ॥ १७ ॥

17. Then Mahālakṣmī said to Mahākālī and Mahāsarasvatī: "Goddesses, bring forth couples, male and female, according to your own natures."

इत्युक्त्वा ते महालक्ष्मीः ससर्ज मिथुनं स्वयम् ।
हिरण्यगर्भौ रुचिरौ स्त्रीपुंसौ कमलासनौ ॥ १८ ॥

18. Having spoken thus, Mahālakṣmī produced her own female and male couple, born of the golden womb, resplendent, and seated on a lotus.

ब्रह्मन्विधे विरिञ्चेति धातरित्याह तं नरम् ।
श्रीः पद्मे कमले लक्ष्मीत्याह माता च तां स्त्रियम ॥ १९ ॥

19. The Mother called the male Brahmā, Vidhi, Viriñca, Dhātṛ; and she called the female Śrī, Padmā, Kamalā, Lakṣmī.

महाकाली भारती च मिथुने सृजतः सह ।
एतयोरपि रूपाणि नामानि च वदामि ते ॥ २० ॥

20. Likewise Mahākālī and Bhāratī each produced a couple. I shall tell you their forms and names.

नीलकण्ठं रक्तबाहुं श्वेताङ्गं चन्द्रशेखरम् ।
जनयामास पुरुषं महाकाली सितां स्त्रियम् ॥ २१ ॥

21. Mahākālī brought forth a blue-throated, red-armed, white-limbed, and moon-crested male, and a white female.

स रुद्रः शङ्करः स्थाणुः कपर्दी च त्रिलोचनः ।
त्रयी विद्या कामधेनुः सा स्त्री भाषाक्षरा स्वरा ॥ २२ ॥

22. He is Rudra, Śaṅkara, Sthāṇu, Kapardī, and Trilocana. The woman is Trayī, Vidyā, Kāmadhenu, Bhāṣākṣarā, and Svarā,

सरस्वती स्त्रियं गौरीं कृष्णं च पुरुषं नृप ।
जनयामास नामानि तयोरपि वदामि ते ॥ २३ ॥

23. [Mahā]sarasvatī brought forth a shining white female and a blue-black male, O king. I shall tell you their names.

विष्णुः कृष्णो हृषीकेशो वासुदेवो जनार्दनः ।
उमा गौरी सती चण्डी सुन्दरी सुभगा शिवा ॥ २४ ॥

24. [His are] Viṣṇu, Kṛṣṇa, Hṛṣīkeśa, Vāsudeva, Janārdana; [hers are] Umā, Gaurī, Satī, Caṇḍī, Sundarī, Subhagā, Śivā.

एवं युवतयः सद्यः पुरुषत्वं प्रपेदिरे ।
चक्षुष्मन्तो नु पश्यन्ति नेतरेऽतद्विदो जनाः ॥ २५ ॥

25. In that way, the three young women at once assumed maleness. Those who are able to see will certainly see, but not the rest who remain uncomprehending.

ब्रह्मणे प्रददौ पत्नीं महालक्ष्मीर्नृप त्रयीम् ।
रुद्राय गौरीं वरदां वासुदेवाय च श्रियम् ॥ २६ ॥

26. Then, O king, Mahālakṣmī presented Trayī as a wife to Brahmā, Gaurī to Rudra, and Śrī to Vāsudeva.

स्वरया सह संभूय विरिञ्चोऽण्डमजीजनत् ।
बिभेद भगवान्रुद्रस्तद्गौर्या सह वीर्यवान् ॥ २७ ॥

27. Viriñca united with Svarā and created an egg. The blessed, heroic Rudra, together with Gaurī, broke it open.

अण्डमध्ये प्रधानादि कार्यजातमभून्नृप ।
महाभूतात्मकं सर्वं जगत्स्थावरजङ्गमम् ॥ २८ ॥

28. Within the egg, O king, was the primary matter, destined to evolve into all the universe, moving and unmoving, consisting of the five gross elements.

पुपोष पालयामास तल्लक्ष्म्या सह केशवः ।
संजहार जगत्सर्वं सह गौर्या महेश्वरः ॥ २९ ॥

29. Keśava, together with Lakṣmī, nourished and protected it. Maheśvara, along with Gaurī, dissolved all the universe.

महालक्ष्मीर्महाराज सर्वसत्त्वमयीश्वरी ।
निराकारा च साकारा सैव नानाभिधानभृत् ॥ ३० ॥

30. O great king, Mahālakṣmī is the supreme sovereign, the true essence of all that is. She is both formless and with form, bearing various names.

नामान्तरैर्निरूप्यैषा नाम्ना नान्येन केनचित् ॥ ३१ ॥

31. She can be described by different names, yet by no other name [can she truly be known].

# Prādhānika Rahasya Commentary

Known as Rahasyas ("secrets"), the three aṅgas usually recited after the Devīmāhātmya form a continuation of King Suratha's dialogue with Medhas and relate to the manifestations of Śakti. If the function of the three preliminary aṅgas is to assure the reciter's safe access to divine power, the purpose of the Rahasyas is to instruct in philosophy and ritual worship. These three closely related texts have been called the "earliest systematic statement of Śākta philosophy."[1]

The Prādhānika Rahasya ("The Secret Relating to Primary Matter," or "The Preeminent Secret") takes as its point of departure the Brahmāstuti's phrase "differentiating into the threefold qualities of everything" (DM 1.78). In considering how the singular ultimate reality assumes the multiple forms of the phenomenal universe, the Prādhānika Rahasya first describes the differentiation of the guṇas as taking place within the Devī herself and remaining at the unmanifest (avyākṛta) stage.[2]

Attempting to describe the indescribable, Medhas paradoxically uses vivid mythological images to refer to unmanifest states of being, beginning with a verbal portrayal of Mahālakṣmī as the supreme, formless "form" of the Devī, containing the three guṇas in perfect, non-manifesting equilibrium (verse 4). He describes the symbols of her powers held in her four hands, and on her head the coiled serpent representing the cosmic cycle of time; the liṅga, symbolizing absolute consciousness; and the yoni, standing for relative consciousness (verse 5).

Alone in an emptiness paradoxically filled with her own light (verse 6), Mahālakṣmī assumes a second form, made from unalloyed tamas. Usually the word *tamas* is translated in this verse as "darkness," which makes a dramatic effect; but it should be remembered that any English word—for example, "darkness, inertia, ignorance, illusion, veiling"—describes only the visible effects of tamas and not the pure energy in itself.

The names of the tamasic, four-armed Mahākālī, revealed in verse 12, encompass proper names, personified qualities, and descriptive epithets. In my translation, I have retained the original Sanskrit forms as capitalized names—indeed, verse 11 announces them as names—but their meanings are significant. Mahāmāyā ("Great Illusion") is the divine power that makes the phenomenal universe cognizable to the senses. Mahākālī ("Great Darkness") signifies pure tamas personified. Mahāmārī ("Great Destroyer") indicates a form of Durgā. The others are Kṣudhā ("Hunger"), Tṛṣā ("Thirst"), Nidrā ("Sleep"), Tṛṣṇā ("Desire"), Ekavīrā ("Foremost Heroine"), Kālarātri ("Dark Night"), Duratyayā and ("Inscrutable One").

Next, Mahālakṣmī assumes a form made of pure sattva (verse 14) and receives her names (verse 16). They are Mahāvidyā ("Great Knowledge"), Mahāvāṇī ("Great Sound"), Bhāratī ("Eloquence"), Vāk ("Speech"), Sarasvatī ("Flowing One"), Āryā ("Noble One"), Brāhmī (the śakti of Brahmā), Kāmadhenu ("Wish-Fulfilling Cow," a reference to the Devī's nurturing aspect), Vedagarbhā ("Womb of the Vedas"), and Dhīśvarī ("Sovereign of Wisdom"). Three of these refer to the creative capacity of sound, speech, and language. *Dhī* in the final epithet signifies thought, especially of a religious nature, such as meditation or prayer, or more generally reflection, intelligence, wisdom, knowledge, or art—all functions associated with sattva.

After differentiation, each guṇa generates a polarized pair of offspring, represented as male and female (verses 17 through 25). This polarization can be thought of as analogous, in the scientific view, to the up and down differentiation of quarks, positive and negative electrical charges, or the north and south poles of a magnet.

Again, there are the names. Mahālakṣmī's male offspring is Brahmā, also called Vidhi ("Creator"), Viriñca (etymology uncertain), and Dhātṛ ("Supporter"); the female is Śrī ("Splendor"), Padmā ("Lotus"), Kamalā ("Lotus") and Lakṣmī ("Good Fortune, Prosperity"). Mahākālī's male offspring is Rudra ("Howling One") or Śiva, also called Śaṅkara ("Causing Prosperity, Beneficent, Auspicious"), Sthāṇu ("Standing Firmly, Motionless"), Kapardī ("He of Matted Locks"), and Trilocana ("Three-Eyed"); the female is Sarasvatī, also called Trayī ("Three [Vedas]"), Vidyā ("Knowledge"), Kāmadhenu ("Wish-Fulfilling Cow"), Bhāṣākṣarā ("Letters of Speech"), and Svarā ("Sound, Speech"). Mahāsarasvatī's male offspring is Viṣṇu, whose other names include Kṛṣṇa ("Dark One"), Hṛṣīkeśa ("He Whose Hair Stands on End [with Joy]"), Vāsudeva ("God of Gods"), and Janārdana ("Exciting, or Agitating, Men"); the female is Umā (a name of Pārvatī), also known as Gaurī ("Shining One"), Satī ("Your Ladyship," a name of Durgā, sometimes described as Truth personified), Caṇḍī ("Fierce, Impetuous"), Sundarī ("Beautiful"), Subhagā ("Possessing Good Fortune, Blessed"), and Śivā ("Auspicious").

The marriages that couple the tamasic Sarasvatī with the rajasic Brahmā, the rajasic Lakṣmī with the sattvic Viṣṇu, and the sattvic Gaurī with the tamasic Rudra signal the beginning of the guṇas' process of interaction (verse 26), which leads to all the activity of the universe. Brahmā and Sarasvatī produce a cosmic egg, which Rudra and Gaurī break open (verse 27), releasing the *pradhāna*—primary, unevolved matter, which will evolve through the further and increasingly complex combining and recombining of the guṇas into the five subtle elements (*tanmātras*) and then into the five gross elements (*mahābhūtas*) of space, air, fire, water and earth. Although the concept of the physical world as consisting of five elements may seem archaic and quaint, note how scientific it truly is. Air, water, and earth represent the three states of matter—gaseous, liquid, and solid. These states are determined by temperature (fire) and can only exist within space.

Then Viṣṇu and Lakṣmī nourished and protected the creation, and Śiva and Gaurī dissolved it back into its source (verse 29). Note that Medhas relates this in the past tense, as if to say that all this happened, happens, and will happen again in a never-ending pulsation of evolution and involution. The Devī is both the ever-changing forms of existence and the formlessness of pure being (verse 30)—that is the pre-eminent secret. According to her manifestations, she is known by many names, yet no name can reveal the fullness of her true nature, which is the infinite Self (verse 31).

# वैकृतिकं रहस्यम्

## VAIKṚTIKA RAHASYA

ऋषिरुवाच ।

The seer said:

ॐ त्रिगुणा तामसी देवी सात्त्विकी या त्रिधोदिता ।
सा शर्वा चण्डिका दुर्गा भद्रा भगवतीर्यते ॥ १ ॥

1. Oṁ. The Devī, who appears manifest in three ways—as containing the three guṇas, as dark, and as brilliantly pure—is called Śarvā, Caṇḍikā, Durgā, Bhadrā, and Bhagavatī.

योगनिद्रा हरेरुक्ता महाकाली तमोगुणा ।
मधुकैटभनाशार्थं यां तुष्टावाम्बुजासनः ॥ २ ॥

2. She is said to be Viṣṇu's mystic sleep, Mahākālī, whose energy is tamas, whom Brahmā, seated on the lotus, praised that she might destroy Madhu and Kaiṭabha.

दशवक्त्रा दशभुजा दशपादाञ्जनप्रभा ।
विशालया राजमाना त्रिंशल्लोचनमालया ॥ ३ ॥

3. She has ten faces, ten arms, and ten feet. She is lustrous as collyrium; she shines radiantly, as if garlanded with her thirty eyes.

स्फुरद्दशनदंष्ट्रा सा भीमरूपापि भूमिप ।
रूपसौभाग्य कान्तीनां सा प्रतिष्ठा महाश्रियः ॥ ४ ॥

4. O king, even though she is of frightful appearance with glistening teeth and fangs, she is the beauty in form, the foundation of all loveliness and great splendor.

खड्गबाणगदाशूलचक्रशङ्खभुशुण्डिभृत् ।
परिघं कार्मुकं शीर्षं निश्च्योतद्रुधिरं दधौ ॥ ५ ॥

5. She bears the sword, arrow, mace, spear, discus, conch, and sling; she carries the iron club and bow and a head dripping with blood.

एषा सा वैष्णवी माया महाकाली दुरत्यया ।
आराधिता वशीकुर्यात्पूजाकर्तुश्चराचरम् ॥ ६ ॥

6. She is Viṣṇu's deluding power, the inscrutable Mahākālī. When pleased, she brings all that is moving and unmoving under her worshiper's control.

सर्वदेवशरीरेभ्यो याऽऽविर्भूतामितप्रभा ।
त्रिगुणा सा महालक्ष्मीः साक्षान्महिषमर्दिनी ॥ ७ ॥

7. She who emerged from the bodies of all the gods as boundless light is Mahālakṣmī, who contains the three energies, and who became embodied as Mahiṣa's slayer.

श्वेतानना नीलभुजा सुश्वेतस्तनमण्डला ।
रक्तमध्या रक्तपादा नीलजङ्घोरुरुन्मदा ॥ ८ ॥

8. White is her face, deep blue her arms, brilliant white the orbs of her breasts, red her waist, red her feet, deep blue her arousing shanks and thighs.

सुचित्रजघना चित्रमाल्याम्बरविभूषणा ।
चित्रानुलेपना कान्तिरूपसौभाग्यशालिनी ॥ ९ ॥

9. Many-colored is her lap. Bedecked with multihued garlands and raiment, she is variously anointed and abounds in a beauty that is pure loveliness.

अष्टादशभुजा पूज्या सा सहस्रभुजा सती ।
आयुधान्यत्र वक्ष्यन्ते दक्षिणाधःकरक्रमात् ॥ १० ॥

10. Although she has a thousand arms, she should be worshiped in eighteen-armed form. The weapons here described proceed in order from her lower right hand:

अक्षमाला च कमलं बाणोऽसिः कुलिशं गदा ।
चक्रं त्रिशूलं परशुः शङ्खो घण्टा च पाशकः ॥ ११ ॥

11. prayer beads, lotus, arrow, sword, thunderbolt, mace, discus, trident, ax, conch, bell, and noose,

शक्तिर्दण्डश्चर्म चापं पानपात्रं कमण्डलुः ।
अलंकृतभुजामेभिरायुधैः कमलासनाम् ॥ १२ ॥

12. spear, staff, shield, bow, drinking-vessel, and waterpot. She whose arms are adorned with these weapons, she who is seated on the lotus,

सर्वदेवमयीमीशां महालक्ष्मीमिमां नृप ।
पूजयेत्सर्वलोकानां स देवानां प्रभुर्भवेत् ॥ १३ ॥

13. the sovereign who encompasses all the gods, this Mahālakṣmī is to be worshiped, O king. Doing so, one becomes the master of all the worlds and of the gods.

गौरीदेहात्समुद्भूता या सत्त्वैकगुणाश्रया ।
साक्षात्सरस्वती प्रोक्ता शुम्भासुर निबर्हिणी ॥ १४ ॥

14. She who was born from the body of Gaurī and who embodies the sole energy of sattva is proclaimed to be [Mahā]sarasvatī, the destroyer of the demon Śumbha.

दधौ चाष्टभुजा बाणमुसले शूलचक्रभृत् ।
शङ्खं घण्टां लाङ्गलं च कार्मुकं वसुधाधिप ॥ १५ ॥

15. In her eight arms she carries the arrow, pestle, spear, discus, conch, bell, ploughshare, and bow, O king.

एषा सम्पूजिता भक्त्या सर्वज्ञत्वं प्रयच्छति ।
निशुम्भमथिनी देवी शुम्भासुरनिबर्हिणी ॥ १६ ॥

16. When worshiped with devotion, she grants omniscience. She is the goddess who crushed Niśumbha and destroyed the demon Śumbha.

इत्युक्तानि स्वरूपाणि मूर्तीनां तव पार्थिव ।
उपासनं जगन्मातुः पृथगासां निशामय ॥ १७ ॥

17. Thus, O king, the true nature of the Devī's embodied forms has been told to you. Hear how the mother of the world is worshiped in her individual forms.

महालक्ष्मीर्यदा पूज्या महाकाली सरस्वती ।
दक्षिणोत्तरयोः पूज्ये पृष्ठतो मिथुनत्रयम् ॥ १८ ॥

18. When Mahālakṣmī is worshiped, Mahākālī and [Mahā]sarasvatī are to be worshiped on her right and left. At the back are the three couples:

विरञ्चिः स्वरया मध्ये रुद्रो गौर्या च दक्षिणे ।
वामे लक्ष्म्या हृषीकेशः पुरतो देवतात्रयम् ॥ १९ ॥

19. Brahmā and Sarasvatī in the middle, Rudra and Gaurī on their right, and Viṣṇu and Lakṣmī on their left, with the three goddesses standing forward.

अष्टादशभुजा मध्ये वामे चास्या दशानना ।
दक्षिणेऽष्टभुजा लक्ष्मीर्महतीति समर्चयेत् ॥ २० ॥

20. The eighteen-armed [Mahālakṣmī] is in the middle, the ten-faced [Mahākālī] on the left, and the eight-armed [Mahāsarasvatī] on the right. [Mahā]lakṣmī is to be worshiped as the primary deity.

अष्टादशभुजा चैषा यदा पूज्या नराधिप ।
दशानना चाष्टभुजा दक्षिणोत्तरयोस्तदा ॥ २१ ॥

21. When this eighteen-armed form is worshiped, O king, along with the ten-faced and eight-armed forms, then on the right and left,

कालमृत्यू च सम्पूज्यौ सर्वारिष्टप्रशान्तये ।
यदा चाष्टभुजा पूज्या शुम्भासुरनिबर्हिणी ॥ २२ ॥

22. time and death should be worshiped to allay all misfortune. When the eight-armed slayer of the demon Śumbha is worshiped,

नवास्याः शक्तयः पूज्यास्तदा रुद्रविनायकौ ।
नमो देव्या इति स्तोत्रैर्महालक्ष्मीं समर्चयेत् ॥ २३

23. her nine śaktis should be worshiped and also Rudra and Viṇāyaka. With the hymn that begins "Salutation to the Devī" [the Aparājitāstuti] one should honor Mahālakṣmī.

अवतारत्रयार्चायां स्तोत्रमन्त्रास्तदाश्रयाः ।
अष्टादशभुजा चैषा पूज्या महिषमर्दिनी ॥ २४ ॥

24. In the worship of the three manifestations, the verses of their respective hymns should be uttered. The eighteen-armed slayer of Mahiṣa is to be worshiped [as foremost, for]

महालक्ष्मीर्महाकाली सैव प्रोक्ता सरस्वती ।
ईश्वरी पुण्यपापानां सर्वलोकमहेश्वरी ॥ २५ ॥

25. she herself is proclaimed as Mahālakṣmī, Mahākālī, and [Mahā]sarasvatī, the great ruler of all worlds, reigning over the virtuous and the wicked.

महिषान्तकरी येन पूजिता स जगत्प्रभुः ।
पूजयेज्जगतां धात्रीं चण्डिकां भक्तवत्सलाम् ॥ २६ ॥

26. One who worships Mahiṣa's slayer becomes master of the world. To Caṇḍikā, the upholder of the worlds, who is tender toward her devotees, one should offer worship

अर्घ्यादिभिरलंकारैर्गन्धपुष्पैस्तथाक्षतैः ।
धूपैर्दीपैश्च नैवेद्यैर्नानाभक्ष्यसमन्वितैः ॥ २७ ॥

27. with oblations and the like, with adornments, with flowers perfumed with sandal paste, with whole blossoms, incense and lights, and with all manner of food offerings,

रुधिराक्तेन बलिना मांसेन सुरया नृप ।
प्रणामाचमनीयेन चन्दनेन सुगन्धिना ॥ २८ ॥

28. with blood sacrifice, flesh, and wine, O king, and with prostrations, the ritual sipping of water, and sweetly fragrant sandalwood,

सकर्पूरैश्च ताम्बूलैर्भक्तिभावसमन्वितैः ।
वामभागेऽग्रतो देव्याश्छिन्नशीर्षं महासुरम् ॥ २९ ॥

29. with offerings of camphor and betel nut, all made with complete devotion. On the left side in front of the Devī, the great decapitated demon,

पूजयेन्महिषं येन प्राप्तं सायुज्यमीशया ।
दक्षिणे पुरतः सिंहं समग्रं धर्ममीश्वरम् ॥ ३० ॥

30. Mahiṣa, should be honored, having attained union with her who is supreme. On the right side in front, the lion, who is the whole and mighty dharma,

वाहनं पूजयेद्देव्या धृतं येन चराचरम् ।
कुर्याच्च स्तवनं धीमांस्तस्या एकाग्रमानसः ॥ ३१ ॥

31. the Devī's mount, should be worshiped, for he sustains all that is moving and unmoving. With one-pointed mind the wise one should sing her praises,

ततः कृताञ्जलिर्भूत्वा स्तुवीत चरितैरिमैः ।
एकेन वा मध्यमेन नैकेनेतरयोरिह ॥ ३२ ॥

32. then, with folded hands, should praise her with these episodes [of the Devīmāhātmya] or by the middle one alone, but not by one only of the other two

चरितार्धं तु न जपेज्जपञ्छिद्रमवाप्नुयात् ।
प्रदक्षिणानमस्कारान् कृत्वा मूर्ध्नि कृताञ्जलिः ॥ ३३ ॥

33. or by chanting half an episode, for that would create a weak point in the recitation. Circumambulating the deity reverently with hands folded on the head,

क्षमापयेज्जगद्धात्रीं मुहुर्मुहुरतन्द्रितः ।
प्रतिश्लोकं च जुहुयात्पायसं तिलसर्पिषा ॥ ३४ ॥

34. one should vigorously ask for forgiveness again and again from the sustainer of the world. With each verse should one make an oblation of milk, sesame, and ghee.

जुहुयात्स्तोत्रमन्त्रैर्वा चण्डिकायै शुभं हविः ।
भूयो नामपदैर्देवीं पूजयेत्सुसमाहितः ॥ ३५ ॥

35. Or, one can make an auspicious offering to Caṇḍikā with the verses of the [Devīmāhātmya's] hymns. With the mind turned inward and fully concentrated, one should worship the Devī with the "salutation verses" [the Aparājitāstuti].

प्रयतः प्राञ्जलिः प्रह्वः प्रणम्यारोप्य चात्मनि ।
सुचिरं भावयेदीशां चण्डिकां तन्मयो भवेत् ॥ ३६ ॥

36. Intent on devotion, with hands folded and head bowed in reverence, deeply collected in oneself, one should meditate on the supreme Caṇḍikā for a long while and become filled with her.

एवं यः पूजयेद्भक्त्या प्रत्यहं परमेश्वरीम् ।
भुक्त्वा भोगान्यथाकामं देवीसायुज्यमाप्नुयात् ॥ ३७ ॥

37. One who daily worships the supreme sovereign in this way, having accordingly experienced all enjoyment with dispassion, attains union with the Devī.

यो न पूजयते नित्यं चण्डिकां भक्तवत्सलाम् ।
भस्मीकृत्यास्य पुण्यानि निर्दहेत्परमेश्वरी ॥ ३८ ॥

38. If one does not always worship Caṇḍikā, who is tender toward her devotees, his merits will the supreme sovereign burn to ashes.

तस्मात्पूजय भूपाल सर्वलोकमहेश्वरीम् ।
यथोक्तेन विधानेन चण्डिकां सुखमाप्स्यसि ॥ ३९ ॥

39. Therefore, O king, worship Caṇḍikā, the great ruler of all the worlds, in the prescribed manner, and you will attain happiness.

## Vaikṛtika Rahasya Commentary

The Vaikṛtika Rahasya ("The Secret Relating to Transformation") concentrates on the supreme Devī's modification (vikṛti) from formlessness to perceptible form. The opening verse asserts that she who is known by such names as Durgā and Caṇḍikā, assumes three aspects: one containing all three guṇas, one expressing pure tamas, and one expressing pure sattva. This cosmogony reflects the text's Vaiṣṇava Tantric stance; instead of characterizing Mahālakṣmī as the purely rajasic emanation of the Absolute, comparable to the tamasic Mahākālī and the sattvic Mahāsarasvatī, it presents her as triguṇā and therefore foremost of the three.

The description of the dark, ten-armed Mahākālī (verses 2 through 6), slayer of Madhu and Kaiṭabha, corresponds to that of the dhyāna that precedes the Devīmāhātmya's first chapter. Likewise, verses 7 through 13 agree with the description of the eighteen-armed Mahālakṣmī in the dhyāna preceding the second chapter, portraying her as the goddess of boundless light, who took form in order to slay Mahiṣāsura. Note that her white, dark blue (or black), and red features symbolize the three guṇas (verse 8), and that she is variously hued (*citrā*), her full range of colors proceeding from the subsequent combining and recombining of the primary guṇas (verse 9). The description of the sattvic, eight-armed Mahāsarasvatī, the slayer of Śumbha, likewise corresponds to the dhyāna that introduces the Devīmāhātmya's third carita at Chapter 5.

The remainder of the Vaikṛtika Rahasya is concerned with formal worship through visualization, meditation, ritual offerings, and the chanting of the Devīmāhātmya, with emphasis on the special importance of the Aparājitāstuti.

# मूर्तिरहस्यम्

## MŪRTIRAHASYA

ऋषिरुवाच ।

The seer said:

ॐ नन्दा भगवती नाम या भविष्यति नन्दजा ।
स्तुता सा पूजिता भक्त्या वशीकुर्याज्जगत्त्रयम् ॥ १ ॥

1. Oṁ. She who will be born to Nanda and named Nandā Bhagavatī, when praised and worshiped with devotion, will grant mastery over the three worlds.

कनकोत्तमकान्तिः सा सुकान्तिकनकाम्बरा ।
देवी कनकवर्णाभा कनकोत्तमभूषणा ॥ २ ॥

2. Her beauty shines like the finest gold, her garments are of golden brilliance. Golden is the Devī's splendor, and of pure gold are her adornments.

कमलाङ्कुशपाशाब्जैरलंकृतचतुर्भुजा ।
इन्दिरा कमला लक्ष्मीः सा श्री रुक्माम्बुजासना ॥ ३ ॥

3. Lotus, goad, noose, and conch grace her four arms. She is Indirā, Kamalā, Lakṣmī, Śrī, seated on a resplendent lotus.

या रक्तदन्तिका नाम देवी प्रोक्ता मयानघ ।
तस्याः स्वरूपं वक्ष्यामि शृणु सर्वभयापहम् ॥ ४ ॥

4. O faultless one, the goddess of whom I now speak is called Raktadantikā. I will describe her true nature; listen, for it allays all fears.

रक्ताम्बरा रक्तवर्णा रक्तसर्वाङ्गभूषणा ।
रक्तायुधा रक्तनेत्रा रक्तकेशातिभीषणा ॥ ५ ॥

5. Red is her clothing, red her body, red the ornaments on all her limbs, red her weapons, red her eyes, and red her hair. Great indeed is the terror she inspires.

रक्ततीक्ष्णनखा रक्तदशना रक्तदन्तिका ।
पतिं नारीवानुरक्ता देवी भक्तं भजेज्जनम् ॥ ६ ॥

6. Red are her rending talons, red her teeth, and red her fangs. As a wife is loving toward her husband, the Devī loves the person who is devoted to her.

वसुधेव विशाला सा सुमेरुयुगलस्तनी ।
दीर्घौ लम्बावतिस्थूलौ तावतीव मनोहरौ ॥ ७ ॥

7. She is expansive like the earth, and her two breasts are like Mount Meru—full, heavy, massive, and alluring.

कर्कशावतिकान्तौ तौ सर्वानन्दपयोनिधी ।
भक्तान्सम्पाययेद्देवी सर्वकामदुघौ स्तनौ ॥ ८ ॥

8. Firm and exquisite, they hold the milk of perfect bliss. With these breasts that satisfy all wants, the Devī nourishes her devotees.

खड्गं पात्रं च मुसलं लाङ्गलं च बिभर्ति सा ।
आख्याता रक्तचामुण्डा देवी योगेश्वरीति च ॥ ९ ॥

9. She carries sword, drinking vessel, pestle, and plough, the Devī known as the red Cāmuṇḍā and Yogeśvarī.

अनया व्याप्तमखिलं जगत्स्थावरजङ्गमम् ।
इमां यः पूजयेद्भक्त्या स व्याप्नोति चराचरम् ॥ १० ॥

10. She pervades the entire world, unmoving and moving. One who worships her with devotion extends throughout the universe.

अधीते य इमं नित्यं रक्तदन्त्या वपुःस्तवम् ।
तं सा परिचरेद्देवी पतिं प्रियमिवाङ्गना ॥ ११ ॥

11. As a woman attends her beloved, the Devī attends one who constantly turns the mind to this wonderful hymn to Raktadantikā.

शाकम्भरी नीलवर्णा नीलोत्पलविलोचना ।
गम्भीरनाभिस्त्रिवलीविभूषिततनूदरी ॥ १२ ॥

12. Śākambharī's color is blue, her eyes like a blue lotus, her navel deep, and her slender waist adorned with three folds of skin.

सुकर्कशसमोत्तुङ्गवृत्तपीनघनस्तनी ।
मुष्टिं शिलीमुखापूर्णं कमलं कमलालया ॥ १३ ॥

13. Her breasts are firm, even, and full, rounded, plump and solid. Reposing on a lotus, she holds a handful of arrows, a lotus blossom,

पुष्पपल्लवमूलादिफलाढ्यं शाकसञ्चयम् ।
काम्यानन्तरसैर्युक्तं क्षुत्तृण्मृत्युभयापहम् ॥ १४ ॥

14. and all manner of flowers, tender plants, roots, fruits, and vegetables in dazzling abundance, with tastes to please every palate, said to remove all fear of hunger, thirst, and death.

कार्मुकं च स्फुरत्कान्ति बिभ्रती परमेश्वरी ।
शाकम्भरी शताक्षी सा सैव दुर्गा प्रकीर्तिता ॥ १५ ॥

15. The supreme sovereign bears a bow of glittering splendor. She is celebrated as Śākambharī, Śatākṣī, and Durgā herself.

विशोका दुष्टदमनी शमनी दुरितापदाम् ।
उमा गौरी सती चण्डी कालिका सा च पार्वती ॥ १६ ॥

16. Free from sorrow, subduing evil, allaying difficulty and misfortune, she is Umā, Gaurī, Satī, Caṇḍī, Kālikā, and Pārvatī.

शाकम्भरीं स्तुवन्ध्यायञ्जपन्सम्पूजयन्नमन् ।
अक्षय्यमश्नुते शीघ्रमन्नपानामृतं फलम् ॥ १७ ॥

17. By praising Śākambharī, contemplating her, repeating her name, worshiping her, and surrendering to her, one quickly obtains the everlasting reward of food, drink, and freedom from death.

भीमापि नीलवर्णा सा दंष्ट्रादशनभासुरा ।
विशाललोचना नारी वृत्तपीनपयोधरा ॥ १८ ॥

18. Bhīmā also is colored blue, with shining fangs and teeth. A wide-eyed woman with full, round breasts,

चन्द्रहासं च डमरुं शिरः पात्रं च बिभ्रती ।
एकवीरा कालरात्रिः सैवोक्ता कामदा स्तुता ॥ १९ ॥

19. she holds a glittering scimitar, drum, head, and drinking-vessel. She is called the solitary warrior, Kālarātri, praised as the granter of desires.

तेजोमण्डलदुर्धर्षा भ्रामरी चित्रकान्तिभृत् ।
चित्रानुलेपना देवी चित्राभरणभूषिता ॥ २० ॥

20. Bhrāmarī, inviolable within her encircling light, is a many-splendored goddess, anointed with various perfumes and adorned with multihued gems.

चित्रभ्रमरपाणिः सा महामारीति गीयते ।
इत्येता मूर्तयो देव्या याः ख्याता वसुधाधिप ॥ २१ ॥

21. With multicolored bees in hand, she is sung of as the great pestilence. Thus, O lord of the earth, are explained the incarnations of the Devī,

जगन्मातुश्चण्डिकायाः कीर्तिताः कामधेनवः ।
इदं रहस्यं परमं न वाच्यं कस्यचित्त्वया ॥ २२ ॥

22. of the mother of the world, of Caṇḍikā, renowned for satisfying every desire. This is the supreme secret, which you must not divulge to anyone,

व्याख्यानं दिव्यमूर्तीनामभीष्टफलदायकम् ।
तस्मात्सर्वप्रयत्नेन देवीं जप निरन्तरम् ॥ २३ ॥

23. this explanation of her divine embodiments that yields the desired results. Therefore, with unflagging perseverance, repeat the Devī's name unceasingly.

सप्तजन्मार्जितैर्घोरैर्ब्रह्महत्यासमैरपि ।
पाठमात्रेण मन्त्राणां मुच्यते सर्वकिल्बिषैः ॥ २४ ॥

24. By proper recitation of the verses [of the Devīmāhātmya], you will be released from your offending acts acquired over seven lifetimes, even those as heinous as the slaying of a Brāhmaṇa.

देव्या ध्यानं मया ख्यातं गुह्याद्गुह्यतरं महत् ।
तस्मात्सर्वप्रयत्नेन सर्वकामफलप्रदम् ॥ २५ ॥

25. Meditation on the Devī is, I proclaim, the great secret of secrets, and if you persevere, it will grant the fulfillment of your every desire.

# Mūrtirahasya Commentary

The Mūrtirahasya ("The Secret Relating to Forms") elaborates on the Devī's further earthly manifestations as foretold in Chapter 11 of the Devīmāhātmya. It describes the iconography of these five incarnations and specifies the benefits of worshiping them. Despite the often fierce characteristics ascribed to some of these forms, more important are the Devī's maternal beneficence and salvific power, which show recurring ties to agricultural and other terrestrial themes.

The Mūrtirahasya falls into five sections, each dealing with one of the five incarnations. First is Bhagavatī Nandā or Vindhyavāsinī (verses 1–3, DM 11.41–42). Next comes Raktadantikā (verses 4–11, DM 11.43–45). Her name means "the red-toothed one," and the emphasis on red, the color of blood, underscores her terrifying, rajasic fierceness, even while she is likened to the expansive, fertile earth, a reminder that the energies of nature are both destructive and beneficent. Śākambharī (verses 12–17, DM 11.46–50) is the earth itself, and her body is blue, just as the planet Earth, seen from space, appears blue. A carved seal from Harappa pictures a naked goddess with a plant issuing from her womb, and possibly this artifact, dating back perhaps four and a half millennia, illustrates Śākambharī or her prototype.[1] Śākambharī's abdominal furrows are clearly an agricultural allusion, and she is further described as holding a great variety of edibles brought forth from her own body. The passage identifies her, the great Earth Mother, with Durgā, Umā, Gaurī, Kālikā, and other names of the supreme Devī. Bhīmā (verses 18–19, DM 11.51–52), also blue, represents her dark aspect, with allusions to death and dissolution. And Bhrāmarī (verses 20–21, DM 11.53–55), the fifth embodiment, appears in a dazzling display of light and color. She, too, manifests as both terrible and auspicious, on the one hand being called "the great pestilence," and on the other symbolizing sexual attraction (and therefore procreative power) through the metaphor of the bee.

Medhas's final word to King Suratha summarizes the supreme secret: that constantly repeating Caṇḍikā's name, reciting the Devīmāhātmya, and meditating on the Devī are the way to eternal bliss.

# Part IV
# The Devīmāhātmya
# Sanskrit Text and Transliteration

# प्रथमचरितम्

## महाकालीध्यानम्

ॐ खड्गं चक्रगदेषुचापपरिघान् शूलं भुशुण्डीं शिरः
शङ्खं सन्दधतीं करैस्त्रिनयनां सर्वाङ्गभूषावृताम् ।
यां हन्तुं मधुकैटभौ जलजभूस्तुष्टाव सुप्ते हरौ
नीलाश्मद्युतिमास्यपाददशकां सेवे महाकालिकाम् ॥

Oṁ. khaḍgaṁ cakragadeṣucāpaparighān śūlaṁ bhuṣuṇḍīṁ śiraḥ
śaṅkhaṁ sandadhatīṁ karais trinayanāṁ sarvāṅgabhūṣāvṛtām
yāṁ hantuṁ madhukaiṭabhau jalajabhūs tuṣṭāva supte harau
nīlāśmadyutim āsyapādadaśakāṁ seve mahākālikām

# प्रथमोऽध्यायः

## मधुकैटभवधः

ॐ नमश्चण्डिकायै

Oṁ namaś caṇḍikāyai

ॐ ऐं मार्कण्डेय उवाच ॥ १ ॥

Oṁ aiṁ mārkaṇḍeya uvāca

सावर्णिः सूर्यतनयो यो मनुः कथ्यतेऽष्टमः ।
निशामय तदुत्पत्तिं विस्तराद्गदतो मम ॥ २ ॥

sāvarṇiḥ sūryatanayo yo manuḥ kathyate 'ṣṭamaḥ
niśāmaya tad utpattiṁ vistarād gadato mama

महामायानुभावेन यथा मन्वन्तराधिपः ।
स बभूव महाभागः सावर्णिस्तनयो रवेः ॥ ३ ॥

mahāmāyānubhāvena yathā manvantarādhipaḥ
sa babhūva mahābhāgaḥ sāvarṇis tanayo raveḥ

स्वारोचिषेऽन्तरे पूर्वं चैत्रवंशसमुद्भवः ।
सुरथो नाम राजाभूत्समस्ते क्षितिमण्डले ॥ ४ ॥

svārociṣe 'ntare pūrvaṁ caitravaṁśasamudbhavaḥ
suratho nāma rājābhūt samaste kṣitimaṇḍale

तस्य पालयतः सम्यक् प्रजाः पुत्रानिवौरसान् ।
बभूवुः शत्रवो भूपाः कोलाविध्वंसिनस्तदा ॥ ५ ॥

tasya pālayataḥ samyak prajāḥ putrānivaurasān
babhūvuḥ śatravo bhūpāḥ kolāvidhvaṁsinas tadā

तस्य तैरभवद्युद्धमतिप्रबलदण्डिनः ।
न्यूनैरपि स तैर्युद्धे कोलाविध्वंसिभिर्जितः ॥ ६ ॥

tasya tair abhavad yuddham atiprabaladaṇḍinaḥ
nyūnair api sa tair yuddhe kolāvidhvaṁsibhir jitaḥ

ततः स्वपुरमायातो निजदेशाधिपोऽभवत् ।
आक्रान्तः स महाभागस्तैस्तदा प्रबलारिभिः ॥ ७ ॥

tataḥ svapuram āyāto nijadeśādhipo ’bhavat
ākrāntaḥ sa mahābhāgas tais tadā prabalāribhiḥ

अमात्यैर्बलिभिर्दुष्टैर्दुर्बलस्य दुरात्मभिः ।
कोशो बलं चापहृतं तत्रापि स्वपुरे ततः ॥ ८ ॥

amātyair balibhir duṣṭair durbalasya durātmabhiḥ
kośo balaṁ cāpahṛtaṁ tatrāpi svapure tataḥ

ततो मृगयाव्याजेन हृतस्वाम्यः स भूपतिः ।
एकाकी हयमारुह्य जगाम गहनं वनम् ॥ ९ ॥

tato mṛgayāvyājena hṛtasvāmyaḥ sa bhūpatiḥ
ekākī hayam āruhya jagāma gahanaṁ vanam

स तत्राश्रममद्राक्षीद्द्विजवर्यस्य मेधसः ।
प्रशान्तश्वापदाकीर्णं मुनिशिष्योपशोभितम् ॥ १० ॥

sa tatrāśramam adrākṣīd dvijavaryasya medhasaḥ
praśāntaśvāpadākīrṇaṁ muniśiṣyopaśobhitam

तस्थौ कञ्चित्स कालं च मुनिना तेन सत्कृतः ।
इतश्चेतश्च विचरंस्तस्मिन् मुनिवराश्रमे ॥ ११ ॥

tasthau kañcit sa kālaṁ ca muninā tena satkṛtaḥ
itaś cetaś ca vicaraṁs tasmin munivarāśrame

सोऽचिन्तयत्तदा तत्र ममत्वाकृष्टमानसः ॥ १२ ॥

so ’cintayat tadā tatra mamatvākṛṣṭamānasaḥ

मत्पूर्वैः पालितं पूर्वं मया हीनं पुरं हि तत् ।
मद्भृत्यैस्तैरसद्वृत्तैर्धर्मतः पाल्यते न वा ॥ १३ ॥

matpūrvaiḥ pālitaṁ pūrvaṁ mayā hīnaṁ puraṁ hi tat
madbhṛtyais tair asadvṛttair dharmataḥ pālyate na vā

न जाने स प्रधानो मे शूरो हस्ती सदामदः ।
मम वैरिवशं यातः कान् भोगानुपलप्स्यते ॥ १४ ॥

na jāne sa pradhāno me śūro hastī sadāmadaḥ
mama vairivaśaṁ yātaḥ kān bhogān upalapsyate

ये ममानुगता नित्यं प्रसादधनभोजनैः ।
अनुवृत्तिं ध्रुवं तेऽद्य कुर्वन्त्यन्यमहीभृताम् ॥ १५ ॥

ye mamānugatā nityaṁ prasādadhanabhojanaiḥ
anuvṛttiṁ dhruvaṁ te 'dya kurvanty anyamahībhṛtām

असम्यग्व्ययशीलैस्तैः कुर्वद्भिः सततं व्ययम् ।
सञ्चितः सोऽतिदुःखेन क्षयं कोशो गमिष्यति ॥ १६ ॥

asamyagvyayaśīlais taiḥ kurvadbhiḥ satataṁ vyayam
sañcitaḥ so 'tiduḥkhena kṣayaṁ kośo gamiṣyati

एतच्चान्यच्च सततं चिन्तयामास पार्थिवः ।
तत्र विप्राश्रमाभ्याशे वैश्यमेकं ददर्श सः ॥ १७ ॥

etac cānyac ca satataṁ cintayāmāsa pārthivaḥ
tatra viprāśramābhyāśe vaiśyam ekaṁ dadarśa saḥ

स पृष्टस्तेन कस्त्वं भो हेतुश्चागमनेऽत्र कः ।
सशोक इव कस्मात्त्वं दुर्मना इव लक्ष्यसे ॥ १८ ॥

sa pṛṣṭas tena kastvaṁ bho hetuś cāgamane 'tra kaḥ
saśoka iva kasmāt tvaṁ durmanā iva lakṣyase

इत्याकर्ण्य वचस्तस्य भूपतेः प्रणयोदितम् ।
प्रत्युवाच स तं वैश्यः प्रश्रयावनतो नृपम् ॥ १९ ॥

ity ākarṇya vacas tasya bhūpateḥ praṇayoditam
pratyuvāca sa taṁ vaiśyaḥ praśrayāvanato nṛpam

वैश्य उवाच ॥ २० ॥

vaiśya uvāca

समाधिर्नाम वैश्योऽहमुत्पन्नो धनिनां कुले ।
पुत्रदारैर्निरस्तश्च धनलोभादसाधुभिः ॥ २१ ॥

samādhir nāma vaiśyo 'ham utpanno dhaninām kule
putradārair nirastaś ca dhanalobhād asādhubhiḥ

विहीनश्च धनैर्दारैः पुत्रैरादाय मे धनम् ।
वनमभ्यागतो दुःखी निरस्तश्चाप्तबन्धुभिः ॥ २२ ॥

vihīnaś ca dhanair dāraiḥ putrair ādāya me dhanam
vanam abhyāgato duḥkhī nirastaś cāptabandhubhiḥ

सोऽहं न वेद्मि पुत्राणां कुशलाकुशलात्मिकाम् ।
प्रवृत्तिं स्वजनानां च दाराणां चात्र संस्थितः ॥ २३ ॥

so 'haṁ na vedmi putrāṇāṁ kuśalākuśalātmikām
pravṛttiṁ svajanānāṁ ca dārāṇāṁ cātra saṁsthitaḥ

किं नु तेषां गृहे क्षेममक्षेमं किं नु साम्प्रतम् ॥ २४ ॥
कथं ते किं नु सद्वृत्ता दुर्वृत्ताः किं नु मे सुताः ॥२५ ॥

kiṁ nu teṣāṁ gṛhe kṣemam akṣemaṁ kiṁ nu sāmpratam
kathaṁ te kiṁ nu sadvṛttā durvṛttāḥ kiṁ nu me sutāḥ

राजोवाच ॥ २६ ॥

rājovāca

यैर्निरस्तो भवाँल्लुब्धैः पुत्रदारादिभिर्धनैः ॥ २७ ॥
तेषु किं भवतः स्नेहमनुबध्नाति मानसम् ॥ २८ ॥

yair nirasto bhavāṁl lubdhaiḥ putradārādibhir dhanaiḥ
teṣu kiṁ bhavataḥ sneham anubadhnāti mānasam

वैश्य उवाच ॥ २९ ॥

vaiśya uvāca

एवमेतद्यथा प्राह भवानस्मद्गतं वचः ।
किं करोमि न बध्नाति मम निष्ठुरतां मनः ॥ ३० ॥

evam etad yathā prāha bhavān asmad gataṁ vacaḥ
kiṁ karomi na badhnāti mama niṣṭhuratāṁ manaḥ

यैः सन्त्यज्य पितृस्नेहं धनलुब्धैर्निराकृतः ।
पतिः स्वजनहार्दं च हार्दितेष्वेव मे मनः ॥ ३१ ॥

yaiḥ santyajya pitṛsnehaṁ dhanalubdhair nirākṛtaḥ
patiḥ svajanahārdaṁ ca hārdi teṣv eva me manaḥ

किमेतन्नाभिजानामि जानन्नपि महामते ।
यत्प्रेमप्रवणं चित्तं विगुणेष्वपि बन्धुषु ॥ ३२ ॥

kim etan nābhijānāmi jānann api mahāmate
yat premapravaṇaṁ cittaṁ viguṇeṣv api bandhuṣu

तेषां कृते मे निःश्वासो दौर्मनस्यं च जायते ॥ ३३ ॥
करोमि किं यन्न मनस्तेष्वप्रीतिषु निष्ठुरम् ॥ ३४ ॥

teṣāṁ kṛte me niḥśvāso daurmanasyaṁ ca jāyate
karomi kiṁ yan na manasteṣv aprītiṣu niṣṭhuram

मार्कण्डेय उवाच ॥ ३५ ॥

mārkaṇḍeya uvāca

ततस्तौ सहितौ विप्र तं मुनिं समुपस्थितौ ॥ ३६ ॥
समाधिर्नाम वैश्योऽसौ स च पार्थिवसत्तमः ॥ ३७ ॥

tatas tau sahitau vipra taṁ muniṁ samupasthitau
samādhir nāma vaiśyo 'sau sa ca pārthivasattamaḥ

कृत्वा तु तौ यथान्यायं यथार्हं तेन संविदम् ।
उपविष्टौ कथाः काश्चिच्चक्रतुर्वैश्यपार्थिवौ ॥ ३८ ॥

kṛtvā tu tau yathānyāyaṁ yathārhaṁ tena saṁvidam
upaviṣṭau kathāḥ kāścic cakratur vaiśyapārthivau

राजोवाच ॥ ३९ ॥

rājovāca

भगवंस्त्वामहं प्रष्टुमिच्छाम्येकं वदस्व तत् ॥ ४० ॥
दुःखाय यन्मे मनसः स्वचित्तायत्ततां विना ॥ ४१ ॥

bhagavaṁs tvām ahaṁ praṣṭum icchāmy ekaṁ vadasva tat
duḥkhāya yan me manasaḥ svacittāyattatāṁ vinā

ममत्वं गतराज्यस्य राज्याङ्गेऽष्वखिलेष्वपि ।
जानतोऽपि यथाज्ञस्य किमेतन्मुनिसत्तम ॥ ४२ ॥

mamatvaṁ gatarājyasya rājyāṅgeṣv akhileṣvapi
jānato 'pi yathājñasya kim etan munisattama

अयं च निकृतः पुत्रैर्दारैर्भृत्यैस्तथोज्झितः ।
स्वजनेन च सन्त्यक्तस्तेषु हार्दी तथाप्यति ॥ ४३ ॥

ayaṁ ca nikṛtaḥ putrair dārair bhṛtyais tathojjhitaḥ
svajanena ca santyaktas teṣu hārdī tathāpyati

एवमेष तथाहं च द्वावप्यत्यन्तदुःखितौ ।
दृष्टदोषेऽपि विषये ममत्वाकृष्टमानसौ ॥ ४४ ॥

evam eṣa tathāhaṁ ca dvāvapyatyantaduḥkhitau
dṛṣṭadoṣe 'pi viṣaye mamatvākṛṣṭamānasau

तत्केनैतन्महाभाग यन्मोहो ज्ञानिनोरपि ।
ममास्य च भवत्येषा विवेकान्धस्य मूढता ॥ ४५ ॥

tat kenaitan mahābhāga yan moho jñāninor api
mamāsya ca bhavaty eṣā vivekāndhasya mūḍhatā

ऋषिरुवाच ॥ ४६ ॥

ṛṣir uvāca

ज्ञानमस्ति समस्तस्य जन्तोर्विषयगोचरे ।
विषयाश्च महाभाग यान्ति चैवं पृथक्पृथक् ॥ ४७ ॥

jñānam asti samastasya jantor viṣayagocare
viṣayāś ca mahābhāga yānti caivaṁ pṛthak pṛthak

दिवान्धाः प्राणिनः केचिद्रात्रावन्धास्तथापरे ।
केचिद्दिवा तथा रात्रौ प्राणिनस्तुल्यदृष्टयः ॥ ४८ ॥

divāndhāḥ prāṇinaḥ kecid rātrāv andhās tathāpare
kecid divā tathā rātrau prāṇinas tulyadṛṣṭayaḥ

ज्ञानिनो मनुजाः सत्यं किन्तु ते न हि केवलम् ।
यतो हि ज्ञानिनः सर्वे पशुपक्षिमृगादयः ॥ ४९ ॥

jñānino manujāḥ satyaṁ kintu te na hi kevalam
yato hi jñāninaḥ sarve paśupakṣimṛgādayaḥ

ज्ञानं च तन्मनुष्याणां यत्तेषां मृगपक्षिणाम् ।
मनुष्याणां च यत्तेषां तुल्यमन्यत्तथोभयोः ॥ ५० ॥

jñānaṁ ca tan manuṣyāṇāṁ yat teṣāṁ mṛgapakṣiṇām
manuṣyāṇāṁ ca yat teṣāṁ tulyam anyat tathobhayoḥ

ज्ञानेऽपि सति पश्यैतान् पतङ्गाञ्छावचञ्चुषु ।
कणमोक्षादृतान् मोहात्पीड्यमानानपि क्षुधा ॥ ५१ ॥

jñāne 'pi sati paśyaitān pataṅgāñ chāvacañcuṣu
kaṇamokṣād ṛtān mohāt pīḍyamānān api kṣudhā

मानुषा मनुजव्याघ्र साभिलाषाः सुतान् प्रति ।
लोभात् प्रत्युपकाराय नन्वेतान् किं न पश्यसि ॥ ५२ ॥

mānuṣā manujavyāghra sābhilāṣāḥ sutān prati
lobhāt pratyupakārāya nanv etān kiṁ na paśyasi

तथापि ममतावर्ते मोहगर्ते निपातिताः ।
महामायाप्रभावेण संसारस्थितिकारिणा ॥ ५३ ॥

tathāpi mamatāvarte mohagarte nipātitāḥ
mahāmāyāprabhāveṇa saṁsārasthitikāriṇā

तन्नात्र विस्मयः कार्यो योगनिद्रा जगत्पतेः ।
महामाया हरेश्चैषा तया सम्मोह्यते जगत् ॥ ५४ ॥

tan nātra vismayaḥ kāryo yoganidrā jagatpateḥ
mahāmāyā hareś caiṣā tayā sammohyate jagat

ज्ञानिनामपि चेतांसि देवी भगवती हि सा ।
बलादाकृष्य मोहाय महामाया प्रयच्छति ॥ ५५ ॥

jñāninām api cetāṁsi devī bhagavatī hi sā
balād ākṛṣya mohāya mahāmāyā prayacchati

तया विसृज्यते विश्वं जगदेतच्चराचरम् ।
सैषा प्रसन्ना वरदा नृणां भवति मुक्तये ॥ ५६ ॥

tayā visṛjyate viśvaṁ jagad etac carācaram
saiṣā prasannā varadā nṛṇāṁ bhavati muktaye

सा विद्या परमा मुक्तेर्हेतुभूता सनातनी ॥ ५७ ॥
संसारबन्धहेतुश्च सैव सर्वेश्वरेश्वरी ॥ ५८ ॥

sā vidyā paramā mukter hetubhūtā sanātanī
saṁsārabandhahetuś ca saiva sarveśvareśvarī

राजोवाच ॥ ५९ ॥

rājovāca

भगवन् का हि सा देवी महामायेति यां भवान् ।
ब्रवीति कथमुत्पन्ना सा कर्मास्याश्च किं द्विज ॥ ६० ॥

bhagavan kā hi sā devī mahāmāyeti yāṁ bhavān
bravīti katham utpannā sā karmāsyāś ca kiṁ dvija

यत्प्रभावा च सा देवी यत्स्वरूपा यदुद्भवा ॥ ६१ ॥
तत्सर्वं श्रोतुमिच्छामि त्वत्तो ब्रह्मविदां वर ॥ ६२ ॥

yat prabhāvā ca sā devī yat svarūpā yad udbhavā
tat sarvaṁ śrotum icchāmi tvat to brahmavidāṁ vara

ऋषिरुवाच ॥ ६३ ॥

ṛṣir uvāca

नित्यैव सा जगन्मूर्तिस्तया सर्वमिदं ततम् ॥ ६४ ॥
तथापि तत्समुत्पत्तिर्बहुधा श्रूयतां मम ॥ ६५ ॥

nityaiva sā jaganmūrtis tayā sarvam idaṁ tatam
tathāpi tat samutpattir bahudhā śrūyatāṁ mama

देवानां कार्यसिद्ध्यर्थमाविर्भवति सा यदा ।
उत्पन्नेति तदा लोके सा नित्याप्यभिधीयते ॥ ६६ ॥

devānāṁ kāryasiddhyartham āvirbhavati sā yadā
utpanneti tadā loke sā nityāpy abhidhīyate

योगनिद्रां यदा विष्णुर्जगत्येकार्णवीकृते ।
आस्तीर्य शेषमभजत्कल्पान्ते भगवान् प्रभुः ॥ ६७ ॥

yoganidrāṁ yadā viṣṇur jagaty ekārṇavīkṛte
āstīrya śeṣam abhajat kalpānte bhagavān prabhuḥ

तदा द्वावसुरौ घोरौ विख्यातौ मधुकैटभौ ।
विष्णुकर्णमलोद्भूतौ हन्तुं ब्रह्माणमुद्यतौ ॥ ६८ ॥

tadā dvāv asurau ghorau vikhyātau madhukaiṭabhau
viṣṇukarṇamalodbhūtau hantuṁ brahmāṇam udyatau

स नाभिकमले विष्णोः स्थितो ब्रह्मा प्रजापतिः ।
दृष्ट्वा तावसुरौ चोग्रौ प्रसुप्तं च जनार्दनम् ॥ ६९ ॥

sa nābhikamale viṣṇoḥ sthito brahmā prajāpatiḥ
dṛṣṭvā tāv asurau cograu prasuptaṁ ca janārdanam

तुष्टाव योगनिद्रां तामेकाग्रहृदयः स्थितः ।
विबोधनार्थाय हरेर्हरिनेत्रकृतालयाम् ॥ ७० ॥

tuṣṭāva yoganidrāṁ tām ekāgrahṛdayaḥ sthitaḥ
vibodhanārthāya harer harinetrakṛtālayām

विश्वेश्वरीं जगद्धात्रीं स्थितिसंहारकारिणीम् ।
निद्रां भगवतीं विष्णोरतुलां तेजसः प्रभुः ॥ ७१ ॥

viśveśvarīṁ jagaddhātrīṁ sthitisaṁhārakāriṇīm
nidrāṁ bhagavatīṁ viṣṇor atulāṁ tejasaḥ prabhuḥ

ब्रह्मोवाच ॥ ७२ ॥

brahmovāca

त्वं स्वाहा त्वं स्वधा त्वं हि वषट्कारः स्वरात्मिका ।
सुधा त्वमक्षरे नित्ये त्रिधामात्रात्मिका स्थिता ॥७३॥

tvaṁ svāhā tvaṁ ṣvadhā tvaṁ hi vaṣaṭkāraḥ svarātmikā
sudhā tvam akṣare nitye tridhāmātrātmikā sthitā

अर्धमात्रा स्थिता नित्या यानुच्चार्याविशेषतः ।
त्वमेव सा त्वं सावित्री त्वं देवजननी परा ॥७४॥

ardhamātrā sthitā nityā yānuccāryāviśeṣataḥ
tvam eva sā tvaṁ sāvitrī tvaṁ devajananī parā

त्वयैतद्धार्यते विश्वं त्वयैतत्सृज्यते जगत् ।
त्वयैतत्पाल्यते देवि त्वमत्स्यन्ते च सर्वदा ॥७५॥

tvayaitad dhāryate viśvaṁ tvayaitat sṛjyate jagat
tvayaitat pālyate devi tvam atsy ante ca sarvadā

विसृष्टौ सृष्टिरूपा त्वं स्थितिरूपा च पालने ।
तथा संहृतिरूपान्ते जगतोऽस्य जगन्मये ॥७६॥

visṛṣṭau sṛṣṭirūpā tvaṁ sthitirūpā ca pālane
tathā saṁhṛtirūpānte jagato 'sya jaganmaye

महाविद्या महामाया महामेधा महास्मृतिः ।
महामोहा च भवती महादेवी महासुरी ॥७७॥

mahāvidyā mahāmāyā mahāmedhā mahāsmṛtiḥ
mahāmohā ca bhavatī mahādevī mahāsurī

प्रकृतिस्त्वं च सर्वस्य गुणत्रयविभाविनी ।
कालरात्रिर्महारात्रिर्मोहरात्रिश्च दारुणा ॥७८॥

prakṛtis tvaṁ ca sarvasya guṇatrayavibhāvinī
kālarātrir mahārātrir moharātriś ca dāruṇā

त्वं श्रीस्त्वमीश्वरी त्वं ह्रीस्त्वं बुद्धिर्बोधलक्षणा ।
लज्जा पुष्टिस्तथा तुष्टिस्त्वं शान्तिः क्षान्तिरेव च ॥७९॥

tvaṁ śrīs tvam īśvarī tvaṁ hrīs tvaṁ buddhir bodhalakṣaṇā
lajjā puṣṭis tathā tuṣṭis tvaṁ śāntiḥ kṣāntir eva ca

खड्गिनी शूलिनी घोरा गदिनी चक्रिणी तथा ।
शङ्खिनी चापिनी बाणभुशुण्डीपरिघायुधा ॥८०॥

khaḍginī śūlinī ghorā gadinī cakriṇī tathā
śaṅkhinī cāpinī bāṇabhuśuṇḍīparighāyudhā

सौम्या सौम्यतराशेषसौम्येभ्यस्त्वतिसुन्दरी ।
परापराणां परमा त्वमेव परमेश्वरी ॥८१॥

saumyā saumyatarāśeṣasaumyebhyas tv atisundarī
parāparāṇāṁ paramā tvam eva parameśvarī

यच्च किञ्चित्क्वचिद्वस्तु सदसद्वाखिलात्मिके ।
तस्य सर्वस्य या शक्तिः सा त्वं किं स्तूयसे मया ॥८२॥

yac ca kiñcit kvacid vastu sadasadvākhilātmike
tasya sarvasya yā śaktiḥ sā tvaṁ kiṁ stūyase mayā

यया त्वया जगत्स्रष्टा जगत्पातात्ति यो जगत् ।
सोऽपि निद्रावशं नीतः कस्त्वां स्तोतुमिहेश्वरः ॥८३॥

yayā tvayā jagatsraṣṭā jagatpātātti yo jagat
so 'pi nidrāvaśaṁ nītaḥ kastvāṁ stotum iheśvaraḥ

विष्णुः शरीरग्रहणमहमीशान एव च ।
कारितास्ते यतोऽतस्त्वां कः स्तोतुं शक्तिमान् भवेत् ॥८४॥

viṣṇuḥ śarīragrahaṇam aham īśāna eva ca
kāritāste yato 'tas tvāṁ kaḥ stotuṁ śaktimān bhavet

सा त्वमित्थं प्रभावैः स्वैरुदारैर्देवि संस्तुता ।
मोहयैतौ दुराधर्षावसुरौ मधुकैटभौ ॥८५॥

sā tvam itthaṁ prabhāvaiḥ svair udārair devi saṁstutā
mohayaitau durādharṣāv asurau madhukaiṭabhau

प्रबोधं च जगत्स्वामी नीयतामच्युतो लघु ॥८६॥
बोधश्च क्रियतामस्य हन्तुमेतौ महासुरौ ॥८७॥

prabodhaṁ ca jagatsvāmī nīyatām acyuto laghu
bodhaś ca kriyatāmasya hantum etau mahāsurau

ऋषिरुवाच ॥ ८८ ॥

ṛṣir uvāca

एवं स्तुता तदा देवी तामसी तत्र वेधसा ।
विष्णोः प्रबोधनार्थाय निहन्तुं मधुकैटभौ ॥ ८९ ॥

evaṁ stutā tadā devī tāmasī tatra vedhasā
viṣṇoḥ prabodhanārthāya nihantuṁ madhukaiṭabhau

नेत्रास्यनासिकाबाहुहृदयेभ्यस्तथोरसः ।
निर्गम्य दर्शने तस्थौ ब्रह्मणोऽव्यक्तजन्मनः ॥ ९० ॥

netrāsyanāsikābāhuhṛdayebhyas tathorasaḥ
nirgamya darśane tasthau brahmaṇo 'vyaktajanmanaḥ

उत्तस्थौ च जगन्नाथस्तया मुक्तो जनार्दनः ।
एकार्णवेऽहिशयनात्ततः स ददृशे च तौ ॥ ९१ ॥

uttasthau ca jagannāthas tayā mukto janārdanaḥ
ekārṇave 'hiśayanāt tataḥ sa dadṛśe ca tau

मधुकैटभौ दुरात्मानावतिवीर्यपराक्रमौ ।
क्रोधरक्तेक्षणावत्तुं ब्रह्माणं जनितोद्यमौ ॥ ९२ ॥

madhukaiṭabhau durātmānāv ativīryaparākramau
krodharaktekṣaṇāv attuṁ brahmāṇaṁ janitodyamau

समुत्थाय ततस्ताभ्यां युयुधे भगवान् हरिः ।
पञ्चवर्षसहस्राणि बाहुप्रहरणो विभुः ॥ ९३ ॥

samutthāya tatas tābhyāṁ yuyudhe bhagavān hariḥ
pañcavarṣasahasrāṇi bāhupraharaṇo vibhuḥ

तावप्यतिबलोन्मत्तौ महामायाविमोहितौ ॥ ९४ ॥
उक्तवन्तौ वरोऽस्मत्तो व्रियतामिति केशवम् ॥ ९५ ॥

tāv apyatibalonmattau mahāmāyāvimohitau
uktavantau varo 'smatto vriyatām iti keśavam

श्रीभगवानुवाच ॥ ९६ ॥

śrī bhagavān uvāca

भवेतामद्य मे तुष्टौ मम वध्यावुभावपि ॥ ९७ ॥
किमन्येन वरेणात्र एतावद्धि वृतं मम ॥ ९८ ॥

bhavetām adya me tuṣṭau mama vadhyāv ubhāv api
kim anyena vareṇātra etāvad dhi vṛtaṁ mama

ऋषिरुवाच ॥ ९९ ॥

ṛṣir uvāca

वञ्चिताभ्यामिति तदा सर्वमापोमयं जगत् ।
विलोक्य ताभ्यां गदितो भगवान् कमलेक्षणः ॥ १०० ॥

vañcitābhyām iti tadā sarvam āpomayaṁ jagat
vilokya tābhyāṁ gadito bhagavān kamalekṣaṇaḥ

आवां जहि न यत्रोर्वी सलिलेन परिप्लुता ॥ १०१ ॥

āvāṁ jahi na yatrorvī salilena pariplutā

ऋषिरुवाच ॥ १०२ ॥

ṛṣir uvāca

तथेत्युक्त्वा भगवता शङ्खचक्रगदाभृता ।
कृत्वा चक्रेण वै छिन्ने जघने शिरसी तयोः ॥ १०३ ॥

tathety uktvā bhagavatā śaṅkhacakragadābhṛtā
kṛtvā cakreṇa vai chinne jaghane śirasī tayoḥ

एवमेषा समुत्पन्ना ब्रह्मणा संस्तुता स्वयम् ।
प्रभावमस्या देव्यास्तु भूयः शृणु वदामि ते ॥ १०४ ॥

evam eṣā samutpannā brahmaṇā saṁstutā svayam
prabhāvam asyā devyās tu bhūyaḥ śṛṇu vadāmi te

# मध्यमचरितम्

## महालक्ष्मीध्यानम्

ॐ अक्षस्रक्परशुं गदेषुकुलिशं पद्मं धनुः कुण्डिकां
दण्डं शक्तिमसिं च चर्म जलजं घण्टां सुराभाजनम् ।
शूलं पाशसुदर्शने च दधतीं हस्तैः प्रवालप्रभां
सेवे सैरिभमर्दिनीमिह महालक्ष्मीं सरोजस्थिताम् ॥

Oṁ. akṣasrakparaṣuṁ gadeṣukuliśaṁ padmaṁ dhanuḥ kuṇḍikāṁ
daṇḍaṁ śaktimasiṁ ca carma jalajaṁ ghaṇṭāṁ surābhājanam
śūlaṁ pāśasudarśane ca dadhatīṁ hastaiḥ pravālaprabhāṁ
seve sairibhamardinīmiha mahālakṣmīṁ sarojasthitām

# द्वितीयोऽध्यायः

## महिषासुरसैन्यवधः

ॐ ह्रीं ऋषिरुवाच ॥ १ ॥

Oṁ hrīṁ ṛṣir uvāca

देवासुरमभूद्युद्धं पूर्णमब्दशतं पुरा ।
महिषेऽसुराणामधिपे देवानां च पुरन्दरे ॥ २ ॥

devāsuram abhūd yuddhaṁ pūrṇam abdaśataṁ purā
mahiṣe 'surāṇām adhipe devānāṁ ca purandare

तत्रासुरैर्महावीर्यैर्देवसैन्यं पराजितम् ।
जित्वा च सकलान् देवानिन्द्रोऽभून्महिषासुरः ॥ ३ ॥

tatrāsurair mahāvīryair devasainyaṁ parājitam
jitvā ca sakalān devān indro 'bhūn mahiṣāsuraḥ

ततः पराजिता देवाः पद्मयोनिं प्रजापतिम् ।
पुरस्कृत्य गतास्तत्र यत्रेशगरुडध्वजौ ॥ ४ ॥

tataḥ parājitā devāḥ padmayoniṁ prajāpatim
puraskṛtya gatās tatra yatreśagaruḍadhvajau

यथावृत्तं तयोस्तद्वन्महिषासुरचेष्टितम् ।
त्रिदशाः कथयामासुर्देवाभिभवविस्तरम् ॥ ५ ॥

yathāvṛttaṁ tayos tadvan mahiṣāsuraceṣṭitam
tridaśāḥ kathayāmāsur devābhibhavavistaram

सूर्येन्द्राग्न्यनिलेन्दूनां यमस्य वरुणस्य च ।
अन्येषां चाधिकारान्स स्वयमेवाधितिष्ठति ॥ ६ ॥

sūryendrāgnyanilendūnāṁ yamasya varuṇasya ca
anyeṣām cādhikārān sa svayam evādhitiṣṭhati

स्वर्गान्निराकृताः सर्वे तेन देवगणा भुवि ।
विचरन्ति यथा मर्त्या महिषेण दुरात्मना ॥ ७ ॥

svargān nirākṛtāḥ sarve tena devagaṇā bhuvi
vicaranti yathā martyā mahiṣeṇa durātmanā

एतद्वः कथितं सर्वममरारिविचेष्टितम् ।
शरणं वः प्रपन्नाः स्मो वधस्तस्य विचिन्त्यताम् ॥ ८ ॥

etad vaḥ kathitaṁ sarvam amarārivіceṣṭitam
śaraṇaṁ vaḥ prapannāḥ smo vadhastasya vicintyatām

इत्थं निशम्य देवानां वचांसि मधुसूदनः ।
चकार कोपं शम्भुश्च भ्रुकुटीकुटिलाननौ ॥ ९ ॥

itthaṁ niśamya devānāṁ vacāṁsi madhusūdanaḥ
cakāra kopaṁ śambhuś ca bhrukuṭīkuṭilānanau

ततोऽतिकोपपूर्णस्य चक्रिणो वदनात्ततः ।
निश्चक्राम महत्तेजो ब्रह्मणः शङ्करस्य च ॥ १० ॥

tato 'tikopapūrṇasya cakriṇo vadanāt tataḥ
niścakrāma mahat tejo brahmaṇaḥ śaṅkarasya ca

अन्येषां चैव देवानां शक्रादीनां शरीरतः ।
निर्गतं सुमहत्तेजस्तच्चैक्यं समगच्छत ॥ ११ ॥

anyeṣāṁ caiva devānāṁ śakrādīnāṁ śarīrataḥ
nirgataṁ sumahat tejas tac caikyaṁ samagacchata

अतीव तेजसः कूटं ज्वलन्तमिव पर्वतम् ।
ददृशुस्ते सुरास्तत्र ज्वालाव्याप्तदिगन्तरम् ॥ १२ ॥

atīva tejasaḥ kūṭaṁ jvalantam iva parvatam
dadṛśus te surās tatra jvālāvyāptadigantaram

अतुलं तत्र तत्तेजः सर्वदेवशरीरजम् ।
एकस्थं तदभून्नारी व्याप्तलोकत्रयं त्विषा ॥ १३ ॥

atulaṁ tatra tat tejaḥ sarvadevaśarīrajam
ekasthaṁ tadabhūn nārī vyāptalokatrayaṁ tviṣā

यदभूच्छाम्भवं तेजस्तेनाजायत तन्मुखम् ।
याम्येन चाभवन् केशा बाहवो विष्णुतेजसा ॥ १४ ॥

yad abhūc chāmbhavaṁ tejas tenājāyata tan mukham
yāmyena cābhavan keśā bāhavo viṣṇutejasā

सौम्येन स्तनयोर्युग्मं मध्यं चैन्द्रेण चाभवत् ।
वारुणेन च जङ्घोरू नितम्बस्तेजसा भुवः ॥ १५ ॥

saumyena stanayor yugmaṁ madhyaṁ caindreṇa cābhavat
vāruṇena ca jaṅghorū nitambas tejasā bhuvaḥ

ब्रह्मणस्तेजसा पादौ तदङ्गुल्योऽर्कतेजसा ।
वसूनां च कराङ्गुल्यः कौबेरेण च नासिका ॥ १६ ॥

brahmaṇas tejasā pādau tad aṅgulyo 'rkatejasā
vasūnāṁ ca karāṅgulyaḥ kaubereṇa ca nāsikā

तस्यास्तु दन्ताः सम्भूताः प्राजापत्येन तेजसा ।
नयनत्रितयं जज्ञे तथा पावकतेजसा ॥ १७ ॥

tasyāstu dantāḥ sambhūtāḥ prājāpatyena tejasā
nayanatritayaṁ jajñe tathā pāvakatejasā

भ्रुवौ च सन्ध्ययोस्तेजः श्रवणावनिलस्य च ।
अन्येषां चैव देवानां सम्भवस्तेजसां शिवा ॥ १८ ॥

bhruvau ca sandhyayos tejaḥ śravaṇāv anilasya ca
anyeṣāṁ caiva devānāṁ sambhavas tejasāṁ śivā

ततः समस्तदेवानां तेजोराशिसमुद्भवाम् ।
तां विलोक्य मुदं प्रापुरमरा महिषार्दिताः ॥ १९ ॥

tataḥ samastadevānāṁ tejorāśisamudbhavām
tāṁ vilokya mudaṁ prāpur amarā mahiṣārditāḥ

ततो देवा ददुस्तस्यै स्वानि स्वान्यायुधानि च ।
शूलं शूलाद्विनिष्कृष्य ददौ तस्यै पिनाकधृक् ॥ २० ॥

tato devā dadus tasyai svāni svānyāyudhāni ca
śūlaṁ śūlād viniṣkṛṣya dadau tasyai pinākadhṛk

चक्रं च दत्तवान् कृष्णः समुत्पाट्य स्वचक्रतः ।
शङ्खं च वरुणः शक्तिं ददौ तस्यै हुताशनः ॥ २१ ॥

cakraṁ ca dattavān kṛṣṇaḥ samutpāṭya svacakrataḥ
śaṅkhaṁ ca varuṇaḥ śaktiṁ dadau tasyai hutāśanaḥ

मारुतो दत्तवांश्चापं बाणपूर्णे तथेषुधी ।
वज्रमिन्द्रः समुत्पाट्य कुलिशादमराधिपः ॥ २२ ॥

māruto dattavāṁś cāpaṁ bāṇapūrṇe tatheṣudhī
vajram indraḥ samutpāṭya kuliśād amarādhipaḥ

ददौ तस्यै सहस्राक्षो घण्टामैरावताद्गजात् ।
कालदण्डाद्यमो दण्डं पाशं चाम्बुपतिर्ददौ ॥ २३ ॥

dadau tasyai sahasrākṣo ghaṇṭām airāvatād gajāt
kāladaṇḍād yamo daṇḍaṁ pāśaṁ cāmbupatir dadau

प्रजापतिश्चाक्षमालां ददौ ब्रह्मा कमण्डलुम् ।
समस्तरोमकूपेषु निजरश्मीन् दिवाकरः ॥ २४ ॥

prajāpatiś cākṣamālāṁ dadau brahmā kamaṇḍalum
samastaromakūpeṣu nijaraśmīn divākaraḥ

कालश्च दत्तवान् खड्गं तस्याश्चर्म च निर्मलम् ।
क्षीरोदश्चामलं हारमजरे च तथाम्बरे ॥ २५ ॥

kālaś ca dattavān khaḍgaṁ tasyāś carma ca nirmalam
kṣīrodaś cāmalaṁ hāram ajare ca tathāmbare

चूडामणिं तथा दिव्यं कुण्डले कटकानि च ।
अर्धचन्द्रं तथा शुभ्रं केयूरान् सर्वबाहुषु ॥ २६ ॥

cūḍāmaṇiṁ tathā divyaṁ kuṇḍale kaṭakāni ca
ardhacandraṁ tathā śubhraṁ keyūrān sarvabāhuṣu

नूपुरौ विमलौ तद्वद् ग्रैवेयकमनुत्तमम् ।
अङ्गुलीयकरत्नानि समस्तास्वङ्गुलीषु च ॥ २७ ॥

nūpurau vimalau tadvad graiveyakam anuttamam
aṅgulīyakaratnāni samastāsvaṅgulīṣu ca

विश्वकर्मा ददौ तस्यै परशुं चातिनिर्मलम् ।
अस्त्राण्यनेकरूपाणि तथाऽभेद्यं च दंशनम् ॥ २८ ॥

viśvakarmā dadau tasyai paraśuṁ cātinirmalam
astrāṇy anekarūpāṇi tathā 'bhedyaṁ ca daṁśanam

अम्लानपङ्कजां मालां शिरस्युरसि चापराम् ।
अददज्जलधिस्तस्यै पङ्कजं चातिशोभनम् ॥ २९ ॥

amlānapaṅkajāṁ mālāṁ śirasy urasi cāparām
adadaj jaladhis tasyai paṅkajaṁ cātiśobhanam

हिमवान् वाहनं सिंहं रत्नानि विविधानि च ।
ददावशून्यं सुरया पानपात्रं धनाधिपः ॥ ३० ॥

himavān vāhanaṁ siṁhaṁ ratnāni vividhāni ca
dadāv aśūnyaṁ surayā pānapātraṁ dhanādhipaḥ

शेषश्च सर्वनागेशो महामणिविभूषितम् ।
नागहारं ददौ तस्यै धत्ते यः पृथिवीमिमाम् ॥ ३१ ॥

śeṣaś ca sarvanāgeśo mahāmaṇivibhūṣitam
nāgahāraṁ dadau tasyai dhatte yaḥ pṛthivīmimām

अन्यैरपि सुरैर्देवी भूषणैरायुधैस्तथा ।
सम्मानिता ननादोच्चैः साट्टहासं मुहुर्मुहुः ॥ ३२ ॥

anyair api surair devī bhūṣaṇair āyudhais tathā
sammānitā nanādoccaiḥ sāṭṭahāsaṁ muhur muhuḥ

तस्या नादेन घोरेण कृत्स्नमापूरितं नभः ।
अमायतातिमहता प्रतिशब्दो महानभूत् ॥ ३३ ॥

tasyā nādena ghoreṇa kṛtsnam āpūritaṁ nabhaḥ
amāyatātimahatā pratiśabdo mahānabhūt

चुक्षुभुः सकला लोकाः समुद्राश्च चकम्पिरे ।
चचाल वसुधा चेलुः सकलाश्च महीधराः ॥ ३४ ॥

cukṣubhuḥ sakalā lokāḥ samudrāś ca cakampire
cacāla vasudhā celuḥ sakalāś ca mahīdharāḥ

जयेति देवाश्च मुदा तामूचुः सिंहवाहिनीम् ।
तुष्टुवुर्मुनयश्चैनां भक्तिनम्रात्ममूर्तयः ॥ ३५ ॥

jayeti devāś ca mudā tām ūcuḥ siṁhavāhinīm
tuṣṭuvur munayaś caināṁ bhaktinamrātmamūrtayaḥ

दृष्ट्वा समस्तं संक्षुब्धं त्रैलोक्यममरारयः ।
सन्नद्धाखिलसैन्यास्ते समुत्तस्थुरुदायुधाः ॥ ३६ ॥

dṛṣṭvā samastaṁ saṁkṣubdhaṁ trailokyam amarārayaḥ
sannaddhākhilasainyāste samuttasthur udāyudhāḥ

आः किमेतदिति क्रोधादाभाष्य महिषासुरः ।
अभ्यधावत तं शब्दमशेषैरसुरैर्वृतः ॥ ३७ ॥

āḥ kim etad iti krodhād ābhāṣya mahiṣāsuraḥ
abhyadhāvata taṁ śabdam aśeṣair asurair vṛtaḥ

स ददर्श ततो देवीं व्याप्तलोकत्रयां त्विषा ।
पादाक्रान्त्या नतभुवं किरीटोल्लिखिताम्बराम् ॥ ३८ ॥

sa dadarśa tato devīṁ vyāptalokatrayāṁ tviṣā
pādākrāntyā natabhuvaṁ kirīṭollikhitāmbarām

क्षोभिताशेषपातालां धनुर्ज्यानिःस्वनेन ताम् ।
दिशो भुजसहस्रेण समन्ताद्व्याप्य संस्थिताम् ॥ ३९ ॥

kṣobhitāśeṣapātālāṁ dhanurjyāniḥsvanena tām
diśo bhujasahasreṇa samantād vyāpya saṁsthitām

ततः प्रववृते युद्धं तया देव्या सुरद्विषाम् ।
शस्त्रास्त्रैर्बहुधा मुक्तैरादीपितदिगन्तरम् ॥ ४० ॥

tataḥ pravavṛte yuddhaṁ tayā devyā suradviṣām
śastrāstrair bahudhā muktair ādīpitadigantaram

महिषासुरसेनानीश्चिक्षुराख्यो महासुरः ।
युयुधे चामरश्चान्यैश्चतुरङ्गबलान्वितः ॥ ४१ ॥

mahiṣāsurasenānīś cikṣurākhyo mahāsuraḥ
yuyudhe cāmaraś cānyaiś caturaṅgabalānvitaḥ

रथानामयुतैः षड्भिरुदग्राख्यो महासुरः ।
अयुध्यतायुतानां च सहस्रेण महाहनुः ॥ ४२ ॥

rathānāmayutaiḥ ṣaḍbhir udagrākhyo mahāsuraḥ
ayudhyatāyutānāṁ ca sahasreṇa mahāhanuḥ

पञ्चाशद्भिश्च नियुतैरसिलोमा महासुरः ।
अयुतानां शतैः षड्भिर्बाष्कलो युयुधे रणे ॥ ४३ ॥

pañcāśadbhiś ca niyutair asilomā mahāsuraḥ
ayutānāṁ śataiḥ ṣaḍbhir bāṣkalo yuyudhe raṇe

गजवाजिसहस्रौघैरनेकैः परिवारितः ।
वृतो रथानां कोट्या च युद्धे तस्मिन्नयुध्यत ॥ ४४ ॥

gajavājisahasraughair anekaiḥ parivāritaḥ
vṛto rathānāṁ koṭyā ca yuddhe tasminn ayudhyata

बिडालाख्योऽयुतानां च पञ्चाशद्भिरथायुतैः ।
युयुधे संयुगे तत्र रथानां परिवारितः ॥ ४५ ॥

biḍālākhyo 'yutānāṁ ca pañcāśadbhir athāyutaiḥ
yuyudhe saṁyuge tatra rathānāṁ parivāritaḥ

अन्ये च तत्रायुतशो रथनागहयैर्वृताः ।
युयुधुः संयुगे देव्या सह तत्र महासुराः ॥ ४६ ॥

anye ca tatrāyutaśo rathanāgahayair vṛtāḥ
yuyudhuḥ saṁyuge devyā saha tatra mahāsurāḥ

कोटिकोटिसहस्रैस्तु रथानां दन्तिनां तथा ।
हयानां च वृतो युद्धे तत्राभून्महिषासुरः ॥ ४७ ॥

koṭikoṭisahasrais tu rathānāṁ dantināṁ tathā
hayānāṁ ca vṛto yuddhe tatrābhūn mahiṣāsuraḥ

तोमरैर्भिन्दिपालैश्च शक्तिभिर्मुसलैस्तथा ।
युयुधुः संयुगे देव्या खड्गैः परशुपट्टिशैः ॥ ४८ ॥

tomarair bhindipālaiś ca śaktibhir musalais tathā
yuyudhuḥ saṁyuge devyā khaḍgaiḥ paraśupaṭṭiśaiḥ

केचिच्च चिक्षिपुः शक्तीः केचित् पाशांस्तथापरे ।
देवीं खड्गप्रहारैस्तु ते तां हन्तुं प्रचक्रमुः ॥ ४९ ॥

kecic ca cikṣipuḥ śaktīḥ kecit pāśāṁs tathāpare
devīṁ khaḍgaprahārais tu te tāṁ hantuṁ pracakramuḥ

सापि देवी ततस्तानि शस्त्राण्यस्त्राणि चण्डिका ।
लीलयैव प्रचिच्छेद निजशस्त्रास्त्रवर्षिणी ॥ ५० ॥

sāpi devī tatas tāni śastrāṇy astrāṇi caṇḍikā
līlayaiva praciccheda nijaśastrāstravarṣiṇī

अनायस्तानना देवी स्तूयमाना सुरर्षिभिः ।
मुमोचासुरदेहेषु शस्त्राण्यस्त्राणि चेश्वरी ॥ ५१ ॥

anāyastānanā devī stūyamānā surarṣibhiḥ
mumocāsuradeheṣu śastrāṇyastrāṇi ceśvarī

सोऽपि क्रुद्धो धुतसटो देव्या वाहनकेसरी ।
चचारासुरसैन्येषु वनेष्विव हुताशनः ॥ ५२ ॥

so 'pi kruddho dhutasaṭo devyā vāhanakesarī
cacārāsurasainyeṣu vaneṣv iva hutāśanaḥ

निःश्वासान् मुमुचे यांश्च युध्यमाना रणेऽम्बिका ।
त एव सद्यः सम्भूता गणाः शतसहस्रशः ॥ ५३ ॥

niḥśvāsān mumuce yāṁś ca yudhyamānā raṇe 'mbikā
ta eva sadyaḥ sambhūtā gaṇāḥ śatasahasraśaḥ

युयुधुस्ते परशुभिर्भिन्दिपालासिपट्टिशैः ।
नाशयन्तोऽसुरगणान् देवीशक्त्युपबृंहिताः ॥ ५४ ॥

yuyudhus te paraśubhir bhindipālāsipaṭṭiśaiḥ
nāśayanto 'suragaṇān devīśaktyupabṛṁhitāḥ

अवादयन्त पटहान् गणाः शङ्खांस्तथापरे ।
मृदङ्गांश्च तथैवान्ये तस्मिन्युद्धमहोत्सवे ॥ ५५ ॥

avādayanta paṭahān gaṇāḥ śaṅkhāṁs tathāpare
mṛdaṅgāṁś ca tathaivānye tasmin yuddhamahotsave

ततो देवी त्रिशूलेन गदया शक्तिवृष्टिभिः ।
खड्गादिभिश्च शतशो निजघान महासुरान् ॥ ५६ ॥

tato devī triśūlena gadayā śaktivṛṣṭibhiḥ
khaḍgādibhiś ca śataśo nijaghāna mahāsurān

पातयामास चैवान्यान् घण्टास्वनविमोहितान् ।
असुरान् भुवि पाशेन बद्ध्वा चान्यानकर्षयत् ॥ ५७ ॥

pātayāmāsa caivānyān ghaṇṭāsvanavimohitān
asurān bhuvi pāśena baddhvā cānyān akarṣayat

केचिद् द्विधाकृतास्तीक्ष्णैः खड्गपातैस्तथापरे ।
विपोथिता निपातेन गदया भुवि शेरते ॥ ५८ ॥

kecid dvidhākṛtās tīkṣṇaiḥ khaḍgapātais tathāpare
vipothitā nipātena gadayā bhuvi śerate

वेमुश्च केचिद्रुधिरं मुसलेन भृशं हताः ।
केचिन्निपतिता भूमौ भिन्नाः शूलेन वक्षसि ॥ ५९ ॥

vemuś ca kecid rudhiraṁ musalena bhṛśaṁ hatāḥ
kecin nipatitā bhūmau bhinnāḥ śūlena vakṣasi

निरन्तराः शरौघेण कृताः केचिद्रणाजिरे ।
शल्यानुकारिणः प्राणान्मुमुचुस्त्रिदशार्दनाः ॥ ६० ॥

nirantarāḥ śaraugheṇa kṛtāḥ kecid raṇājire
śalyānukāriṇaḥ prāṇān mumucus tridaśārdanāḥ

केषाञ्चिद्बाहवश्छिन्नाश्छिन्नग्रीवास्तथापरे ।
शिरांसि पेतुरन्येषामन्ये मध्ये विदारिताः ॥ ६१ ॥

keṣāñcid bāhavaś chinnāś chinnagrīvās tathāpare
śirāṁsi petur anyeṣām anye madhye vidāritāḥ

विच्छिन्नजङ्घास्त्वपरे पेतुरुर्व्यां महासुराः ।
एकबाहवक्षिचरणाः केचिद्देव्या द्विधाकृताः ॥ ६२ ॥

vicchinnajaṅghās tv apare petur urvyāṁ mahāsurāḥ
ekabāhvakṣicaraṇāḥ kecid devyā dvidhākṛtāḥ

छिन्नेऽपि चान्ये शिरसि पतिताः पुनरुत्थिताः ।
ननृतुश्चापरे तत्र युद्धे तूर्यलयाश्रिताः ॥ ६३ ॥

chinne 'pi cānye śirasi patitāḥ punar utthitāḥ
nanṛtuś cāpare tatra yuddhe tūryalayāśritāḥ

कबन्धाश्छिन्नशिरसः खड्गशक्त्यृष्टिपाणयः ।
तिष्ठ तिष्ठेति भाषन्तो देवीमन्ये महासुराः ॥ ६४ ॥

kabandhāś chinnaśirasaḥ khaḍgaśaktyṛṣṭipāṇayaḥ
tiṣṭha tiṣṭheti bhāṣanto devīm anye mahāsurāḥ

पातितै रथनागाश्वैरसुरैश्च वसुन्धरा ।
अगम्या साभवत्तत्र यत्राभूत् स महारणः ॥ ६५ ॥

pātitai rathanāgāśvair asuraiś ca vasundharā
agamyā sābhavat tatra yatrābhūt sa mahāraṇaḥ

शोणितौघा महानद्यः सद्यस्तत्र विसुस्रुवुः ।
मध्ये चासुरसैन्यस्य वारणासुरवाजिनाम् ॥ ६६ ॥

śoṇitaughā mahānadyaḥ sadyas tatra visusruvuḥ
madhye cāsurasainyasya vāraṇāsuravājinām

क्षणेन तन्महासैन्यमसुराणां तथाम्बिका ।
निन्ये क्षयं यथा वह्निस्तृणदारुमहाचयम् ॥ ६७ ॥

kṣaṇena tan mahāsainyam asurāṇām tathāmbikā
ninye kṣayaṁ yathā vahnistṛṇadārumahācayam

स च सिंहो महानादमुत्सृजन् धुतकेसरः ।
शरीरेभ्योऽमरारीणामसूनिव विचिन्वति ॥ ६८ ॥

sa ca siṁho mahānādam utsṛjan dhutakesaraḥ
śarīrebhyo 'marārīṇām asūn iva vicinvati

देव्या गणैश्च तैस्तत्र कृतं युद्धं तथासुरैः ।
यथैषां तुष्टुवुर्देवाः पुष्पवृष्टिमुचो दिवि ॥ ६९ ॥

devyā gaṇaiś ca tais tatra kṛtaṁ yuddhaṁ tathāsuraiḥ
yathaiṣāṁ tuṣṭuvur devāḥ puṣpavṛṣṭimuco divi

# तृतीयोऽध्यायः

## महिषासुरवधः

ऋषिरुवाच ॥ १ ॥

ṛṣir uvāca

निहन्यमानं तत्सैन्यमवलोक्य महासुरः ।
सेनानीश्चिक्षुरः कोपाद्ययौ योद्धुमथाम्बिकाम् ॥ २ ॥

nihanyamānaṁ tat sainyam avalokya mahāsuraḥ
senānīś cikṣuraḥ kopād yayau yoddhum athāmbikām

स देवीं शरवर्षेण ववर्ष समरेऽसुरः ।
यथा मेरुगिरेः शृङ्गं तोयवर्षेण तोयदः ॥ ३ ॥

sa devīṁ śaravarṣeṇa vavarṣa samare 'suraḥ
yathā merugireḥ śṛṅgaṁ toyavarṣeṇa toyadaḥ

तस्य छित्वा ततो देवी लीलयैव शरोत्करान् ।
जघान तुरगान्बाणैर्यन्तारं चैव वाजिनाम् ॥ ४ ॥

tasya chitvā tato devī līlayaiva śarotkarān
jaghāna turagān bāṇair yantāraṁ caiva vājinām

चिच्छेद च धनुः सद्यो ध्वजं चातिसमुच्छ्रितम् ।
विव्याध चैव गात्रेषु छिन्नधन्वानमाशुगैः ॥ ५ ॥

ciccheda ca dhanuḥ sadyo dhvajaṁ cātisamucchritam
vivyādha caiva gātreṣu chinnadhanvānam āśugaiḥ

स छिन्नधन्वा विरथो हताश्वो हतसारथिः ।
अभ्यधावत तां देवीं खड्गचर्मधरोऽसुरः ॥ ६ ॥

sa chinnadhanvā viratho hatāśvo hatasārathiḥ
abhyadhāvata tāṁ devīṁ khaḍgacarmadharo 'suraḥ

सिंहमाहत्य खड्गेन तीक्ष्णधारेण मूर्धनि ।
आजघान भुजे सव्ये देवीमप्यतिवेगवान् ॥ ७ ॥

siṁham āhatya khaḍgena tīkṣṇadhāreṇa mūrdhani
ājaghāna bhuje savye devīm apyativegavān

तस्याः खड्गो भुजं प्राप्य पफाल नृपनन्दन ।
ततो जग्राह शूलं स कोपादरुणलोचनः ॥ ८ ॥

tasyāḥ khadgo bhujaṁ prāpya paphāla nṛpanandana
tato jagrāha śūlaṁ sa kopād aruṇalocanaḥ

चिक्षेप च ततस्तत्तु भद्रकाल्यां महासुरः ।
जाज्वल्यमानं तेजोभी रविबिम्बमिवाम्बरात् ॥ ९ ॥

cikṣepa ca tatas tat tu bhadrakālyāṁ mahāsuraḥ
jājvalyamānaṁ tejobhī ravibimbam ivāmbarāt

दृष्ट्वा तदापतच्छूलं देवी शूलममुञ्चत ।
तच्छूलं शतधा तेन नीतं स च महासुरः ॥ १० ॥

dṛṣṭvā tad āpatac chūlaṁ devī śūlam amuñcata
tac chūlaṁ śatadhā tena nītaṁ sa ca mahāsuraḥ

हते तस्मिन्महावीर्ये महिषस्य चमूपतौ ।
आजगाम गजारूढश्चामरस्त्रिदशार्दनः ॥ ११ ॥

hate tasmin mahāvīrye mahiṣasya camūpatau
ājagāma gajārūḍhaś cāmaras tridaśārdanaḥ

सोऽपि शक्तिं मुमोचाथ देव्यास्तामम्बिका द्रुतम् ।
हुङ्काराभिहतां भूमौ पातयामास निष्प्रभाम् ॥ १२ ॥

so 'pi śaktiṁ mumocātha devyās tām ambikā drutam
huṅkārābhihatāṁ bhūmau pātayāmāsa niṣprabhām

भग्नां शक्तिं निपतितां दृष्ट्वा क्रोधसमन्वितः ।
चिक्षेप चामरः शूलं बाणैस्तदपि साच्छिनत् ॥ १३ ॥

bhagnāṁ śaktiṁ nipatitāṁ dṛṣṭvā krodhasamanvitaḥ
cikṣepa cāmaraḥ śūlaṁ bāṇais tad api sācchinat

ततः सिंहः समुत्पत्य गजकुम्भान्तरस्थितः ।
बाहुयुद्धेन युयुधे तेनोच्चैस्त्रिदशारिणा ॥ १४ ॥

tataḥ siṁhaḥ samutpatya gajakumbhāntarasthitaḥ
bāhuyuddhena yuyudhe tenocchais tridaśāriṇā

युध्यमानौ ततस्तौ तु तस्मान्नागान्महीं गतौ ।
युयुधातेऽतिसंरब्धौ प्रहारैरतिदारुणैः ॥ १५ ॥

yudhyamānau tatas tau tu tasmān nāgān mahīṁ gatau
yuyudhāte 'tisaṁrabdhau prahārair atidāruṇaiḥ

ततो वेगात् खमुत्पत्य निपत्य च मृगारिणा ।
करप्रहारेण शिरश्चामरस्य पृथक् कृतम् ॥ १६ ॥

tato vegāt kham utpatya nipatya ca mṛgāriṇā
karaprahāreṇa śiraś cāmarasya pṛthak kṛtam

उदग्रश्च रणे देव्या शिलावृक्षादिभिर्हतः ।
दन्तमुष्टितलैश्चैव करालश्च निपातितः ॥ १७ ॥

udagraś ca raṇe devyā śilāvṛkṣādibhir hataḥ
dantamuṣṭitalaiś caiva karālaś ca nipātitaḥ

देवी क्रुद्धा गदापातैश्चूर्णयामास चोद्धतम् ।
बाष्कलं भिन्दिपालेन बाणैस्ताम्रं तथान्धकम् ॥ १८ ॥

devī kruddhā gadāpātaiś cūrṇayāmāsa coddhatam
bāṣkalaṁ bhindipālena bāṇais tāmraṁ tathāndhakam

उग्रास्यमुग्रवीर्यं च तथैव च महाहनुम् ।
त्रिनेत्रा च त्रिशूलेन जघान परमेश्वरी ॥ १९ ॥

ugrāsyam ugravīryaṁ ca tathaiva ca mahāhanum
trinetrā ca triśūlena jaghāna parameśvarī

बिडालस्यासिना कायात् पातयामास वै शिरः ।
दुर्धरं दुर्मुखं चोभौ शरैर्निन्ये यमक्षयम् ॥ २० ॥

bidālasyāsinā kāyāt pātayāmāsa vai śiraḥ
durdharaṁ durmukhaṁ cobhau śarair ninye yamakṣayam

एवं संक्षीयमाणे तु स्वसैन्ये महिषासुरः ।
माहिषेण स्वरूपेण त्रासयामास तान् गणान् ॥ २१ ॥

evaṁ saṁkṣīyamāṇe tu svasainye mahiṣāsuraḥ
māhiṣeṇa svarūpeṇa trāsayāmāsa tān gaṇān

कांश्चित्तुण्डप्रहारेण खुरक्षेपैस्तथापरान् ।
लाङ्गूलताडितांश्चान्यान् शृङ्गाभ्यां च विदारितान् ॥ २२ ॥

kāṁścit tuṇḍaprahāreṇa khurakṣepais tathāparān
lāṅgūlatāḍitāṁś cānyān śṛṅgābhyāṁ ca vidāritān

वेगेन कांश्चिदपरान्नादेन भ्रमणेन च ।
निःश्वासपवनेनान्यान्पातयामास भूतले ॥ २३ ॥

vegena kāṁścid aparān nādena bhramaṇena ca
niḥśvāsapavanenānyān pātayāmāsa bhūtale

निपात्य प्रमथानीकमभ्यधावत सोऽसुरः ।
सिंहं हन्तुं महादेव्याः कोपं चक्रे ततोऽम्बिका ॥ २४ ॥

nipātya pramathānīkam abhyadhāvata so 'suraḥ
siṁhaṁ hantuṁ mahādevyāḥ kopaṁ cakre tato 'mbikā

सोऽपि कोपान्महावीर्यः खुरक्षुण्णमहीतलः ।
शृङ्गाभ्यां पर्वतानुच्चांश्चिक्षेप च ननाद च ॥ २५ ॥

so 'pi kopān mahāvīryaḥ khurakṣuṇṇamahītalaḥ
śṛṅgābhyāṁ parvatān uccāṁś cikṣepa ca nanāda ca

वेगभ्रमणविक्षुण्णा मही तस्य व्यशीर्यत ।
लाङ्गूलेनाहतश्चाब्धिः प्लावयामास सर्वतः ॥ २६ ॥

vegabhramaṇavikṣuṇṇā mahī tasya vyaśīryata
lāṅgūlenāhataś cābdhiḥ plāvayāmāsa sarvataḥ

धुतशृङ्गविभिन्नाश्च खण्डं खण्डं ययुर्घनाः ।
श्वासानिलास्ताः शतशो निपेतुर्नभसोऽचलाः ॥ २७ ॥

dhutaśṛṅgavibhinnāś ca khaṇḍaṁ khaṇḍaṁ yayur ghanāḥ
śvāsānilāstāḥ śataśo nipetur nabhaso 'calāḥ

इति क्रोधसमाध्मातमापतन्तं महासुरम् ।
दृष्ट्वा सा चण्डिका कोपं तद्वधाय तदाकरोत् ॥ २८ ॥

iti krodhasamādhmātam āpatantaṁ mahāsuram
dṛṣṭvā sā caṇḍikā kopaṁ tad vadhāya tadākarot

सा क्षिप्त्वा तस्य वै पाशं तं बबन्ध महासुरम् ।
तत्याज माहिषं रूपं सोऽपि बद्धो महामृधे ॥ २९ ॥

sā kṣiptvā tasya vai pāśaṁ taṁ babandha mahāsuraṁ
tatyāja māhiṣaṁ rūpaṁ so 'pi baddho mahāmṛdhe

ततः सिंहोऽभवत्सद्यो यावत्तस्याम्बिका शिरः ।
छिनत्ति तावत् पुरुषः खड्गपाणिरदृश्यत ॥ ३० ॥

tataḥ siṁho 'bhavat sadyo yāvat tasyāmbikā śiraḥ
chinatti tāvat puruṣaḥ khaḍgapāṇir adṛśyata

तत एवाशु पुरुषं देवी चिच्छेद सायकैः ।
तं खड्गचर्मणा सार्धं ततः सोऽभून्महागजः ॥ ३१ ॥

tata evāśu puruṣaṁ devī ciccheda sāyakaiḥ
taṁ khaḍgacarmaṇā sārdhaṁ tataḥ so 'bhūn mahāgajaḥ

करेण च महासिंहं तं चकर्ष जगर्ज च ।
कर्षतस्तु करं देवी खड्गेन निरकृन्तत ॥ ३२ ॥

kareṇa ca mahāsiṁhaṁ taṁ cakarṣa jagarja ca
karṣatas tu karaṁ devī khaḍgena nirakṛntata

ततो महासुरो भूयो माहिषं वपुरास्थितः ।
तथैव क्षोभयामास त्रैलोक्यं सचराचरम् ॥ ३३ ॥

tato mahāsuro bhūyo māhiṣaṁ vapurāsthitaḥ
tathaiva kṣobhayāmāsa trailokyaṁ sacarācaram

ततः क्रुद्धा जगन्माता चण्डिका पानमुत्तमम् ।
पपौ पुनः पुनश्चैव जहासारुणलोचना ॥ ३४ ॥

tataḥ kruddhā jaganmātā caṇḍikā pānam uttamam
papau punaḥ punaś caiva jahāsāruṇalocanā

नननर्द चासुरः सोऽपि बलवीर्यमदोद्धतः ।
विषाणाभ्यां च चिक्षेप चण्डिकां प्रति भूधरान् ॥ ३५ ॥

nanarda cāsuraḥ so 'pi balavīryamadoddhataḥ
viṣāṇābhyāṁ ca cikṣepa caṇḍikāṁ prati bhūdharān

सा च तान्प्रहितांस्तेन चूर्णयन्ती शरोत्करैः ।
उवाच तं मदोद्धूतमुखरागाकुलाक्षरम् ॥ ३६ ॥

sā ca tān prahitāṁs tena cūrṇayantī śarotkaraiḥ
uvāca taṁ madoddhūtamukharāgākulākṣaram

देव्युवाच ॥ ३७ ॥

devy uvāca

गर्ज गर्ज क्षणं मूढ मधु यावत्पिबाम्यहम् ।
मया त्वयि हतेऽत्रैव गर्जिष्यन्त्याशु देवताः ॥ ३८ ॥

garja garja kṣaṇaṁ mūḍha madhu yāvat pibāmy aham
mayā tvayi hate 'traiva garjiṣyanty āśu devatāḥ

ऋषिरुवाच ॥ ३९ ॥

ṛṣir uvāca

एवमुक्त्वा समुत्पत्य सारूढा तं महासुरम् ।
पादेनाक्रम्य कण्ठे च शूलेनैनमताडयत् ॥ ४० ॥

evam uktvā samutpatya sārūḍhā taṁ mahāsuram
pādenākramya kaṇṭhe ca śulenainam atāḍayat

ततः सोऽपि पदाक्रान्तस्तया निजमुखात्ततः ।
अर्धनिष्क्रान्त एवासीद्देव्या वीर्येण संवृतः ॥ ४१ ॥

tataḥ so 'pi padākrāntas tayā nijamukhāt tataḥ
ardhaniṣkrānta evāsīd devyā vīryeṇa saṁvṛtaḥ

अर्धनिष्क्रान्त एवासौ युध्यमानो महासुरः ।
तया महासिना देव्या शिरश्छित्त्वा निपातितः ॥ ४२ ॥

ardhaniṣkrānta evāsau yudhyamāno mahāsuraḥ
tayā mahāsinā devyā śiraśchittvā nipātitaḥ

ततो हाहाकृतं सर्वं दैत्यसैन्यं ननाश तत् ।
प्रहर्षं च परं जग्मुः सकला देवतागणाः ॥ ४३ ॥

tato hāhākṛtaṁ sarvaṁ daityasainyaṁ nanāśa tat
praharṣaṁ ca paraṁ jagmuḥ sakalā devatāgaṇāḥ

तुष्टुवुस्तां सुरा देवीं सह दिव्यैर्महर्षिभिः ।
जगुर्गन्धर्वपतयो ननृतुश्चाप्सरोगणाः ॥ ४४ ॥

tuṣṭuvus tāṁ surā devīṁ saha divyair maharṣibhiḥ
jagur gandharvapatayo nanṛtuś cāpsarogaṇāḥ

# चतुर्थोऽध्यायः

## शक्रादिस्तुतिः

ऋषिरुवाच ॥ १ ॥

ṛṣir uvāca

शक्रादयः सुरगणा निहतेऽतिवीर्ये
तस्मिन्दुरात्मनि सुरारिबले च देव्या ।
तां तुष्टुवुः प्रणतिनम्रशिरोधरांसा
वाग्भिः प्रहर्षपुलकोद्गमचारुदेहाः ॥ २ ॥

śakrādayaḥ suragaṇā nihate 'tivīrye
tasmin durātmani surāribale ca devyā
tāṁ tuṣṭuvuḥ praṇatinamraśirodharāṁsā
vāgbhiḥ praharṣapulakodgamacārudehāḥ

देव्या यया ततमिदं जगदात्मशक्त्या
निःशेषदेवगणशक्तिसमूहमूर्त्या ।
तामम्बिकामखिलदेवमहर्षिपूज्यां
भक्त्या नताः स्म विदधातु शुभानि सा नः ॥ ३ ॥

devyā yayā tatam idaṁ jagad ātmaśaktyā
niḥśeṣadevagaṇaśaktisamūhamūrtyā
tāṁ ambikām akhiladevamaharṣipūjyāṁ
bhaktyā natāḥ sma vidadhātu śubhāni sā naḥ

यस्याः प्रभावमतुलं भगवाननन्तो
ब्रह्मा हरश्च न हि वक्तुमलं बलं च ।
सा चण्डिकाखिलजगत्परिपालनाय
नाशाय चाशुभभयस्य मतिं करोतु ॥ ४ ॥

yasyāḥ prabhāvam atulaṁ bhagavān ananto
brahmā haraś ca na hi vaktum alaṁ balaṁ ca
sā caṇḍikākhilajagat paripālanāya
nāśāya cāśubhabhayasya matiṁ karotu

या श्रीः स्वयं सुकृतिनां भवनेष्वलक्ष्मीः
पापात्मनां कृतधियां हृदयेषु बुद्धिः ।
श्रद्धा सतां कुलजनप्रभवस्य लज्जा
तां त्वां नताः स्म परिपालय देवि विश्वम् ॥ ५ ॥

yā śrīḥ svayaṁ sukṛtināṁ bhavaneṣvalakṣmīḥ
pāpātmanāṁ kṛtadhiyāṁ hṛdayeṣu buddhiḥ
śraddhā satāṁ kulajanaprabhavasya lajjā
tāṁ tvāṁ natāḥ sma paripālaya devi viśvam

किं वर्णयाम तव रूपमचिन्त्यमेतत्
किञ्चातिवीर्यमसुरक्षयकारि भूरि ।
किं चाहवेषु चरितानि तवाति यानि
सर्वेषु देव्यसुरदेवगणादिकेषु ॥ ६ ॥

kiṁ varṇayāma tava rūpam acintyam etat
kiñ cātivīryam asurakṣayakāri bhūri
kiṁ cāhaveṣu caritāni tavāti yāni
sarveṣu devy asuradevagaṇādikeṣu

हेतुः समस्तजगतां त्रिगुणापि दोषै-
र्न ज्ञायसे हरिहरादिभिरप्यपारा ।
सर्वाश्रयाखिलमिदं जगदंशभूत-
मव्याकृता हि परमा प्रकृतिस्त्वमाद्या ॥ ७ ॥

hetuḥ samastajagatāṁ triguṇāpi doṣair
na jñāyase hariharādibhir apyapārā
sarvāśrayākhilam idaṁ jagad aṁśabhūtam
avyākṛtā hi paramā prakṛtis tvam ādyā

यस्याः समस्तसुरता समुदीरणेन
तृप्तिं प्रयाति सकलेषु मखेषु देवि ।

स्वाहासि वै पितृगणस्य च तृप्तिहेतु-
रुच्चार्यसे त्वमत एव जनैः स्वधा च ॥ ८ ॥

yasyāḥ samastasuratā samudīraṇena
tṛptiṁ prayāti sakaleṣu makheṣu devi
svāhāsi vai pitṛgaṇasya ca tṛptihetur
uccāryase tvam ata eva janaiḥ svadhā ca

या मुक्तिहेतुरविचिन्त्यमहाव्रता त्वं
अभ्यस्यसे सुनियतेन्द्रियतत्त्वसारैः ।
मोक्षार्थिभिर्मुनिभिरस्तसमस्तदोषै-
र्विद्यासि सा भगवती परमा हि देवि ॥ ९ ॥

yā muktihetur avicintyamahāvratā tvaṁ
abhyasyase suniyatendriyatattvasāraiḥ
mokṣārthibhir munibhir astasamastadoṣair
vidyāsi sā bhagavatī paramā hi devi

शब्दात्मिका सुविमलर्ग्यजुषां निधान-
मुद्गीथरम्यपदपाठवतां च साम्नाम् ।
देवी त्रयी भगवती भवभावनाय
वार्ता च सर्वजगतां परमार्तिहन्त्री ॥ १० ॥

śabdātmikā suvimalargyajuṣāṁ nidhānam
udgītharamyapadapāṭhavatāṁ ca sāmnām
devī trayī bhagavatī bhavabhāvanāya
vārtā ca sarvajagatāṁ paramārtihantrī

मेधासि देवि विदिताखिलशास्त्रसारा
दुर्गासि दुर्गभवसागरनौरसङ्गा ।
श्रीः कैटभारिहृदयैककृताधिवासा
गौरी त्वमेव शशिमौलिकृतप्रतिष्ठा ॥ ११ ॥

medhāsi devi viditākhilaśāstrasārā
durgāsi durgabhavasāgaranaur asaṅgā
śrīḥ kaiṭabhārihṛdayaikakṛtādhivāsā
gaurī tvaṁ eva śaśimaulikṛtapratiṣṭhā

ईषत्सहासममलं परिपूर्णचन्द्र-
बिम्बानुकारि कनकोत्तमकान्तिकान्तम् ।
अत्यद्भुतं प्रहृतमात्तरुषा तथापि
वक्त्रं विलोक्य सहसा महिषासुरेण ॥ १२ ॥

īṣatsahāsam amalaṁ paripūrṇacandra-
bimbānukāri kanakottamakāntikāntam
atyadbhutaṁ prahṛtam āttaruṣā tathāpi
vaktraṁ vilokya sahasā mahiṣāsureṇa

दृष्ट्वा तु देवि कुपितं भ्रुकुटीकराल-
मुद्यच्छशाङ्कसदृशच्छवि यन्न सद्यः ।
प्राणान् मुमोच महिषस्तदतीव चित्रं
कैर्जीव्यते हि कुपितान्तकदर्शनेन ॥ १३ ॥

dṛṣṭvā tu devi kupitaṁ bhrukuṭīkarālam
udyacchaśāṅkasadṛśacchavi yan na sadyaḥ
prāṇān mumoca mahiṣas tad atīva citraṁ
kair jīvyate hi kupitāntakadarśanena

देवि प्रसीद परमा भवती भवाय
सद्यो विनाशयसि कोपवती कुलानि ।
विज्ञातमेतदधुनैव यदस्तमेतन्
नीतं बलं सुविपुलं महिषासुरस्य ॥ १४ ॥

devi prasīda paramā bhavatī bhavāya
sadyo vināśayasi kopavatī kulāni
vijñātam etad adhunaiva yad astam etan
nītaṁ balaṁ suvipulaṁ mahiṣāsurasya

ते सम्मता जनपदेषु धनानि तेषां
तेषां यशांसि न च सीदति धर्मवर्गः ।
धन्यास्त एव निभृतात्मजभृत्यदारा
येषां सदाभ्युदयदा भवती प्रसन्ना ॥ १५ ॥

te sammatā janapadeṣu dhanāni teṣāṁ
teṣāṁ yaśāṁsi na ca sīdati dharmavargaḥ

dhanyāsta eva nibhṛtātmajabhṛtyadārā
    yeṣāṁ sadābhyudayadā bhavatī prasannā

धर्म्याणि देवि सकलानि सदैव कर्मा-
    ण्यत्याद्दतः प्रतिदिनं सुकृती करोति ।
स्वर्गं प्रयाति च ततो भवती प्रसादा-
    ल्लोकत्रयेऽपि फलदा ननु देवि तेन ॥ १६ ॥

dharmyāṇi devi sakalāni sadaiva karmāṇy
    atyādṛtaḥ pratidinaṁ sukṛtī karoti
svargaṁ prayāti ca tato bhavatī prasādāl-
    lokatraye 'pi phaladā nanu devi tena

दुर्गे स्मृता हरसि भीतिमशेषजन्तोः
    स्वस्थैः स्मृता मतिमतीव शुभां ददासि ।
दारिद्र्यदुःखभयहारिणि का त्वदन्या
    सर्वोपकारकरणाय सदार्द्रचित्ता ॥ १७ ॥

durge smṛtā harasi bhītim aśeṣajantoḥ
    svasthaiḥ smṛtā matim atīva śubhāṁ dadāsi
dāridryaduḥkhabhayahāriṇi kā tvad anyā
    sarvopakārakaraṇāya sadārdracittā

एभिर्हतैर्जगदुपैति सुखं तथैते
    कुर्वन्तु नाम नरकाय चिराय पापम् ।
संग्राममृत्युमधिगम्य दिवं प्रयान्तु
    मत्वेति नूनमहितान्विनिहंसि देवि ॥ १८ ॥

ebhir hatair jagad upaiti sukhaṁ tathaite
    kurvantu nāma narakāya cirāya pāpam
saṁgrāma mṛtyum adhigamya divaṁ prayāntu
    matveti nūnam ahitān vinihaṁsi devi

दृष्ट्वैव किं न भवती प्रकरोति भस्म
    सर्वासुरानरिषु यत्प्रहिणोषि शस्त्रम् ।
लोकान्प्रयान्तु रिपवोऽपि हि शस्त्रपूता
    इत्थं मतिर्भवति तेष्वपि तेऽतिसाध्वी ॥ १९ ॥

dṛṣṭvaiva kiṁ na bhavatī prakaroti bhasma
sarvāsurān ariṣu yat prahiṇoṣi śastram
lokān prayāntu ripavo 'pi hi śastrapūtā
itthaṁ matir bhavati teṣv api te 'tisādhvī

खड्गप्रभानिकरविस्फुरणैस्तथोग्रैः
शूलाग्रकान्तिनिवहेन दृशोऽसुराणाम् ।
यन्नागता विलयमंशुमदिन्दुखण्ड-
योग्याननं तव विलोकयतां तदेतत् ॥ २० ॥

khaḍgaprabhānikaravisphuraṇais tathograiḥ
śūlāgrakāntinivahena dṛśo 'surāṇām
yan nāgatā vilayam aṁśumad indukhaṇḍa-
yogyānanaṁ tava vilokayatāṁ tad etat

दुर्वृत्तवृत्तशमनं तव देवि शीलं
रूपं तथैतदविचिन्त्यमतुल्यमन्यैः ।
वीर्यं च हन्तृ हृतदेवपराक्रमाणां
वैरिष्वपि प्रकटितैव दया त्वयेत्थम् ॥ २१ ॥

durvṛttavṛttaśamanaṁ tava devi śīlaṁ
rūpaṁ tathaitad avicintyam atulyam anyaiḥ
vīryaṁ ca hantṛ hṛtadevaparākramāṇāṁ
vairiṣv api prakaṭitaiva dayā tvayettham

केनोपमा भवतु तेऽस्य पराक्रमस्य
रूपं च शत्रुभयकार्यतिहारि कुत्र ।
चित्ते कृपा समरनिष्ठुरता च दृष्टा
त्वय्येव देवि वरदे भुवनत्रयेऽपि ॥ २२ ॥

kenopamā bhavatu te 'sya parākramasya
rūpaṁ ca śatrubhayakāry atihāri kutra
citte kṛpā samaraniṣṭhuratā ca dṛṣṭā
tvayy eva devi varade bhuvanatraye 'pi

त्रैलोक्यमेतदखिलं रिपुनाशनेन
त्रातं त्वया समरमूर्धनि तेऽपि हत्वा ।

नीता दिवं रिपुगणा भयमप्यपास्त-
मस्माकमुन्मदसुरारिभवं नमस्ते ॥ २३ ॥

trailokyam etad akhilaṁ ripunāśanena
trātaṁ tvayā samaramūrdhani te 'pi hatvā
nītā divaṁ ripugaṇā bhayam apy apāstam
asmākam unmada surāribhavaṁ namaste

शूलेन पाहि नो देवि पाहि खड्गेन चाम्बिके ।
घण्टास्वनेन नः पाहि चापज्यानिस्स्वनेन च ॥ २४ ॥

śūlena pāhi no devi pāhi khaḍgena cāmbike
ghaṇṭāsvanena naḥ pāhi cāpajyānissvanena ca

प्राच्यां रक्ष प्रतीच्यां च चण्डिके रक्ष दक्षिणे ।
भ्रामणेनात्मशूलस्य उत्तरस्यां तथेश्वरि ॥ २५ ॥

prācyāṁ rakṣa pratīcyāṁ ca caṇḍike rakṣa dakṣine
bhrāmaṇenātmaśūlasya uttarasyāṁ tatheśvari

सौम्यानि यानि रूपाणि त्रैलोक्ये विचरन्ति ते ।
यानि चात्यन्तघोराणि तै रक्षास्मांस्तथा भुवम् ॥ २६ ॥

saumyāni yāni rūpāṇi trailokye vicaranti te
yāni cātyantaghorāṇi tai rakṣāsmāṁs tathā bhuvam

खड्गशूलगदादीनि यानि चास्त्राणि तेऽम्बिके ।
करपल्लवसङ्गीनि तैरस्मान्रक्ष सर्वतः ॥ २७ ॥

khaḍgaśūlagadādīni yāni cāstrāṇi te 'mbike
karapallavasaṅgīni tair asmān rakṣa sarvataḥ

ऋषिरुवाच ॥ २८ ॥

ṛṣir uvāca

एवं स्तुता सुरैर्दिव्यैः कुसुमैर्नन्दनोद्भवैः ।
अर्चिता जगतां धात्री तथा गन्धानुलेपनैः ॥ २९ ॥

evaṁ stutā surair divyaiḥ kusumair nandanodbhavaiḥ
arcitā jagatāṁ dhātrī tathā gandhānulepanaiḥ

भक्त्या समस्तैस्त्रिदशैर्दिव्यैर्धूपैः सुधूपिता ।
प्राह प्रसादसुमुखी समस्तान् प्रणतान् सुरान् ॥ ३० ॥

bhaktyā samastais tridaśair divyair dhūpaiḥ sudhūpitā
prāha prasādasumukhī samastān praṇatān surān

देव्युवाच ॥ ३१ ॥

devy uvāca

व्रियतां त्रिदशाः सर्वे यदस्मत्तोऽभिवाञ्छितम् ।
ददाम्यहमतिप्रीत्या स्तवैरेभिः सुपूजिता ॥ ३२ ॥

vriyatāṁ tridaśāḥ sarve yad asmatto 'bhivāñchitam
dadāmy aham atiprītyā stavair ebhiḥ supūjitā

देवा ऊचुः ॥ ३३ ॥

devā ūcuḥ

भगवत्या कृतं सर्वं न किञ्चिदवशिष्यते ।
यदयं निहतः शत्रुरस्माकं महिषासुरः ॥ ३४ ॥

bhagavatyā kṛtaṁ sarvaṁ na kiñcid avaśiṣyate
yad ayaṁ nihataḥ śatrur asmākaṁ mahiṣāsuraḥ

यदि चापि वरो देयस्त्वयाऽस्माकं महेश्वरि ।
संस्मृता संस्मृता त्वं नो हिंसेथाः परमापदः ॥ ३५ ॥

yadi cāpi varo deyas tvayā 'smākaṁ maheśvari
saṁsmṛtā saṁsmṛtā tvaṁ no hiṁsethāḥ paramāpadaḥ

यश्च मर्त्यः स्तवैरेभिस्त्वां स्तोष्यत्यमलानने ।
तस्य वित्तर्द्धिविभवैर्धनदारादिसम्पदाम् ॥ ३६ ॥

yaś ca martyaḥ stavair ebhis tvāṁ stoṣyaty amalānane
tasya vittarddhivibhavair dhanadārādisampadām

वृद्धयेऽस्मत्प्रसन्ना त्वं भवेथाः सर्वदाम्बिके ॥ ३७ ॥

vṛddhaye 'smat prasannā tvaṁ bhavethāḥ sarvadāmbike

ऋषिरुवाच ॥ ३८ ॥

ṛṣir uvāca

इति प्रसादिता देवैर्जगतोऽर्थे तथात्मनः ।
तथेत्युक्त्वा भद्रकाली बभूवान्तर्हिता नृप ॥ ३९ ॥

iti prasāditā devair jagato 'rthe tathātmanaḥ
tathety uktvā bhadrakālī babhuvāntarhitā nṛpa

इत्येतत्कथितं भूप सम्भूता सा यथा पुरा ।
देवी देवशरीरेभ्यो जगत्त्रयहितैषिणी ॥ ४० ॥

ity etat kathitaṁ bhūpa sambhūtā sā yathā purā
devī devaśarīrebhyo jagattrayahitaiṣinī

पुनश्च गौरीदेहात्सा समुद्भूता यथाभवत् ।
वधाय दुष्टदैत्यानां तथा शुम्भनिशुम्भयोः ॥ ४१ ॥

punaś ca gaurīdehāt sā samudbhūtā yathābhavat
vadhāya duṣṭadaityānāṁ tathā śumbhaniśumbhayoḥ

रक्षणाय च लोकानां देवानामुपकारिणी ।
तच्छृणुष्व मयाख्यातं यथावत्कथयामि ते ॥ ४२ ॥

rakṣaṇāya ca lokānāṁ devānām upakāriṇī
tac chṛṇuṣva mayākhyātaṁ yathāvat kathayāmi te

# उत्तमचरितम्

## महासरस्वतीध्यानम्

ॐ घण्टाशूलहलानि शङ्खमुसले चक्रं धनुः सायकं
हस्ताब्जैर्दधतीं घनान्तविलसच्छीतांशुतुल्यप्रभाम् ।
गौरीदेहसमुद्भवां त्रिजगतामाधारभूतां महा-
पूर्वामत्र सरस्वतीमनुभजे शुम्भादिदैत्यार्दिनीम् ॥

Oṁ. ghaṇṭāśūlahalāni śaṅkhamusale cakraṁ dhanuḥ sāyakaṁ
hastābjair dadhatīṁ ghanāntavilasacchītāṁśutulyaprabhām
gaurīdehasamudbhavāṁ trijagatāmādhārabhūtāṁ mahā-
pūrvām atra sarasvatīm anubhaje śumbhādidaityārdinīm

# पञ्चमोऽध्यायः

## देव्या दूतसंवादः

ॐ क्लीं ऋषिरुवाच ॥ १ ॥

Oṁ klīṁ ṛṣir uvāca

पुरा शुम्भनिशुम्भाभ्यामसुराभ्यां शचीपतेः ।
त्रैलोक्यं यज्ञभागाश्च हृता मदबलाश्रयात् ॥ २ ॥

purā śumbhaniśumbhābhyām asurābhyāṁ śacīpateḥ
trailokyaṁ yajñabhāgāś ca hṛtā madabalāśrayāt

तावेव सूर्यतां तद्वदधिकारं तथैन्दवम् ।
कौबेरमथ याम्यं च चक्राते वरुणस्य च ॥ ३ ॥

tāv eva sūryatāṁ tadvad adhikāraṁ tathaindavam
kauberam atha yāmyaṁ ca cakrāte varuṇasya ca

तावेव पवनर्द्धिं च चक्रतुर्वह्निकर्म च ।
ततो देवा विनिर्धूता भ्रष्टराज्याः पराजिताः ॥ ४ ॥

tāv eva pavanarddhiṁ ca cakratur vahnikarma ca
tato devā vinirdhūtā bhraṣṭarājyāḥ parājitāḥ

हृताधिकारास्त्रिदशास्ताभ्यां सर्वे निराकृताः ।
महासुराभ्यां तां देवीं संस्मरन्त्यपराजिताम् ॥ ५ ॥

hṛtādhikārās tridaśās tābhyāṁ sarve nirākṛtāḥ
mahāsurābhyāṁ tāṁ devīṁ saṁsmaranty aparājitāṁ

तयास्माकं वरो दत्तो यथापत्सु स्मृताखिलाः ।
भवतां नाशयिष्यामि तत्क्षणात्परमापदः ॥ ६ ॥

tayāsmākaṁ varo datto yathāpatsu smṛtākhilāḥ
bhavatāṁ nāśayiṣyāmi tatkṣaṇāt paramāpadaḥ

इति कृत्वा मतिं देवा हिमवन्तं नगेश्वरम् ।
जग्मुस्तत्र ततो देवीं विष्णुमायां प्रतुष्टुवुः ॥ ७ ॥

iti kṛtvā matiṁ devā himavantaṁ nageśvaram
jagmus tatra tato devīṁ viṣṇumāyāṁ pratuṣṭuvuḥ

देवा ऊचुः ॥ ८ ॥

devā ūcuḥ

नमो देव्यै महादेव्यै शिवायै सततं नमः ।
नमः प्रकृत्यै भद्रायै नियताः प्रणताः स्म ताम् ॥ ९ ॥

namo devyai mahādevyai śivāyai satataṁ namaḥ
namaḥ prakṛtyai bhadrāyai niyatāḥ praṇatāḥ sma tām

रौद्रायै नमो नित्यायै गौर्यै धात्र्यै नमो नमः ।
ज्योत्स्नायै चेन्दुरूपिण्यै सुखायै सततं नमः ॥ १० ॥

raudrāyai namo nityāyai gauryai dhātryai namo namaḥ
jyotsnāyai cendurūpiṇyai sukhāyai satataṁ namaḥ

कल्याण्यै प्रणता वृद्ध्यै सिद्ध्यै कुर्मो नमो नमः ।
नैर्ऋत्यै भूभृतां लक्ष्म्यै शर्वाण्यै ते नमो नमः ॥ ११ ॥

kalyāṇyai praṇatā vṛddhyai siddhyai kurmo namo namaḥ
nairṛtyai bhūbhṛtāṁ lakṣmyai śarvāṇyai te namo namaḥ

दुर्गायै दुर्गपारायै सारायै सर्वकारिण्यै ।
ख्यात्यै तथैव कृष्णायै धूम्रायै सततं नमः ॥ १२ ॥

durgāyai durgapārāyai sārāyai sarvakāriṇyai
khyātyai tathaiva kṛṣṇāyai dhūmrāyai satataṁ namaḥ

अतिसौम्यातिरौद्रायै नतास्तस्यै नमो नमः ।
नमो जगत्प्रतिष्ठायै देव्यै कृत्यै नमो नमः ॥ १३ ॥

atisaumyātiraudrāyai natās tasyai namo namaḥ
namo jagatpratiṣṭhāyai devyai kṛtyai namo namaḥ

या देवी सर्वभूतेषु विष्णुमायेति शब्दिता ।
नमस्तस्यै नमस्तस्यै नमस्तस्यै नमो नमः ॥ १४–१६ ॥

yā devī sarvabhūteṣu viṣṇumāyeti śabditā
namas tasyai namas tasyai namas tasyai namo namaḥ

या देवी सर्वभूतेषु चेतनेत्यभिधीयते ।
नमस्तस्यै नमस्तस्यै नमस्तस्यै नमो नमः ॥ १७–१९ ॥

yā devī sarvabhūteṣu cetanety abhidhīyate
namas tasyai namas tasyai namas tasyai namo namaḥ

या देवी सर्वभूतेषु बुद्धिरूपेण संस्थिता ।
नमस्तस्यै नमस्तस्यै नमस्तस्यै नमो नमः ॥ २०–२२ ॥

yā devī sarvabhūteṣu buddhirūpeṇa saṁsthitā
namas tasyai namas tasyai namas tasyai namo namaḥ

या देवी सर्वभूतेषु निद्रारूपेण संस्थिता ।
नमस्तस्यै नमस्तस्यै नमस्तस्यै नमो नमः ॥ २३–२५ ॥

yā devī sarvabhūteṣu nidrārūpeṇa saṁsthitā
namas tasyai namas tasyai namas tasyai namo namaḥ

या देवी सर्वभूतेषु क्षुधारूपेण संस्थिता ।
नमस्तस्यै नमस्तस्यै नमस्तस्यै नमो नमः ॥ २६–२८ ॥

yā devī sarvabhūteṣu kṣudhārūpeṇa saṁsthitā
namas tasyai namas tasyai namas tasyai namo namaḥ

या देवी सर्वभूतेषु च्छायारूपेण संस्थिता ।
नमस्तस्यै नमस्तस्यै नमस्तस्यै नमो नमः ॥ २९–३१ ॥

yā devī sarvabhūteṣu chāyārūpeṇa saṁsthitā
namas tasyai namas tasyai namas tasyai namo namaḥ

या देवी सर्वभूतेषु शक्तिरूपेण संस्थिता ।
नमस्तस्यै नमस्तस्यै नमस्तस्यै नमो नमः ॥ ३२–३४ ॥

yā devī sarvabhūteṣu śaktirūpeṇa saṁsthitā
namas tasyai namas tasyai namas tasyai namo namaḥ

या देवी सर्वभूतेषु तृष्णारूपेण संस्थिता ।
नमस्तस्यै नमस्तस्यै नमस्तस्यै नमो नमः ॥ ३५-३७ ॥

yā devī sarvabhūteṣu tṛṣṇārūpeṇa saṁsthitā
namas tasyai namas tasyai namas tasyai namo namaḥ

या देवी सर्वभूतेषु क्षान्तिरूपेण संस्थिता ।
नमस्तस्यै नमस्तस्यै नमस्तस्यै नमो नमः ॥ ३८-४० ॥

yā devī sarvabhūteṣu kṣāntirūpeṇa saṁsthitā
namas tasyai namas tasyai namas tasyai namo namaḥ

या देवी सर्वभूतेषु जातिरूपेण संस्थिता ।
नमस्तस्यै नमस्तस्यै नमस्तस्यै नमो नमः ॥ ४१-४३ ॥

yā devī sarvabhūteṣu jātirūpeṇa saṁsthitā
namas tasyai namas tasyai namas tasyai namo namaḥ

या देवी सर्वभूतेषु लज्जारूपेण संस्थिता ।
नमस्तस्यै नमस्तस्यै नमस्तस्यै नमो नमः ॥ ४४-४६ ॥

yā devī sarvabhūteṣu lajjārūpeṇa saṁsthitā
namas tasyai namas tasyai namas tasyai namo namaḥ

या देवी सर्वभूतेषु शान्तिरूपेण संस्थिता ।
नमस्तस्यै नमस्तस्यै नमस्तस्यै नमो नमः ॥ ४७-४९ ॥

yā devī sarvabhūteṣu śāntirūpeṇa saṁsthitā
namas tasyai namas tasyai namas tasyai namo namaḥ

या देवी सर्वभूतेषु श्रद्धारूपेण संस्थिता ।
नमस्तस्यै नमस्तस्यै नमस्तस्यै नमो नमः ॥ ५०-५२ ॥

yā devī sarvabhūteṣu śraddhārūpeṇa saṁsthitā
namas tasyai namas tasyai namas tasyai namo namaḥ

या देवी सर्वभूतेषु कान्तिरूपेण संस्थिता ।
नमस्तस्यै नमस्तस्यै नमस्तस्यै नमो नमः ॥ ५३-५५ ॥

yā devī sarvabhūteṣu kāntirūpeṇa saṁsthitā
namas tasyai namas tasyai namas tasyai namo namaḥ

या देवी सर्वभूतेषु लक्ष्मीरूपेण संस्थिता ।
नमस्तस्यै नमस्तस्यै नमस्तस्यै नमो नमः ॥ ५६-५८ ॥

yā devī sarvabhūteṣu lakṣmīrūpeṇa saṁsthitā
namas tasyai namas tasyai namas tasyai namo namaḥ

या देवी सर्वभूतेषु वृत्तिरूपेण संस्थिता ।
नमस्तस्यै नमस्तस्यै नमस्तस्यै नमो नमः ॥ ५९-६१ ॥

yā devī sarvabhūteṣu vṛttirūpeṇa saṁsthitā
namas tasyai namas tasyai namas tasyai namo namaḥ

या देवी सर्वभूतेषु स्मृतिरूपेण संस्थिता ।
नमस्तस्यै नमस्तस्यै नमस्तस्यै नमो नमः ॥ ६२-६४ ॥

yā devī sarvabhūteṣu smṛtirūpeṇa saṁsthitā
namas tasyai namas tasyai namas tasyai namo namaḥ

या देवी सर्वभूतेषु दयारूपेण संस्थिता ।
नमस्तस्यै नमस्तस्यै नमस्तस्यै नमो नमः ॥ ६५-६७ ॥

yā devī sarvabhūteṣu dayārūpeṇa saṁsthitā
namas tasyai namas tasyai namas tasyai namo namaḥ

या देवी सर्वभूतेषु तुष्टिरूपेण संस्थिता ।
नमस्तस्यै नमस्तस्यै नमस्तस्यै नमो नमः ॥ ६८-७० ॥

yā devī sarvabhūteṣu tuṣṭirūpeṇa saṁsthitā
namas tasyai namas tasyai namas tasyai namo namaḥ

या देवी सर्वभूतेषु मातृरूपेण संस्थिता ।
नमस्तस्यै नमस्तस्यै नमस्तस्यै नमो नमः ॥ ७१-७३ ॥

yā devī sarvabhūteṣu mātṛrūpeṇa saṁsthitā
namas tasyai namas tasyai namas tasyai namo namaḥ

या देवी सर्वभूतेषु भ्रान्तिरूपेण संस्थिता ।
नमस्तस्यै नमस्तस्यै नमस्तस्यै नमो नमः ॥ ७४-७६ ॥

yā devī sarvabhūteṣu bhrāntirūpeṇa saṁsthitā
namas tasyai namas tasyai namas tasyai namo namaḥ

इन्द्रियाणामधिष्ठात्री भूतानां चाखिलेषु या ।
भूतेषु सततं तस्यै व्याप्तिदेव्यै नमो नमः ॥ ७७ ॥

indriyāṇāṁ adhiṣṭhātrī bhūtānāṁ cākhileṣu yā
bhūteṣu satataṁ tasyai vyāptidevyai namo namaḥ

चितिरूपेण या कृत्स्नमेतद्व्याप्य स्थिता जगत् ।
नमस्तस्यै नमस्तस्यै नमस्तस्यै नमो नमः ॥ ७८–८० ॥

citirūpeṇa yā kṛtsnam etad vyāpya sthitā jagat
namas tasyai namas tasyai namas tasyai namo namaḥ

स्तुता सुरैः पूर्वमभीष्टसंश्रया–
त्तथा सुरेन्द्रेण दिनेषु सेविता ।
करोतु सा नः शुभहेतुरीश्वरी
शुभानि भद्राण्यभिहन्तु चापदः ॥ ८१ ॥

stutā suraiḥ pūrvam abhīṣṭasaṁśrayāt tathā surendreṇa dineṣu sevitā
karotu sā naḥ śubhahetur īśvarī śubhāni bhadrāṇy abhihantu cāpadaḥ

या साम्प्रतं चोद्धतदैत्यतापितै–
रस्माभिरीशा च सुरैर्नमस्यते ।
या च स्मृता तत्क्षणमेव हन्ति नः
सर्वापदो भक्तिविनम्रमूर्तिभिः ॥ ८२ ॥

yā sāmprataṁ coddhatadaityatāpitair asmābhir īśā ca surair namasyate
yā ca smṛtā tat kṣaṇam eva hanti naḥ sarvāpado bhaktivinamramūrtibhiḥ

ऋषिरुवाच ॥ ८३ ॥

ṛṣir uvāca

एवं स्तवादियुक्तानां देवानां तत्र पार्वती ।
स्नातुमभ्याययौ तोये जाह्नव्या नृपनन्दन ॥ ८४ ॥

evaṁ stavādiyuktānāṁ devānāṁ tatra pārvatī
snātum abhyāyayau toye jāhnavyā nṛpanandana

साब्रवीत्तान् सुरान् सुभ्रूर्भवद्भिः स्तूयतेऽत्र का ।
शरीरकोशतश्चास्याः समुद्भूताऽब्रवीच्छिवा ॥ ८५ ॥

sābravīt tān surān subhrūr bhavadbhiḥ stūyate 'tra kā
śarīrakośataś cāsyāḥ samudbhūtā 'bravīc chivā

स्तोत्रं ममैतत्क्रियते शुम्भदैत्यनिराकृतैः ।
देवैः समेतैः समरे निशुम्भेन पराजितैः ॥ ८६ ॥

stotraṁ mamaitat kriyate śumbhadaityanirākṛtaiḥ
devaiḥ sametaiḥ samare niśumbhena parājitaiḥ

शरीरकोशाद्यत्तस्याः पार्वत्या निःसृताम्बिका ।
कौशिकीति समस्तेषु ततो लोकेषु गीयते ॥ ८७ ॥

śarīrakośād yat tasyāḥ pārvatyā niḥsṛtāmbikā
kauśikīti samasteṣu tato lokeṣu gīyate

तस्यां विनिर्गतायां तु कृष्णाभूत्सापि पार्वती ।
कालिकेति समाख्याता हिमाचलकृताश्रया ॥ ८८ ॥

tasyāṁ vinirgatāyāṁ tu kṛṣṇābhūt sāpi pārvatī
kāliketi samākhyātā himācalakṛtāśrayā

ततोऽम्बिकां परं रूपं बिभ्राणां सुमनोहरम् ।
ददर्श चण्डो मुण्डश्च भृत्यौ शुम्भनिशुम्भयोः ॥ ८९ ॥

tato 'mbikāṁ paraṁ rūpaṁ bibhrāṇāṁ sumanoharam
dadarśa caṇḍo muṇḍaś ca bhṛtyau śumbhaniśumbhayoḥ

ताभ्यां शुम्भाय चाख्याता सातीव सुमनोहरा ।
काप्यास्ते स्त्री महाराज भासयन्ती हिमाचलम् ॥ ९० ॥

tābhyāṁ śumbhāya cākhyātā sātīva sumanoharā
kāpyāste strī mahārāja bhāsayantī himācalam

नैव तादृक् क्वचिद्रूपं दृष्टं केनचिदुत्तमम् ।
ज्ञायतां काप्यसौ देवी गृह्यतां चासुरेश्वर ॥ ९१ ॥

naiva tādṛk kvacid rūpaṁ dṛṣṭaṁ kenacid uttamam
jñāyatāṁ kāpy asau devī gṛhyatāṁ cāsureśvara

स्त्रीरत्नमतिचार्वङ्गी द्योतयन्ती दिशस्त्विषा ।
सा तु तिष्ठति दैत्येन्द्र तां भवान् द्रष्टुमर्हति ॥ ९२ ॥

strīratnam aticārvaṅgī dyotayantī diśas tviṣā
sā tu tiṣṭhati daityendra tāṁ bhavān draṣṭum arhati

यानि रत्नानि मणयो गजाश्वादीनि वै प्रभो ।
त्रैलोक्ये तु समस्तानि साम्प्रतं भान्ति ते गृहे ॥ ९३ ॥

yāni ratnāni maṇayo gajāśvādīni vai prabho
trailokye tu samastāni sāmpratam bhānti te gṛhe

ऐरावतः समानीतो गजरत्नं पुरन्दरात् ।
पारिजाततरुश्चायं तथैवोच्चैःश्रवा हयः ॥ ९४ ॥

airāvataḥ samānīto gajaratnaṁ purandarāt
pārijātataruś cāyaṁ tathaivoccaiḥśravā hayaḥ

विमानं हंससंयुक्तमेतत्तिष्ठति तेऽङ्गणे ।
रत्नभूतमिहानीतं यदासीद्वेधसोऽद्भुतम् ॥ ९५ ॥

vimānaṁ haṁsasaṁyuktam etat tiṣṭhati te 'ṅgaṇe
ratnabhūtam ihānītaṁ yadāsīd vedhaso 'dbhutam

निधिरेष महापद्मः समानीतो धनेश्वरात् ।
किञ्जल्किनीं ददौ चाब्धिर्मालामम्लानपङ्कजाम् ॥ ९६ ॥

nidhir eṣa mahāpadmaḥ samānīto dhaneśvarāt
kiñjalkinīṁ dadau cābdhir mālām amlānapaṅkajām

छत्रं ते वारुणं गेहे काञ्चनस्रावि तिष्ठति ।
तथाऽयं स्यन्दनवरो यः पुरासीत्प्रजापतेः ॥ ९७ ॥

chatraṁ te vāruṇaṁ gehe kāñcanasrāvi tiṣṭhati
tathā 'yaṁ syandanavaro yaḥ purāsīt prajāpateḥ

मृत्योरुत्क्रान्तिदा नाम शक्तिरीश त्वया हृता ।
पाशः सलिलराजस्य भ्रातुस्तव परिग्रहे ॥ ९८ ॥

mṛtyor utkrāntidā nāma śaktir īśa tvayā hṛtā
pāśaḥ salilarājasya bhrātus tava parigrahe

निशुम्भस्याब्धिजाताश्च समस्ता रत्नजातयः ।
वह्निश्चापि ददौ तुभ्यमग्निशौचे च वाससी ॥ ९९ ॥

niśumbhasyābdhijātāś ca samastā ratnajātayaḥ
vahniś cāpi dadau tubhyam agniśauce ca vāsasī

एवं दैत्येन्द्र रत्नानि समस्तान्याहृतानि ते ।
स्त्रीरत्नमेषा कल्याणी त्वया कस्मान्न गृह्यते ॥ १०० ॥

evaṁ daityendra ratnāni samastany āhṛtāni te
strīratnam eṣā kalyāṇī tvayā kasmān na gṛhyate

ऋषिरुवाच ॥ १०१ ॥

ṛṣir uvāca

निशम्येति वचः शुम्भः स तदा चण्डमुण्डयोः ।
प्रेषयामास सुग्रीवं दूतं देव्या महासुरम् ॥ १०२ ॥

niśamyeti vacaḥ śumbhaḥ sa tadā caṇḍamuṇḍayoḥ
preṣayāmāsa sugrīvaṁ dūtaṁ devyā mahāsuram

इति चेति च वक्तव्या सा गत्वा वचनान्मम ।
यथा चाभ्येति सम्प्रीत्या तथा कार्यं त्वया लघु ॥ १०३ ॥

iti ceti ca vaktavyā sā gatvā vacanān mama
yathā cābhyeti samprītyā tathā kāryaṁ tvayā laghu

स तत्र गत्वा यत्रास्ते शैलोद्देशेऽतिशोभने ।
सा देवी तां ततः प्राह श्लक्ष्णं मधुरया गिरा ॥ १०४ ॥

sa tatra gatvā yatrāste śailoddeśe 'tiśobhane
sā devī tāṁ tataḥ prāha ślakṣṇaṁ madhurayā girā

दूत उवाच ॥ १०५ ॥

dūta uvāca

देवि दैत्येश्वरः शुम्भस्त्रैलोक्ये परमेश्वरः ।
दूतोऽहं प्रेषितस्तेन त्वत्सकाशमिहागतः ॥ १०६ ॥

devi daityeśvaraḥ śumbhas trailokye parameśvaraḥ
duto 'haṁ preṣitas tena tvat sakāśam ihāgataḥ

अव्याहताज्ञः सर्वासु यः सदा देवयोनिषु ।
निर्जिताखिलदैत्यारिः स यदाह शृणुष्व तत् ॥ १०७ ॥

avyāhatājñaḥ sarvāsu yaḥ sadā devayoniṣu
nirjitākhiladaityāriḥ sa yadāha śṛṇuṣva tat

मम त्रैलोक्यमखिलं मम देवा वशानुगाः ।
यज्ञभागानहं सर्वानुपाश्नामि पृथक् पृथक् ॥ १०८ ॥

mama trailokyam akhilaṁ mama devā vaśānugāḥ
yajñabhāgān ahaṁ sarvān upāśnāmi pṛthak pṛthak

त्रैलोक्ये वररत्नानि मम वश्यान्यशेषतः ।
तथैव गजरत्नं च हृतं देवेन्द्रवाहनम् ॥ १०९ ॥

trailokye vararatnāni mama vaśyāny aśeṣataḥ
tathaiva gajaratnaṁ ca hṛtaṁ devendravāhanam

क्षीरोदमथनोद्भूतमश्वरत्नं ममामरैः ।
उच्चैःश्रवससंज्ञं तत्प्रणिपत्य समर्पितम् ॥ ११० ॥

kṣīrodamathanodbhūtam aśvaratnaṁ mamāmaraiḥ
uccaiḥśravasasaṁjñaṁ tat praṇipatya samarpitam

यानि चान्यानि देवेषु गन्धर्वेषूरगेषु च ।
रत्नभूतानि भूतानि तानि मय्येव शोभने ॥ १११ ॥

yāni cānyāni deveṣu gandharveṣūrageṣu ca
ratnabhūtāni bhūtāni tāni mayy eva śobhane

स्त्रीरत्नभूतां त्वां देवि लोके मन्यामहे वयम् ।
सा त्वमस्मानुपागच्छ यतो रत्नभुजो वयम् ॥ ११२ ॥

strīratnabhūtāṁ tvāṁ devi loke manyāmahe vayam
sā tvam asmān upāgaccha yato ratnabhujo vayam

मां वा ममानुजं वापि निशुम्भमुरुविक्रमम् ।
भज त्वं चञ्चलापाङ्गि रत्नभूतासि वै यतः ॥ ११३ ॥

māṁ vā mamānujaṁ vāpi niśumbham uruvikramam
bhaja tvaṁ cañcalāpāṅgi ratnabhūtāsi vai yataḥ

परमैश्वर्यमतुलं प्राप्स्यसे मत्परिग्रहात् ।
एतद्बुद्ध्या समालोच्य मत्परिग्रहतां व्रज ॥ ११४ ॥

paramaiśvaryam atulaṁ prāpsyase matparigrahāt
etad buddhyā samālocya matparigrahatāṁ vraja

ऋषिरुवाच ॥ ११५ ॥

ṛṣir uvāca

इत्युक्ता सा तदा देवी गम्भीरान्तःस्मिता जगौ ।
दुर्गा भगवती भद्रा ययेदं धार्यते जगत् ॥ ११६ ॥

ity uktā sā tadā devī gambhīrāntaḥsmitā jagau
durgā bhagavatī bhadrā yayedaṁ dhāryate jagat

देव्युवाच ॥ ११७ ॥

devy uvāca

सत्यमुक्तं त्वया नात्र मिथ्या किञ्चित्त्वयोदितम् ।
त्रैलोक्याधिपतिः शुम्भो निशुम्भश्चापि तादृशः ॥ ११८ ॥

satyam uktaṁ tvayā nātra mithyā kiñcit tvayoditam
trailokyādhipatiḥ śumbho niśumbhaś cāpi tādṛśaḥ

किं त्वत्र यत्परिज्ञातं मिथ्या तत्क्रियते कथम् ।
श्रूयतामल्पबुद्धित्वात्प्रतिज्ञा या कृता पुरा ॥ ११९ ॥

kiṁ tvatra yat parijñātaṁ mithyā tat kriyate katham
śrūyatām alpabuddhitvāt pratijñā yā kṛtā purā

यो मां जयति संग्रामे यो मे दर्पं व्यपोहति ।
यो मे प्रतिबलो लोके स मे भर्ता भविष्यति ॥ १२० ॥

yo māṁ jayati saṅgrāme yo me darpaṁ vyapohati
yo me pratibalo loke sa me bhartā bhaviṣyati

तदागच्छतु शुम्भोऽत्र निशुम्भो वा महासुरः ।
मां जित्वा किं चिरेणात्र पाणिं गृह्णातु मे लघु ॥ १२१ ॥

tadāgacchatu śumbho 'tra niśumbho vā mahāsuraḥ
māṁ jitvā kiṁ cireṇātra pāṇiṁ gṛhṇātu me laghu

दूत उवाच ॥ १२२ ॥

dūta uvāca

अवलिप्तासि मैवं त्वं देवि ब्रूहि ममाग्रतः ।
त्रैलोक्ये कः पुमांस्तिष्ठेदग्रे शुम्भनिशुम्भयोः ॥ १२३ ॥

avaliptāsi maivaṁ tvaṁ devi brūhi mamāgrataḥ
trailokye kaḥ pumāṁs tiṣṭhed agre śumbhaniśumbhayoḥ

अन्येषामपि दैत्यानां सर्वे देवा न वै युधि ।
तिष्ठन्ति सम्मुखे देवि किं पुनः स्त्री त्वमेकिका ॥ १२४ ॥

anyeṣām api daityānāṁ sarve devā na vai yudhi
tiṣṭhanti sammukhe devi kiṁ punaḥ strī tvam ekikā

इन्द्राद्याः सकला देवास्तस्थुर्येषां न संयुगे ।
शुम्भादीनां कथं तेषां स्त्री प्रयास्यसि सम्मुखम् ॥ १२५ ॥

indrādyāḥ sakalā devās tasthur yeṣāṁ na saṁyuge
śumbhādīnāṁ kathaṁ teṣāṁ strī prayāsyasi sammukham

सा त्वं गच्छ मयैवोक्ता पार्श्वं शुम्भनिशुम्भयोः ।
केशाकर्षणनिर्धूतगौरवा मा गमिष्यसि ॥ १२६ ॥

sā tvaṁ gaccha mayaivoktā pārśvaṁ śumbhaniśumbhayoḥ
keśākarṣaṇanirdhūtagauravā mā gamiṣyasi

देव्युवाच ॥ १२७ ॥

devy uvāca

एवमेतद् बली शुम्भो निशुम्भश्चातिवीर्यवान् ।
किं करोमि प्रतिज्ञा मे यदनालोचिता पुरा ॥ १२८ ॥

evam etad balī śumbho niśumbhaś cātivīryavān
kiṁ karomi pratijñā me yad anālocitā purā

स त्वं गच्छ मयोक्तं ते यदेतत्सर्वमादृतः ।
तदाचक्ष्वासुरेन्द्राय स च युक्तं करोतु यत् ॥ १२९ ॥

sa tvaṁ gaccha mayoktaṁ te yad etat sarvam ādṛtaḥ
tad ācakṣvāsurendrāya sa ca yuktaṁ karotu yat

# षष्ठोऽध्यायः

## धूम्रलोचनवधः

ऋषिरुवाच ॥ १ ॥

ṛṣir uvāca

इत्याकर्ण्य वचो देव्याः स दूतोऽमर्षपूरितः ।
समाचष्ट समागम्य दैत्यराजाय विस्तरात् ॥ २ ॥

ity ākarṇya vaco devyāḥ sa dūto 'marṣapūritaḥ
samācaṣṭa samāgamya daityarājāya vistarāt

तस्य दूतस्य तद्वाक्यमाकर्ण्यासुरराट् ततः ।
सक्रोधः प्राह दैत्यानामधिपं धूम्रलोचनम् ॥ ३ ॥

tasya dūtasya tad vākyam ākarṇyāsurarāṭ tataḥ
sakrodhaḥ prāha daityānām adhipaṁ dhūmralocanam

हे धूम्रलोचनाशु त्वं स्वसैन्यपरिवारितः ।
तामानय बलाद्दुष्टां केशाकर्षणविह्वलाम् ॥ ४ ॥

he dhūmralocanāśu tvaṁ svasainyaparivāritaḥ
tām ānaya balād duṣṭāṁ keśākarṣaṇavihvalām

तत्परित्राणदः कश्चिद्यदि वोत्तिष्ठतेऽपरः ।
स हन्तव्योऽमरो वापि यक्षो गन्धर्व एव वा ॥ ५ ॥

tat paritrāṇadaḥ kaścid yadi vottiṣṭhate 'paraḥ
sa hantavyo 'maro vāpi yakṣo gandharva eva vā

ऋषिरुवाच ॥ ६ ॥

ṛṣir uvāca

तेनाज्ञप्तस्ततः शीघ्रं स दैत्यो धूम्रलोचनः ।
वृतः षष्ट्या सहस्राणामसुराणां द्रुतं ययौ ॥ ७ ॥

teṇājñaptas tataḥ śīghraṁ sa daityo dhūmralocanaḥ
vṛtaḥ ṣaṣṭyā sahasrāṇām asurāṇāṁ drutaṁ yayau

स दृष्ट्वा तां ततो देवीं तुहिनाचलसंस्थिताम् ।
जगादोच्चैः प्रयाहीति मूलं शुम्भनिशुम्भयोः ॥ ८ ॥

sa dṛṣṭvā tāṁ tato devīṁ tuhinācalasaṁsthitām
jagādoccaiḥ prayāhīti mūlaṁ śumbhaniśumbhayoḥ

न चेत्प्रीत्याद्य भवती मद्भर्तारमुपैष्यति ।
ततो बलान्नयाम्येष केशाकर्षणविह्वलाम् ॥ ९ ॥

na cet prītyādya bhavatī madbhartāram upaiṣyati
tato balān nayāmy eṣa keśākarṣaṇavihvalām

देव्युवाच ॥ १० ॥

devy uvāca

दैत्येश्वरेण प्रहितो बलवान्बलसंवृतः ।
बलान्नयसि मामेवं ततः किं ते करोम्यहम् ॥ ११ ॥

daityeśvareṇa prahito balavān balasaṁvṛtaḥ
balān nayasi mām evaṁ tataḥ kiṁ te karomy aham

ऋषिरुवाच ॥ १२ ॥

ṛṣir uvāca

इत्युक्तः सोऽभ्यधावत्तामसुरो धूम्रलोचनः ।
हुङ्कारेणैव तं भस्म सा चकाराम्बिका ततः ॥ १३ ॥

ity uktaḥ so 'bhyadhāvat tām asuro dhūmralocanaḥ
huṅkāreṇaiva taṁ bhasma sā cakārāmbikā tataḥ

अथ क्रुद्धं महासैन्यमसुराणां तथाम्बिकाम् ।
ववर्ष सायकैस्तीक्ष्णैस्तथा शक्तिपरश्वधैः ॥ १४ ॥

atha kruddhaṁ mahāsainyam asurāṇāṁ tathāmbikām
vavarṣa sāyakais tīkṣṇais tathā śaktiparaśvadhaiḥ

ततो धुतसटः कोपात्कृत्वा नादं सुभैरवम् ।
पपातासुरसेनायां सिंहो देव्याः स्ववाहनः ॥ १५ ॥

tato dhutasaṭaḥ kopāt kṛtvā nādaṁ subhairavam
papātāsurasenāyāṁ siṁho devyāḥ svavāhanaḥ

कांश्चित्करप्रहारेण दैत्यानास्येन चापरान् ।
आक्रान्त्या चाधरेणान्यान् स जघान महासुरान् ॥ १६ ॥

kāṁścit karaprahāreṇa daityān āsyena cāparān
ākrāntyā cādhareṇānyān sa jaghāna mahāsurān

केषाञ्चित्पाटयामास नखैः कोष्ठानि केसरी ।
तथा तलप्रहारेण शिरांसि कृतवान्पृथक् ॥ १७ ॥

keṣāñcit pāṭayāmāsa nakhaiḥ koṣṭhāni kesarī
tathā talaprahāreṇa śirāṁsi kṛtavān pṛthak

विच्छिन्नबाहुशिरसः कृतास्तेन तथापरे ।
पपौ च रुधिरं कोष्ठादन्येषां धुतकेसरः ॥ १८ ॥

vicchinnabāhuśirasaḥ kṛtās tena tathāpare
papau ca rudhiraṁ koṣṭhād anyeṣāṁ dhutakesaraḥ

क्षणेन तद्बलं सर्वं क्षयं नीतं महात्मना ।
तेन केसरिणा देव्या वाहनेनातिकोपिना ॥ १९ ॥

kṣaṇena tad balaṁ sarvaṁ kṣayaṁ nītaṁ mahātmanā
tena kesariṇā devyā vāhanenātikopinā

श्रुत्वा तमसुरं देव्या निहतं धूम्रलोचनम् ।
बलं च क्षयितं कृत्स्नं देवीकेसरिणा ततः ॥ २० ॥

śrutvā tam asuraṁ devyā nihataṁ dhūmralocanam
balaṁ ca kṣayitaṁ kṛtsnaṁ devīkesariṇā tataḥ

चुकोप दैत्याधिपतिः शुम्भः प्रस्फुरिताधरः ।
आज्ञापयामास च तौ चण्डमुण्डौ महासुरौ ॥ २१ ॥

cukopa daityādhipatiḥ śumbhaḥ prasphuritādharaḥ
ājñāpayāmāsa ca tau caṇḍamuṇḍau mahāsurau

हे चण्ड हे मुण्ड बलैर्बहुलैः परिवारितौ ।
तत्र गच्छतं गत्वा च सा समानीयतां लघु ॥ २२ ॥

he caṇḍa he muṇḍa balair bahulaiḥ parivāritau
tatra gacchataṁ gatvā ca sā samānīyatāṁ laghu

केशेष्वाकृष्य बद्ध्वा वा यदि वः संशयो युधि ।
तदाशेषायुधैः सर्वैरसुरैर्विनिहन्यताम् ॥ २३ ॥

keśeṣvākṛṣya baddhvā vā yadi vaḥ saṁśayo yudhi
tadāśeṣāyudhaiḥ sarvair asurair vinihanyatām

तस्यां हतायां दुष्टायां सिंहे च विनिपातिते ।
शीघ्रमागम्यतां बद्ध्वा गृहीत्वा तामथाम्बिकाम् ॥ २४ ॥

tasyāṁ hatāyāṁ duṣṭāyāṁ siṁhe ca vinipātite
śīghram āgamyatāṁ baddhvā gṛhītvā tām athāmbikām

# सप्तमोऽध्यायः

## चण्डमुण्डवधः

ऋषिरुवाच ॥ १ ॥

ṛṣir uvāca

आज्ञप्तास्ते ततो दैत्याश्चण्डमुण्डपुरोगमाः ।
चतुरङ्गबलोपेता ययुरभ्युद्यतायुधाः ॥ २ ॥

ājñaptāste tato daityāś caṇḍamuṇḍapurogamāḥ
caturaṅgabalopetā yayur abhyudyatāyudhāḥ

ददृशुस्ते ततो देवीमीषद्धासां व्यवस्थिताम् ।
सिंहस्योपरि शैलेन्द्रशृङ्गे महति काञ्चने ॥ ३ ॥

dadṛśus te tato devīm īṣaddhāsāṁ vyavasthitām
siṁhasyopari śailendraśṛṅge mahati kāñcane

ते दृष्ट्वा तां समादातुमुद्यमञ्चक्रुरुद्यताः ।
आकृष्टचापासिधरास्तथान्ये तत्समीपगाः ॥ ४ ॥

te dṛṣṭvā tāṁ samādātum udyam añcakrur udyatāḥ
ākṛṣṭacāpāsidharās tathānye tat samīpagāḥ

ततः कोपं चकारोच्चैरम्बिका तानरीन्प्रति ।
कोपेन चास्या वदनं मषीवर्णमभूत्तदा ॥ ५ ॥

tataḥ kopaṁ cakāroccair ambikā tān arīn prati
kopena cāsyā vadanaṁ maṣīvarṇam abhūt tadā

भ्रुकुटीकुटिलात्तस्या ललाटफलकाद्द्रुतम् ।
काली करालवदना विनिष्क्रान्तासिपाशिनी ॥ ६ ॥

bhrukuṭīkuṭilāt tasyā lalāṭaphalakād drutam
kālī karālavadanā viniṣkrāntāsipāśinī

विचित्रखट्वाङ्गधरा नरमालाविभूषणा ।
द्वीपिचर्मपरीधाना शुष्कमांसातिभैरवा ॥ ७ ॥

vicitrakhaṭvāṅgadharā naramālāvibhūṣaṇā
dvīpicarmaparīdhānā śuṣkamāṁsātibhairavā

अतिविस्तारवदना जिह्वाललनभीषणा ।
निमग्नारक्तनयना नादापूरितदिङ्मुखा ॥ ८ ॥

ativistāravadanā jihvālalanabhīṣaṇā
nimagnāraktanayanā nādāpūritadiṅmukhā

सा वेगेनाभिपतिता घातयन्ती महासुरान् ।
सैन्ये तत्र सुरारीणामभक्षयत तद्बलम् ॥ ९ ॥

sā vegenābhipatitā ghātayantī mahāsurān
sainye tatra surārīṇām abhakṣayata tad balam

पार्ष्णिग्राहाङ्कुशग्राहियोधघण्टासमन्वितान् ।
समादायैकहस्तेन मुखे चिक्षेप वारणान् ॥ १० ॥

pārṣṇigrāhāṅkuśagrāhiyodhaghaṇṭāsamanvitān
samādāyaikahastena mukhe cikṣepa vāraṇān

तथैव योधं तुरगै रथं सारथिना सह ।
निक्षिप्य वक्त्रे दशनैश्चर्वयत्यतिभैरवम् ॥ ११ ॥

tathaiva yodhaṁ turagai rathaṁ sārathinā saha
nikṣipya vaktre daśanaiś carvayaty atibhairavam

एकं जग्राह केशेषु ग्रीवायामथ चापरम् ।
पादेनाक्रम्य चैवान्यमुरसान्यमपोथयत् ॥ १२ ॥

ekaṁ jagrāha keśeṣu grīvāyām atha cāparam
pādenākramya caivānyam urasānyam apothayat

तैर्मुक्तानि च शस्त्राणि महास्त्राणि तथासुरैः ।
मुखेन जग्राह रुषा दशनैर्मथितान्यपि ॥ १३ ॥

tair muktāni ca śastrāṇi mahāstrāṇi tathāsuraiḥ
mukhena jagrāha ruṣā daśanair mathitāny api

बलिनां तद्बलं सर्वमसुराणां दुरात्मनाम् ।
ममर्दाभक्षयच्चान्यानन्यांश्चाताडयत्तथा ॥ १४ ॥

balināṁ tad balaṁ sarvam asurāṇāṁ durātmanām
mamardābhakṣayac cānyān anyāṁś cātāḍayat tathā

असिना निहताः केचित्केचित्खट्वाङ्गताडिताः ।
जग्मुर्विनाशमसुरा दन्ताग्राभिहतास्तथा ॥ १५ ॥

asinā nihatāḥ kecit kecit khaṭvāṅgatāḍitāḥ
jagmur vināśam asurā dantāgrābhihatās tathā

क्षणेन तद्बलं सर्वमसुराणां निपातितम् ।
दृष्ट्वा चण्डोऽभिदुद्राव तां कालीमतिभीषणाम् ॥ १६ ॥

kṣaṇena tad balaṁ sarvam asurāṇāṁ nipātitam
dṛṣṭvā caṇḍo 'bhidudrāva tāṁ kālīm atibhīṣaṇām

शरवर्षैर्महाभीमैर्भीमाक्षीं तां महासुरः ।
छादयामास चक्रैश्च मुण्डः क्षिप्तैः सहस्रशः ॥ १७ ॥

śaravarṣair mahābhīmair bhīmākṣīṁ tāṁ mahāsuraḥ
chādayāmāsa cakraiś ca muṇḍaḥ kṣiptaiḥ sahasraśaḥ

तानि चक्राण्यनेकानि विशमानानि तन्मुखम् ।
बभुर्यथाऽर्कबिम्बानि सुबहूनि घनोदरम् ॥ १८ ॥

tāni cakrāṇy anekāni viśamānāni tan mukham
babhur yathā 'rkabimbāni subahūni ghanodaram

ततो जहासातिरुषा भीमं भैरवनादिनी ।
काली करालवक्त्रान्तर्दुर्दर्शदशनोज्ज्वला ॥ १९ ॥

tato jahāsātiruṣā bhīmaṁ bhairavanādinī
kālī karālavaktrāntar durdarśadaśanojjvalā

उत्थाय च महासिंहं देवी चण्डमधावत ।
गृहीत्वा चास्य केशेषु शिरस्तेनासिनाच्छिनत् ॥ २० ॥

utthāya ca mahāsiṁhaṁ devī caṇḍam adhāvata
gṛhītvā cāsya keśeṣu śiras tenāsinācchinat

अथ मुण्डोऽभ्यधावत्तां दृष्ट्वा चण्डं निपातितम् ।
तमप्यपातयद्भूमौ सा खड्गाभिहतं रुषा ॥ २१ ॥

atha muṇḍo 'bhyadhāvat tāṁ dṛṣṭvā caṇḍaṁ nipātitam
tam apyapātayad bhūmau sā khaḍgābhihataṁ ruṣā

हतशेषं ततः सैन्यं दृष्ट्वा चण्डं निपातितम् ।
मुण्डं च सुमहावीर्यं दिशो भेजे भयातुरम् ॥ २२ ॥

hataśeṣaṁ tataḥ sainyaṁ dṛṣṭvā caṇḍaṁ nipātitam
muṇḍaṁ ca sumahāvīryaṁ diśo bheje bhayāturam

शिरश्चण्डस्य काली च गृहीत्वा मुण्डमेव च ।
प्राह प्रचण्डाट्टहासमिश्रमभ्येत्य चण्डिकाम् ॥ २३ ॥

śiraś caṇḍasya kālī ca gṛhītvā muṇḍam eva ca
prāha pracaṇḍāṭṭahasamiśram abhyetya caṇḍikām

मया तवात्रोपहृतौ चण्डमुण्डौ महापशू ।
युद्धयज्ञे स्वयं शुम्भं निशुम्भं च हनिष्यसि । २४ ॥

mayā tavātropahṛtau caṇḍamuṇḍau mahāpaśū
yuddhayajñe svayaṁ śumbhaṁ niśumbhaṁ ca haniṣyasi

ऋषिरुवाच ॥ २५ ॥

ṛṣir uvāca

तावानीतौ ततो दृष्ट्वा चण्डमुण्डौ महासुरौ ।
उवाच कालीं कल्याणी ललितं चण्डिका वचः ॥ २६ ॥

tāv ānītau tato dṛṣṭvā caṇḍamuṇḍau mahāsurau
uvāca kālīṁ kalyāṇī lalitaṁ caṇḍikā vacaḥ

यस्माच्चण्डं च मुण्डं च गृहीत्वा त्वमुपागता ।
चामुण्डेति ततो लोके ख्याता देवि भविष्यसि ॥ २७ ॥

yasmāc caṇḍaṁ ca muṇḍaṁ ca gṛhītvā tvam upāgatā
cāmuṇḍeti tato loke khyātā devi bhaviṣyasi

# अष्टमोऽध्यायः

## रक्तबीजवधः

ऋषिरुवाच ॥ १ ॥

ṛṣir uvāca

चण्डे च निहते दैत्ये मुण्डे च विनिपातिते ।
बहुलेषु च सैन्येषु क्षयितेष्वसुरेश्वरः ॥ २ ॥

caṇḍe ca nihate daitye muṇḍe ca vinipātite
bahuleṣu ca sainyeṣu kṣayiteṣv asureśvaraḥ

ततः कोपपराधीनचेताः शुम्भः प्रतापवान् ।
उद्योगं सर्वसैन्यानां दैत्यानामादिदेश ह ॥ ३ ॥

tataḥ kopaparādhīnacetāḥ śumbhaḥ pratāpavān
udyogaṁ sarvasainyānāṁ daityānām ādideśa ha

अद्य सर्वबलैर्दैत्याः षडशीतिरुदायुधाः ।
कम्बूनां चतुरशीतिर्निर्यान्तु स्वबलैर्वृताः ॥ ४ ॥

adya sarvabalair daityāḥ ṣaḍaśītir udāyudhāḥ
kambūnāṁ caturaśītir niryāntu svabalair vṛtāḥ

कोटिवीर्याणि पञ्चाशदसुराणां कुलानि वै ।
शतं कुलानि धौम्राणां निर्गच्छन्तु ममाज्ञया ॥ ५ ॥

koṭivīryāṇi pañcāśad asurāṇāṁ kulāni vai
śataṁ kulāni dhaumrāṇāṁ nirgacchantu mamājñayā

कालका दौर्हृदा मौर्याः कालकेयास्तथासुराः ।
युद्धाय सज्जा निर्यान्तु आज्ञया त्वरिता मम ॥ ६ ॥

kālakā daurhṛdā mauryāḥ kālakeyās tathāsurāḥ
yuddhāya sajjā niryāntu ājñayā tvaritā mama

इत्याज्ञाप्यासुरपतिः शुम्भो भैरवशासनः ।
निर्जगाम महासैन्यसहस्रैर्बहुभिर्वृतः ॥ ७ ॥

ity ājñāpyāsurapatiḥ śumbho bhairavaśāsanaḥ
nirjagāma mahāsainyasahasrair bahubhir vṛtaḥ

आयान्तं चण्डिका दृष्ट्वा तत्सैन्यमतिभीषणम् ।
ज्यास्वनैः पूरयामास धरणीगगनान्तरम् ॥ ८ ॥

āyāntaṁ caṇḍikā dṛṣṭvā tat sainyam atibhīṣaṇam
jyāsvanaiḥ pūrayāmāsa dharaṇīgaganāntaram

ततः सिंहो महानादमतीव कृतवान्नृप ।
घण्टास्वनेन तान्नादानम्बिका चोपबृंहयत् ॥ ९ ॥

tataḥ siṁho mahānādam atīva kṛtavān nṛpa
ghaṇṭāsvanena tān nādān ambikā copabṛṁhayat

धनुर्ज्यासिंहघण्टानां नादापूरितदिङ्मुखा ।
निनादैर्भीषणैः काली जिग्ये विस्तारितानना ॥ १० ॥

dhanurjyāsiṁhaghaṇṭānāṁ nādāpūritadiṅmukhā
ninādair bhīṣanaiḥ kālī jigye vistāritānanā

तं निनादमुपश्रुत्य दैत्यसैन्यैश्चतुर्दिशम् ।
देवी सिंहस्तथा काली सरोषैः परिवारिताः ॥ ११ ॥

taṁ ninādam upaśrutya daityasainyaiś caturdiśam
devī siṁhas tathā kālī saroṣaiḥ parivāritāḥ

एतस्मिन्नन्तरे भूप विनाशाय सुरद्विषाम् ।
भवायामरसिंहानामतिवीर्यबलान्विताः ॥ १२ ॥

etasminn antare bhūpa vināśāya suradviṣām
bhavāyāmarasiṁhānām ativīryabalānvitāḥ

ब्रह्मेशगुहविष्णूनां तथेन्द्रस्य च शक्तयः ।
शरीरेभ्यो विनिष्क्रम्य तद्रूपैश्चण्डिकां ययुः ॥ १३ ॥

brahmeśaguhaviṣṇūnāṁ tathendrasya ca śaktayaḥ
śarīrebhyo viniṣkramya tadrūpaiś caṇḍikāṁ yayuḥ

यस्य देवस्य यद्रूपं यथा भूषणवाहनम् ।
तद्वदेव हि तच्छक्तिरसुरान्योद्धुमाययौ ॥ १४ ॥

yasya devasya yadrūpaṁ yathā bhūṣaṇavāhanam
tad vad eva hi tac chaktir asurān yoddhum āyayau

हंसयुक्तविमानाग्रे साक्षसूत्रकमण्डलुः ।
आयाता ब्रह्मणः शक्तिर्ब्रह्माणी साभिधीयते ॥ १५ ॥

haṁsayuktavimānāgre sākṣasūtrakamaṇḍaluḥ
āyātā brahmaṇaḥ śaktir brahmāṇī sābhidhīyate

माहेश्वरी वृषारूढा त्रिशूलवरधारिणी ।
महाहिवलया प्राप्ता चन्द्ररेखाविभूषणा ॥ १६ ॥

māheśvarī vṛṣārūḍhā triśūlavaradhāriṇī
mahāhivalayā prāptā candrarekhāvibhūṣaṇā

कौमारी शक्तिहस्ता च मयूरवरवाहना ।
योद्धुमभ्याययौ दैत्यानम्बिका गुहरूपिणी ॥ १७ ॥

kaumārī śaktihastā ca mayūravaravāhanā
yoddhum abhyāyayau daityān ambikā guharūpiṇī

तथैव वैष्णवी शक्तिर्गरुडोपरि संस्थिता ।
शङ्खचक्रगदाशार्ङ्गखड्गहस्ताभ्युपाययौ ॥ १८ ॥

tathaiva vaiṣṇavī śaktir garuḍopari saṁsthitā
śaṅkhacakragadāśārṅgakhaḍgahastābhyupāyayau

यज्ञवाराहमतुलं रूपं या बिभ्रतो हरेः ।
शक्तिः साप्याययौ तत्र वाराहीं बिभ्रती तनुम् ॥ १९ ॥

yajñavārāham atulaṁ rūpaṁ yā bibhrato hareḥ
śaktiḥ sāpyāyayau tatra vārāhīṁ bibhratī tanum

नारसिंही नृसिंहस्य बिभ्रती सदृशं वपुः ।
प्राप्ता तत्र सटाक्षेपक्षिप्तनक्षत्रसंहतिः ॥ २० ॥

nārasiṁhī nṛsiṁhasya bibhratī sadṛśaṁ vapuḥ
prāptā tatra saṭākṣepakṣiptanakṣatrasaṁhatiḥ

वज्रहस्ता तथैवैन्द्री गजराजोपरि स्थिता ।
प्राप्ता सहस्रनयना यथा शक्रस्तथैव सा ॥ २१ ॥

vajrahastā tathaivaindrī gajarājopari sthitā
prāptā sahasranayanā yathā śakrastathaiva sā

ततः परिवृतस्ताभिरीशानो देवशक्तिभिः ।
हन्यन्तामसुराः शीघ्रं मम प्रीत्याह चण्डिकाम् ॥ २२ ॥

tataḥ parivṛtas tābhir īśāno devaśaktibhiḥ
hanyantām asurāḥ śīghraṁ mama prītyāha caṇḍikām

ततो देवीशरीरात्तु विनिष्क्रान्तातिभीषणा ।
चण्डिकाशक्तिरत्युग्रा शिवाशतनिनादिनी ॥ २३ ॥

tato devīśarīrāt tu viniṣkrāntātibhīṣaṇā
caṇḍikāśaktir atyugrā śivāśataninādinī

सा चाह धूम्रजटिलमीशानमपराजिता ।
दूतस्त्वं गच्छ भगवन्पार्श्वं शुम्भनिशुम्भयोः ॥ २४ ॥

sā cāha dhūmrajaṭilam īśānam aparājitā
dūtas tvaṁ gaccha bhagavan pārśvaṁ śumbhaniśumbhayoḥ

ब्रूहि शुम्भं निशुम्भं च दानवावतिगर्वितौ ।
ये चान्ये दानवास्तत्र युद्धाय समुपस्थिताः ॥ २५ ॥

brūhi śumbhaṁ niśumbhaṁ ca dānavav atigarvitau
ye cānye dānavās tatra yuddhāya samupasthitāḥ

त्रैलोक्यमिन्द्रो लभतां देवाः सन्तु हविर्भुजः ।
यूयं प्रयात पातालं यदि जीवितुमिच्छथ ॥ २६ ॥

trailoyam indro labhatāṁ devāḥ santu havirbhujaḥ
yūyaṁ prayāta pātālaṁ yadi jīvitum icchatha

बलावलेपादथ चेद्भवन्तो युद्धकाङ्क्षिणः ।
तदागच्छत तृप्यन्तु मच्छिवाः पिशितेन वः ॥ २७ ॥

balāvalepād atha ced bhavanto yuddhakāṅkṣiṇaḥ
tadāgacchata tṛpyantu macchivāḥ piśitena vaḥ

यतो नियुक्तो दौत्येन तया देव्या शिवः स्वयम् ।
शिवदूतीति लोकेऽस्मिंस्ततः सा ख्यातिमागता ॥ २८ ॥

yato niyukto dautyena tayā devyā śivaḥ svayam
śivadūtīti loke 'smiṁs tataḥ sā khyātimāgatā

तेऽपि श्रुत्वा वचो देव्याः शर्वाख्यातं महासुराः ।
अमर्षापूरिता जग्मुर्यतः कात्यायनी स्थिता ॥ २९ ॥

te 'pi śrutvā vaco devyāḥ śarvākhyātaṁ mahāsurāḥ
amarṣāpūritā jagmur yataḥ kātyāyanī sthitā

ततः प्रथममेवाग्रे शरशक्त्यृष्टिवृष्टिभिः ।
ववर्षुरुद्धतामर्षास्तां देवीममरारयः ॥ ३० ॥

tataḥ prathamam evāgre śaraśaktyṛṣṭivṛṣṭibhiḥ
vavarṣur uddhatāmarṣās tāṁ devīṁ amarārayaḥ

सा च तान् प्रहितान् बाणाञ्छूलशक्तिपरश्वधान् ।
चिच्छेद लीलयाध्मातधनुर्मुक्तैर्महेषुभिः ॥ ३१ ॥

sā ca tān prahitān bāṇāñ chūlaśaktiparaśvadhān
ciccheda līlayādhmātadhanurmuktair maheṣubhiḥ

तस्याग्रतस्तथा काली शूलपातविदारितान् ।
खट्वाङ्गपोथितांश्चारीन्कुर्वती व्यचरत्तदा ॥ ३२ ॥

tasyāgratas tathā kālī śūlapātavidāritān
khaṭvāṅgapothitāṁś cārīn kurvatī vyacarat tadā

कमण्डलुजलाक्षेपहतवीर्यान् हतौजसः ।
ब्रह्माणी चाकरोच्छत्रून्येन येन स्म धावति ॥ ३३ ॥

kamaṇḍalujalākṣepahatavīryān hataujasaḥ
brahmāṇī cākaroc chatrūn yena yena sma dhāvati

माहेश्वरी त्रिशूलेन तथा चक्रेण वैष्णवी ।
दैत्याञ्जघान कौमारी तथा शक्त्यातिकोपना ॥ ३४ ॥

māheśvarī triśūlena tathā cakreṇa vaiṣṇavī
daityāñ jaghāna kaumārī tathā śaktyātikopanā

ऐन्द्री कुलिशपातेन शतशो दैत्यदानवाः ।
पेतुर्विदारिताः पृथ्व्यां रुधिरौघप्रवर्षिणः ॥ ३५ ॥

aindrī kuliśapātena śataśo daityadānavāḥ
petur vidāritāḥ pṛthvyāṁ rudhiraughapravarṣiṇaḥ

तुण्डप्रहारविध्वस्ता दंष्ट्राग्रक्षतवक्षसः ।
वाराहमूर्त्या न्यपतंश्चक्रेण च विदारिताः ॥ ३६ ॥

tuṇḍaprahāravidhvastā daṁṣṭrāgrakṣatavakṣasaḥ
vārāhamūrtyā nyapataṁś cakreṇa ca vidāritāḥ

नखैर्विदारितांश्चान्यान् भक्षयन्ती महासुरान् ।
नारसिंही चचाराजौ नादापूर्णदिगम्बरा ॥ ३७ ॥

nakhair vidāritāṁś cānyān bhakṣayantī mahāsurān
nārasiṁhī cacārājau nādāpūrṇadigambarā

चण्डाट्टहासैरसुराः शिवदूत्यभिदूषिताः ।
पेतुः पृथिव्यां पतितांस्तांश्चखादाथ सा तदा ॥ ३८ ॥

caṇḍāṭṭahāsair asurāḥ śivadūty abhidūṣitāḥ
petuḥ pṛthivyāṁ patitāṁs tāṁś cakhādātha sā tadā

इति मातृगणं क्रुद्धं मर्दयन्तं महासुरान् ।
दृष्ट्वाभ्युपायैर्विविधैर्नेशुर्देवारिसैनिकाः ॥ ३९ ॥

iti mātṛgaṇaṁ kruddhaṁ mardayantaṁ mahāsurān
dṛṣṭvābhyupāyair vividhair neśur devārisainikāḥ

पलायनपरान्दृष्ट्वा दैत्यान्मातृगणार्दितान् ।
योद्धुमभ्याययौ क्रुद्धो रक्तबीजो महासुरः ॥ ४० ॥

palāyanaparān dṛṣṭvā daityān mātṛgaṇārditān
yoddhum abyāyayau kruddho raktabījo mahāsuraḥ

रक्तबिन्दुर्यदा भूमौ पतत्यस्य शरीरतः ।
समुत्पतति मेदिन्यां तत्प्रमाणस्तदासुरः ॥ ४१ ॥

raktabindur yadā bhūmau pataty asya śarīrataḥ
samutpatati medinyāṁ tatpramāṇas tadāsuraḥ

युयुधे स गदापाणिरिन्द्रशक्त्या महासुरः ।
ततश्चैन्द्री स्ववज्रेण रक्तबीजमताडयत् ॥ ४२ ॥

yuyudhe sa gadāpāṇir indraśaktyā mahāsuraḥ
tataś caindrī svavajreṇa raktabījam aṭādayat

कुलिशेनाहतस्याशु बहु सुस्राव शोणितम् ।
समुत्तस्थुस्ततो योधास्तद्रूपास्तत्पराक्रमाः ॥ ४३ ॥

kuliśenāhatasyāśu bahu susrāva śoṇitam
samuttasthus tato yodhās tadrūpās tatparākramāḥ

यावन्तः पतितास्तस्य शरीराद्रक्तबिन्दवः ।
तावन्तः पुरुषा जातास्तद्वीर्यबलविक्रमाः ॥ ४४ ॥

yāvantaḥ patitās tasya śarīrād raktabindavaḥ
tāvantaḥ puruṣā jātās tadvīryabalavikramāḥ

ते चापि युयुधुस्तत्र पुरुषा रक्तसम्भवाः ।
समं मातृभिरत्युग्रशस्त्रपातातिभीषणम् ॥ ४५ ॥

te cāpi yuyudhus tatra puruṣā raktasambhavāḥ
samaṁ mātṛbhir atyugraśastrapātātibhīṣaṇam

पुनश्च वज्रपातेन क्षतमस्य शिरो यदा ।
ववाह रक्तं पुरुषास्ततो जाताः सहस्रशः ॥ ४६ ॥

punaś ca vajrapātena kṣatam asya śiro yadā
vavāha raktaṁ puruṣās tato jātāḥ sahasraśaḥ

वैष्णवी समरे चैनं चक्रेणाभिजघान ह ।
गदया ताडयामास ऐन्द्री तमसुरेश्वरम् ॥ ४७ ॥

vaiṣṇavī samare cainaṁ cakreṇābhijaghāna ha
gadayā tāḍayāmāsa aindrī tam asureśvaram

वैष्णवीचक्रभिन्नस्य रुधिरस्रावसम्भवैः ।
सहस्रशो जगद्व्याप्तं तत्प्रमाणैर्महासुरैः ॥ ४८ ॥

vaiṣṇavīcakrabhinnasya rudhirasrāvasambhavaiḥ
sahasraśo jagad vyāptaṁ tatpramāṇair mahāsuraiḥ

शक्त्या जघान कौमारी वाराही च तथासिना ।
माहेश्वरी त्रिशूलेन रक्तबीजं महासुरम् ॥ ४९ ॥

śaktyā jaghāna kaumārī vārāhī ca tathāsinā
māheśvarī triśūlena raktabījaṁ mahāsuram

स चापि गदया दैत्यः सर्वा एवाहनत् पृथक् ।
मातृः कोपसमाविष्टो रक्तबीजो महासुरः ॥ ५० ॥

sa cāpi gadayā daityaḥ sarvā evāhanat pṛthak
mātṝḥ kopasamāviṣṭo raktabījo mahāsuraḥ

तस्याहतस्य बहुधा शक्तिशूलादिभिर्भुवि ।
पपात यो वै रक्तौघस्तेनासञ्छतशोऽसुराः ॥ ५१ ॥

tasyāhatasya bahudhā śaktiśūlādibhir bhuvi
papāta yo vai raktaughas tenāsañ chataśo 'surāḥ

तैश्चासुरासृक्सम्भूतैरसुरैः सकलं जगत् ।
व्याप्तमासीत्ततो देवा भयमाजग्मुरुत्तमम् ॥ ५२ ॥

taiś cāsurāsṛksambhūtair asuraiḥ sakalaṁ jagat
vyāptam āsīt tato devā bhayam ājagmur uttamam

तान् विषण्णान् सुरान् दृष्ट्वा चण्डिका प्राहसत्त्वरा ।
उवाच कालीं चामुण्डे विस्तीर्णं वदनं कुरु ॥ ५३ ॥

tān viṣaṇṇān surān dṛṣṭvā caṇḍikā prāhasat tvarā
uvāca kālīṁ cāmuṇḍe vistīrṇaṁ vadanaṁ kuru

मच्छस्त्रपातसम्भूतान् रक्तबिन्दून्महासुरान् ।
रक्तबिन्दोः प्रतीच्छ त्वं वक्त्रेणानेन वेगिता ॥ ५४ ॥

macchastrapātasambhūtān raktabindūn mahāsurān
raktabindoḥ pratīccha tvaṁ vaktreṇānena vegitā

भक्षयन्ती चर रणे तदुत्पन्नान्महासुरान् ।
एवमेष क्षयं दैत्यः क्षीणरक्तो गमिष्यति ॥ ५५ ॥

bhakṣayantī cara raṇe tadutpannān mahāsurān
evam eṣa kṣayaṁ daityaḥ kṣīṇarakto gamiṣyati

भक्ष्यमाणास्त्वया चोग्रा न चोत्पत्स्यन्ति चापरे ।
इत्युक्त्वा तां ततो देवी शूलेनाभिजघान तम् ॥ ५६ ॥

bhakṣyamāṇās tvayā cogrā na cotpatsyanti cāpare
ity uktvā tāṁ tato devī śūlenābhijaghāna tam

मुखेन काली जगृहे रक्तबीजस्य शोणितम् ।
ततोऽसावाजघानाथ गदया तत्र चण्डिकाम् ॥ ५७ ॥

mukhena kālī jagṛhe raktabījasya śoṇitam
tato 'sāvājaghānātha gadayā tatra caṇḍikām

न चास्या वेदनां चक्रे गदापातोऽल्पिकामपि ।
तस्याहतस्य देहात्तु बहु सुस्राव शोणितम् ॥ ५८ ॥

na cāsyā vedanāṁ cakre gadāpāto 'lpikām api
tasyāhatasya dehāt tu bahu susrāva śoṇitam

यतस्ततस्तद्वक्त्रेण चामुण्डा सम्प्रतीच्छति ।
मुखे समुद्गता येऽस्या रक्तपातान्महासुराः ॥ ५९ ॥

yatas tatas tad vaktreṇa cāmuṇḍā sampratīcchati
mukhe samudgatā ye 'syā raktapātān mahāsurāḥ

तांश्चखादाथ चामुण्डा पपौ तस्य च शोणितम् ॥ ६० ॥

tāṁś cakhādātha cāmuṇḍā papau tasya ca śoṇitam

देवी शूलेन वज्रेण बाणैरसिभिर्ऋष्टिभिः ।
जघान रक्तबीजं तं चामुण्डापीतशोणितम् ॥ ६१ ॥

devī śūlena vajreṇa bāṇair asibhir ṛṣṭibhiḥ
jaghāna raktabījaṁ taṁ cāmuṇḍāpītaśoṇitam

स पपात महीपृष्ठे शस्त्रसङ्घसमाहतः ।
नीरक्तश्च महीपाल रक्तबीजो महासुरः ॥ ६२ ॥

sa papāta mahīpṛṣṭhe śastrasaṁghasamāhataḥ
nīraktaś ca mahīpāla raktabījo mahāsuraḥ

ततस्ते हर्षमतुलमवापुस्त्रिदशा नृप ।
तेषां मातृगणो जातो ननर्तासृङ्मदोद्धतः ॥ ६३ ॥

tatas te harṣam atulam avāpus tridaśā nṛpa
teṣāṁ mātṛgaṇo jāto nanartāsṛṅmadoddhataḥ

# नवमोऽध्यायः

## निशुम्भवधः

राजोवाच ॥ १ ॥

rājovāca

विचित्रमिदमाख्यातं भगवन् भवता मम ।
देव्याश्चरितमाहात्म्यं रक्तबीजवधाश्रितम् ॥ २ ॥

vicitram idam ākhyātaṁ bhagavan bhavatā mama
devyāś caritamāhātmyaṁ raktabījavadhāśritam

भूयश्चेच्छाम्यहं श्रोतुं रक्तबीजे निपातिते ।
चकार शुम्भो यत्कर्म निशुम्भश्चातिकोपनः ॥ ३ ॥

bhūyaś cecchāmy ahaṁ śrotuṁ raktabīje nipātite
cakāra śumbho yatkarma niśumbhaś cātikopanaḥ

ऋषिरुवाच ॥ ४ ॥

ṛṣir uvāca

चकार कोपमतुलं रक्तबीजे निपातिते ।
शुम्भासुरो निशुम्भश्च हतेष्वन्येषु चाहवे ॥ ५ ॥

cakāra kopam atulaṁ raktabīje nipātite
śumbhāsuro niśumbhaś ca hateṣv anyeṣu cāhave

हन्यमानं महासैन्यं विलोक्यामर्षमुद्वहन् ।
अभ्यधावन्निशुम्भोऽथ-मुख्ययासुरसेनया ॥ ६ ॥

hanyamānaṁ mahāsainyaṁ vilokyāmarṣam udvahan
abhyadhāvan niśumbho 'tha mukhyayāsurasenayā

तस्याग्रतस्तथा पृष्ठे पार्श्वयोश्च महासुराः ।
सन्दष्टौष्ठपुटाः क्रुद्धा हन्तुं देवीमुपाययुः ॥ ७ ॥

tasyāgratas tathā pṛṣṭhe pārśvayoś ca mahāsurāḥ
sandaṣṭauṣṭhapuṭāḥ kruddhā hantuṁ devīm upāyayuḥ

आजगाम महावीर्यः शुम्भोऽपि स्वबलैर्वृतः ।
निहन्तुं चण्डिकां कोपात्कृत्वा युद्धं तु मातृभिः ॥ ८ ॥

ājagāma mahāvīryaḥ śumbho 'pi svabalair vṛtaḥ
nihantuṁ caṇḍikāṁ kopāt kṛtvā yuddhaṁ tu mātṛbhiḥ

ततो युद्धमतीवासीद्देव्या शुम्भनिशुम्भयोः ।
शरवर्षमतीवोग्रं मेघयोरिव वर्षतोः ॥ ९ ॥

tato yuddham atīvāsīd devyā śumbhaniśumbhayoḥ
śaravarṣam atīvograṁ meghayor iva varṣatoḥ

चिच्छेदास्ताञ्छरांस्ताभ्यां चण्डिका स्वशरोत्करैः ।
ताडयामास चाङ्गेषु शस्त्रौघैरसुरेश्वरौ ॥ १० ॥

cicchedāstāñ charāṁs tābhyāṁ caṇḍikā svaśarotkaraiḥ
tāḍayāmāsa cāṅgeṣu śastraughair asureśvarau

निशुम्भो निशितं खड्गं चर्म चादाय सुप्रभम् ।
अताडयन्मूर्ध्नि सिंहं देव्या वाहनमुत्तमम् ॥ ११ ॥

niśumbho niśitaṁ khaḍgaṁ carma cādāya suprabham
atāḍayan mūrdhni siṁhaṁ devyā vāhanam uttamam

ताडिते वाहने देवी क्षुरप्रेणासिमुत्तमम् ।
निशुम्भस्याशु चिच्छेद चर्म चाप्यष्टचन्द्रकम् ॥ १२ ॥

tāḍite vāhane devī kṣurapreṇāsim uttamam
niśumbhasyāśu ciccheda carma cāpyaṣṭacandrakam

छिन्ने चर्मणि खड्गे च शक्तिं चिक्षेप सोऽसुरः ।
तामप्यस्य द्विधा चक्रे चक्रेणाभिमुखागताम् ॥ १३ ॥

chinne carmaṇi khaḍge ca śaktiṁ cikṣepa so 'suraḥ
tām apy asya dvidhā cakre cakreṇābhimukhāgatām

कोपाध्मातो निशुम्भोऽथ शूलं जग्राह दानवः ।
आयान्तं मुष्टिपातेन देवी तच्चाप्यचूर्णयत् ॥ १४ ॥

kopādhmāto niśumbho 'tha śūlaṁ jagrāha dānavaḥ
āyāntaṁ muṣṭipātena devī tac cāpy acūrṇayat

आविध्याथ गदां सोऽपि चिक्षेप चण्डिकां प्रति ।
सापि देव्या त्रिशूलेन भिन्ना भस्मत्वमागता ॥ १५ ॥

āvidhyātha gadāṁ so 'pi cikṣepa caṇḍikāṁ prati
sāpi devyā triśūlena bhinnā bhasmatvam āgatā

ततः परशुहस्तं तमायान्तं दैत्यपुङ्गवम् ।
आहत्य देवी बाणौघैरपातयत भूतले ॥ १६ ॥

tataḥ paraśuhastaṁ tam āyāntaṁ daityapuṅgavam
āhatya devī bāṇaughair apātayata bhūtale

तस्मिन्निपतिते भूमौ निशुम्भे भीमविक्रमे ।
भ्रातर्यतीव संक्रुद्धः प्रययौ हन्तुमम्बिकाम् ॥ १७ ॥

tasmin nipatite bhūmau niśumbhe bhīmavikrame
bhrātary atīva saṁkruddhaḥ prayayau hantum ambikām

स रथस्थस्तथात्युच्चैर्गृहीतपरमायुधैः ।
भुजैरष्टाभिरतुलैर्व्याप्याशेषं बभौ नभः ॥ १८ ॥

sa rathasthas tathāty uccair gṛhītaparamāyudhaiḥ
bhujair aṣṭābhir atulair vyāpyāśeṣaṁ babhau nabhaḥ

तमायान्तं समालोक्य देवी शङ्खमवादयत् ।
ज्याशब्दं चापि धनुषश्चकारातीव दुःसहम् ॥ १९ ॥

tam āyāntaṁ samālokya devī śaṅkham avādayat
jyāśabdaṁ cāpi dhanuṣaś cakārātīva duḥsaham

पूरयामास ककुभो निजघण्टास्वनेन च ।
समस्तदैत्यसैन्यानां तेजोवधविधायिना ॥ २० ॥

pūrayāmāsa kakubho nijaghaṇṭāsvanena ca
samastadaityasainyānāṁ tejovadhavidhāyinā

ततः सिंहो महानादैस्त्याजितेभमहामदैः ।
पूरयामास गगनं गां तथोपदिशो दश ॥ २१ ॥

tataḥ siṁho mahānādais tyājitebhamahāmadaiḥ
pūrayāmāsa gaganaṁ gāṁ tathopadiśo daśa

ततः काली समुत्पत्य गगनं क्ष्मामताडयत् ।
कराभ्यां तन्निनादेन प्राक्स्वनास्ते तिरोहिताः ॥ २२ ॥

tataḥ kālī samutpatya gaganaṁ kṣmām atāḍayat
karābhyāṁ tan ninādena prāksvanāste tirohitāḥ

अट्टाट्टहासमशिवं शिवदूती चकार ह ।
तैः शब्दैरसुरास्त्रेसुः शुम्भः कोपं परं ययौ ॥ २३ ॥

aṭṭāṭṭahāsam aśivaṁ śivadūtī cakāra ha
taiḥ śabdair asurās tresuḥ śumbhaḥ kopaṁ paraṁ yayau

दुरात्मंस्तिष्ठ तिष्ठेति व्याजहाराम्बिका यदा ।
तदा जयेत्यभिहितं देवैराकाशसंस्थितैः ॥ २४ ॥

durātmaṁs tiṣṭha tiṣṭheti vyājahārāmbikā yadā
tadā jayety abhihitaṁ devair ākāśasaṁsthitaiḥ

शुम्भेनागत्य या शक्तिर्मुक्ता ज्वालातिभीषणा ।
आयान्ती वह्निकूटाभा सा निरस्ता महोल्कया ॥ २५ ॥

śumbhenāgatya yā śaktir muktā jvālātibhīṣaṇā
āyāntī vahnikūṭābhā sā nirastā maholkayā

सिंहनादेन शुम्भस्य व्याप्तं लोकत्रयान्तरम् ।
निर्घातनिःस्वनो घोरो जितवानवनीपते ॥ २६ ॥

siṁhanādena śumbhasya vyāptaṁ lokatrayāntaram
nirghātaniḥsvano ghoro jitavān avanīpate

शुम्भमुक्ताञ्छरान्देवी शुम्भस्तत्प्रहिताञ्छरान् ।
चिच्छेद स्वशरैरुग्रैः शतशोऽथ सहस्रशः ॥ २७ ॥

śumbhamuktāñ charān devī śumbhas tatprahitāñ charān
ciccheda svaśarair ugraiḥ śataśo 'tha sahasraśaḥ

ततः सा चण्डिका क्रुद्धा शूलेनाभिजघान तम् ।
स तदाभिहतो भूमौ मूर्च्छितो निपपात ह ॥ २८ ॥

tataḥ sā caṇḍikā kruddhā śūlenābhijaghāna tam
sa tadābhihato bhūmau mūrcchito nipapāta ha

ततो निशुम्भः सम्प्राप्य चेतनामात्तकार्मुकः ।
आजघान शरैर्देवीं कालीं केसरिणं तथा ॥ २९ ॥

tato niśumbhaḥ samprāpya cetanām āttakārmukaḥ
ājaghāna śarair devīṁ kālīṁ kesariṇaṁ tathā

पुनश्च कृत्वा बाहूनामयुतं दनुजेश्वरः ।
चक्रायुधेन दितिजश्छादयामास चण्डिकाम् ॥ ३० ॥

punaś ca kṛtvā bāhūnām ayutaṁ danujeśvaraḥ
cakrāyudhena ditijaś chādayāmāsa caṇḍikām

ततो भगवती क्रुद्धा दुर्गा दुर्गार्तिनाशिनी ।
चिच्छेद तानि चक्राणि स्वशरैः सायकांश्च तान् ॥ ३१ ॥

tato bhagavatī kruddhā durgā durgārtināśinī
ciccheda tāni cakrāṇi svaśaraiḥ sāyakāṁś ca tān

ततो निशुम्भो वेगेन गदामादाय चण्डिकाम् ।
अभ्यधावत वै हन्तुं दैत्यसेनासमावृतः ॥ ३२ ॥

tato niśumbho vegena gadām ādāya caṇḍikām
abhyadhāvata vai hantuṁ daityasenāsamāvṛtaḥ

तस्यापतत एवाशु गदां चिच्छेद चण्डिका ।
खड्गेन शितधारेण स च शूलं समाददे ॥ ३३ ॥

tasyāpatata evāśu gadāṁ ciccheda caṇḍikā
khaḍgena śitadhāreṇa sa ca śūlaṁ samādade

शूलहस्तं समायान्तं निशुम्भममरार्दनम् ।
हृदि विव्याध शूलेन वेगाविद्धेन चण्डिका ॥ ३४ ॥

śūlahastaṁ samāyāntaṁ niśumbham amarārdanam
hṛdi vivyādha śūlena vegāviddhena caṇḍikā

भिन्नस्य तस्य शूलेन हृदयान्निःसृतोऽपरः ।
महाबलो महावीर्यस्तिष्ठेति पुरुषो वदन् ॥ ३५ ॥

bhinnasya tasya śūlena hṛdayān niḥsṛto 'paraḥ
mahābalo mahāvīryas tiṣṭheti puruṣo vadan

तस्य निष्क्रामतो देवी प्रहस्य स्वनवत्ततः ।
शिरश्चिच्छेद खड्गेन ततोऽसावपतद्भुवि ॥ ३६ ॥

tasya niṣkrāmato devī prahasya svanavat tataḥ
śiraś ciccheda khaḍgena tato 'sāvapatad bhuvi

ततः सिंहश्चखादोग्रदंष्ट्राक्षुण्णशिरोधरान् ।
असुरांस्तांस्तथा काली शिवदूती तथापरान् ॥ ३७ ॥

tataḥ siṁhaś cakhādogradaṁṣṭrākṣuṇṇaśirodharān
asurāṁs tāṁs tathā kālī śivadūtī tathāparān

कौमारीशक्तिनिर्भिन्नाः केचिन्नेशुर्महासुराः ।
ब्रह्माणीमन्त्रपूतेन तोयेनान्ये निराकृताः ॥ ३८ ॥

kaumārīśaktinirbhinnāḥ kecin neśur mahāsurāḥ
brahmāṇīmantrapūtena toyenānye nirākṛtāḥ

माहेश्वरीत्रिशूलेन भिन्नाः पेतुस्तथापरे ।
वाराहीतुण्डघातेन केचिच्चूर्णीकृता भुवि ॥ ३९ ॥

māheśvarītriśūlena bhinnāḥ petus tathāpare
vārāhītuṇḍaghātena kecic cūrṇīkṛtā bhuvi

खण्डं खण्डं च चक्रेण वैष्णव्या दानवाः कृताः ।
वज्रेण चैन्द्रीहस्ताग्रविमुक्तेन तथापरे ॥ ४० ॥

khaṇḍaṁ khaṇḍaṁ ca cakreṇa vaiṣṇavyā dānavāḥ kṛtāḥ
vajreṇa caindrīhastāgravimuktena tathāpare

केचिद्विनेशुरसुराः केचिन्नष्टा महाहवात् ।
भक्षिताश्चापरे कालीशिवदूतीमृगाधिपैः ॥ ४१ ॥

kecid vineśur asurāḥ kecin naṣṭā mahāhavāt
bhakṣitāś cāpare kālīśivadūtīmṛgādhipaiḥ

# दशमोऽध्यायः

## शुम्भवधः

ऋषिरुवाच ॥ १ ॥

ṛṣir uvāca

निशुम्भं निहतं दृष्ट्वा भ्रातरं प्राणसम्मितम् ।
हन्यमानं बलं चैव शुम्भः क्रुद्धोऽब्रवीद्वचः ॥ २ ॥

niśumbhaṁ nihataṁ dṛṣṭvā bhrātaraṁ prāṇasammitam
hanyamānaṁ balaṁ caiva śumbhaḥ kruddho 'bravīd vacaḥ

बलावलेपदुष्टे त्वं मा दुर्गे गर्वमावह ।
अन्यासां बलमाश्रित्य युद्ध्यसे यातिमानिनी ॥ ३ ।

balāvalepaduṣṭe tvaṁ mā durge garvam āvaha
anyāsāṁ balam āśritya yuddhyase yātimāninī

देव्युवाच ॥ ४ ॥

devy uvāca

एकैवाहं जगत्यत्र द्वितीया का ममापरा ।
पश्यैता दुष्ट मय्येव विशन्त्यो मद्विभूतयः ॥ ५ ॥

ekaivāhaṁ jagaty atra dvitīyā kā mamāparā
paśyaitā duṣṭa mayy eva viśantyo madvibhūtayaḥ

ततः समस्तास्ता देव्यो ब्रह्माणीप्रमुखा लयम् ।
तस्या देव्यास्तनौ जग्मुरेकैवासीत्तदाम्बिका ॥ ६ ॥

tataḥ samastās tā devyo brahmāṇīpramukhā layam
tasyā devyās tanau jagmur ekaivāsīt tadāmbikā

देव्युवाच ॥ ७ ॥

devy uvāca

अहं विभूत्या बहुभिरिह रूपैर्यदास्थिता ।
तत्संहृतं मयैकैव तिष्ठाम्याजौ स्थिरो भव ॥ ८ ॥

ahaṁ vibhūtyā bahubhir iha rūpair yadāsthitā
tat saṁhṛtaṁ mayaikaiva tiṣṭhāmy ājau sthiro bhava

ऋषिरुवाच ॥ ९ ॥

ṛṣir uvāca

ततः प्रववृते युद्धं देव्याः शुम्भस्य चोभयोः ।
पश्यतां सर्वदेवानामसुराणां च दारुणम् ॥ १० ॥

tataḥ pravavṛte yuddhaṁ devyāḥ śumbhasya cobhayoḥ
paśyatāṁ sarvadevānām asurāṇāṁ ca dāruṇam

शरवर्षैः शितैः शस्त्रैस्तथास्त्रैश्चैव दारुणैः ।
तयोर्युद्धमभूद्भूयः सर्वलोकभयङ्करम् ॥ ११ ॥

śaravarṣaiḥ śitaiḥ śastrais tathāstraiś caiva dāruṇaiḥ
tayor yuddham abhūd bhūyaḥ sarvalokabhayaṅkaram

दिव्यान्यस्त्राणि शतशो मुमुचे यान्यथाम्बिका ।
बभञ्ज तानि दैत्येन्द्रस्तत्प्रतीघातकर्तृभिः ॥ १२ ॥

divyāny astrāṇi śataśo mumuce yāny athāmbikā
babhañja tāni daityendras tatpratīghātakartṛbhiḥ

मुक्तानि तेन चास्त्राणि दिव्यानि परमेश्वरी ।
बभञ्ज लीलयैवोग्रहुङ्कारोच्चारणादिभिः ॥ १३ ॥

muktāni tena cāstrāṇi divyāni parameśvarī
babhañja līlayaivograhuṅkāroccāraṇādibhiḥ

ततः शरशतैर्देवीमाच्छादयत सोऽसुरः ।
सापि तत्कुपिता देवी धनुश्चिच्छेद चेषुभिः ॥ १४ ॥

tataḥ śaraśatair devīm ācchādayata so 'suraḥ
sāpi tatkupitā devī dhanuś ciccheda ceṣubhiḥ

छिन्ने धनुषि दैत्येन्द्रस्तथा शक्तिमथाददे ।
चिच्छेद देवी चक्रेण तामप्यस्य करे स्थिताम् ॥ १५ ॥

chinne dhanuṣi daityendras tathā śaktim athādade
ciccheda devī cakreṇa tām apy asya kare sthitām

ततः खड्गमुपादाय शतचन्द्रं च भानुमत् ।
अभ्यधावत्तदा देवीं दैत्यानामधिपेश्वरः ॥ १६ ॥

tataḥ khaḍgam upādāya śatacandraṁ ca bhānumat
abhyadhāvat tadā devīṁ daityānām adhipeśvaraḥ

तस्यापतत एवाशु खड्गं चिच्छेद चण्डिका ।
धनुर्मुक्तैः शितैर्बाणैश्चर्म चार्ककरामलम् ॥ १७ ॥

tasyāpatata evāśu khaḍgaṁ ciccheda caṇḍikā
dhanurmuktaiḥ śitair bāṇaiś carma cārkakarāmalam

हताश्वः स तदा दैत्यश्छिन्नधन्वा विसारथिः ।
जग्राह मुद्गरं घोरमम्बिकानिधनोद्यतः ॥ १८ ॥

hatāśvaḥ sa tadā daityaś chinnadhanvā visārathiḥ
jagrāha mudgaraṁ ghoram ambikānidhanodyataḥ

चिच्छेदापततस्तस्य मुद्गरं निशितैः शरैः ।
तथापि सोऽभ्यधावत्तां मुष्टिमुद्यम्य वेगवान् ॥ १९ ॥

cicchedāpatatas tasya mudgaraṁ niśitaiḥ śaraiḥ
tathāpi so 'bhyadhāvat tāṁ muṣṭim udyamya vegavān

स मुष्टिं पातयामास हृदये दैत्यपुङ्गवः ।
देव्यास्तं चापि सा देवी तलेनोरस्यताडयत् ॥ २० ॥

sa muṣṭim pātayāmāsa hṛdaye daityapuṅgavaḥ
devyās taṁ cāpi sā devī talenorasy atāḍayat

तलप्रहाराभिहतो निपपात महीतले ।
स दैत्यराजः सहसा पुनरेव तथोत्थितः ॥ २१ ॥

talaprahārābhihato nipapāta mahītale
sa daityarājaḥ sahasā punareva tathotthitaḥ

उत्पत्य च प्रगृह्योच्चैर्देवीं गगनमास्थितः ।
तत्रापि सा निराधारा युयुधे तेन चण्डिका ॥ २२ ॥

utpatya ca pragṛhyoccair devīṁ gaganam āsthitaḥ
tatrāpi sā nirādhārā yuyudhe tena caṇḍikā

नियुद्धं खे तदा दैत्यश्चण्डिका च परस्परम् ।
चक्रतुः प्रथमं सिद्धमुनिविस्मयकारकम् ॥ २३ ॥

niyuddhaṁ khe tadā daityaś caṇḍikā ca parasparam
cakratuḥ prathamaṁ siddhamunivismayakārakam

ततो नियुद्धं सुचिरं कृत्वा तेनाम्बिका सह ।
उत्पाट्य भ्रामयामास चिक्षेप धरणीतले ॥ २४ ॥

tato niyuddhaṁ suciraṁ kṛtvā tenāmbikā saha
utpāṭya bhrāmayāmāsa cikṣepa dharaṇītale

स क्षिप्तो धरणीं प्राप्य मुष्टिमुद्यम्य वेगतः ।
अभ्यधावत दुष्टात्मा चण्डिकानिधनेच्छया ॥ २५ ॥

sa kṣipto dharaṇīṁ prāpya muṣṭim udyamya vegataḥ
abhyadhāvata duṣṭātmā caṇḍikānidhanecchayā

तमायान्तं ततो देवी सर्वदैत्यजनेश्वरम् ।
जगत्यां पातयामास भित्वा शूलेन वक्षसि ॥ २६ ॥

tam āyāntaṁ tato devī sarvadaityajaneśvaram
jagaty āṁ pātayāmāsa bhitvā śūlena vakṣasi

स गतासुः पपातोर्व्यां देवी शूलाग्रविक्षतः ।
चालयन् सकलां पृथ्वीं साब्धिद्वीपां सपर्वताम् ॥ २७ ॥

sa gatāsuḥ papātorvyāṁ devī śūlāgravikṣataḥ
cālayan sakalāṁ pṛthvīṁ sābdhidvīpāṁ saparvatām

ततः प्रसन्नमखिलं हते तस्मिन् दुरात्मनि ।
जगत्स्वास्थ्यमतीवाप निर्मलं चाभवन्नभः ॥ २८ ॥

tataḥ prasannam akhilaṁ hate tasmin durātmani
jagat svāsthyam atīvāpa nirmalaṁ cābhavan nabhaḥ

उत्पातमेघाः सोल्का ये प्रागासंस्ते शमं ययुः ।
सरितो मार्गवाहिन्यस्तथासंस्तत्र पातिते ॥ २९ ॥

utpātameghāḥ solkā ye prāgāsaṁs te śamaṁ yayuḥ
sarito mārgavāhinyas tathāsaṁs tatra pātite

ततो देवगणाः सर्वे हर्षनिर्भरमानसाः ।
बभूवुर्निहते तस्मिन् गन्धर्वा ललितं जगुः ॥ ३० ॥

tato devagaṇāḥ sarve harṣanirbharamānasāḥ
babhūvur nihate tasmin gandharvā lalitaṁ jaguḥ

अवादयंस्तथैवान्ये ननृतुश्चाप्सरोगणाः ।
ववुः पुण्यास्तथा वाताः सुप्रभोऽभूद्दिवाकरः ॥ ३१ ॥

avādayaṁs tathaivānye nanṛtuś cāpsaroganāḥ
vavuḥ puṇyās tathā vātāḥ suprabho 'bhūd divākaraḥ

जज्वलुश्चाग्नयः शान्ताः शान्तदिग्जनितस्वनाः ॥ ३२ ॥

jajvaluś cāgnayaḥ śāntāḥ śāntadigjanitasvanāḥ

# एकादशोऽध्यायः

## नारायणीस्तुतिः

ऋषिरुवाच ॥ १ ॥

ṛṣir uvāca

देव्या हते तत्र महासुरेन्द्रे
सेन्द्राः सुरा वह्निपुरोगमास्ताम् ।
कात्यायनीं तुष्टुवुरिष्टलाभा-
द्विकासिवक्त्राब्जविकासिताशाः ॥ २ ॥

devyā hate tatra mahāsurendre sendrāḥ surā vahnipurogamās tām
kātyāyanīṁ tuṣṭuvur iṣṭalābhād vikāsivaktrābjavikāsitāśāḥ

देवि प्रपन्नार्तिहरे प्रसीद
प्रसीद मातर्जगतोऽखिलस्य ।
प्रसीद विश्वेश्वरि पाहि विश्वं
त्वमीश्वरी देवि चराचरस्य ॥ ३ ॥

devi prapannārtihare prasīda prasīda mātar jagato 'khilasya
prasīda viśveśvari pāhi viśvaṁ tvam īśvarī devi carācarasya

आधारभूता जगतस्त्वमेका
महीस्वरूपेण यतः स्थितासि ।
अपां स्वरूपस्थितया त्वयैत-
दाप्यायते कृत्स्नमलङ्घ्यवीर्ये ॥ ४ ॥

ādhārabhūtā jagatas tvam ekā mahīsvarūpeṇa yataḥ stithāsi
apāṁ svarūpasthitayā tvayaitad āpyāyate kṛtsnam alaṅghyavīrye

त्वं वैष्णवी शक्तिरनन्तवीर्या
विश्वस्य बीजं परमासि माया ।
सम्मोहितं देवि समस्तमेत-
त्त्वं वै प्रसन्ना भुवि मुक्तिहेतुः ॥ ५ ॥

tvaṁ vaiṣṇavī śaktir anantavīryā viśvasya bījaṁ paramāsi māyā
sammohitaṁ devi samastam etat tvaṁ vai prasannā bhuvi muktihetuḥ

विद्याः समस्तास्तव देवि भेदाः
स्त्रियः समस्ताः सकला जगत्सु ।
त्वयैकया पूरितमम्बयैतत्
का ते स्तुतिः स्तव्यपरापरोक्तिः ॥ ६ ॥

vidyāḥ samastās tava devi bhedāḥ striyaḥ samastāḥ sakalā jagatsu
tvayaikayā pūritam ambayaitat kā te stutiḥ stavyaparāparoktiḥ

सर्वभूता यदा देवी भुक्तिमुक्तिप्रदायिनी ।
त्वं स्तुता स्तुतये का वा भवन्तु परमोक्तयः ॥ ७ ॥

sarvabhūtā yadā devī bhuktimuktipradāyinī
tvaṁ stutā stutaye kā vā bhavantu paramoktayaḥ

सर्वस्य बुद्धिरूपेण जनस्य हृदि संस्थिते ।
स्वर्गापवर्गदे देवि नारायणि नमोऽस्तु ते ॥ ८ ॥

sarvasya buddhirūpeṇa janasya hṛdi saṁsthite
svargāpavargade devi nārāyaṇī namo 'stu te

कलाकाष्ठादिरूपेण परिणामप्रदायिनि ।
विश्वस्योपरतौ शक्ते नारायणि नमोऽस्तु ते ॥ ९ ॥

kalākāṣṭhādirūpeṇa pariṇāmapradāyini
viśvasyoparatau śakte nārāyaṇi namo 'stu te

सर्वमङ्गलमाङ्गल्ये शिवे सर्वार्थसाधिके ।
शरण्ये त्र्यम्बके गौरि नारायणि नमोऽस्तु ते ॥ १० ॥

sarvamaṅgalamāṅgalye śive sarvārthasādhike
śaraṇye tryambake gauri nārāyaṇi namo 'stu te

सृष्टिस्थितिविनाशानां शक्तिभूते सनातनि ।
गुणाश्रये गुणमये नारायणि नमोऽस्तु ते ॥ ११ ॥

sṛṣṭisthitivināśānāṁ śaktibhūte sanātani
guṇāśraye guṇamaye nārāyaṇi namo 'stu te

शरणागतदीनार्तपरित्राणपरायणे ।
सर्वस्यार्तिहरे देवि नारायणि नमोऽस्तु ते ॥ १२ ॥

śaraṇāgatadīnārtaparitrāṇaparāyaṇe
sarvasyārtihare devi nārāyaṇi namo 'stu te

हंसयुक्तविमानस्थे ब्रह्माणीरूपधारिणि ।
कौशाम्भःक्षरिके देवि नारायणि नमोऽस्तु ते ॥ १३ ॥

haṁsayuktavimānasthe brahmāṇīrūpadhāriṇi
kauśāmbhaḥkṣarike devi nārāyaṇi namo 'stu te

त्रिशूलचन्द्राहिधरे महावृषभवाहिनि ।
माहेश्वरीस्वरूपेण नारायणि नमोऽस्तु ते ॥ १४ ॥

triśūlacandrāhidhare mahāvṛṣabhavāhini
māheśvarīsvarūpeṇa nārāyaṇi namo 'stu te

मयूरकुक्कुटवृते महाशक्तिधरेऽनघे ।
कौमारीरूपसंस्थाने नारायणि नमोऽस्तु ते ॥ १५ ॥

mayūrakukkuṭavṛte mahāśaktidhare 'naghe
kaumārīrūpasaṁsthāne nārāyaṇi namo 'stu te

शङ्खचक्रगदाशार्ङ्गगृहीतपरमायुधे ।
प्रसीद वैष्णवीरूपे नारायणि नमोऽस्तु ते ॥ १६ ॥

śaṅkhacakragadāśārṅgagṛhītaparamāyudhe
prasīda vaiṣṇavīrūpe nārāyaṇi namo 'stu te

गृहीतोग्रमहाचक्रे दंष्ट्रोद्धृतवसुन्धरे ।
वराहरूपिणि शिवे नारायणि नमोऽस्तु ते ॥ १७ ॥

gṛhītogramahācakre daṁṣṭroddhṛtavasundhare
varāharūpiṇi śive nārāyaṇi namo 'stu te

नृसिंहरूपेणोग्रेण हन्तुं दैत्यान् कृतोद्यमे ।
त्रैलोक्यत्राणसहिते नारायणि नमोऽस्तु ते ॥ १८ ॥

nṛsiṁharūpeṇogreṇa hantuṁ daityān kṛtodyame
trailokyatrāṇasahite nārāyaṇi namo 'stu te

किरीटिनि महावज्रे सहस्रनयनोज्ज्वले ।
वृत्रप्राणहरे चैन्द्रि नारायणि नमोऽस्तु ते ॥ १९ ॥

kirīṭini mahāvajre sahasranayanojjvale
vṛtraprāṇahare caindri nārāyaṇi namo 'stu te

शिवदूतीस्वरूपेण हतदैत्यमहाबले ।
घोररूपे महारावे नारायणि नमोऽस्तु ते ॥ २० ॥

śivadūtīsvarūpeṇa hatadaityamahābale
ghorarūpe mahārāve nārāyaṇi namo 'stu te

दंष्ट्राकरालवदने शिरोमालाविभूषणे ।
चामुण्डे मुण्डमथने नारायणि नमोऽस्तु ते ॥ २१ ॥

daṁṣṭrākarālavadane śiromālāvibhūṣaṇe
cāmuṇḍe muṇḍamathane nārāyaṇi namo 'stu te

लक्ष्मि लज्जे महाविद्ये श्रद्धे पुष्टि स्वधे ध्रुवे ।
महारात्रि महामाये नारायणि नमोऽस्तु ते ॥ २२ ॥

lakṣmi lajje mahāvidye śraddhe puṣṭi svadhe dhruve
mahārātri mahāmāye nārāyaṇi namo 'stu te

मेधे सरस्वति वरे भूति बाभ्रवि तामसि ।
नियते त्वं प्रसीदेशे नारायणि नमोऽस्तु ते ॥ २३ ॥

medhe sarasvati vare bhūti bābhravi tāmasi
niyate tvaṁ prasīdeśe nārāyaṇi namo 'stu te

सर्वस्वरूपे सर्वेशे सर्वशक्तिसमन्विते ।
भयेभ्यस्त्राहि नो देवि दुर्गे देवि नमोऽस्तु ते ॥ २४ ॥

sarvasvarūpe sarveśe sarvaśaktisamanvite
bhayebhyas trāhi no devi durge devi namo 'stu te

एतत्ते वदनं सौम्यं लोचनत्रयभूषितम् ।
पातु नः सर्वभूतेभ्यः कात्यायनि नमोऽस्तु ते ॥ २५ ॥

etat te vadanaṁ saumyaṁ locanatrayabhūṣitam
pātu naḥ sarvabhūtebhyaḥ kātyāyani namo 'stu te

ज्वालाकरालमत्युग्रमशेषासुरसूदनम् ।
त्रिशूलं पातु नो भीतेर्भद्रकालि नमोऽस्तु ते ॥ २६ ॥

jvālākarālam atyugram aśeṣāsurasūdanam
triśūlaṁ pātu no bhīter bhadrakāli namo 'stu te

हिनस्ति दैत्यतेजांसि स्वनेनापूर्य या जगत् ।
सा घण्टा पातु नो देवि पापेभ्यो नः सुतानिव ॥ २७ ॥

hinasti daityatejāṁsi svanenāpūrya yā jagat
sā ghaṇṭā pātu no devi pāpebhyo naḥ sutān iva

असुरासृग्वसापङ्कचर्चितस्ते करोज्ज्वलः ।
शुभाय खड्गो भवतु चण्डिके त्वां नता वयम् ॥ २८ ॥

asurāsṛgvasāpaṅkacarcitas te karojjvalaḥ
śubhāya khaḍgo bhavatu caṇḍike tvāṁ natā vayam

रोगानशेषानपहंसि तुष्टा
रुष्टा तु कामान् सकलानभीष्टान् ।
त्वामाश्रितानां न विपन्नराणां
त्वामाश्रिता ह्याश्रयतां प्रयान्ति ॥ २९ ॥

rogān aśeṣān apahaṁsi tuṣṭā ruṣṭā tu kāmān sakalān abhīṣṭān
tvām āśritānāṁ na vipannarāṇāṁ tvām āśritā hy āśrayatāṁ prayānti

एतत्कृतं यत्कदनं त्वयाद्य
धर्मद्विषां देवि महासुराणाम् ।
रूपैरनेकैर्बहुधात्ममूर्तिं
कृत्वाम्बिके तत्प्रकरोति कान्या ॥ ३० ॥

etat kṛtaṁ yat kadanaṁ tvayādya dharmadviṣāṁ devi mahāsurāṇām
rūpair anekair bahudhātmamūrtiṁ kṛtvāmbike tat prakaroti kānyā

विद्यासु शास्त्रेषु विवेकदीपे-
ष्वाद्येषु वाक्येषु च का त्वदन्या ।
ममत्वगर्तेऽतिमहान्धकारे
विभ्रामयत्येतदतीव विश्वम् ॥ ३१ ॥

vidyāsu śāstreṣu vivekadīpeṣv ādyeṣu vākyeṣu ca kā tvad anyā
mamatvagarte 'timahāndhakāre vibhrāmayaty etad atīva viśvam

रक्षांसि यत्रोग्रविषाश्च नागा
यत्रारयो दस्युबलानि यत्र ।
दावानलो यत्र तथाब्धिमध्ये
तत्र स्थिता त्वं परिपासि विश्वम् ॥ ३२ ॥

rakṣāṁsi yatrogra viṣāś ca nāgā yatrārayo dasyubalāni yatra
dāvānalo yatra tathābdhimadhye tatra sthitā tvaṁ paripāsi viśvam

विश्वेश्वरि त्वं परिपासि विश्वं
विश्वात्मिका धारयसीति विश्वम् ।
विश्वेशवन्द्या भवती भवन्ति
विश्वाश्रया ये त्वयि भक्तिनम्राः ॥ ३३ ॥

viśveśvari tvaṁ paripāsi viśvaṁ viśvātmikā dhārayasīti viśvam
viśveśavandyā bhavatī bhavanti viśvāśrayā ye tvayi bhaktinamrāḥ

देवि प्रसीद परिपालय नोऽरिभीते-
र्नित्यं यथासुरवधादधुनैव सद्यः ।
पापानि सर्वजगतां प्रशमं नयाशु
उत्पातपाकजनितांश्च महोपसर्गान् ॥ ३४ ॥

devi prasīda paripālaya no 'ribhīter nityaṁ yathāsuravadhād adhunaiva
sadyaḥ
pāpāni sarvajagatāṁ praśamaṁ nayāśu utpātapākajanitāṁś ca
mahopasargān

प्रणतानां प्रसीद त्वं देवि विश्वार्तिहारिणि ।
त्रैलोक्यवासिनामीड्ये लोकानां वरदा भव ॥ ३५ ॥

praṇatānāṁ prasīda tvaṁ devi viśvārtihāriṇi
trailokyavāsinām īḍye lokānāṁ varadā bhava

देव्युवाच ॥ ३६ ॥

devy uvāca

वरदाहं सुरगणा वरं यन्मनसेच्छथ ।
तं वृणुध्वं प्रयच्छामि जगतामुपकारकम् ॥ ३७ ॥

varadāhaṁ suragaṇā varaṁ yan manasecchatha
taṁ vṛṇudhvaṁ prayacchāmi jagatām upakārakam

देवा ऊचुः ॥ ३८ ॥

devā ūcuḥ

सर्वाबाधाप्रशमनं त्रैलोक्यस्याखिलेश्वरि ।
एवमेव त्वया कार्यमस्मद्वैरिविनाशनम् ॥ ३९ ॥

sarvābādhāpraśamanaṁ trailokyasyākhileśvari
evam eva tvayā kāryam asmadvairivināśanam

देव्युवाच ॥ ४० ॥

devy uvāca

वैवस्वतेऽन्तरे प्राप्ते अष्टाविंशतिमे युगे ।
शुम्भो निशुम्भश्चैवान्यावुत्पत्स्येते महासुरौ ॥ ४१ ॥

vaivasvate 'ntare prāpte aṣṭāviṁśatime yuge
śumbho niśumbhaś caivānyāv utpatsyete mahāsurau

नन्दगोपगृहे जाता यशोदागर्भसम्भवा ।
ततस्तौ नाशयिष्यामि विन्ध्याचलनिवासिनी ॥ ४२ ॥

nandagopagṛhe jātā yaśodāgarbhasambhavā
tatas tau nāśayiṣyāmi vindhyācalanivāsinī

पुनरप्यतिरौद्रेण रूपेण पृथिवीतले ।
अवतीर्य हनिष्यामि वैप्रचित्तांस्तु दानवान् ॥ ४३ ॥

punar apy atiraudreṇa rūpeṇa pṛthivītale
avatīrya haniṣyāmi vaipracittāṁs tu dānavān

भक्षयन्त्याश्च तानुग्रान् वैप्रचित्तान् महासुरान् ।
रक्ता दन्ता भविष्यन्ति दाडिमीकुसुमोपमाः ॥ ४४ ॥

bhakṣayantyāś ca tān ugrān vaipracittān mahāsurān
raktā dantā bhaviṣyanti dāḍimīkusumopamāḥ

ततो मां देवताः स्वर्गे मर्त्यलोके च मानवाः ।
स्तुवन्तो व्याहरिष्यन्ति सततं रक्तदन्तिकाम् ॥ ४५ ॥

tato māṁ devatāḥ svarge martyaloke ca mānavāḥ
stuvanto vyāhariṣyanti satataṁ raktadantikām

भूयश्च शतवार्षिक्यामनावृष्ट्यामनम्भसि ।
मुनिभिः संस्तुता भूमौ सम्भविष्याम्ययोनिजा ॥ ४६ ॥

bhūyaś ca śatavārṣikyām anāvṛṣṭyām anambhasi
munibhiḥ saṁstutā bhūmau sambhaviṣyāmy ayonijā

ततः शतेन नेत्राणां निरीक्षिष्यामि यन्मुनीन् ।
कीर्तयिष्यन्ति मनुजाः शताक्षीमिति मां ततः ॥ ४७ ॥

tataḥ śatena netrāṇāṁ nirīkṣiṣyāmi yan munīn
kīrtayiṣyanti manujāḥ śatākṣīm iti māṁ tataḥ

ततोऽहमखिलं लोकमात्मदेहसमुद्भवैः ।
भरिष्यामि सुराः शाकैरावृष्टेः प्राणधारकैः ॥ ४८ ॥

tato 'ham akhilaṁ lokam ātmadehasamudbhavaiḥ
bhariṣyāmi surāḥ śākair āvṛṣṭeḥ prāṇadhārakaiḥ

शाकम्भरीति विख्यातिं तदा यास्याम्यहं भुवि ॥ ४९ ॥

śākambharīti vikhyātiṁ tadā yāsyāmy ahaṁ bhuvi

तत्रैव च वधिष्यामि दुर्गमाख्यं महासुरम् ।
दुर्गादेवीति विख्यातं तन्मे नाम भविष्यति ॥ ५० ॥

tatraiva ca vadhiṣyāmi durgamākhyaṁ mahāsuram
durgādevīti vikhyātaṁ tan me nāma bhaviṣyati

पुनश्चाहं यदा भीमं रूपं कृत्वा हिमाचले ।
रक्षांसि क्षययिष्यामि मुनीनां त्राणकारणात् ॥ ५१ ॥

punaś cāhaṁ yadā bhīmaṁ rūpaṁ kṛtvā himācale
rakṣāṁsi kṣayayiṣyāmi munīnāṁ trāṇakāraṇāt

तदा मां मुनयः सर्वे स्तोष्यन्त्यानम्रमूर्तयः ।
भीमादेवीति विख्यातं तन्मे नाम भविष्यति ॥ ५२ ॥

tadā māṁ munayaḥ sarve stoṣyanty ānamramūrtayaḥ
bhīmādevīti vikhyātaṁ tan me nāma bhaviṣyati

यदारुणाख्यस्त्रैलोक्ये महाबाधां करिष्यति ।
तदाहं भ्रामरं रूपं कृत्वासङ्ख्येयषट्पदम् ॥ ५३ ॥

yadāruṇākhyas trailokye mahābādhāṁ kariṣyati
tadāhaṁ bhrāmaraṁ rūpaṁ kṛtvāsaṅkhyeyaṣaṭpadam

त्रैलोक्यस्य हितार्थाय वधिष्यामि महासुरम् ।
भ्रामरीति च मां लोकास्तदा स्तोष्यन्ति सर्वतः ॥ ५४ ॥

trailokyasya hitārthāya vadhiṣyāmi mahāsuram
bhrāmarīti ca māṁ lokāstadā stoṣyanti sarvataḥ

इत्थं यदा यदा बाधा दानवोत्था भविष्यति ।
तदा तदावतीर्याहं करिष्याम्यरिसंक्षयम् ॥ ५५ ॥

itthaṁ yadā yadā bādhā dānavotthā bhaviṣyati
tadā tadāvatīryāhaṁ kariṣyāmy arisaṁkṣayam

# द्वादशोऽध्यायः

## फलस्तुतिः

देव्युवाच ॥ १ ॥

devy uvāca

एभिः स्तवैश्च मां नित्यं स्तोष्यते यः समाहितः ।
तस्याहं सकलां बाधां नाशयिष्याम्यसंशयम् ॥ २ ॥

ebhiḥ stavaiś ca māṁ nityaṁ stoṣyate yaḥ samāhitaḥ
tasyāhaṁ sakalāṁ bādhāṁ nāśayiṣyāmy asaṁśayam

मधुकैटभनाशं च महिषासुरघातनम् ।
कीर्तयिष्यन्ति ये तद्वद्वधं शुम्भनिशुम्भयोः ॥ ३ ॥

madhukaiṭabhanāśaṁ ca mahiṣāsuraghātanam
kīrtayiṣyanti ye tadvad vadhaṁ śumbhaniśumbhayoḥ

अष्टम्यां च चतुर्दश्यां नवम्यां चैकचेतसः ।
श्रोष्यन्ति चैव ये भक्त्या मम माहात्म्यमुत्तमम् ॥ ४ ॥

aṣṭamyāṁ ca caturdaśyāṁ navamyāṁ caikacetasaḥ
śroṣyanti caiva ye bhaktyā mama māhātmyam uttamam

न तेषां दुष्कृतं किञ्चिद्दुष्कृतोत्था न चापदः ।
भविष्यति न दारिद्र्यं न चैवेष्टवियोजनम् ॥ ५ ॥

na teṣāṁ duṣkṛtaṁ kiñcid duṣkṛtotthā na cāpadaḥ
bhaviṣyati na dāridryaṁ na caiveṣṭaviyojanam

शत्रुतो न भयं तस्य दस्युतो वा न राजतः ।
न शस्त्रानलतोयौघात्कदाचित्सम्भविष्यति ॥ ६ ॥

śatruto na bhayaṁ tasya dasyuto vā na rājataḥ
na śastrānalatoyaughāt kadācit sambhaviṣyati

तस्मान्ममैतन्माहात्म्यं पठितव्यं समाहितैः ।
श्रोतव्यं च सदा भक्त्या परं स्वस्त्ययनं हि तत् ॥ ७ ॥

tasmān mamaitan māhātmyaṁ paṭhitavyaṁ samāhitaiḥ
śrotavyaṁ ca sadā bhaktyā paraṁ svastyayanaṁ hi tat

उपसर्गानशेषांस्तु महामारीसमुद्भवान् ।
तथा त्रिविधमुत्पातं माहात्म्यं शमयेन्मम ॥ ८ ॥

upasargān aśeṣāṁs tu mahāmārīsamudbhavān
tathā trividham utpātaṁ māhātmyaṁ śamayen mama

यत्रैतत्पठ्यते सम्यङ्नित्यमायतने मम ।
सदा न तद्विमोक्ष्यामि सान्निध्यं तत्र मे स्थितम् ॥ ९ ॥

yatraitat paṭhyate samyaṅ nityam āyatane mama
sadā na tad vimokṣyāmi sānnidhyaṁ tatra me sthitam

बलिप्रदाने पूजायामग्निकार्ये महोत्सवे ।
सर्वं ममैतच्चरितमुच्चार्यं श्राव्यमेव च ॥ १० ॥

balipradāne pūjāyām agnikārye mahotsave
sarvaṁ mamaitac caritam uccāryaṁ śrāvyam eva ca

जानताजानता वापि बलिपूजां तथा कृताम् ।
प्रतीच्छिष्याम्यहं प्रीत्या वह्निहोमं तथाकृतम् ॥ ११ ॥

jānatājānatā vāpi balipūjāṁ tathā kṛtām
pratīcchiṣyāmy ahaṁ prītyā vahnihomaṁ tathākṛtam

शरत्काले महापूजा क्रियते या च वार्षिकी ।
तस्यां ममैतन्माहात्म्यं श्रुत्वा भक्तिसमन्वितः ॥ १२ ॥

śaratkāle mahāpūjā kriyate yā ca vārṣikī
tasyāṁ mamaitan māhātmyaṁ śrutvā bhaktisamanvitaḥ

सर्वाबाधाविनिर्मुक्तो धनधान्यसुतान्वितः ।
मनुष्यो मत्प्रसादेन भविष्यति न संशयः ॥ १३ ॥

sarvābādhāvinirmukto dhanadhānyasutānvitaḥ
manuṣyo matprasādena bhaviṣyati na saṁśayaḥ

श्रुत्वा ममैतन्माहात्म्यं तथा चोत्पत्तयः शुभाः ।
पराक्रमं च युद्धेषु जायते निर्भयः पुमान् ॥ १४ ॥

śrutvā mamaitan māhātmyaṁ tathā cotpattayaḥ śubhāḥ
parākramaṁ ca yuddheṣu jāyate nirbhayaḥ pumān

रिपवः संक्षयं यान्ति कल्याणं चोपपद्यते ।
नन्दते च कुलं पुंसां माहात्म्यं मम शृण्वताम् ॥ १५ ॥

ripavaḥ saṁkṣayaṁ yānti kalyāṇaṁ copapadyate
nandate ca kulaṁ puṁsāṁ māhātmyaṁ mama śṛṇvatām

शान्तिकर्मणि सर्वत्र तथा दुःस्वप्नदर्शने ।
ग्रहपीडासु चोग्रासु माहात्म्यं शृणुयान्मम ॥ १६ ॥

śāntikarmaṇi sarvatra tathā duḥsvapnadarśane
grahapīḍāsu cogrāsu māhātmyaṁ śṛṇuyān mama

उपसर्गाः शमं यान्ति ग्रहपीडाश्च दारुणाः ।
दुःस्वप्नं च नृभिर्दृष्टं सुस्वप्नमुपजायते ॥ १७ ॥

upasargāḥ śamaṁ yānti grahapīḍāś ca dāruṇāḥ
duḥsvapnaṁ ca nṛbhir dṛṣṭaṁ susvapnam upajāyate

बालग्रहाभिभूतानां बालानां शान्तिकारकम् ।
सङ्घातभेदे च नृणां मैत्रीकरणमुत्तमम् ॥ १८ ॥

bālagrahābhibhūtānāṁ bālānāṁ śāntikārakam
saṅghātabhede ca nṛṇāṁ maitrīkaraṇam uttamam

दुर्वृत्तानामशेषाणां बलहानिकरं परम् ।
रक्षोभूतपिशाचानां पठनादेव नाशनम् ॥ १९ ॥

durvṛttānām aśeṣāṇāṁ balahānikaraṁ param
rakṣobhūtapiśācānāṁ paṭhanād eva nāśanam

सर्वं ममैतन्माहात्म्यं मम सन्निधिकारकम् ॥ २० ॥

sarvaṁ mamaitan māhātmyaṁ mama sannidhikārakam

पशुपुष्पार्घ्यधूपैश्च गन्धदीपैस्तथोत्तमैः ।
विप्राणां भोजनैर्होमैः प्रोक्षणीयैरहर्निशम् ॥ २१ ॥

paśupuṣpārghyadhūpaiś ca gandhadīpais tathottamaiḥ
viprāṇāṁ bhojanair homaiḥ prokṣaṇīyair aharniśam

अन्यैश्च विविधैर्भोगैः प्रदानैर्वत्सरेण या ।
प्रीतिर्मे क्रियते सास्मिन्सकृत्सुचरिते श्रुते ॥ २२ ॥

anyaiś ca vividhair bhogaiḥ pradānair vatsareṇa yā
prītir me kriyate sāsmin sakṛt sucarite śrute

श्रुतं हरति पापानि तथारोग्यं प्रयच्छति ।
रक्षां करोति भूतेभ्यो जन्मनां कीर्तनं मम ॥ २३ ॥

śrutaṁ harati pāpāni tathārogyaṁ prayacchati
rakṣāṁ karoti bhūtebhyo janmanāṁ kīrtanaṁ mama

युद्धेषु चरितं यन्मे दुष्टदैत्यनिबर्हणम् ।
तस्मिञ्छ्रुते वैरिकृतं भयं पुंसां न जायते ॥ २४ ॥

yuddheṣu caritaṁ yanme duṣṭadaityanibarhaṇam
tasmiñc chrute vairikṛtaṁ bhayaṁ puṁsāṁ na jāyate

युष्माभिः स्तुतयो याश्च याश्च ब्रह्मर्षिभिः कृताः ।
ब्रह्मणा च कृतास्तास्तु प्रयच्छन्ति शुभां मतिम् ॥ २५ ॥

yuṣmābhiḥ stutayo yāś ca yāś ca brahmarṣibhiḥ kṛtāḥ
brahmaṇā ca kṛtās tās tu prayacchanti śubhāṁ matim

अरण्ये प्रान्तरे वापि दावाग्निपरिवारितः ।
दस्युभिर्वा वृतः शून्ये गृहीतो वापि शत्रुभिः ॥ २६ ॥

araṇye prāntare vāpi dāvāgniparivāritaḥ
dasyubhir vā vṛtaḥ śūnye gṛhīto vāpi śatrubhiḥ

सिंहव्याघ्रानुयातो वा वने वा वनहस्तिभिः ।
राज्ञा क्रुद्धेन चाज्ञप्तो वध्यो बन्धगतोऽपि वा ॥ २७ ॥

siṁhavyāghrānuyāto vā vane vā vanahastibhiḥ
rājñā kruddhena cājñapto vadhyo bandhagato 'pi vā

आघूर्णितो वा वातेन स्थितः पोते महार्णवे ।
पतत्सु चापि शस्त्रेषु संग्रामे भृशदारुणे ॥ २८ ॥

āghūrṇito vā vātena sthitaḥ pote mahārṇave
patatsu cāpi śastreṣu saṁgrāme bhṛśadāruṇe

सर्वाबाधासु घोरासु वेदनाभ्यर्दितोऽपि वा ।
स्मरन्ममैतच्चरितं नरो मुच्येत सङ्कटात् ॥ २९ ॥

sarvābādhāsu ghorāsú vedanābhyardito 'pi vā
smaran mamaitac caritaṁ naro mucyeta saṅkaṭāt

मम प्रभावात्सिंहाद्या दस्यवो वैरिणस्तथा ।
दूरादेव पलायन्ते स्मरतश्चरितं मम ॥ ३० ॥

mama prabhāvāt siṁhādyā dasyavo vairiṇas tathā
dūrād eva palāyante smarataś caritaṁ mama

ऋषिरुवाच ॥ ३१ ॥

ṛṣir uvāca

इत्युक्त्वा सा भगवती चण्डिका चण्डविक्रमा ।
पश्यतामेव देवानां तत्रैवान्तरधीयत ॥ ३२ ॥

ity uktvā sā bhagavatī caṇḍikā caṇḍavikramā
paśyatām eva devānāṁ tatraivāntaradhīyata

तेऽपि देवा निरातङ्काः स्वाधिकारान्यथा पुरा ।
यज्ञभागभुजः सर्वे चक्रुर्विनिहतारयः ॥ ३३ ॥

te 'pi devā nirātaṅkāḥ svādhikārān yathā purā
yajñabhāgabhujaḥ sarve cakrur vinihatārayaḥ

दैत्याश्च देव्या निहते शुम्भे देवरिपौ युधि ।
जगद्विध्वंसिनि तस्मिन् महोग्रेऽतुलविक्रमे ॥ ३४ ॥

daityāś ca devyā nihate śumbhe devaripau yudhi
jagadvidhvaṁsini tasmin mahogre 'tulavikrame

निशुम्भे च महावीर्ये शेषाः पातालमाययुः ॥ ३५ ॥

niśumbhe ca mahāvīrye śeṣāḥ pātālam āyayuḥ

एवं भगवती देवी सा नित्यापि पुनः पुनः ।
सम्भूय कुरुते भूप जगतः परिपालनम् ॥ ३६ ॥

evaṁ bhagavatī devī sā nityāpi punaḥ punaḥ
sambhūya kurute bhūpa jagataḥ paripālanam

तयैतन्मोह्यते विश्वं सैव विश्वं प्रसूयते ।
सा याचिता च विज्ञानं तुष्टा ऋद्धिं प्रयच्छति ॥ ३७ ॥

tayaitan mohyate viśvaṁ saiva viśvaṁ prasūyate
sā yācitā ca vijñānaṁ tuṣṭā ṛddhiṁ prayacchati

व्याप्तं तयैतत्सकलं ब्रह्माण्डं मनुजेश्वर ।
महाकाल्या महाकाले महामारीस्वरूपया ॥ ३८ ॥

vyāptaṁ tayaitat sakalaṁ brahmāṇḍaṁ manujeśvara
mahākālyā mahākāle mahāmārīsvarūpayā

सैव काले महामारी सैव सृष्टिर्भवत्यजा ।
स्थितिं करोति भूतानां सैव काले सनातनी ॥ ३९ ॥

saiva kāle mahāmārī saiva sṛṣṭir bhavaty ajā
sthitiṁ karoti bhūtānāṁ saiva kāle sanātanī

भवकाले नृणां सैव लक्ष्मीर्वृद्धिप्रदा गृहे ।
सैवाभावे तथालक्ष्मीर्विनाशायोपजायते ॥ ४० ॥

bhavakāle nṛṇāṁ saiva lakṣmīr vṛddhipradā gṛhe
saivābhāve tathālakṣmīr vināśāyopajāyate

स्तुता सम्पूजिता पुष्पैर्धूपगन्धादिभिस्तथा ।
ददाति वित्तं पुत्रांश्च मतिं धर्मे गतिं शुभाम् ॥ ४१ ॥

stutā sampūjitā puṣpair dhūpagandhādibhis tathā
dadāti vittaṁ putrāṁś ca matim dharme gatim śubhām

# त्रयोदशोऽध्यायः

## सुरथवैश्ययोर्वरप्रदानम्

ऋषिरुवाच ॥ १ ॥

ṛṣir uvāca

एतत्ते कथितं भूप देवीमाहात्म्यमुत्तमम् ॥ २ ॥

etat te kathitaṁ bhūpa devīmāhātmyam uttamam

एवम्प्रभावा सा देवी ययेदं धार्यते जगत् ।
विद्या तथैव क्रियते भगवद्विष्णुमायया ॥ ३ ॥

evamprabhāvā sā devī yayedaṁ dhāryate jagat
vidyā tathaiva kriyate bhagavadviṣṇumāyayā

तया त्वमेष वैश्यश्च तथैवान्ये विवेकिनः ।
मोह्यन्ते मोहिताश्चैव मोहमेष्यन्ति चापरे ॥ ४ ॥

tayā tvam eṣa vaiśyaś ca tathaivānye vivekinaḥ
mohyante mohitāś caiva moham eṣyanti cāpare

तामुपैहि महाराज शरणं परमेश्वरीम् ।
आराधिता सैव नृणां भोगस्वर्गापवर्गदा ॥ ५ ॥

tām upaihi mahārāja śaraṇam parameśvarīm
ārādhitā saiva nṛṇāṁ bhogasvargāpavargadā

मार्कण्डेय उवाच ॥ ६ ॥

mārkaṇḍeya uvāca

इति तस्य वचः श्रुत्वा सुरथः स नराधिपः ।
प्रणिपत्य महाभागं तमृषिं संशितव्रतम् ॥ ७ ॥

iti tasya vacaḥ śrutvā surathaḥ sa narādhipaḥ
praṇipatya mahābhāgaṁ tam ṛṣiṁ saṁśitavratam

निर्विण्णोऽतिममत्वेन राज्यापहरणेन च ।
जगाम सद्यस्तपसे स च वैश्यो महामुने ॥ ८ ॥

nirviṇṇo ’timamatvena rājyāpaharaṇena ca
jagāma sadyas tapase sa ca vaiśyo mahāmune

सन्दर्शनार्थमम्बाया नदीपुलिनसंस्थितः ।
स च वैश्यस्तपस्तेपे देवीसूक्तं परं जपन् ॥ ९ ॥

sandarśanārtham ambāyā nadīpulinasaṁsthitaḥ
sa ca vaiśyas tapas tepe devīsūktaṁ paraṁ japan

तौ तस्मिन् पुलिने देव्याः कृत्वा मूर्तिं महीमयीम् ।
अर्हणां चक्रतुस्तस्याः पुष्पधूपाग्नितर्पणैः ॥ १० ॥

tau tasmin puline devyāḥ kṛtvā mūrtiṁ mahīmayīm
arhaṇāṁ cakratus tasyāḥ puṣpadhūpāgnitarpaṇaiḥ

निराहारौ यताहारौ तन्मनस्कौ समाहितौ ।
ददतुस्तौ बलिं चैव निजगात्रासृगुक्षितम् ॥ ११ ॥

nirāhārau yatāhārau tanmanaskau samāhitau
dadatus tau baliṁ caiva nijagātrāsṛgukṣitam

एवं समाराधयतोस्त्रिभिर्वर्षैर्यतात्मनोः ।
परितुष्टा जगद्धात्री प्रत्यक्षं प्राह चण्डिका ॥ १२ ॥

evaṁ samārādhayatos tribhir varṣair yatātmanoḥ
parituṣṭā jagaddhātrī pratyakṣaṁ prāha caṇḍikā

देव्युवाच ॥ १३ ॥

devy uvāca

यत्प्रार्थ्यते त्वया भूप त्वया च कुलनन्दन ॥ १४ ॥
मत्तस्तत्प्राप्यतां सर्वं परितुष्टा ददामि तत् ॥ १५ ॥

yat prārthyate tvayā bhūpa tvayā ca kulanandana
mat tas tat prāpyatāṁ sarvaṁ parituṣṭā dadāmi tat

मार्कण्डेय उवाच ॥ १६ ॥

mārkaṇḍeya uvāca

ततो वव्रे नृपो राज्यमविभ्रंश्यन्यजन्मनि ।
अत्र चैव निजं राज्यं हतशत्रुबलं बलात् ॥ १७ ॥

tato vavre nṛpo rājyam avibhraṁśyanyajanmani
atra caiva nijaṁ rājyaṁ hataśatrubalaṁ balāt

सोऽपि वैश्यस्ततो ज्ञानं वव्रे निर्विण्णमानसः ।
ममेत्यहमिति प्राज्ञः सङ्गविच्युतिकारकम् ॥ १८ ॥

so 'pi vaiśyas tato jñānaṁ vavre nirviṇṇamānasaḥ
mametyaham iti prājñaḥ saṅgavicyutikārakam

देव्युवाच ॥ १९ ॥

devy uvāca

स्वल्पैरहोभिर्नृपते स्वराज्यं प्राप्स्यते भवान् ॥ २० ॥
हत्वा रिपूनस्खलितं तव तत्र भविष्यति ॥ २१ ॥

svalpair ahobhir nṛpate svarājyaṁ prāpsyate bhavān
hatvā ripūn askhalitaṁ tava tatra bhaviṣyati

मृतश्च भूयः सम्प्राप्य जन्म देवाद्विवस्वतः ॥ २२ ॥
सावर्णिको नाम मनुर्भवान्भुवि भविष्यति ॥ २३ ॥

mṛtaś ca bhūyaḥ samprāpya janma devād vivasvataḥ
sāvarṇiko nāma manur bhavān bhuvi bhaviṣyati

वैश्यवर्य त्वया यश्च वरोऽस्मत्तोऽभिवाञ्छितः ॥ २४ ॥
तं प्रयच्छामि संसिद्ध्यै तव ज्ञानं भविष्यति ॥ २५ ॥

vaiśyavarya tvayā yaś ca varo 'smatto 'bhivāñchitaḥ
taṁ prayacchāmi saṁsiddhyai tava jñānaṁ bhaviṣyati

मार्कण्डेय उवाच ॥ २६ ॥

mārkaṇḍeya uvāca

इति दत्वा तयोर्देवी यथाभिलषितं वरम् ।
बभूवान्तर्हिता सद्यो भक्त्या ताभ्यामभिष्टुता ॥ २७ ॥

iti datvā tayor devī yathābhilaṣitaṁ varam
babhūvāntarhitā sadyo bhaktyā tābhyām abhiṣṭutā

एवं देव्या वरं लब्ध्वा सुरथः क्षत्रियर्षभः ।
सूर्याज्जन्म समासाद्य सावर्णिर्भविता मनुः ॥ २८ ॥

evaṁ devyā varaṁ labdhvā surathaḥ kṣatriyarṣabhaḥ
sūryāj janma samāsādya sāvarṇir bhavitā manuḥ

सावर्णिर्भविता मनुः क्लीं ओम् ॥ २९ ॥

sāvarṇir bhavitā manuḥ klīṁ Oṁ

श्रीसप्तशतीदेवीमाहात्म्यं समाप्तम्

śrīsaptaśatīdevīmāhātmyaṁ samāptam

ओं तत् सत् ओम् ॥

Oṁ tat sat Oṁ

# NOTES

## PART I: ORIGINS AND CONTEXT OF THE DEVĪMĀHĀTMYA

### A Brief History

1. J. Desmond Clark and Martin A. J. Williams, "Paleoenvironments and Prehistory in North Central India: A Preliminary Report," in *Studies in the Archaeology of India and Pakistan*, Jerome Jacobson, ed. (New Dehli: Oxford & IBH Publishing Co., 1986), pp. 31–32.
2. Clark and Williams, "Paleoenvironments," p. 39.
3. Prithvi Kumar Agrawala, *Goddesses in Ancient India* (New Delhi: Abhinav Publications, 1984), pp. 26–27.
4. Savitri Dhawan, *Mother Goddesses in Early Indian Religion* (Jaipur and New Delhi: National Publishing House, 1997), p. 14.
5. Agrawala, *Goddesses*, p. 27.
6. Agrawala, *Goddesses*, p. 16.
7. Dilip K. Chakrabarti, *The Archaeology of Ancient Indian Cities* (Delhi: Oxford University Press, 1995), p. 123.
8. Agrawala, *Goddesses*, p. 24.
9. Jonathan Mark Kenoyer, *Ancient Cities of the Indus Valley Civilization* (Karachi: Oxford University Press, American Institute of Pakistan Studies, 1998), pp. 105–106.
10. Ibid.
11. Agrawala, *Goddesses*, pp. 35–36.
12. Agrawala, *Goddesses*, p. 33.
13. Jonathan Z. Smith and William Scott Green, eds., *The HarperCollins Dictionary of Religion* (San Francisco: HarperCollins, 1995), 483.
14. Agrawala, *Goddesses*, p. 46.
15. Ibid.
16. Agrawala, *Goddesses*, p. 79.
17. Agrawala, *Goddesses*, p. 48.
18. Agrawala, *Goddesses*, p. 93.
19. Agrawala, *Goddesses*, p. 96.
20. Ralph T. H. Griffith, trans., *Hinduism: The Rig Veda,* Sacred Writings, vol. 5 (New York: Book-of-the-Month Club, 1992), pp. 640–641.
21. Agrawala, *Goddesses*, p. 57.

22. Ibid.
23. Ibid.
24. Tracy Pintchman, *The Rise of the Goddess in the Hindu Tradition* (Albany: State University of New York Press, 1994), p. 32.
25. Agrawala, *Goddesses*, pp. 56–60.
26. Thomas B. Coburn, *Devī-Māhātmya: The Crystallization of the Goddess Tradition* (Delhi: Motilal Banarsidass, 1984), p. 255.
27. Kenoyer, *Ancient Cities*, p. 183.
28. Kenoyer, *Ancient Cities*, p. 29.
29. Griffith, *Hinduism*, p. 3 n. 10.
30. Chakrabarti, *Archaeology of Ancient Indian Cities*, pp. 90–91.
31. Griffith, *Hinduism*, p. 3 n. 12.
32. Agrawala, *Goddesses*, p. 89.
33. Brian M. Fagan, ed., *The Oxford Companion to Archaeology* (New York: Oxford University Press, 1996), p. 351.
34. Paul G. Bahn, *The Cambridge Illustrated History of Archaeology* (Cambridge: Cambridge University Press, 1996), p. 258.
35. Sir John Woodroffe (Arthur Avalon), *Shakti and Shakta* (New York: Dover Publications, 1978), pp. 136–138.
36. Thomas B. Coburn, *Encountering the Goddess: A Translation of the Devī-Māhātmya and a Study of Its Interpretation* (Albany: State University of New York Press, 1991), p. 125.
37. Georg Feuerstein, *Tantra: The Path of Ecstasy* (Boston and London: Shambhala, 1998), pp. 1–2.
38. Woodroffe, *Shakti and Shakta*, p. 206.
39. Coburn, *Devī-Māhātmya,* p. 20.

**The Devīmāhātmya's Origins, Structure, and Context**

1. C. Mackenzie Brown, *The Triumph of the Goddess: The Canonical Models and Theological Visions of the* Devī-Bhāgavata Purāṇa (Albany: State University of New York Press, 1990), p. 159.
2. Coburn, *Encountering the Goddess,* p. 8.
3. John Michael Greer, "Myth, History and Pagan Origins," *The Pomegranate* 9 (1999): 45.
4. Ibid.
5. John Bowker, ed., *The Oxford Dictionary of World Religions* (Oxford and New York: Oxford University Press, 1997), p. 673.
6. Coburn, *Encountering the Goddess*, p. 138.
7. Brown, *Triumph of the Goddess,* p. 90.
8. Woodroffe, *Shakti and Shakta*, p. 259.
9. Swami Vivekananda, *Inspired Talks* (New York: Ramakrishna-Vivekananda Center, 1970), p. 48.
10. Woodroffe, *Shakti and Shakta*, p. 290.
11. Swami Satprakashananda, *The Universe, God, and God-Realization: From the Viewpoint of Vedanta* (St. Louis: The Vedanta Society, 1977), pp. 110–111.

12. Woodroffe, *Shakti and Shakta*, p. 274.
13. David Kinsley, *The Goddesses' Mirror: Visions of the Divine from East and West* (Albany: State University of New York Press, 1989), p. 4.
14. Coburn, *Devī-Māhātmya,* p. 116.
15. Coburn, *Devī-Māhātmya,* p. 119.
16. Coburn, *Devī-Māhātmya,* pp. 227–229
17. Coburn, *Devī-Māhātmya,* p. 120.
18. Brian Hayden, "An Archeological Evaluation of the Gimbutas Paradigm," *The Pomegranate* 6 (1998): 38–39.
19. Kenoyer, *Ancient Cities*, pp. 114–115.
20. Coburn, *Devī-Māhātmya,* p. 222.
21. Coburn, *Encountering the Goddess,* p. 24.
22. Coburn, *Devī-Māhātmya,* p. 249.
23. Coburn, *Devī-Māhātmya,* p. 120 n. 19.
24. Coburn, *Devī-Māhātmya,* pp. 275–281.
25. Thomas B. Coburn, "Devī, The Great Goddess," in *Devī: Goddesses of India,* John Stratton Hawley and Donna Marie Wulff, eds. (Berkeley and Los Angeles: University of California Press, 1996), p. 41.
26. Coburn, *Devī-Māhātmya*, pp. 267–275.
27. Coburn, *Devī-Māhātmya*, p. 221.
28. Coburn, *Encountering the Goddess,* p. 24.
29. Cynthia Ann Humes, "Vindhyavāsinī" in *Devi: Goddesses of India,* John Stratton Hawley and Donna Marie Wulff, eds. (Berkeley: University of California Press, 1996), p. 49.
30. Humes, "Vindhyavāsinī," pp. 51–52.
31. N. N. Bhattacharyya, *The Indian Mother Goddess,* 3rd enlarged ed. (New Delhi: Manohar Publishers, 1999), p. 63.
32. Humes, "Vindhyavāsinī," p. 57.
33. David R. Kinsley, "Kālī: Blood and Death Out of Place," in *Devī: Goddesses of India,* Hawley and Wulff, eds., p. 78.
34. Kinsley, "Kālī," p. 78.
35. Coburn, *Devī-Māhātmya*, p. 111.
36. Coburn, *Devī-Māhātmya*, p. 325.
37. David Kinsley, *Hindu Goddesses: Visions of the Divine Feminine in the Hindu Religious Tradition* (Berkeley and Los Angeles: University of California Press, 1986), p. 156.
38. Coburn, *Devī-Māhātmya,* p. 325.
39. Kinsley, *Hindu Goddesses,* p. 159.
40. Coburn, *Devī-Māhātmya,* p. 325.
41. Kinsley, *Hindu Goddesses,* p. 159.
42. Kinsley, *Hindu Goddesses,* p. 160.
43. Ibid.
44. Agrawala, *Goddesses,* p. 136.
45. Kinsley, *Hindu Goddesses*, p. 155.
46. Coburn, *Encountering the Goddess,* p. 154.

47. Coburn, *Encountering the Goddess,* p. 100.
48. Brown, *Triumph of the Goddess*, p. 137.
49. Coburn, *Devī-Māhātmya,* p. 101.
50. Coburn, *Encountering the Goddess,* p. 106.
51. Coburn, *Encountering the Goddess,* p. 108.
52. Coburn, *Encountering the Goddess,* p. 110.
53. Kinsley, *The Goddesses' Mirror*, p. 14.
54. C. Mackenzie Brown, *The Devī Gītā: The Song of the Goddess: A Translation, Annotation, and Commentary* (Albany: State University of New York Press, 1998), p. 260 n. 2.
55. *Glory of the Mother* (Bombay: Central Chinmaya Mission Trust, 1991), p. 7.

**The Śri Durgāsaptaślokīstotra**

1. S. Shankaranarayanan, trans., *Glory of the Divine Mother (Devīmāhātmyam),* 2nd ed. (Pondicherry: Dipti Publications, 1973), p. 77.

## PART II: COMMENTARY NOTES

**Chapter 1**

1. Thomas B. Coburn, *Encountering the Goddess: A Translation of the Devī-Māhātmya and a Study of Its Interpretation* (Albany: State University of New York Press, 1991), pp. 112–114.
2. C. Mackenzie Brown, *The Devī Gītā: The Song of the Goddess* (Albany: State University of New York Press, 1998), pp. 65–66.
3. Coburn, *Encountering the Goddess,* p. 79.
4. Coburn, *Encountering the Goddess,* p. 95.
5. Coburn, *Encountering the Goddess,* p. 134.
6. Coburn, *Encountering the Goddess,* p. 133.
7. Brown, *The Devī Gītā,* p. 97 n. 6.
8. Coburn, *Encountering the Goddess,* pp. 134–135.
9. C. Mackenzie Brown, *The Triumph of the Goddess: The Canonical Models and Theological Visions of the Devī-Bhāgavata Purāṇa* (Albany: State University of New York Press, 1990), p. 137.
10. Thomas B. Coburn, *Devī-Māhātmya: The Crystallization of the Goddess Tradition* (Delhi: Motilal Banarsidass, 1984), pp. 130–131.
11. Brown, *The Devī Gītā,* p. 73.

**Chapter 2**

1. Sir John Woodroffe (Arthur Avalon), *Shakti and Shakta* (New York: Dover Publications, 1978), p. 224.
2. Brown, *The Devī Gītā*, pp. 97–98.
3. Coburn, *Devī-Māhātmya,* p. 230.
4. Coburn, *Devī-Māhātmya,* pp. 98–99.
5. Thomas B. Coburn, "Devī, The Great Goddess," in *Devī: Goddesses of India,* John Stratton Hawley and Donna Marie Wulff, eds. (Berkeley and Los Angeles: University of California Press, 1996), p. 40.

6. Sir Monier Monier-Williams, *A Sanskrit-English Dictionary* (Oxford: Oxford University Press, 1899), p. 83.

**Chapter 3**

1. Prithvi Kumar Agrawala, *Goddesses in Ancient India* (New Delhi: Abhinav Publications, 1984), p. 120.
2. Sarah Caldwell, "Bhagavati, Ball of Fire," in *Devī: Goddesses of India,* Hawley and Wulff, eds., p. 196.

**Chapter 4**

1. F. Eden Pargiter, trans., *The Mārkaṇḍeya Purāṇa* (Delhi and Varanasi: Indological Book House, 1995), p. 482.
2. Coburn, *Encountering the Goddess*, p. 48.
3. Coburn, *Devī-Māhātmya,* p. 167.
4. Coburn, *Devī-Māhātmya,* p. 158 n. 294.
5. Coburn, *Devī-Māhātmya,* p. 162.
6. Coburn, *Devī-Māhātmya,* p. 171.
7. Coburn, *Devī-Māhātmya,* p. 173.
8. John Bowker, ed., *The Oxford Dictionary of World Religions* (Oxford and New York: Oxford University Press, 1997), p. 487.
9. Woodroffe, *Shakti and Shakta*, p. 13.
10. Woodroffe, *Shakti and Shakta*, p. 478.
11. Woodroffe, *Shakti and Shakta*, p. 700.
12. Mahendranath Gupta (M.), *The Gospel of Sri Ramakrishna,* Swami Nikhilananda, trans. (New York: Ramakrishna-Vivekananda Center, 1942), pp. 499–500.
13. Swami Satprakashananda, *The Universe, God and God-Realization: From the Viewpoint of Vedanta* (St. Louis: Vedanta Society of St. Louis, 1977), p. 132.
14. Sir John Woodroffe, *The Garland of Letters: Studies in the Mantra-Śāstra,* 9th ed. (Pondicherry: Ganesh & Company, 1989), p. 30.
15. Satprakashananda, *The Universe*, p. 134.
16. Swami Prabhavananda, *The Eternal Companion: Brahmananda, Teachings and Reminiscences with a Biography,* 3rd rev. ed. (Hollywood, CA: Vedanta Press, 1970), p. 5.
17. Swāmī Jagadīśvarānanda, trans., *Devi Mahatmyam (Glory of the Divine Mother): Seven-Hundred Mantras on Sri Durga* (Mylapore, Madras: Sri Ramakrishna Math, 1969) p. 56 n. 7.
18. Satprakashananda, *The Universe*, p. 139.
19. Coburn, *Devī-Māhātmya,* p. 203.
20. Coburn, *Devī-Māhātmya,* p. 116.

**Chapter 5**

1. Coburn, *Devī-Māhātmya,* p. 222.
2. Coburn, *Devī-Māhātmya,* p. 239.
3. Cynthia Ann Humes, "Vindhyavāsinī: Local Goddess Yet Great Goddess," in *Devī: Goddesses of India,* Hawley and Wulff, eds., p. 68.

4. Coburn, *Devī-Māhātmya,* p. 232.
5. Humes, "Vindhyavāsinī," pp. 68–69.
6. Coburn, *Devī-Māhātmya,* p. 196.
7. T. V. Narayana Menon, *The Thousand Names of the Divine Mother: Śrī Lalitā Sahasranāma with Commentary,* N. M. Namboodiri, trans. (San Ramon, CA: Mata Amritanandamyai Center, 1996), p. 159.
8. Menon, *Thousand Names*, p. 159.
9. Coburn, *Devī-Māhātmya,* pp. 197–198.
10. Brown, *The Devī-Gītā,* p. 4.
11. Brown, *The Devī-Gītā,* p. 86.
12. Coburn, *Devī-Māhātmya,* pp. 174–175.
13. Agrawala, *Goddesses*, pp. 111–112.
14. Agrawala, *Goddesses*, p. 13.
15. Swami Siddhanathananda, trans., *Devi Mahatmyam (*Bombay: Bharatiya Vidya Bhavan, 1995), p. 159.
16. Coburn, *Devī-Māhātmya,* p. 273.
17. Coburn, *Devī-Māhātmya,* p. 280.
18. Coburn, *Devī-Māhātmya,* pp. 274–275.
19. Coburn, *Devī-Māhātmya,* p. 278.
20. Coburn, *Devī-Māhātmya,* p. 275.
21. Swami Satprakashananda, *Methods of Knowledge: Perceptual, Non-perceptual, and Transcendental, According to Advaita Vedanta* (London: George Allen & Unwin, 1965), 107.
22. Satprakashananda, *Methods of Knowledge*, p. 108.
23. Coburn, *Devī-Māhātmya,* p. 270.
24. Ajit Mookerjee, *Ritual Art of India* (New York: Thames & Hudson, 1985), p. 170.

**Chapter 6**

1. Swami Atmajnanananda, personal correspondence dated March 16, 1998.

**Chapter 7**

1. Gupta, *Gospel of Sri Ramakrishna*, p. 135.
2. Coburn, *Devī-Māhātmya,* pp. 135–136.
3. David Kinsley, *Hindu Goddesses: Visions of the Divine Feminine in the Hindu Religious Tradition* (Berkeley and Los Angeles: University of California Press, 1986), p. 148.
4. Coburn, *Encountering the Goddess,* pp. 136–137.

**Chapter 8**

1. Swami Harshananda, *Hindu Gods and Goddesses,* 2nd ed. (Mylapore, Madras: Sri Ramakrishna Math, 1982), p. xiv.
2. Harshananda, *Hindu Gods and Goddesses,* p. xiv.
3. Ibid.
4. Harshananda, *Hindu Gods and Goddesses,* p. 63.

5. Harshananda, *Hindu Gods and Goddesses,* p. 81.
6. Coburn, *Devī-Māhātmya,* pp. 132–133.
7. Coburn, *Devī-Māhātmya,* p. 186.
8. Coburn, *Devī-Māhātmya,* p. 325.
9. Coburn, *Devī-Māhātmya,* p. 232.
10. Harshananda, *Hindu Gods and Goddesses,* pp. 98–99.

**Chapter 9**

1. Coburn, *Encountering the Goddess,* pp. 102–103.
2. Pushpendra Kumar, *Sakti and Her Episodes: On the Basis of Ancient Indian Tradition and Mythology,* 2nd rev. ed. (Delhi: Eastern Book Linkers, 1986), p. 77.

**Chapter 10**

1. S. Shankaranarayanan, trans., *Glory of the Divine Mother,* 2nd ed. (Pondicherry: Dipti Publications, 1973), p. 6.

**Chapter 11**

1. Harshananda, *Hindu Gods and Goddesses,* p. 124.
2. Barbara Powell, *Windows into the Infinite: A Guide to the Hindu Scriptures* (Fremont, CA: Asian Humanities Press, 1996) p. 340.
3. Agrawala, *Goddesses*, pp. 62–63.
4. Swami Yatiswarananda, *Universal Prayers: Selected and Translated from Sanskrit Religious Literature* (Mylapore, Madras: Sri Ramakrishna Math, 1977), p. 141.
5. Pargiter, *The Mārkaṇḍeya Purāṇa*, p. 512.
6. Atmajnanananda, personal correspondence, March 16, 1998.
7. Powell, *Windows into the Infinite*, p. 334.
8. Woodroffe, *Shakti and Shakta,* p. 138.
9. Woodroffe, *Shakti and Shakta,* p. 171.
10. Mookerjee, *Ritual Art of India*, p. 37.
11. Coburn, *Devī-Māhātmya,* p. 107.
12. Coburn, *Devī-Māhātmya,* p. 264.
13. Harshananda, *Hindu Gods and Goddesses*, pp. 97–98.
14. Kinsley, *Hindu Goddesses,* pp. 67, 188.
15. Woodroffe, *Shakti and Shakta,* p 34.
16. Woodroffe, *Shakti and Shakta,* p 39.
17. Ralph T. H. Griffith, trans., *Hinduism: The Rig Veda* (New York: Book-of-the-Month Club, 1992), p. 3 n. 12.
18. Agrawala, *Goddesses*, p. 89.
19. Coburn, *Encountering the Goddess,* p. 139.
20. N. N. Bhattacharyya, *The Indian Mother Goddess,* 3rd enlarged ed. (New Delhi: Manohar Publications, 1999), p. 59.
21. Brown, *The Triumph of the Goddess, p.* 293 n. 17.
22. Kinsley, *Hindu Goddesses*, p. 161.

23. Kinsley, *Hindu Goddesses*, pp. 171–172.
24. Kinsley, *Hindu Goddesses*, p. 162.
25. Kinsley, *Hindu Goddesses*, p. 239 n. 23.
26. Kinsley, *Hindu Goddesses*, p. 143.

**Chapter 12**

1. Coburn, *Devi-Māhātmya*, p. 120.

## PART III: THE AṄGAS

**Devyāh Kavacam**

1. Swami Sarvadevananda, personal interview, August 7, 1999.
2. Swami Satprakashananda, *The Universe, God and God-Realization: From the Viewpoint of Vedanta* (St. Louis: Vedanta Society of St. Louis, 1977), pp. 122–123.

**Argalāṣtotra**

1. Thomas B. Coburn, *Encountering the Goddess: A Translation of the Devī-Māhātmya and a Study of Its Interpretation* (Albany: State University of New York Press, 1991), p. 107.

**Kīlakastotra**

1. Swami Satyananda Saraswati, *Chaṇḍī Pāṭh: She Who Tears Apart Thought* (Delhi: Motilal Banarsidass, 1995), 89.

**Rātrisūkta**

1. Thomas B. Coburn, *Devī-Māhātmya: The Crystallization of the Goddess Tradition* (Delhi: Motilal Banarsidass, 1984), pp. 265–266.
2. Sir John Woodroffe (Arthur Avalon), *Shakti and Shakta* (New York: Dover Publications, 1978), p. 110.
3. S. Shankaranarayanan, trans., *Glory of the Divine Mother (Devīmāhātmya)*, 2nd ed. (Pondicherry: Dipti Publications, 1973), p. 123.
4. Ibid.

**Devīsūkta**

1. Woodroffe, *Shakti and Shakta*, p. 110.
2. Huston Smith, *Essays on World Religion*, M. Darrol Bryant, ed. (New York: Paragon House, 1992), pp. 135–153.
3. Vasudeva S. Agrawala, *Devī-Māhātmyam: The Glorification of the Great Goddess* (Ramnagar, Varanasi: All-India Kashiraj Trust, 1963), p. 226.
4. Agrawala, *Devī-Māhātmyam*, p. 231.
5. Sarvadevananda, personal interview, August 7, 1999.

**Prādhānika Rahasya**

1. Coburn, *Encountering the Goddess*, p. 108.

2. Coburn, *Encountering the Goddess,* p. 109.

**Mūrtirahasya**

1. Narendra Nath Bhattacharyya, *History of the Śākta Religion* (New Delhi: Munshiram Manoharlal, 1996), pp. 15–16.

# GLOSSARY

**adharma**—unrighteousness; absence of virtue; that which reverses or is contrary to the divinely established order; the opposite of → dharma.*

**Aditi**—one of the most ancient goddesses of the → Ṛgveda. Her name, meaning "boundless" or "undivided," characterizes her as infinite consciousness and freedom and the inexhaustible source of the universe.

**advaita**—nondualism; the philosophical view that ultimate reality is an infinite and undifferentiated unity, that God, soul, and the universe are one.

**Advaita Vedānta**—the school of → Vedānta developed by → Śaṁkarācārya, who taught that → Brahman alone is real, and that the world, although experienced as real because of → māyā, is only an appearance. Advaita Vedānta views → ātman (the Self) and Brahman (the unity underlying all manifold appearance) as one.

**Ādyā Śakti**—the supreme reality according to → Śākta doctrine, corresponding to → Brahman; divine consciousness seen as the primal power.

**Agni**—the Vedic god of fire, who acts as the mediator between humans and the gods by conveying sacrifices through his sacred fire.

**ahaṁkāra**—literally "I-maker"; the ego, the consciousness of being a unique and separate entity which claims perceptions, emotions, and acts of will as its own.

**Aindrī**—the → śakti of → Indra; one of the → Saptamātṛkās. The Devīmāhātmya employs this name for Indra's feminine counterpart instead of the usual name, Indrāṇī, to emphasize the → Śākta understanding of goddess-as-power rather than goddess-as-consort.

**Alakṣmī**—misfortune personified as a goddess; the mirror-image of → Lakṣmī.

**Ambikā**—an affectionate name for the → Devī, frequently employed in the Devīmāhātmya and meaning "Mother."

**Āmbhṛṇī**—the female seer of the → Ṛgveda through whom the Devī → Vāk proclaims her own glory in the → Devīsūkta.

**aṅga**—"limb"; one of six texts (→ Kavaca, Argalāstotra, Kīlakastotra, Prādhānika Rahasya, Vaikṛtika Rahasya, Mūrtirahasya) appended to the Devīmāhātmya around the 14th century for ritual and exegetic purposes.

**anuṣṭubh**—the classic meter of Sanskrit epic and narrative poetry; the primary meter of the Devīmāhātmya. A verse (→ śloka) consists of four quarter-verses (→ pāda) of eight syllables each.

---

* An arrow (→) indicates a cross-reference within the glossary.

**Aparājitāstuti**—("Hymn to the Invincible Devī"); the third hymn of the Devīmāhātmya (5.9–82), which praises the Devi's immanence as consciousness abiding in various forms in all beings.

**Argalāstotra**—("Hymn of the Bolt"); the Devīmāhātmya's second → aṅga, consisting of a series of invocations requesting the Devī's assurance that ritual recitation will bring success.

**Ārya**—noble; the name applied to groups of Indo-European-speaking tribes who began entering India around 4500 BCE. Their dialects evolved into the Vedic, later Sanskrit, language. Some current scholars, especially in India, reject this ethnic definition and propose instead that the term designates the moral nobility of people whose lives exemplified the teachings of the → Vedas.

**asura**—a demon. In Hindu mythology, the battle between good and evil is often expressed as an allegorical war between gods and demons, who symbolize the divine and evil tendencies within human consciousness.

**ātman**—the true Self, identical with → Brahman, as distinct from the finite self or ego (→ ahaṁkāra).

**avatāra**—"descent"; the earthly manifestation or incarnation of a deity.

**āvaraṇa**—concealment; the veiling power of ignorance (→ avidyā) to conceal the boundless unity of the Absolute.

**avidyā**—ignorance, nescience. Avidyā is individual or cosmic ignorance, the non-knowing of → Brahman, or the inability to distinguish between the real and the unreal. Cosmic ignorance is also called → māyā.

**avidyāmāyā**—the aspect of → māyā that binds one to worldly existence. It produces entangling passions such as anger and greed. Māyā's other aspect, → vidyāmāyā, produces qualities such as kindness, purity, and selflessness, which lead to liberation. Both forms of māyā belong to the relative, phenomenal world.

**Bhadrakālī**—"the propitious Kālī"; an aspect of the Divine Mother associated with the blessing of the household.

**Bhagavadgītā**—("The Song of God"); a sacred text forming eighteen chapters (700 verses) of the sixth book of the → Mahābhārata and containing the teachings of Śrī → Kṛṣṇa to his disciple Arjuna on Self-realization through the paths of knowledge (→ jñāna), devotion (→ bhakti), selfless action, and meditation.

**Bhagavatī**—"the blessed one"; a name of the Divine Mother.

**bhakti**—devotion; love for one's chosen ideal of the divine, usually in the personalized form of a particular god or goddess.

**Bhāskararāya**—author of the → *Guptavatī,* the most important commentary on the Devīmāhātmya. Writing from the → Śākta perspective, Bhāskararāya (fl. late 17th to mid-18th century) understood the Devī as the supreme, nondual reality (→ advaita) and the manifest universe as her actual transformation (→ pariṇāma).

**Bhīmadevī**—a particularly terrible, but protective, form of the Devī, described in DM 11.51–52 and MR 18–19.

**Bhrāmarī**—the Devī in her bee-like form, described in DM 11.53–54 and MR 20–21.

**bhukti**—worldly enjoyment or, more broadly, worldly experience.

**bīja**—"seed"; a nonlexical, mystical symbol vibrating with the concentrated power of a particular deity or divine energy. In Tantric Hinduism, the bīja is the essential component of any → mantra.
**bindu**—concentrated → Śakti as the point of potentiality from which the material universe emanates at the time of creation and into which it collapses at the time of cosmic dissolution.
**Brahmā**—the creator god. He is the first in a triad (→ Trimūrti) with → Viṣṇu, the preserver, and → Śiva, the destroyer.
**Brahman**—the Absolute beyond all attributes, which is the immutable substratum of phenomenal existence; the impersonal ultimate reality transcending time and space.
**brāhmaṇa**—a member of the highest Hindu caste, which comprises priests and custodians of sacred knowledge. In the Devīmāhātmya, the seer → Medhas represents this caste.
**Brāhmaṇa**—a sacred text forming part of the → Vedas and primarily concerned with ritual practices and rules of conduct.
**Brahmāṇī**—the divine consort or → śakti of → Brahmā; in the Devīmāhātmya, she is one of the → Saptamātṛkās.
**Brahmāstuti**—("Brahmā's Hymn"); the first hymn of the Devīmāhātmya (1.73–87), addressed to the Devī's tamasic aspect, → Mahākālī, and concerned primarily with cosmogony.
**buddhi**—intellect, intelligence; the determinative faculty that categorizes and interprets sensory data and is responsible for reason and will. According to → Advaita Vedānta, buddhi is not conscious but merely reflects the consciousness of the ātman; in distinction, the Śākta philosophy considers buddhi a finite form of the infinite consciousness, veiled and limited by → māyā.
**Cāmuṇḍā**—a particularly terrible form of → Kālī, who slew the demons Caṇḍa and Muṇḍa (DM 7.6–27) and Raktabīja (DM 8.40–62). She represents the power of concentrated awareness and the awakening of spiritual consciousness.
**Caṇḍa**—together with Muṇḍa, one of Śumbha's flattering, scheming servants in the Devīmāhātmya's fifth through seventh chapters.
**Caṇḍī**—1. an alternate title of the Devīmāhātmya, common in Bengal. 2. a name of the Divine Mother, also → Caṇḍikā.
**Caṇḍikā**—"the violent, impetuous one"; after the name Devī itself, the Devīmāhātmya's most frequently employed name for the Divine Mother.
**Candra**—the Vedic god of the moon.
**carita**—one of the three divisions or episodes of the Devīmāhātmya, consisting of Chapter 1, Chapters 2–4, and Chapters 5–13. Literally, the term means "acts, deeds, behavior."
**daitya**—a demon, said to be the son of → Diti. In the Devīmāhātmya, the term is used interchangeably with → asura and → dānava.
**dānava**—a demon (→ asura, daitya).
**deva**—a god.
**Devī**—the supreme Goddess, who manifests in many forms and is known by many names. Among her principal forms are → Durgā, → Pārvatī and → Kālī.

**Devīsūkta**—an important hymn of the → Ṛgveda (ṚV 10.125) in which the Devī extols her own greatness. This hymn of eight verses is regarded by many Indian scholars as the source from which the entire Devīmāhātmya developed.
**dharma**—righteousness, virtue, morality; religious duty; truth; the order by which the universe is upheld.
**Dhūmralocana**—the thuggish demon chieftain sent by Śumbha to abduct the Devī, who instead is slain by her (DM 6.1–13).
**dhyāna**—1. meditation, the state in which the mind is fixed on its object, like the unbroken flow of oil from one vessel into another. 2. one of three texts that introduce each of the Devīmāhātmya's three → caritas, immediately preceding Chapters 1, 2, and 5.
**Diti**—the ancient earth goddess and mother of the → daityas. She represents the opposite of → Aditi.
**Durgā**—the primary deity of the Devīmāhātmya. Usually represented as ten-armed and riding upon a lion, Durgā is at once the warrior goddess who destroys evil, the fiercely protective yet infinitely compassionate mother, and the bestower of unconditional, all-redeeming grace.
**Durgāstava**—an early hymn to Durgā, found in MBh 4.5, important for containing numerous divine epithets and themes found later in the Devīmāhātmya.
**Durgāstotra**—a second hymn to Durgā, found in MBh 6.22 immediately before the → Bhagavadgītā. Recited by Arjuna on Kṛṣṇa's instruction for the sake of assuring victory in battle, the hymn contains themes and traditions that reappear throughout the Devīmāhātmya.
**Garuḍa**—the mythical half-man, half-bird that is the → vāhana of → Viṣṇu.
**Gaurī**—"the shining one, the white one"; a name of the Divine Mother.
**guṇa**—one of the three basic forces operative in the universe (→ sattva, rajas, tamas).
***Guptavatī***—("Confirming What Is Hidden"); the title of one of the most important commentaries on the Devīmāhātmya, written around 1741 by the great Tantric authority → Bhāskararāya.
**Harivaṁśa**—a later supplement to the → Mahābhārata, datable in part to as early as the second century BCE.
**Himālaya**—"abode of snow"; the Himālaya mountain range personified as the father of the goddesses → Pārvatī and Gaṅgā (the river Ganges).
**icchā**—the initial divine will to create, cooperative with → jñāna, the knowledge, and → kriyā, the action for doing so.
**Indra**—the supreme Vedic god; the lord of the atmosphere, revered as the giver of life-sustaining rain and feared as the all-powerful god of storms.
**Īśvara**—"Lord, Ruler, Sovereign"; the personal but formless God (→ sāguṇa Brahman) that is the human mind's highest possible understanding of the impersonal Absolute. According to → Vedānta, Īśvara is → Brahman united with → māyā and acts as the creator, preserver, and destroyer of the universe.
**Īśvarī**—(female) Sovereign. The term is often compounded, as in Parameśvarī ("Supreme Sovereign"), Māheśvarī ("Great Sovereign," the śakti of Śiva), Viśveśvarī ("Ruler of the Universe")—frequently employed epithets of the Devī.

**jagat**—"that which moves"; the world.
**japa**—repetition of a divine name or → mantra.
**jñāna**—knowledge; the direct experience of the transcendental Absolute.
**Kaiṭabha**—together with → Madhu, one of the two stupid, brutish demons of the Devīmāhātmya's first chapter.
**Kāla**—the Vedic god of time; time personified as the universal destroyer.
**kālarātri**—"dark night"; in Purāṇic cosmology, a period of cosmic nonmanifestation, lasting 4,320,000,000 human years, during which the universe remains in a state of potentiality. It alternates with an equally long period of cosmic manifestation, known as a day of Brahmā.
**Kālarātri**—the Divine Mother characterized as a solitary warrior and fulfiller of desires (MR 19).
**Kālī**—one of the most powerful and complex aspects of the Devī, representing primal energy or the dynamic aspect of ultimate reality. Often associated with the terrifying power of death and the relentlessness of all-devouring time, Kālī is also adored by her devotees as a loving mother.
**Kālikā**—another name of → Kālī.
**Kalyānī**—an aspect of the Devī signifying auspiciousness and beauty.
**karma**—any mental or physical act or the collective consequences of one's actions in the present and previous lives. Determining an individual's character and experience of joy and sorrow, karma operates as the law of cause and effect in the continuing cycle of birth, death, and rebirth.
**Kātyāyanī**—a name of the Divine Mother, associating her with the Kātyas, a venerated clan of Vedic sages.
**Kaumārī**—the śakti of the war god Kumāra (→ Skanda); one of the → Saptamātṛkās.
**Kauśikī**—an aspect of the Divine Mother, so named because she emerged from the body (kośa) of → Pārvatī (DM 5.85–87).
**Kavaca**—the first → aṅga associated with the Devīmāhātmya, more correctly called the Devyāḥ Kavacam ("Armor of the Devī"). It serves to invoke her protective energy throughout the body in preparation for the ritual recitation of the Devīmāhātmya.
**Kīlakastotra**—("Hymn of the Pin"); the Devīmāhātmya's third → aṅga, intended to remove the restraint put upon the text by Śiva and to grant access to its full power.
**kriyā**—the divine action by which the universe is created, following upon → icchā (divine will) and → jñāna (divine knowledge).
**Kṛṣṇa**—an → avatāra of → Viṣṇu and one of the most widely worshiped aspects of God in Hinduism. The → Bhagavadgītā contains his teachings to his disciple Arjuna.
**kṣatriya**—a member of the royal or warrior caste, represented in the Devīmāhātmya by → Suratha.
**Kubera**—the Vedic god of wealth.
**lakṣmī**—good fortune, prosperity, happiness, wealth, success, beauty, splendor.
**Lakṣmī**—an auspicious aspect of the Divine Mother as the goddess of prosperity and good fortune; the consort of → Viṣṇu.

**līlā**—the divine play by which the supreme deity creates the universe. The concept of līlā implies the freedom, joy, and inexhaustible creativity that pervade and direct the cosmic drama of the universe, which for the deity is pure sport.

**Madhu**—together with → Kaiṭabha, one of the two foolish demons of the Devīmāhātmya's first chapter.

**Mahābhārata**—the immense Hindu epic (and world's longest epic poem), comprising well over 100,000 verses and containing the → Bhagavadgītā. Ascribed to the sage Vyāsa, the Mahābhārata in fact took shape between the fifth century BCE and the second century CE. Divided into eighteen books, it is a vast and well-loved repository of spiritual knowledge, moral instruction, and cultural tradition.

**Mahākālī**—a powerful, cosmic aspect of the Divine Mother (→ vyaṣṭi) as the pure energy of → tamas; the presiding deity of the Devīmāhātmya's first → carita.

**Mahālakṣmī**—1. a powerful, cosmic aspect of the Divine Mother (→ vyaṣṭi) as the pure energy of → rajas; the presiding deity of the Devīmāhātmya's second → carita. 2. According to → Vaiṣṇava Tantric usage, the supreme (→ samaṣṭi, triguṇa) form of the Devī.

**Mahāmāyā**—the Divine Mother's deluding power, which causes the unitary, infinite consciousness to appear as the seemingly real, phenomenal universe.

**Mahāsarasvatī**—a powerful, cosmic aspect of the Divine Mother (→ vyaṣṭi) as the pure energy of → sattva; the presiding deity of the Devīmāhātmya's third → carita.

**māhātmya**—a literary composition extolling the majesty or exalted state of a deity, holy place, or object worthy of veneration.

**Māheśvarī**—the → śakti of Maheśvara (Śiva); one of the → Saptamātṛkās.

**Mahiṣāsura**—the primary demon of the Devīmāhātmya's second → carita; depicted as a buffalo that creates chaos on a cosmic scale, he is slain by → Durgā.

**Mahiṣāsuramardinī**—"the crusher of the buffalo demon"; a name of → Durgā.

**mamatā, mamatva**—"I-ness"; the sense of attachment that attends upon the ego.

**manas**—"mind," specifically, the mental organ that acts as a receptor of sensory data. According to → Sāṁkhya philosophy, manas, → ahaṁkāra, and → buddhi constitute the antaḥkāraṇa ("inner instrument").

**mantra**—a syllable, series of syllables, or a verse that embodies divine power, used in ritual and meditation; a name of a god or goddess, repeated as a form of spiritual practice designed to merge the individual's consciousness with the chosen deity.

**manu**—in mythology, a semi-divine progenitor of humanity and ruler over the earth for a period known as a → manvantara.

**Manusmṛti**—the Laws of Manu, a Sanskrit legal text dealing with the nature of good and evil, a woman's role in society, dietary regulations, political conduct, caste, → karma, and aspects of criminal, civil, and domestic law.

**manvantara**—in Purāṇic cosmology, a world-age. Fourteen manvantaras constitute a day of Brahmā (4,320,000,000 human years) or period of cosmic manifestation. Each manvantara is ruled by a particular → manu: the framing story of the Devīmāhātmya is set in the second manvantara (that of Svarociṣa), the present age is the seventh manvantara (that of Vaivasvata) and the eighth will be ruled by King → Suratha, reborn as the manu Sāvarṇi (13.22–23, 28–29).

**Mārkaṇḍeyapurāṇa**—an early → Purāṇa containing the teachings of the sage Mārkaṇḍeya on the history of the world during past and future → manvantaras. Chapters 81–93 constitute the Devīmāhātmya.
**mātṛgaṇa**—"band of mothers"; another name for → the Saptamātṛkās.
**māyā**—the veiling or deluding power of the Absolute, responsible for the appearance of the relative, phenomenal universe. The → Vedānta philosophy pairs the terms → Brahman and māyā to denote the Absolute and its inseparable power; with shades of philosophical difference, Sāṁkhya calls these puruṣa and → prakṛti, and Śākta doctrine calls them → Śiva and → Śakti.
**Medhas**—the sage in the Devīmāhātmya, who as the teacher to → Suratha and → Samādhi, relates the three tales of the Devī's battles with the demons.
**moha**—delusion; the finitization of consciousness that causes one to take appearance for reality.
**mukti**—release; final liberation from the limitations of body, mind, and worldly bondage through knowledge of the ultimate reality, or union with the Divine.
**Muṇḍa**—one of Śumbha's two demon servants (→ Caṇḍa) in the Devīmāhātmya's fifth through seventh chapters.
**Mūrtirahasya**—("The Secret Relating to Forms"); the sixth of the Devīmāhātmya's → aṅgas, which elaborates upon the Devī's predicted manifestations in DM 11.40–55.
**Nanda**—the cowherd into whose family the Devī was born as → Vindhyavāsinī, and who became the foster father of → Kṛṣṇa.
**Nārasiṁhī**—the śakti of Narasiṁha, the man-lion incarnation of → Viṣṇu; one of the → Saptamātṛkās.
**Nārāyaṇī**—the śakti of → Viṣṇu, who is also known as Nārāyaṇa.
**Nārāyaṇīstuti**—("Hymn to Nārāyaṇī"); the fourth hymn of the Devīmāhātmya (11.3–35), which presents a comprehensive summation of → Śākta theology. Emphasizing the Devī's motherhood, sovereignty, and protective intervention in human affairs, the hymn praises her various aspects, including the → Saptamātṛkās.
**Navarātri**—the great autumn festival in honor of → Durgā and her victory over evil. (A spring Navarātri similarly commemorates Rāma's defeat of the demon Rāvaṇa.)
**Navārṇamantra**—a Tantric mantra of great importance in the worship of the Devī. According to the commentator → Bhāskararāya, it is an appeal for her to undo the knot of ignorance that precludes the individual's knowledge of oneness with the Absolute.
**nirguṇa**—without qualities, in distinction to → saguṇa, with qualities.
**nirguṇa Brahman**—the impersonal Absolute, which transcends time and space and is beyond all thought; the supreme reality.
**Nirṛti**—an abstract, but nevertheless dreaded, Vedic goddess whose name means "decay" and who personifies adversity, calamity, disease, and death.
**nirvāṇa**—extinction of the individual self; enlightenment; transcendental bliss.
**Niśumbha**—the younger brother of → Śumbha and one of the two main demons of the Devīmāhātmya's third → carita. He represents the ego's sense of attachment.
**nitya**—eternal. The term carries the connotation of permanence and immutability.

**Oṁ**—the → bīja or sound-symbol of → Brahman. Representing both the impersonal Absolute (→ nirguṇa Brahman) and the personal divinity (→ Īśvara, saguṇa Brahman), Oṁ is the creative Word which produces all manifestation.

**pāda**—in Sanskrit prosody, a quarter-verse or half-line of poetry.

**pāramārthika**—according to → Advaita Vedānta, the category of the absolutely real, which is the changeless → Brahman.

**pariṇāma**—transformation, change. Pariṇāmavāda is the doctrine, accepted by the adherents of → Śākta philosophy, that the phenomenal universe is an actual transformation of divinity and not a mere appearance (→ vivarta). It teaches that the effect exists potentially within the cause and that creation is a transformation from potentiality to actuality.

**Pārvatī**—the Divine Mother as → Śiva's auspicious consort.

**Paśupati**—"Lord of Beasts"; a name usually applied to → Śiva.

**Patañjali**—the philosopher who systematized a science of meditation in his → Yogasūtra in the second or third century BCE.

**phalaśruti**—a literary composition that details the benefits of reciting or hearing a sacred text; the form of the Devīmāhātmya's twelfth chapter.

**Prādhānika Rahasya**—("The Secret Relating to Primary Matter"); the Devīmāhātmya's fourth → aṅga, concerned with the philosophical question of how the One manifests as the many.

**Prajāpati**—"Lord of Creatures"; a name applied to various deities. In the Devīmāhātmya, it refers to Brahmā.

**prakṛti**—the primal "nature" or "matter" of the universe. Prakṛti should be thought of as a dynamic process, which manifests all the names and forms within creation. Technically, the term belongs to the → Sāṁkhya system of philosophy, but it is used more or less synonymously with → māyā and → śakti.

**prātibhāsika**—according to → Advaita Vedānta, the category of appearance or unreality.

**Pṛthivī**—the earth, personified as a goddess in the → Vedas and often evoked in connection with Dyaus (heaven).

**pūjā**—ritual worship, designed to connect the worshiper with the Divine.

**Purāṇa**—a class of Hindu scriptures with a strongly devotional outlook. Containing myths and legends of gods and goddesses, kings, sages, and devotees, the Purāṇas are a vast repository of popular Hindu religion and cultural tradition.

**rajas**—one of the three → guṇas or basic energies of the universe. Rajas is activity, manifesting as restlessness, impurity, urgency, and passion. It is symbolized by the color red.

**Raktabīja**—one of the major demons of the Devīmāhātmya, appearing in the eighth chapter (8.40–63). His name, "he whose seed is blood," denotes an amazing replicative ability that symbolizes the insatiability of desire or, on a deeper level, the untamed thought-waves (→ vṛtti) within the mind.

**Raktadantikā**—a completely red manifestation of the Devī, predicted in the Devīmāhātmya (11.43–45) as the destroyer of evil and further defined in the Mūrtirahasya (MR 4–11) as beneficent and protective.

**Rāmakṛṣṇa, Śrī**—an Indian holy man (1836–1886) and priest of Kālī at the Dakśineśvar temple. The Ramakrishna Math and Mission, a monastic order founded by his disciples in 1887, presents a revitalized vision of → Vedānta to the modern world, teaches the inherent divinity of humankind and the harmony of all religions, and carries out extensive social work as worship of God through service to one's fellow human beings.

**Rātrisūkta**—("Hymn to Night"); an ancient hymn of the → Ṛgveda (ṚV 10.127), praising the deified night as the goddess Rātri. Underlying its exquisite natural imagery is the implication that she is the substratum and mother of creation.

**Ṛgveda**—the oldest and largest of the four → Vedas, its → saṁhitā portion containing 1,028 hymns in ten books (*maṇḍalas*). Composed in archaic Sanskrit, probably over hundreds of years, most of the hymns address deities who are personifications of natural forces, but the texts can be interpreted as allegories conveying deeper knowledge. Some of the later hymns rise to rarefied heights of metaphysical inquiry. Customarily, Western scholars date the Ṛgveda Saṁhitā to 1500–1200 BCE, but recent research, combined with internal evidence from the texts, supports the traditional Hindu claim of far greater antiquity.

**ṛta**—truth, law, order; the eternal principle of cosmic and moral order at work in the universe, also linked in the → Vedas with natural order, such as the passage of the seasons (*ṛtu*). Ṛta anticipates the doctrine of → karma and generally is replaced by → dharma in later Sanskrit texts.

**Rudra**—a Vedic storm god, associated with agricultural fertility but more often with destruction. In post-Vedic times he became identified with → Śiva.

**saccidānanda**—being-consciousness-bliss (sat-cit-ānanda); a threefold epithet attempting to describe the unitary, indescribable → Brahman.

**sādhana**—spiritual practice; in Tantra, a prescribed path leading to liberation (→ mukti) through worship (→ pūjā), → mantra repetition (→ japa), and meditation (→ dhyāna).

**saguṇa**—with qualities, the opposite of → nirguṇa.

**saguṇa Brahman**—the Absolute associated with → māyā and personified as → Īśvara.

**Śaiva**—referring to the theistic tradition that regards → Śiva as the supreme being. The Śaiva tradition may be non-Vedic in origin, and it tends to be more ascetic and oriented toward → jñāna than the → Vaiṣṇava.

**Śākambharī**—a nurturing manifestation of the Devī as the earth itself, described in the Devīmāhātmya (11.46–50) and Mūrtirahasya (MR 12–17).

**Śakrādistuti**—("Praise by Indra and the Other Gods"); the second hymn of the Devīmāhātmya (4.3–27). Eloquent and philosophically profound, it views the Devī as the ultimate reality, the creator, the fierce defender of → dharma, and the Divine Mother who grants universal redemption through her unconditional love.

**Śākta**—1. referring to the tradition that centers on the worship of → Śakti, the supreme power and ultimate reality, conceptualized as the Divine Mother who creates, sustains, and dissolves the universe. Śākta religion originated in pre- and non-Vedic goddess cults and eventually became assimilated to the Vedic tradition. 2. an adherent of the Śākta religion.

**śakti**—1. power, energy, ability. 2. the individual power of a god, usually represented as his female counterpart. 3. a spear.
**Śakti**—the supreme being according to the → Śākta tradition; consciousness in its dynamic, creative aspect, in distinction to → Śiva, its static aspect as the ground of existence. The two, seemingly different, are ultimately nondifferent aspects of the indivisible ultimate unity, the transcendent → Ādyā Śakti. Śakti assumes all the forms in the universe and is worshiped devotionally as the Divine Mother in many manifestations, among them → Kālī and → Durgā.
**samādhi**—total absorption in the object of meditation. The highest samādhi, called nirvikalpa samādhi, is the transcendental consciousness or identity with the impersonal Absolute.
**Samādhi**—the dispossessed merchant in the Devīmāhātmya, so named because his dispassion to the world leads him, through the Divine Mother's grace, to → samādhi and liberation.
**samaṣṭi**—aggregate; the samaṣṭi form of the Devī is her supreme aspect from which the three → vyaṣṭi or → guṇa forms proceed.
**saṁhitā**—"collection"; the initial portion of each of the four → Vedas, consisting of hymns to the deities.
**Śaṁkarācārya**—one of India's greatest philosophers and saints and the primary exponent of → Advaita Vedānta. In addition to important devotional hymns, Śaṁkarācārya (788–820), or simply Śaṁkara, composed numerous philosophical works and commentaries representing the pinnacle of nondualistic thought.
**Sāṁkhya**—one of six orthodox schools of Hindu philosophy, attributed to the sage Kapila and dating to before 500 BCE. Sāṁkhya is dualistic, teaching that the universe comes into being through the union of puruṣa (conscious spirit) and prakṛti (unconscious, primordial matter), which are two eternal principles.
**saṁsāra**—the ever-repeating cycle of birth, death, and rebirth, perpetuated by → karma.
**saṁskāra**—an impression created in an individual's consciousness by a thought or action in the present or a previous life, collectively forming one's character.
**Saptamātṛkās**—"Seven Little Mothers"; individualized, generally fierce manifestations of the Devī's power (→ śakti), whom the Devīmāhātmya identifies as → Brahmāṇī, → Māheśvarī, → Kaumārī, → Vaiṣṇavī, → Vārāhī, → Nārasiṁhī, and → Aindrī.
**Sarasvatī**—an auspicious form of the Divine Mother as the goddess of knowledge and creativity and the consort of → Brahmā. Originally a deified river, Sarasvatī is one of the most ancient Hindu goddesses, understood on a deeper level as the flow of consciousness itself. In early times she became identified with → Vāk.
**Śarvāṇī**—the Devī as → Śiva's consort in her destructive aspect, presiding over cosmic dissolution.
**Śatākṣī**—"hundred-eyed"; a manifestation of the Devī also called → Śākambharī (DM 11.46–50 and MR 12–17).
**sattva**—one of the three → guṇas or basic energies of the universe; the Devī's revealing power. Sattva is repose, manifesting as light, calmness, purity, goodness, and wisdom. It is symbolized by the color white.

**Sāvitrī**—the wife of Brahmā, considered the mother of the Vedas.

**Śeṣa**—the seven-headed serpent upon whom → Viṣṇu rests on the primordial ocean during periods of cosmic nonmanifestation.

**Śiva**—God in his aspect as destroyer, the third member of the → Trimūrti. For the → Śaivas, he is the supreme reality, the Great God (Mahādeva) who embodies compassion and renunciation and grants the liberating knowledge of the individual's identity with the Absolute. For the → Śāktas, Śiva is the static ground of all being, inseparable and ultimately nondifferent from → Śakti, the dynamic creative energy.

**Śivadūtī**—"she whose messenger is Śiva"; the Devī's own fierce → śakti, so named because she sent → Śiva as her messenger to → Śumbha and → Niśumbha (DM 8.22–28).

**Skanda**—the son of → Śiva and god of war, also known as Kārttikeya and Kumāra, the latter characterized as a chaste youth.

**śloka**—a stanza of Sanskrit poetry; the name of the epic meter, also called → anuṣṭubh.

**śraddhā**—faith. In the Hindu understanding, śraddhā does not mean unquestioning acceptance but implies trust, expectation, and a reciprocity between the human and the Divine.

**Śraddhā**—faith (→ śraddhā) personified as a goddess.

**śrī**—1. light, luster, radiance, splendor, glory, beauty, prosperity, good fortune, auspiciousness. 2. a quality of inner radiance or splendor attributed to a god or goddess in the → Ṛgveda.

**Śrī**—the quality of → śrī personified as a goddess, later identified with → Lakṣmī.

**Śrī Durgāsaptaśati**—("Seven Hundred Verses to Śrī Durgā"); an alternate title of the Devīmāhātmya.

**Śrīsūkta**—an important hymn appended to the → Ṛgveda in late Vedic times and the earliest known text to celebrate Vedic → Śrī and non-Vedic → Lakṣmī as one and the same goddess.

**Sugrīva**—Śumbha's messenger, who delivered a proposal of marriage to the Devī (DM 5.102–129).

**Śumbha**—the central demon of the Devīmāhātmya's third → carita, symbolizing the human ego; the older brother of → Niśumbha, who represents attachment.

**Suratha**—the deposed king who, together with the merchant → Samādhi, becomes a disciple of the seer → Medhas and receives his teachings.

**Sūrya**—the Vedic sun god, who is extremely brilliant and rides across the sky in a chariot drawn by seven horses. His light, shining like a jewel in the sky, produces the day and energizes all living beings.

**sūtra**—"thread"; an aphorism or set of aphorisms that contains philosophical teaching in compressed form and requires elaboration to make it comprehensible. The six schools of Hindu philosophy originally transmitted their teachings in sūtra form, an example being the → Yogasūtra of → Patañjali.

**svadhā**—a → mantra uttered when an oblation to departed ancestors is poured into the sacrificial fire, sometimes personified as the goddess Svadhā.

**svāhā**—a → mantra uttered when an oblation to the gods is poured into the sacrificial fire, sometimes personified as the goddess Svāhā.

**tamas**—one of the three → guṇas or basic energies of the universe; the Ḍevī's concealing power. Tamas is inertia, manifesting as darkness, heaviness, dullness, ignorance, error, and negativity. It is symbolized by the color black.

**Tantra**—1. the non-Vedic, often esoteric, element of Hindu tradition, which centers on divine power, usually seen as feminine (→ Śakti, Śākta), and prescribes spiritual practices (→ sādhana) and ritual as the means to liberation. 2. any of a group of sacred texts that transmit such teaching, cast in the form of a dialogue between → Śiva and the → Devī.

**tejas**—fiery brilliance; in the Devīmāhātmya, the Divine Mother's own radiance that emerged from the bodies of the gods and united in the form of → Durgā (2.9–19).

**triguṇa**—characterized by the three → guṇas: → sattva, → rajas and → tamas.

**Trimūrti**—the representation of → Īśvara as three gods in one, → Brahmā symbolizing → rajas or creative passion, → Viṣṇu symbolizing → sattva or sustaining goodness, and → Śiva symbolizing → tamas or the energy of cosmic dissolution. With Brahmā's diminished importance in post-Vedic theism, the threefold activity was ascribed entirely to → Viṣṇu, → Śiva or the → Devī by their respective devotees.

**upādhi**—limiting adjunct, association, attribute; a term employed by → Vedānta to denote any object, quality, or circumstance from which the ego forms a sense of personal identity.

**Upaniṣad**—a text belonging to the final, philosophical portion of the → Vedas. Recording the spiritual truths revealed to sages in ancient times through the direct experience of transcendental consciousness, the Upaniṣads proclaim the identity of → ātman (the Self) and → Brahman (ultimate reality). The principal Upaniṣads are the Īśa, Kena, Kaṭha, Praśna, Muṇḍaka, Māṇḍūkya, Chāndogya, Bṛhadāraṇyaka, Aitareya, Taittirīya, Kauṣītaki, and Śvetāśvatara. They date to before 400 BCE, and the earliest are of great antiquity.

**vāk**—speech, voice, language; the primal creative force or Word, roughly analogous to the ancient Greek and early Christian Logos.

**Vāk**—the Vedic goddess of creative speech, later identified with → Sarasvatī and → Durgā. In the Ṛgveda, she lauds herself in a first-person hymn, the → Devīsūkta.

**vāhana**—the mount or vehicle of a deity, revealing an aspect of that god or goddess's power. For example, → Durgā rides upon a lion, symbolizing → dharma.

**Vaikṛtika Rahasya**—("The Secret Relating to Transformation"), the Devīmāhātmya's fifth → aṅga, concerned with the subsequent modifications of divine consciousness after initial differentiation.

**Vaiṣṇava**—referring to the theistic tradition that regards → Viṣṇu as the supreme being and centers its worship primarily on his incarnations as Rāma and → Kṛṣṇa.

**Vaiṣṇavī**—the → śakti of → Viṣṇu; one of the → Saptamātṛkās.

**vaiṣya**—a member of the mercantile and agricultural caste, represented in the Devīmāhātmya by the merchant → Samādhi.

**Vārāhī**—the → śakti of Varāha or → Viṣṇu in his boar incarnation; one of the Saptamātṛkās.

**Varuṇa**—one of the oldest Vedic gods, personifying the all-encompassing firmament. Often associated with clouds, water, and the ocean, Varuṇa presides over the starry night, watching humanity with a thousand eyes. His function as the lord of → ṛta is to preserve cosmic and moral order.

**Vasus**—a group of eight Vedic gods who serve → Indra and personify the waters, the Pole Star, the moon, the earth, wind, fire, light, and dawn.

**Vāyu**—the Vedic god of the wind, who rides in a chariot driven by → Indra.

**Vedas**—the most ancient and authoritative Hindu texts and probably the world's oldest sacred literature. There are four Vedas: Ṛk (→ Ṛgveda), Sāma, Yajus and Atharva. Each consists of four divisions: → Saṁhitā (collected hymns), Brāhmaṇas (texts concerned primarily with ritual), Āraṇyakas (reinterpretations of external ritual as internal spiritual practice), and → Upaniṣads (the philosophical essence of the Vedas).

**Vedānta**—one of the six orthodox schools of Hindu philosophy, systematized from the teachings of the → Upaniṣads and codified in the Vedāntasūtra (Brahmasūtra) of Bādarāyaṇa, dated to between the fifth and first centuries BCE. Subsequently, distinct branches of Vedānta developed, including the strictly nondual → Advaita Vedānta of → Śaṁkarācārya.

**vidyā**—knowledge; a term often used interchangeably with → jñāna.

**vidyāmāyā**—that aspect of → māyā that leads toward knowledge and liberation, as opposed to → avidyāmāyā, which produces the bondage of ego-consciousness.

**vikṛti**—change, alteration, modification; the transformation by which the formless, unitary consciousness manifests as the multiple forms of the phenomenal universe.

**vikṣepa**—the power by which → māyā or → avidyā projects the manifold experience of the universe, often mentioned in connection with → āvaraṇa.

**Vindhyavāsinī**—"dweller in the Vindhya [Mountains]"; an aspect of the Devī, identified with → Mahāmāyā, who figures in the birth narrative of Śrī → Kṛṣṇa, in the Devīmāhātmya (11.41–42) and in the Mūrtirahasya (MR 1–3).

**Viṣṇu**—God in his aspect as preserver, the second member of the → Trimūrti. For members of the → Vaiṣṇava devotional sect, he is the supreme god, who incarnates in every age as the guardian of → dharma to deliver humanity from ignorance and evil.

**Viṣṇumāyā**—an epithet of the Devī expressing her nature as the supreme being's inscrutable power.

**viśva**—"all"; a word used to signify the universe.

**Viśvakarman**—a Vedic god and aspect of Brahmā as architect of the world. His name means "maker of all [this universe]," and he is represented as four-headed, holding prayer beads, book, the sacred kuśa grass, and ascetic's waterpot in his four hands, and riding upon a swan.

**vivarta**—appearance, apparent change. Vivartavāda is the doctrine, advanced by Śaṁkarācārya, that the phenomenal universe is only an apparant superimposition (adhyāsa) on the changeless reality of → Brahman. This view contrasts with the doctrine of → pariṇāma, favored by → Śākta philosophy, which regards the universe as an actual transformation of divine consciousness and therefore another aspect of reality.

**Vṛtra**—a demon in the → Ṛgveda who withheld life-giving water from the earth until his strongholds, the clouds, were breached by → Indra, whose thunderbolt released the rain. The Devīmāhātmya attributes Vṛtra's defeat to Indra's → śakti, → Aindrī (11.19).

**vṛtti**—activity, movement; more specifically, a modification or wave in the mind through which knowledge of the objective world becomes possible. Vṛttis can be positive thoughts that lead toward truth, or restless, distracting, and negative thoughts that deepen ignorance and bondage. According to → Patañjali, one should strive consciously to replace negative vṛttis with positive ones and then go beyond either to the attainment of unmodified, transcendental consciousness.

**vyaṣṭi**—the specific individuality of the Devī's three cosmic → guṇa aspects, personified as → Mahākālī, → Mahālakṣmī and → Mahāsarasvatī. The vyaṣṭis proceed from the supreme Devī's undifferentiated → samaṣṭi form.

**vyāvahārika**—empirical; the term used by → Śaṁkarācārya to denote the world of our experience, which is neither absolutely real (→ pāramārthika) nor wholly illusory (→ prātibhāsika).

**Yama**—the Vedic god of death, whose name literally means "restraint."

**Yaśodā**—the wife of the cowherd → Nanda, → Kṛṣṇa's foster mother, and the earthly mother of → Vindhyavāsinī.

**Yoganidrā**—the Devī personified as the mystic sleep of → Viṣṇu during periods of universal dissolution.

**Yogasūtra**—the classic text on the science of meditation, attributed to → Patañjali.

# BIBLIOGRAPHY


Agrawala, Prithvi Kumar. *Goddesses in Ancient India.* New Delhi: Abhinav Publications, 1984.

Agrawala, Vasudeva S. *Devī-Māhātmyam: The Glorification of the Great Goddess.* Ramnagar, Varanasi: All-India Kashiraj Trust, 1963.

Bahn, Paul G., ed. *The Cambridge Illustrated History of Archaeology.* Cambridge: Cambridge University Press, 1996.

Bandyopadhyay, Pranab. *Gods and Goddesses in Hindu Mythology.* Calcutta: United Writers, 1995.

Bhattacharyya, Narendra Nath. *History of the Śākta Religion.* New Delhi: Munshiram Manoharlal, 1996.

———. *The Indian Mother Goddess.* 3rd enlarged ed. New Delhi: Manohar Publishers, 1999.

Bowker, John, ed. *The Oxford Dictionary of World Religions.* Oxford and New York: Oxford University Press, 1997.

Brooks, Douglas Renfrew. *The Secret of the Three Cities: An Introduction to Hindu Śākta Tantrism.* Chicago and London: University of Chicago Press, 1990.

Brown, C. Mackenzie. *The Devī Gītā: The Song of the Goddess: A Translation, Annotation, and Commentary.* Albany: State University of New York Press, 1998.

———. *The Triumph of the Goddess: The Canonical Models and Theological Visions of the "Devī-Bhāgavata Purāṇa."* Albany: State University of New York Press, 1990.

Bryant, Edwin. *The Quest for the Origins of Vedic Culture: The Indo-Aryan Migration Debate.* Oxford: Oxford University Press, 2001.

Chakrabarti, Dilip K. *The Archaeology of Ancient Indian Cities.* Delhi: Oxford University Press, 1997.

Coburn, Thomas B. *Devī-Māhātmya· The Crystallization of the Goddess Tradition.* Delhi: Motilal Banarsidass, 1988.

———. *Encountering the Goddess: A Translation of the Devī-Māhātmya and a Study of Its Interpretation.* Albany: State University of New York Press, 1991.

Dhawan, Savitri. *Mother Goddesses in Early Indian Religion.* Jaipur and New Delhi: National Publishing House, 1997.

Fagan, Brian M. *The Oxford Companion to Archaeology.* New York and Oxford: Oxford University Press, 1996.

Feuerstein, Georg. *Tantra: The Path of Ecstasy.* Boston and London: Shambala, 1998.

Gambhīrānanda, Swāmī, trans. *Eight Upaniṣads: With the Commentary of Śaṅkarācārya.* 2 vols. 2nd rev. ed. Calcutta: Advaita Ashrama, 1989.

*Glory of the Mother.* Bombay: Central Chinmaya Mission Trust, 1991.

Greer, John Michael. "Myth, History and Pagan Origins." *The Pomegranate* 9: 44–50.

Griffith, Ralph T. H., trans. *Hinduism: The Rig Veda.* Sacred Writings, vol. 5. New York: Book-of-the-Month Club, 1992.

Grimes, John. *A Concise Dictionary of Indian Philosophy: Sanskrit Terms Defined in English.* Albany: State University of New York Press, 1989.

Gupta, Mahendranath (M.). *The Gospel of Sri Ramakrishna.* Translated by Swami Nikhilananda. New York: Ramakrishna-Vivekananda Center, 1942.

Harding, Elizabeth U. *Kali: The Black Goddess of Dakshineswar.* York Beach, ME: Nicolas-Hays, 1993.

Harshananda, Swami. *Hindu Gods and Goddesses.* 2nd ed. Mylapore, Madras: Sri Ramakrishna Math, 1982.

Hawley, John Stratton and Donna Marie Wulff, eds. *Devī, Goddesses of India.* Berkeley and Los Angeles: University of California Press, 1996.

Hayden, Brian. "An Archaeological Evaluation of the Gimbutas Paradigm." *The Pomegranate* 6: 35–46.

Jacobson, Jerome, ed. *Studies in the Archaeology of India and Pakistan.* New Delhi: Oxford & IBH Publishing Co., 1986.

Jagadīśvarānanda, Swāmī, trans. *The Bṛhadāraṇyaka Upaniṣad.* Revised by Swāmī Mādhavānanda. 2nd ed. Mylapore, Madras: Sri Ramakrishna Math, 1951.

———. *Devi Mahatmyam (Glory of the Divine Mother): Seven-Hundred Mantras on Sri Durga.* Mylapore, Madras: Sri Ramakrishna Math, 1969.

Jansen, Eva Rudy. *The Book of Hindu Imagery: Gods, Manifestations and Their Meaning.* Translated by Tony Langham. Havelte, Netherlands: Binkey Kok, 1993.

Jyotirmayananda, Swami. *Mysticism of the Devi Mahatmya: Worship of the Divine Mother.* South Miami: Yoga Research Foundation, 1994.

Kenoyer, Jonathan Mark. *Ancient Cities of the Indus Valley Civilization.* Karachi: Oxford University Press, American Institute of Pakistan Studies, 1998.

———. "Birth of a Civilization." *Archaeology,* January-February 1998: 54–61.

Kinsley, David. *The Goddesses' Mirror: Visions of the Divine from East and West.* Albany: State University of New York Press, 1989.

———. *Hindu Goddesses: Visions of the Divine Feminine in the Hindu Religious Tradition.* Berkeley and Los Angeles: University of California Press, 1986.

Kumar, Pushpendra. *Sakti and Her Episodes: On the Basis of Ancient Indian Tradition and Mythology.* 2nd rev. ed. Delhi: Eastern Book Linkers, 1986.

Lahiri, Nayanjot, ed. *The Decline and Fall of the Indus Civilization.* Delhi: Permanent Black, 2000.

Lal, B. B. *India 1947–1997: New Light on the Indus Civilization.* New Delhi: Aryan Books International, 1998.

Mallory, J. P. *In Search of the Indo-Europeans: Language, Archaeology and Myth.* London: Thames & Hudson, 1989.

Menon, T. V. Narayana. *The Thousand Names of the Divine Mother: Śrī Lalitā Sahasranāma with Commentary.* Translated by N. M. Namboodir. San Ramon, CA: Mata Amritanandamyai Center, 1996.

Monier-Williams, Sir Monier. *A Sanskrit-English Dictionary.* Oxford: Oxford University Press, 1899.

Mookerjee, Ajit. *Ritual Art of India.* New York: Thames & Hudson, 1985.

Nikhilananda, Swami, trans. *The Upanishads.* 4 vols. 4th ed. New York: Ramakrishna-Vivekananda Center, 1977.

Pargiter, F. Eden, trans. *The Mārkaṇḍeya Purāṇa.* Delhi and Varanasi: Indological Book House, 1995.

Pintchman, Tracy. *The Rise of the Goddess in the Hindu Tradition.* Albany: State University of New York Press, 1994.

Powell, Barbara. *Windows into the Infinite: A Guide to the Hindu Scriptures.* Fremont, CA: Asian Humanities Press, 1996.

Prabhavananda, Swami. *The Eternal Companion: Brahmananda,Teachings and Reminiscences with a Biography.* 3rd rev. ed. Hollywood, CA: Vedanta Press, 1970.

———. *The Spiritual Heritage of India.* Hollywood, CA: Vedanta Press, 1969.

Prabhavananda, Swami, and Christopher Isherwood, trans. *Bhagavad-Gita: The Song of God.* London: J. M. Dent & Sons, 1947.

———. *How to Know God: The Yoga Aphorisms of Patanjali.* Hollywood, CA: Vedanta Press, 1953.

Prabhavananda, Swami, and Frederick Manchester, trans. *The Upanishads: Breath of the Eternal.* Hollywood, CA: Vedanta Press, 1947.

Radhakrishnan, Sarvepalli, trans. *The Bhagavadgītā: With an Introductory Essay, Sanskrit Text, English Translation and Notes.* 2nd ed. London: George Allen & Unwin, 1949.

Satprakashananda, Swami. *Methods of Knowledge: Perceptual, Non-perceptual, and Transcendental, According to Advaita Vedanta.* London: George Allen & Unwin, 1965.

———. *The Universe, God and God-Realization: From the Viewpoint of Vedanta.* St. Louis: Vedanta Society of St. Louis, 1977.

Satyananda Saraswati, Swami, trans. *Chaṇḍī Pāṭh: She Who Tears Apart Thought also Known as The Durgā Saptaśatī, The Seven Hundred Verses in Praise of She Who Removes All Difficulties, and The Devī Māhātmyam, The Glory of the Goddess.* Delhi: Motilal Banarsidass, 1995.

Schuhmacher, Stephan and Gert Woerner, eds. *The Encyclopedia of Eastern Philosophy and Religion.* Translated by Michael H. Kohn, et al. Boston: Shambhala, 1989.

Shankaranarayanan, S., trans. *Glory of the Divine Mother.* 2nd ed. Pondicherry: Dipti Publications, 1973.

Sharma, Dipak Kumar. *Durgāsaptaśatī.* Delhi: New Bharatiya Book Corporation, 2000.

Siddhinathananda, Swami, trans. *Devi Mahatmyam.* Bombay: Bharatiya Vidya Bhavan, 1995.

Sivananda, Swami, trans. *The Devi Mahatmya.* Shivanandanagar: The Divine Life Society, 1994.

Sivaraman, E. A. *Devi Mahatmyam: The Greatness of the Supreme Divine Goddess Parasakthi.* Bombay: Bharatiya Vidya Bhavan, 1993.

Smith, Houston. *Essays on World Religion.* Edited by M. Darrol Bryant. New York: Paragon House, 1992.

Smith, Jonathan Z., ed. and William Scott Green, assoc. ed. *The HarperCollins Dictionary of Religion.* San Francisco: HarperCollins, 1995.

Swarupananda, Swami, trans. *Shrimad-Bhagavad-Gita.* Calcutta: Advaita Ashrama, 1909.

Thakur, Manoj K. *Devīmāhātmya: The Glory of the Goddess.* Delhi: World View Publications, 1999.

Tyāgīśānanda, Swāmī, trans. *Śvetāśvatara Upaniṣad.* Mylapore, Madras: Sri Ramakrishna Math, 1979.

Swami Vivekananda. *Inspired Talks.* New York: Ramakrishna-Vivekananda Center, 1970.

Wheeler, Sir Mortimer. *Civilizations of the Indus Valley and Beyond.* New York: McGraw-Hill, 1966.

Woodroffe, Sir John (Arthur Avalon). *The Garland of Letters: Studies in the Mantra-Śāstra.* 9th ed. Pondicherry: Ganesh & Company, 1989.

———. *Shakti and Shakta.* 6th ed. New York: Dover Publications, 1978.

Yatiswarananda, Swami. *Universal Prayers: Selected and Translated from Sanskrit Religious Literature.* Mylapore, Madras: Sri Ramakrishna Math, 1977.

# INDEX

## E



## F



## G

## Q



## R



## S